Orthodoxy and Heresy
in Earliest Christianity

This book is a translation of Walter Bauer's *Rechtgläubigkeit und Ketzerei im ältesten Christentum*, which first appeared in 1934 as volume 10 in the series Beiträge zur historischen Theologie (Tübingen: Mohr/Siebeck), and was reprinted with minor additions and corrections, plus two supplementary essays by Georg Strecker in 1964. A few additional corrections have also been included in the English edition (e.g. 242 n. 3). The translators are listed below, p. xviii.

COPYRIGHT © 1971 BY FORTRESS PRESS

Library of Congress Catalog Card Number 71-141252

ISBN 0-8006-1363-5

First paperback edition 1979

7738A79   Printed in the United States of America   1-1363

Orthodoxy and Heresy in Earliest Christianity

by **WALTER BAUER**

second German edition,
with added appendices, by
GEORG STRECKER

translated by a team from the
Philadelphia Seminar on Christian Origins

and edited by
ROBERT A. KRAFT *and*
GERHARD KRODEL

FORTRESS PRESS   Philadelphia

Dedicated to

FRAU L. BAUER

Contents

CONTENTS

APPENDICES
by Georg Strecker

Foreword to the Second German Edition

In earliest Christianity, orthodoxy and heresy do not stand in relation to one another as primary to secondary, but in many regions heresy is the original manifestation of Christianity. In the present work, Walter Bauer [1] has developed this thesis in a consistent fashion, and not only has called into question in a fundamental way the traditional understanding of the development of church history and the historical foundation of ecclesiastical-orthodox self-understanding, but at the same time has indicated new directions for ecumenical discussion. The unfavorable political situation was, above all, responsible for denying the book a wider influence. Thus in the field of international scholarship, W. Bauer is known far less for being the pioneer of the approach to church history presented herein than as the author of the *Wörterbuch zum Neuen Testament*.[2] Therefore, thanks are all the more due to the publisher for the decision to make the work available

1. On the person and work of Bauer, see the memorial issue NTS, 9 (1962/63): 1-38 (with presentations by F. W. Gingrich, W. Schneemelcher, and E. Fascher); also "In Memoriam Walter Bauer," *Theologische Literaturzeitung*, 86 (1961): 313-316 (addresses by W. Zimmerli and J. Jeremias at the funeral service). Bauer's bibliography can be found in *Theologische Literaturzeitung*, 77 (1952): 501-504; and 86 (1961): 315 f. (compiled by C.-H. Hunzinger), and biographical information in the article "Bauer, W." in RGG[3], 1 (1957): 925 (by W. G. Kümmel).
2. [W. F. Arndt and F. W. Gingrich, *A Greek-English Lexicon of the New Testament and Other Early Christian Literature: a Translation and Adaptation of Walter Bauer's Griechisch-Deutsches Wörterbuch zu den Schriften des Neuen Testaments und der übrigen urchristlichen Literatur, fourth revised and augmented edition, 1952* (Chicago/Cambridge [Eng.]: University Press, 1957). A revised fifth German edition appeared in 1957, and materials for a revised English edition are being gathered.]

once again, and thereby to create the possibility of a new and more thorough appreciation.

Just a few weeks before his unexpected death on 17 November, 1960, Walter Bauer had learned of the proposed new edition and, with kind words, expressed agreement with the plan and with the person of the reviser. The task that faced the undersigned [vi] was first of all to correct typographical errors and other minor oversights, and to introduce such improvements as were envisioned by the author, according to his annotated copy.[3] Apart from these additions, the text of the work has remained unchanged—it was even possible to retain the same pagination. Secondly, it was necessary to deal with the current state of the discussion. This task is undertaken in a double appendix, so as not to infringe upon the character of the original work. Following the original plan, this supplementary material includes a more detailed consideration of Jewish Christianity, and, in addition, an account of the reception of the book. In both parts an effort has been made to indicate possibilities and directions for elaborating Bauer's position and to provide a critical evaluation of more recent investigations of similar orientation.[4]

Thanks are expressed to all who have contributed to the production of this edition; in particular to Prof. D. Philip Vielhauer, from whose suggestion the form of the supplementary material essentially derives, and to Frau L. Bauer, who with constant, kindly assistance made accessible her husband's literary remains, and placed at my disposal the manuscript of the book, notes from three lectures that were delivered in September and October of 1933 on the same subject in Uppsala and Sondershausen, the author's annotated personal copy, and also his collection of reviews. My wife has assisted me in the expansion of the index and in reading proofs, and thus, with the others named, also deserves the thanks of the reader.

GEORG STRECKER

Bonn, September 1963

3. [The addition of two footnotes (51 n. 31, 59 n. 59) and a reference to Josephus at the end of 153 n. 12 should be noted, as well as the inclusion of an index of modern authors.]

4. [The second appendix has been extensively revised and restructured by R. A. Kraft for this English edition.]

Introduction to the English Edition

It is not surprising that Bauer's investigation of "orthodoxy" and "heresy" in early Christianity has had relatively little direct influence on the English-speaking world (see appendix 2), and, despite its obvious significance and its presence on reading lists for advanced study in Christian origins, never has been translated into English. The book was written for a rather limited audience—it is not an introductory volume for the beginner, nor is it a synthesis of modern opinions about the subject matter, but was written for scholars, as an original, front-line contribution to the progress of historical investigation. Bauer presupposes that his readers are conversant with the subject matter at more than an elementary level (see below, xxiv f.). In short, this investigation originally was oriented toward an audience that would be difficult to find today outside the hallways and classrooms of the best institutions of higher learning.

There is also another reason that became increasingly obvious to those who contributed their time and energy in preparing this edition. Quite apart from the difficulty of the subject matter (particularly in chap. 1!), Bauer's German *style* presents a complex and frustrating problem for the translator who hopes to capture something of the "tone" or "flavor" of the original as well as representing accurately its content. Bauer writes in a dynamic and highly sophisticated manner, mixing precision with irony and even insinuation, pictorial language with careful presentation of the historical evidence, hypotheses and caveats with the subtle use of overstatement and understatement in cleverly nuanced expressions. His German is literary but not necessarily formal. Long sentences with closely interrelated parts appear alongside brief, sometimes cryptic or oblique comments couched in clever, often scholarly German idiom. Frequently the presentation flows along rapidly in an exciting manner, despite the difficulties of the subject matter—but its flow is such that the motion is difficult to capture in translation, and is sometimes even difficult to follow in the original, unless one is already completely steeped in the evidence being discussed and in Bauer's general orientation toward it! Nor is it easy to represent the variety and nuances of his choice of vocabulary—e.g. some readers will perhaps cringe at such renderings as "ecclesiastical" for *kirchlich* and related words, but the overuse of "orthodox" to cover even that word group in addition to *rechtgläubig* and *orthodox* seemed less than fair to Bauer's intention. Hopefully his meaning will not be seriously obscured in such instances.

Editorial Modifications in This Edition. A philosophy of translation—and also of scholarly serviceability—underlies this English edition. Translations can be only more or less adequate, and the editors are fully aware of the fact that there will remain room for improvement at various places throughout the volume. This English edition does not aim at "popularization" of the original style (e.g. long sentences are seldom chopped up or radically recast at the expense of Bauer's precision), but attempts to be as faithful as possible to both the content and the "tone" of the original. At the same time, it attempts to increase the potential usefulness of the book for English readers both in the classroom and in the study by a variety of means:

(1) The *pagination* of the original has been retained wherever possible by the use of bracketed bold type numbers inserted into the text at the appropriate places. Thus there should be little difficulty in using this edition to locate material referred to in earlier publications based on the two German editions (except for the footnotes which have been renumbered, and for appendix 2, which has been extensively revised).

(2) English translations (or equivalents) have been supplied for all *non-English material* (ancient or modern) found in Bauer-Strecker, apart from a few Latin or Greek phrases included in standard English dictionaries. It should be noted, however, that although this edition may note the existence of an available ET (English translation) of material which Bauer (or Strecker) cites, the ET of that material which is supplied has been made especially for this volume

with particular regard to the use made of the material in the German edition. This applies to modern as well as to ancient literature (cf. e.g. 44 and n. 1 there). With some exceptions, the Greek, Latin, and Syriac words and passages found in Bauer-Strecker also are retained in this edition (Greek and Syriac in transliteration), and sometimes an ancient text has been expanded or supplied by the editors to help clarify the argument (e.g. xxiii n. 1). In most instances, the ancient sources are referred to by English forms of their titles, rather than Latin or Greek—a practice not without its frustrations, especially for the scholar!

(3) In the case of *ancient texts,* an attempt has been made to refer to standard editions in current use as well as to convenient ETs as available. For texts to which frequent reference is made in various parts of the book, this bibliographical information is included under the appropriate listing in the index; otherwise it is supplied in footnotes at the place of occurrence. Nevertheless, the reader/user will find that such tools as the patrologies of Altaner and/or Quasten, or for the less traveled paths of chap. 1, the *Short Introduction* by Wright, will be indispensable for following the presentation in all its detail (see the index).

(4) Where ETs or new editions of *modern works* mentioned by Bauer-Strecker are known to the editors, they have been included (or sometimes substituted) in the footnotes. Occasionally references to recent discoveries relevant for Bauer's argument also are added (e.g. 42 n. 99).

(5) In general, the original *footnote procedures* have been modified considerably so that cross-references and brief references to ancient sources appear in the text itself, while longer references that might tend to interrupt the presentation unduly are contained in footnotes along with references to modern literature, parenthetical comments, supplementary information, and the like (see e.g. 2 n. 3 for an example of reshuffling and revision). Full bibliographical information normally is provided at the initial reference to modern works; thereafter, the author's name and a short title appear. The index is so constructed as to facilitate locating such bibliographical data.

Use of Brackets. It has proved difficult consistently to alert the reader to the presence of such editorial adjustments at their numerous occurrences in this edition. For some changes, it has seemed unnecessary to do so—e.g. the addition of cross-references, substitution of an English edition for a German title (cf. e.g. 17 n. 34, where Bauer referred to the German translation of Burkitt's book!), explicit mention of certain biblical references implied by Bauer's treatment (e.g. 234). Instances of *substantial* editorial additions, however, consistently have been designated by the *use of brackets;* certain minor supplements also are so marked. But where brackets occur within direct quotations (e.g. 3) or within parentheses, it is not to be assumed that expansion by the American editors is present; on the contrary, such instances usually represent a normal use of brackets under those conditions, and have no special significance.

Editorial Responsibility. Almost without exception, the substantive editorial additions are the responsibility of R. A. Kraft, who has prepared the final form of the manuscript for the press and has attempted to standardize such things as footnote form and to reduce as much as possible any obvious inconsistencies in translation and style. It was the primary editorial responsibility of G. Krodel to check the work of the individual translators for accuracy of their understanding of the German. Translating is, for the most part, a thankless task—and a difficult one if done carefully. Great appreciation is due to the translation team for their unselfish efforts.

Index. The comprehensive index at the end of the volume is an experiment aimed at facilitating efficient use of the book. It includes not only such expected matters as subject and author entries, but also lists abbreviations and provides reference to editions and ETs of ancient sources cited frequently throughout the book. For less frequently cited sources, the material normally appears at the initial footnote reference. The index also is intended as a bibliographical tool for modern works cited, since it directs the user to the appropriate footnote (usually the first mentioned) in which such data is included.

Background of the Translation, Acknowledgements. This English edition of Bauer represents the work of a team of translators from the Philadelphia Seminar on Christian Origins (PSCO). In the spring of 1966, the seminar members voted to devote the forthcoming year to a study of Bauer's book, under the cochairmanship of J. Reumann (Lutheran Theological Seminary, Philadelphia) and R. A. Kraft. Concurrently, a subcommittee was formed to produce a translation of the volume, with Krodel and Kraft designated as final editors. Negotiations with Fortress Press were opened immediately, and by the time the 1966/67 seminar commenced in the fall, Fortress Press had committed itself to the project and was negotiating for translation rights from the German publisher. Originally, it was proposed that two volumes be published: (1) a translation of the original 1934 edition of Bauer, and (2) a volume of supplementary studies including the material added by Strecker in the 1964 edition. Although this plan was abandoned in deference to the wishes of the German editor, it was agreed that the second appendix could be revised for the purposes of this edition, with added attention to the impact of Bauer's book in the English-speaking world.

Meanwhile, it was discovered that John E. Steely of Southeastern Baptist Theological Seminary had been at work independently on a translation of the book. When he learned of the PSCO project, he made his rough draft translation available (extending through the opening pages of appendix 1, without footnotes) and agreed to cooperate as a member of the team in seeing the project through to its completion. His draft proved useful not only as an extra checkpoint in editing the work of the team, but was used as the basic translation for two chapters of this edition. The translation team generously agreed that any monetary profit from the book should be channelled through the PSCO for the establishment of a series of scholarly publications dealing with Christian origins apart from New Testament proper.

Appreciation is due to Fortress Press for encouraging this project and undertaking to publish it, and to the many members and friends of the PSCO who became involved at various levels—including a special debt to Niel J. McEleney of St. Paul's College in Washington D.C. for working through the final draft and offering several valuable suggestions. Professor Strecker also deserves thanks for making himself available by mail, especially in connection with the revision of the second appendix. Finally, for the often thankless task of transforming complicated handwritten materials into the final product presented here, mention should be made of those who, like Joan Krodel and the secretaries from the Department of Religious Thought at the University of Pennsylvania, contributed their time and talents.

ROBERT A. KRAFT, *for the editors and the translation team*
July 1970

LIST OF TRANSLATORS

Paul J. Achtemeier (chap. 9), Kunz Professor of New Testament,
Lancaster Theological Seminary, Lancaster, Pa. 17603

Stephen Benko (chap. 5), Associate Professor of Ancient History
and Coordinator of the Classical Studies Program,
Fresno State College, Fresno, California 93710

Howard N. Bream (chap. 8), Kraft Professor of Biblical Studies,
Lutheran Theological Seminary, Gettysburg, Pa. 17325

Robert F. Evans (chap. 6), Associate Professor of Religious Thought,
University of Pennsylvania, Philadelphia, Pa. 19104

David M. Hay (chap. 2), Assistant Professor of New Testament,
Princeton Theological Seminary, Princeton, New Jersey 08540

Robert A. Kraft (Foreword, Introduction, Appendix 2, coeditor),
Associate Professor of Religious Thought,
University of Pennsylvania, Philadelphia, Pa. 19104

Gerhard Krodel (chaps. 3-4, Appendix 1, coeditor),
Artman Professor of New Testament,
Lutheran Theological Seminary, Philadelphia, Pa. 19118

John J. O'Rourke (chap. 10), Professor of Sacred Scriptures,
St. Charles Borromeo Seminary, Philadelphia, Pa. 19151

John E. Steely (chaps. 1 and 10), Professor of Historical Theology,
Southeastern Baptist Theological Seminary,
Wake Forest, North Carolina 27587

David C. Steinmetz (chap. 7), Assistant Professor of Church History,
Lancaster Theological Seminary, Lancaster, Pa. 17603

Robert L. Wilken (chap. 8), Assistant Professor of Patristics,
Fordham University, New York, NY 10023

Orthodoxy and Heresy in Earliest Christianity

by **WALTER BAUER**

Introduction

"Orthodoxy" and "heresy": we all know what enormous importance is attached to these two concepts for the history of our religion. Usually, however, investigation of this subject tends to focus upon the later epochs. The period of Christian origins is, as a rule, passed over rather briefly. Of course, the "errors" combatted in the earliest literature of Christianity are described and investigated from various points of view, with this or that result. But this is usually done with implicit, or even explicit, assent to the view that any such divergence really is a corruption of Christianity.

But if we follow such a procedure, and simply agree with the judgment of the anti-heretical fathers for the post-New Testament period, do we not all too quickly become dependent upon the vote of but *one* party—that party which perhaps as much through favorable circumstances as by its own merit eventually was thrust into the foreground, and which possibly has at its disposal today the more powerful, and thus the more prevalent voice, only because the chorus of others has been muted? Must not the historian, like the judge, preside over the parties and maintain as a primary principle the dictum *audiatur et altera pars* [let the other side also be heard]? When one side cannot, because of anxiety, confusion, or clumsiness, gain proper recognition, is it not the obligation of the judge—and, *mutatis mutandis* of the historian—to assist it, as best he can, to unfold its case instead of simply submitting to the mental agility and firmness, the sagacity and loquacity of the other? Does either judge or historian dare to act as though whatever cannot be read and understood by everyone as part of the public records never existed, and thus is unimportant for passing sentence?

In our day and age, there is no longer any debate [2] that in terms of a *scientific approach* to history, the New Testament writings cannot be understood properly if one now looks back on them from the end of the process of canonization as sacred books, and prizes them as constituent parts of the celestial charter of salvation, with all the attendant characteristics. We have long since become accustomed to understanding them in terms of their own time—the gospels as more or less successful attempts to relate the life of Jesus; the Pauline letters as occasional writings, connected with specific and unrepeatable situations, and having spatial as well as temporal limitations to their sphere of authority. We must also approach the "heretics" in the same way. We need to understand them also in terms of their own time, and not to evaluate them by means of ecclesiastical doctrine which was developing, or which later became a ready-made norm.

We can determine adequately the significance the "heretics" possessed for nascent and developing Christianity only when we, insofar as it is possible, place ourselves back into the period in which they went about their business, and without hesitation cast all our preconceived ideas aside. We must remain open to all possibilities. What constitutes "truth" in one generation can be out of date in the next—through progress, but also through retrogression into an earlier position. The actual situation in this region may not obtain in that one, and indeed, may never have had general currency.

Perhaps—I repeat, *perhaps*—certain manifestations of Christian life that the authors of the church renounce as "heresies" originally had not been such at all, but, at least here and there, were the only form of the new religion—that is, for those regions they were simply "Christianity." The possibility also exists that their adherents constituted the majority, and that they looked down with hatred and scorn on the orthodox, who for them were the false believers. I do not say this in order to introduce some special use of language for the investigations which follow, so that "orthodoxy" designates the preference of the given majority, while "heresy" is characterized by the fact that only the minority adhere to it. Majority and minority can change places and then such a use of language, which would be able to represent this change only with difficulty, would easily lead to obscurities and misunderstandings. No, even in this book, "orthodoxy" and "heresy" will refer to what one customarily and [3] usually understands them to mean. There is only this proviso, that we will not hear the two of them discussed by the church—that is, by the one party—but by history.

In order to exclude from the outset all modern impressions and judgments, I will proceed from the view concerning the heretics and their doctrines which was cherished already in the second century by the ancient church, and will test its defensibility in hopes of discovering, by means of such a critical procedure, a route to the goal. The ecclesiastical position includes roughly the following main points:

(1) Jesus reveals the pure doctrine to his apostles, partly before his death, and partly in the forty days before his ascension.

(2) After Jesus' final departure, the apostles apportion the world among themselves, and each takes the unadulterated gospel to the land which has been allotted him.

(3) Even after the death of the disciples the gospel branches out further. But now obstacles to it spring up within Christianity itself. The devil cannot resist sowing weeds in the divine wheatfield—and he is successful at it. True Christians blinded by him abandon the pure doctrine. This development takes place in the following sequence: unbelief, right belief, wrong belief. There is scarcely the faintest notion anywhere that unbelief might be changed directly into what the church calls false belief. No, where there is heresy, orthodoxy must have preceded. For example, Origen puts it like this: "All heretics at first are believers; then later they swerve from the rule of faith." [1]

This view is so deeply rooted, and so widely held, that it applies even to such personalities as Mani, who is supposed to have been a presbyter of the church and a valiant warrior against both Jews and pagans, but then left the church because he took it as a personal offence that his students received such scanty recognition (see below, 39). In general, it is an opinion of orthodoxy that only impure motives drive the heretic from the church—indeed, this must be so if

1. *Commentary on the Song of Songs*, 3 (to Cant. 2.2): *omnes enim haeretici primo ad credulitatem veniunt, et post haec ab itinere fidei et dogmatum veritate declinant* (ed. W. A. Baehrens, GCS 33 [1925]; ET by R. P. Lawson, ACW 26 [1957]). See also the fragment from Origen on Proverbs (to 2.16), ed. Lommatzsch 13,228 (= PG 13, 28 f.). Tertullian speaks similarly at the end of *Prescription against Heretics* 36 in his analogy of the wild olive (or fig) tree (= heresy) which springs from a cultivated seed (= orthodox doctrine).

the evil-one is at the bottom of it all. Already Hegesippus, who was in Rome around the year 160, asserts that after the martyr's death of James the Just, Thebutis had begun to corrupt the church, which until then had been a pure virgin, [4] through false belief, because he had not succeeded James as the leader of the Jerusalem community (EH 4.22.4-6). We hear similar things about Valentinus (below, 39 n. 91, and 128), Marcion,[2] and Bardesanes (below, 38 f.).

(4) Of course, right belief is invincible. In spite of all the efforts of Satan and his instruments, it repels unbelief and false belief, and extends its victorious sway ever further.

Scholarship has not found it difficult to criticize these convictions. It knows that the ecclesiastical doctrine was not yet present with Jesus; likewise, that the twelve apostles by no means played the role assigned to them out of consideration for the purity and revealed nature of ecclesiastical dogma. Further, historical thinking that is worthy of this name refuses to employ here the correlatives "true" and "untrue," "bad" and "good." It is not easily convinced of the moral inferiority attributed to the heretics. It recognizes there the same embarrassed, and thus artificial, claim that emanated from Jewish Christianity when it asserted that Paul had sued for the hand of the high priest's daughter and, when it was denied him, began to rage against Torah (Epiphanius Her. 30.16).

Sooner or later, however, a point is reached at which criticism bogs down. For my tastes, it all too easily submits to the ecclesiastical opinion as to what is early and late, original and dependent, essential and unimportant for the earliest history of Christianity. If my impression is correct, even today the overwhelmingly dominant view still is that for the period of Christian origins, ecclesiastical doctrine (of course, only as this pertains to a certain stage in its development) already represents what is primary, while heresies, on the other hand, somehow are a deviation from the genuine. I do not mean to say that this point of view must be false, but neither can I regard it as self-evident, or even as demonstrated and clearly established. Rather, we are confronted here with a problem that merits our attention.

In this way, the subject of my book is defined more precisely, and I am left free to bypass much else that also could be treated under

2. [Epiphanius Her. 42.1.8; see also Tertullian Prescription against Heretics 30 and Against Marcion 4.4, and the Edessene Chronicle 6 (below pp. 14 ff., 38).]

the title I have selected. For example, I do not intend to present once again a description of the tenets of the ancient heresies, but I presuppose that they are well known, along with many other things. We live in a time that demands concise discussion, and repetition of what already has been presented in a suitable manner [5] should not be tolerated. Therefore, he who opens this book in hopes of finding therein a convenient synopsis of what fellow-scholars already have contributed to this or to that aspect of the theme will be disappointed.

As we turn to our task, the New Testament seems to be both too unproductive and too much disputed to be able to serve as a point of departure. The majority of its anti-heretical writings cannot be arranged with confidence either chronologically or geographically; nor can the more precise circumstances of their origin be determined with sufficient precision. It is advisable, therefore, first of all to interrogate other sources concerning the relationship of orthodoxy and heresy, so that, with the insights that may be gained there, we may try to determine the time and place of their origins. I have chosen to begin with Edessa and Egypt so as to obtain a glimpse into the emergence and the original condition of Christianity in regions other than those that the New Testament depicts as affected by this religion.

1

Edessa

After the breakup of the kingdom of Alexander the Great, Mesopotamia, including the region in which Edessa lay, came under the control of Seleucus I Nicator. He reorganized an extant settlement there, Osroë, by mixing the population with westerners who spoke Greek, and gave it the Macedonian name Edessa.[1] In the second half of the second century B.C.E., as the Seleucid kingdom disintegrated in the wars with Parthia (145-129), insubordinate despots seized power for themselves in Edessa and its environs (i.e., in the Osroëne), as was true elsewhere in Mesopotamia (Diodorus *Exc. Escur.* 25), at first under Parthian dominion. Thereafter, they came under the Armenian banner in the time of Tigranes, and then the Roman through Lucullus and Pompey. With the assassination of Caracalla, which occurred in Edessa in 217 C.E., the local dynasty finally came to an end, after various preliminary interludes, when the Osroëne was incorporated into the Roman Empire.[2]

The Greek influence did not have a long or profound effect here. According to the *Chronicle* of Jacob of Edessa, who lived in the seventh century, the Greek part of the population was so greatly diminished already by the year 180 of the Seleucid era (= 133 B.C.E.)

1. Appian *Roman History* 11 (*Syrian Wars*). 57 (ed. and ET by H. White, LCL [1912]). The name Edessa, which is Illyrian in origin, means "water-city"; cf. U. Wilcken, *Alexander the Great* (ET by G. C. Richards from 1931 German, London: Chatto and Windus, 1932), p. 23 (= German 20).
2. A. von Gutschmid, *Untersuchungen über die Geschichte des Königreiches Osroëne*, Mémoires de l'Academie impériale des Sciences de S. Pétersbourg, series 7, vol. 35.1 (St. Petersburg, 1887); E. Meyer, "Edessa," *Paulys Realencyclopädie der classischen Altertumswissenschaft*, ed. G. Wissowa, 5.2 (Stuttgart, 1905), 1933-1938.

that they allowed the native population to have a king from their own midst.[3] The rulers—strictly speaking they were not kings but toparchs, even though the coins occasionally also call them [7] "king" (*basileus*) —even at that time bear predominantly Arabic or Aramaic names: 'Abdu, Ma'nu, Bakru, Abgar, Wâ'il. Moreover, the old Semitic designation of the city is revived at the expense of "Edessa"—it is called Urhâi, modern Urfa (see below, n. 11). There is a corresponding lack of Greek inscriptions for the first centuries of the common era. The native princes use Syriac inscriptions on their coins. Roman gold pieces, which were in circulation in the area from the time of Marcus Aurelius, of course have Greek legends, as do the coins which name the emperor along with a local prince. Only Abgar IX [4] (179-214), the Roman minion, prefers a Greek inscription even for himself alone.[5] This represents only his own attitude, not the national orientation of his subjects.

When we ask how and when Christianity gained influence in this region, it is unnecessary to begin with a survey of the sources—which are in Syriac, Greek, and a few in Latin. Instead, for the sake of convenience, we will combine the information concerning the sources with the evaluation of them and with the collection of discernible data made possible thereby.

The story of King Abgar V Ukkama (= the Black), who ruled from 9-46 C.E., and his relationship to Jesus is well known.[6] It is found in its oldest form in Eusebius, *Ecclesiastical History* [= EH] 1.13, who first tells the story, then introduces the documentation, so as to return once again to the story. The king, who has heard of the miraculous healings performed by Jesus, appeals to him by letter, acknowledges his deity, and begs to be freed from the illness that afflicts him. At the same time, in view of the hostility of the Jews, he offers his own home city to Jesus as a safe dwelling place. Jesus answers

3. Syriac text ed. by E.-W. Brooks, with a Latin translation in the companion volume, by J. B. Chabot, in part 2 of *Chronica minora* (CSCO, Scriptores Syri, series 3, vol. 4, 1903), syr. 281 f., lat. 211.
4. So Gutschmid and others such as F. Haase; but H. Leclercq, following M. Babelon, designates him as Abgar VIII—DACL 4 (1921): 2065 ff. (esp. 2065.7).
5. Gutschmid, *Osroëne*, pp. 37 ff.; G. F. Hill, *Catalogue of Greek Coins in the British Museum: the Greek Coins of Arabia, Mesopotamia and Persia* (London: Longmans, 1922), e.g. p. CI, no. 5.
6. [See also Bauer's treatment of this subject in Hennecke-Schneemelcher, 1: 437 ff. On Edessene Christianity in general, see most recently J. B. Segal, *Edessa: "The Blessed City"* (Oxford and New York: University Press, 1970).]

likewise in writing. He blesses the king for believing without having seen. He must decline the invitation, since he has to fulfill his calling and his earthly life in Palestine. But after his death and ascension a disciple will come who will heal the king and will bring life to him, as well as to his people. Then this actually took place. [8]

Eusebius makes the transition from his account (EH 1.13.1-4) to the *verbatim* reproduction of the two letters as follows (13.5): "There is also documentary evidence of these things, taken from the record office at Edessa, a city which at that time was still ruled by a king. For in the public documents there, which also contain the experiences of Abgar among other events of antiquity, these things also have been found preserved from his time until the present. But there is nothing like listening to the letters themselves, which we have taken from the archives, and which translated literally from the Syriac are as follows."

After reproducing the letters (13.6-10) Eusebius continues: "To these letters the following is appended, in Syriac" (13.11). There follows (13.12-21) the account of how after the ascension "Judas, who is also called Thomas" sends Thaddaeus, one of the seventy disciples, to Edessa. There he heals Abgar and many others, and is requested by the "toparch" (13.13; cf. also 13.6) to tell him about Jesus' life and works. Thaddaeus declares his willingness, but he wants to do so on the following day before the entire populace. Thus all the citizens of the city are summoned (13.20). Still, nothing more is said about the projected apostolic sermon, but the account concludes with the statement: "These things took place in the year 340 [of the Seleucid era = 28/29 c.e.]" (13.22ᵃ). Finally the whole thing ends with the words of Eusebius: "Let this useful story, translated literally from the Syriac, stand here in its proper place" (13.22ᵇ).

The account of the conversion of Edessa, which we have just presented from Eusebius (EH 1.13; cf. 2.1.6-8), can in no way and to no extent be traced back as a report that is earlier than the beginning of the fourth century, when Eusebius' *Ecclesiastical History* originated. On the other hand, toward the end of that century or the beginning of the next, the report underwent further development, which reached a culmination of sorts in the so-called *Doctrina Addai*, a Syriac book which was written in Edessa around the year 400.[7] In it the material

7. G. Phillips, *The Doctrine of Addai the Apostle* (London, 1876).

known from Eusebius reappears, albeit to a considerable measure expanded, among other things, by a detailed account of the activity of the apostolic emissary[8] in Edessa, who preaches, baptizes, and builds the first church. [9]

In surveying this information from the earliest history of Christian Edessa there naturally occurs to us what had been said above xxiii about the ecclesiastical way of thinking. The decisive role that is attributed to Jesus and his apostle is viewed quite ecclesiastically. Indeed, the stronger the ecclesiastical coloring is applied, the more powerfully does doubt assert itself as to the truth of what is stated. In this instance we are in the happy position of not having to investigate the doubts individually. In the twentieth century the conviction has quite generally prevailed that Eusebius is not tracing the actual course of history, but is relating a legend. Today the only thing that remains to be asked is whether the church father's presentation is completely useless for shedding light upon the origin of the Christian church in Edessa, or whether in the justifiable rejection of the whole we may still single out this or that particular trait, in order to derive therefrom some sort of tenable insight for ourselves.

That the latter is legitimate is at present the almost universally acknowledged scholarly view. Thus one may point, for example, to the figure of Tobias, who according to Eusebius, lives in Edessa and mediates the contact between Thaddaeus and Abgar (EH 1.13.11 and 13). From this, one could deduce the historical fact that Christianity in Edessa had ties to Judaism there. Still, this conclusion is quite tenuous in view of the fact that Eusebius says nothing at all about the Judaism of Tobias, but it is left to the reader to draw from the name itself the necessary conclusion as a basis for all the rest.

Much more significant is the wide currency gained, especially through the work of the historian A. von Gutschmid, by the view that it was not Abgar V, the contemporary of Jesus, but in fact a later prince by the same name—Abgar IX (179-214)—who first turned Christian and thereby helped this religion to erupt.[9] Nevertheless, the

---

8. Here he is called Addai, not Thaddeus as in Eusebius.
9. Gutschmid, *Osroëne*, pp. 1 ff. [See also, e.g. H. Lietzmann, *A History of the Early Church* in 4 vols. (ET by B. L. Woolf from the 1932-44 German; London: Lutterworth, 1937-53; reprint New York: Meridian paperback, 1961), 2: 260 (= German p. 266), in conscious disagreement with Bauer. (The date 250 in the ET is a typographical error for 200.)]

grounds for accepting a conversion of this later Abgar appear to me to be overrated, while the counterarguments are not given enough consideration.[10] [10] We must still give serious attention to the fact that without exception the ancient authors who speak of a Christian King Abgar of Edessa mean that one with whom Jesus is supposed to have been in correspondence. The possibility of this ninth Abgar has been uncovered by modern scholarship only as a substitute for the conversion of the fifth Abgar, which at present no one can seriously accept any longer.

The only support for the modern view is, after all, a passage from the *Book of the Laws of the Countries,* one of the oldest monuments of original Syriac prose, a product of the school of Bar Daisan (whom the Greeks call Bardesanes), from the beginning of the third century. Chapter 45 reads: "In Syria and in Urhâi [11] the men used to castrate themselves in honor of Taratha. But when King Abgar became a believer, he commanded that anyone who emasculated himself should have a hand cut off. And from that day to the present no one in Urhâi emasculates himself anymore." [12] Thus we have reference to a Christian King Abgar by an Edessene author at the beginning of the third century. Since, on the basis of what is known, Abgar V does not qualify, one may now think of the ninth Abgar, who probably would have been an early contemporary of that author.

But does a person use the expression "from this day down to mine" to speak of his contemporary? Is not one who speaks in this way looking back to a personality who lived much earlier? But this observation, which serves to shake the opinion that the text refers to Abgar IX, by no means leads to the view that one must now refer it to Abgar V and suppose that the Abgar legend already existed in some form at the time when the *Book of the Laws of the Countries* was written. For that book really offers no guarantee for the presence

10. H. Gompertz opposes the idea that Abgar IX was converted to Christianity in an essay "Hat es jemals in Edessa christliche Könige gegeben?" in the *Archäologisch-epigraphischen Mitteilungen aus Österreich-Ungarn,* 9 (1896): 154-157. Also sceptical is F. Haase, *Altchristliche Kirchengeschichte nach orientalischen Quellen* (Leipzig, 1925), pp. 84 ff.
11. Urhâi is the Aramaic name of the city called Edessa by the Macedonians. The old name later regained its prevalence and still is reflected in the modern name Urfa (see above, 2). [Greek text Eusebius *Pr. Gosp.* 6.10 reads Osroëne.]
12. Ed. by F. Nau in PSyr 1.2 (1907): 606. [Separate ed. by Nau (Paris, 1931). Text and ET by W. Cureton, *Spicilegium Syriacum* (London, 1855); ET by B. P. Pratten, ANF 8:723-734.]

of Christianity within the Edessene royal household, be it earlier or later. The Syriac text from which we have proceeded can not be trusted. The earliest witness for the text of that [11] ancient Syriac writing under consideration is not a codex in that language, but is Eusebius, who has copied the *Book of the Laws* in his *Preparation for the Gospel* 6.10. When he comes to speak of the customs in Edessa, he is in close enough agreement, for the most part, with the Syriac text; but the explanation referring to the faith of the king—that is, the words "when he became a believer" in the passage cited above— cannot be found in Eusebius (6.10.44). But since he knew of a King Abgar of Edessa who had become a believer, as is clear from the *Ecclesiastical History* (see above, 2 f.), and since he had absolutely no reason to eliminate the words which would have been helpful to the Christian cause, the only remaining conclusion is that he did not find them in his source; and the Syriac text doubtless is indebted for them, as an appended postscript, to someone who knew the Abgar legend. If this sort of person heard of such a measure taken by a King Abgar, a measure which from his point of view must have seemed directed against paganism, to what else could he attribute it than the Christian faith of the famous prince Abgar? Actually, the decisive stand of an ancient ruler against emasculation requires no Christian motivation. From the time of Domitian, the pagan emperors proceeded with ever sharper measures against this offense.[13]

The rest of what is adduced in support of a Christian king of Edessa appears to me to be entirely without importance. The Christian Sextus Julius Africanus, who around the year 200 spent some time at the Edessene royal court, once refers to his contemporary Abgar as "a holy person." [14] This is not to be exploited as a Christian

13. Moreover, the measure instituted by that Abgar of whom the *Book of the Laws* speaks (above, n. 12) and to whom we are no longer able to ascribe a number in no way produced the thorough and lasting effect that one is led to expect when he reads the passage devoted to him. Even in the fifth century, Rabbula of Edessa in his rules for priests and clerics must stipulate that no Christian is to emasculate himself: J. J. Overbeck (ed.), *S. Ephraemi Syri Rabulae Episcopi Edesseni, Balaei, aliorumque opera selecta* (Oxford, 1865), p. 221.4. Isaac of Antioch, doubtless an Edessene priest of the fifth century, inveighs mightily against self-mutilation in *Carmen* 37.467 ff. (ed. G. Bickell, *S. Isaaci Antiocheni, doctoris Syrorum, opera omnia*, 2 [Giessen, 1877]: 260 ff. = ed. of P. Bedjan [Paris, 1903], no. 51, pp. 633 ff.)
14. *Hieros anēr*, in George Syncellus, *Chronicle* (*Chronographie*, ed. G. Dindorf [Bonn, 1829], 1: 676.13).

confession, and is understood quite correctly by Eusebius in his *Chronicle* for the year 2235 of Abraham (probably = 218 c.e.), when he says: [12] "Abgar, a *distinguished* man, ruled over Urrha, as Africanus relates." Also from Africanus derives the report of Epiphanius, when in the description of the heresy of Bardesanes he characterizes the contemporary Edessene ruler Abgar as a "most pious and reasonable person" (*anēr hosiōtatos kai logiōtatos, Her.* 56.1.3).

In support of our position is the fact that in a Syriac novel dealing with Julian the Apostate, from a manuscript no later than the seventh century, Satan explains: "From the beginning of the world, there was no nation or kingdom that did not honor me. Only this Constantine reneged."[15] It appears, then, that the original Syrian who is telling this story knows nothing of a Christian prince prior to Constantine; thus he knows of no such tradition from his own, Syriac-speaking area.

Further, two large marble columns are still standing on the citadel in Edessa (Urfa), one of which bears an inscription in honor of the Queen Chelmath, the daughter of Manu.[16] The form of the letters in the inscription is that of approximately 200 c.e. Thus it is quite possible that the princess named was the wife of that Abgar who is supposed to have become a Christian around the turn of the third century.[17] Now H. Pognon suggests what appears to me quite likely, that the columns originally were among those mentioned in an anonymous *Chronicle* that Rahmani has edited from an Edessene codex: "There was in Urhai a great pagan temple, splendidly built, from the time of the great king Seleucus. . . . It was magnificently decorated and in its midst were great marble columns."[18] Later, this temple was remodelled into a church and received the name "Church of our Redeemer." If Pognon's supposition is correct, and people have perpetuated the name of Abgar's wife in a pagan temple to her honor, and the inscription was not removed [13] subsequently, then from

15. T. Nöldeke in *Zeitschrift der Deutschen Morgenländischen Gesellschaft,* 28 (1874): 665 (see 671 on the date of the manuscript). The Syriac text is given in G. Hoffmann, *Julian der Abtrünnige* (Leiden: Brill, 1880), at the end (fol. 53b-54a) [ET by H. Gollancz, *Julian the Apostate, now translated for the first time from the Syriac original* (London: Milford, 1928), p. 260].
16. According to Eusebius EH 2.12.3, several splendid pillars of Queen Helena of Adiabene stand in the suburbs of Aelia [= Jerusalem].
17. So H. Leclercq in DACL 4 (1921): 2102 f.
18. H. Pognon, *Inscriptions sémitiques de la Syrie, de la Mésopotamie et de la Région de Mossoul* (Paris: Lecoffre, 1907), pp. 206 f. I. E. Rahmani (ed.), *Chronicon civile et ecclesiasticum anonymi auctoris* (Mt. Libano, 1904), p. 66.3 ff.

this point of view also, the Christianity of her royal spouse is rendered somewhat doubtful.

Finally, it is to be remembered that Dio Cassius tells of the extraordinary cruelty of this very Abgar.[19] Thus at least in his case, the Christian faith cannot have had a very deep effect.

The purpose of this criticism is to contest the assumption that the presence of a Christian prince and of a state church for Edessa around the year 200 is in any way assured. But also, apart from the problem of the ruler, the existence of ecclesiastically organized Christianity in Edessa at this time cannot be asserted with any confidence, no matter how frequently and from what impressive quarters this is constantly repeated. If we examine the sources for the earliest history of Christianity in Edessa, it will appear to us that in his *Ecclesiastical History,* which went through four editions in the years 311/12 to 324/25,[20] Eusebius ought to be able to give us the best information. The learned bishop even lived in Palestine, not excessively distant from the region with which we are concerned, and he also understood Syriac, the language spoken there. But an investigation of what the "father of church history" knows, or at least communicates, concerning the situation in the Mesopotamian neighborhood before and during his epoch—apart from the impossible Abgar story—discloses a result that is disturbing for its poverty. I enumerate:

a) EH 4.2.5: Trajan has cleared Mesopotamia of the Jews. Eusebius knows this from the Greek historians who tell of Trajan's reign.

b) EH 7.5.2: A letter of Dionysius of Alexandria to the Roman bishop Stephen (255-257) is quoted, in which, among the Oriental churches which earlier were divided and now are united, there are also listed quite summarily "Mesopotamia, and Pontus and Bithynia" (*Mesopotamia Pontos te kai Bithynia*).

c) EH 9.12.1: Under Diocletian the Christians in Mesopotamia, in contrast to other provinces, were hung by the feet over a slow fire.

There is nothing much of significance there. But up to this point we still have not examined [14] *the* passage that always is adduced in order to prove that already in the second century there must have been ecclesiastically organized Christianity of a not-inconsiderable size in Mesopotamia.

19. *Roman History,* Epitome of 78.12.1a (ed. E. Carey, LCL [1927] = Exc. Vales. 369/p. 746); cf. Gutschmid, *Osroëne,* p. 36.
20. Cf. the GCS edition of EH by E. Schwartz, 3: XLVII ff.

d) EH 5.23.4: At the time of the Roman bishop Victor (189-99), gatherings of bishops took place everywhere on the matter of the Easter controversy, and Eusebius still knows of letters in which the church leaders have set down their opinion. In this connection, the following localities are enumerated: Palestine, Rome, Pontus, Gaul, and then the "Osroëne and the cities there." The phrase "and the cities there" is as unusual as it is superfluous. Where else are the Osroëne bishops supposed to have been situated except in the "cities there"? But what speaks even more decisively against these words than this sort of observation is the fact that the earliest witness for the text of Eusebius, the Latin translation of Rufinus, does not contain the words "as well as from those in the Osroëne and the cities there." This cannot be due to tampering with the text by the Italian translator, for whom eastern matters are of no great concern. In those books with which he has supplemented Eusebius' *History*, Rufinus mentions Mesopotamia and Edessa several times (11.5 and 8 at the end; see below, n. 24). Thus the only remaining possibility is that in his copy of EH 5.23.4 he found no reference to the Osroëne, but that we are dealing here with a grammatically awkward interpolation by a later person who noted the omission of Edessa and its environs.

The author of the *Ecclesiastical History* is not well informed about Mesopotamia; this verdict may be rendered without apology. He does mention Julius Africanus and makes excerpts from his *Chronicle*,[21] but without mentioning Mesopotamia or Edessa on such occasions. For him, Bardesanes belongs quite generally to the "land of the two rivers"; he has not learned anything more specific about him (EH 4.30.1). And by his own admission, it is only by hearsay that he is acquainted with the gospel in use by the Christians of that area in his own time, the so-called *Diatessaron* (4.29.6). This indicates to me that ecclesiastical Christianity cannot have been flourishing in Mesopotamia at that time, at least not in a form congenial to Eusebius. Apparently, he never felt the temptation to examine these areas in person, and he was able to secure only a few literary items of information about them. [15]

And for this reason alone he could fall victim to a forgery like the Jesus-Abgar correspondence. What then is the situation? Eusebius

21. See the index of literature cited in the Schwartz edition of EH, 3: 62.

declares often (above, 3) and with emphasis that he is dealing with a document from the archives of Edessa. Although we cannot be absolutely sure from his statement that he himself had translated the material from the Syriac, we can be certain that the material was given to him with the express assurance that it came from the public records of Edessa. It is well to note that it is not Jerome or some other questionable person that is speaking here, but a man whose devotion to truth and whose honesty are above suspicion. Thus for me, what he describes to be the state of affairs is reliable. This means that I proceed from the following assumption: Eusebius has not fabricated this himself, but has been deceived by someone else. And his credulity is explained first of all by his utter ignorance of the entire Mesopotamian situation, and perhaps also because the one who brought him the Syriac manuscript introduced himself in such a way as to preclude any misgivings. Later, we will suggest a possible solution to this problem (below, 35-39).

But first, a few observations. Naturally, based on the principle "Who stands to benefit?", the correspondence with its embellishments stems from Edessa. But it is noteworthy that even long after the appearance of Eusebius' *Ecclesiastical History* the *Edessene* public knows nothing of this exchange of letters. Ephraem of Edessa (d. 373), who praises the conversion of the city with rhetorical exaggeration, knows only of the sending of the apostle Addai, nothing more.[22] At least nothing else seems to him [16] worth mentioning. It is not that

---

22. See F. Haase, *Kirchengeschichte*, pp. 71 f.; R. A. Lipsius, *Die apokryphen Apostelgeschichten und Apostellegenden*, 2.2 (Braunschweig, 1884): 182 ff. Moreover, the only place, to my knowledge, in which Abgar appears in the works of Ephraem—and here not as a letter writer or author, but as a patient of Thaddeus—is in the appendix to his commentary on the *Diatessaron* (preserved in Armenian; Latin tr. by J. B. Aucher with ed. of G. Moesinger, *Evangelii concordantis expositio* [Venice, 1876], p. 287; ed. L. Leloir, CSCO 137/145 = Scriptores Armeniaci 1-2 [1953-54], 350/248; this material is lacking in the Syriac materials—see Leloir's introduction and French translation in SC 121 [1966]), against which one may raise doubts. Immediately after the interpretation of the gospel harmony, this text deals with the origin of the four canonical gospels, with which Ephraem had no close connection (cf. J. Schäfers, *Evangelienzitate in Ephraems des Syrers Kommentar zu den paulinischen Schriften* [Freiburg im B., 1917], especially 47), and adds a catalogue of heretics that has nothing in common with the struggle against false belief exhibited elsewhere by Ephraem, and can scarcely be derived from a treatise of Ephraem "*De Sectis*" (*On the Sects/Heresies*)—essentially it deals with the seven Jewish heresies that were known since the time of Justin and [16] Hegesippus (in EH 4.22.7). Ephraem *Carmina Nisibena* 27.62 (see below, n. 58) alludes to an apostle as the founder of the Edessene church, without saying more.

personal critical principles have determined Ephraem's selection; there is another apocryphal exchange of letters, between Paul and the Corinthians (from the spurious *Acts of Paul*), that he incorporates confidently into his Bible. Not until around the end of the fourth century or the beginning of the fifth do we find evidence that the Edessene Christians are acquainted with the Abgar saga, which has now increased considerably in scope beyond the form known to Eusebius (see above, 2-3)—it is attested by the pilgrim Aetheria,[23] who at the same time shows that her western homeland was acquainted with it, and by the *Doctrina Addai* (above, 3).

From this I conclude that someone in Edessa must have proceeded in an exceptionally cautious fashion. He did not endanger the undertaking by suddenly appearing in Edessa itself with the assertion that nearly three centuries earlier the city had stood in close connection with Jesus in person, which certainly would not have been accepted without contradiction, least of all by the opponents of those circles interested in the legend. Rather, this person made use of the zeal for collecting which characterized the learned and guileless bishop of Caesarea, who was wholly inexperienced with regard to the situation in Mesopotamia, slipped into his hands the "Syrian Acts," cheerfully and justifiably confident that this story soon would find its way back home in improved and enlarged form, now secure against all assaults.

Thus we find the Abgar saga to be a pure fabrication, without any connection with reality, which need not have emerged earlier than the beginning of the fourth century (see below, 35 f.), and which says nothing certain about the Christianity of Edessa in an earlier time. The converted king loses all claim to be taken seriously when one accepts him as a legendary figure and resolutely rejects any thought of a "historical kernel." The apostle Thomas, whose remains rested in Edessa from the fourth century,[24] and whose much earlier *Acts*

---

23. P. Geyer (ed.), *Itinera Hierosolymitana saec. IV-VIII* (CSEL 39, 1898), p. 19 (= 17.1). Cf. A. Bludau, *Die Pilgerreise der Aetheria* (Paderborn: Schöningh, 1927), 245 ff.—dated no earlier than the very end of the fourth century (ca. 394; p. 248).

24. According to Ephraem *Carmina Nisibena* 42.9-40 (see below, n. 58); *Edessene Chronicle* 38, for 22 August 394 (the day on which the shrine in the great church at Edessa, which is still called that of Thomas, was transferred there); [17] Rufinus *Eccl. Hist.* 2.5 (= 11.5 in the Schwartz-Mommsen GCS ed. of EH); Socrates *Eccl. Hist.* 4.18 [ET by A. C. Zenos, NPNF 2, series 2]; Sozomen *Eccl. Hist.* 6.18 [ET by C. D. Hantranft, NPNF 2, series 2].

stems from this region, [17] also converted a king, Gundafor of India (*Acts of Thomas* 24 ff.). This story may have provided inspiration for the fabricator, but it is not necessary to conjecture such a connection.

If Eusebius' *Ecclesiastical History* does not reach back to an earlier period as a source for Edessa, where else do we hear anything about the earlier time? We know that Sextus Julius Africanus, who stayed at the Edessene court as a friend of Abgar IX and companion to his son, was a Christian. But his Christianity could tolerate not only the close association with pagan princes, but even contact with Bardesanes, and in general was of such a sort that one could hardly describe him as a particular "type," and certainly not as a representative of "orthodoxy" in any ecclesiastical sense.[25] But that there were Christians of *another* kind in Edessa at that time does not need to be demonstrated, since we have just mentioned one such example in the person of Bardesanes. I pose the question: With respect to the history of the church of Edessa, how well does the widely held view stand up, that in the various cities at the beginning there existed communities of orthodox Christians—naturally orthodoxy is understood to involve a certain development and unfolding—who form the genuine kernel of Christianity, and alongside are minorities of those who are "off the track" and are regarded and treated as heretics? I raise the question as to how well it stands the test, and find the answer, it stands up poorly. Up to now nothing has spoken in its favor.

Even the *Edessene Chronicle* requires no different interpretation.[26] Quite the contrary. Compiled at the close of the sixth century,[27] [18] the *Chronicle* contains a lengthy account of the great inundation in Edessa in November of 201 C.E. prior to the actual chronology, which

25. See below, 159-165. The same may be said of the scripturally learned Macarius of Edessa, with whom Lucian, the spiritual foster-father of Arius, is supposed to have pursued his first studies according to Suidas and Symeon Metaphrastes (texts in J. Bidez [ed.], *Kirchengeschichte des Philostorgius* [GCS, 1913], p. 184). On the whole, when someone has obtained something from Edessa, it is scented with the odor of heresy, as with Eusebius of Emesa (d. 359) whose astrological inclinations caused the members of his diocese to oppose his installation. For the subtleties of trinitarian orthodoxy, on the other hand, he had no capacity. See G. Krüger, RPTK³ 5 (1898): 618 f.

26. Ed. by I. Guidi in part 1 of *Chronica minora* (CSCO, Scriptores Syri ser. 3, vol. 4, 1903), pp. 1-11. L. Hallier, *Untersuchungen über die Edessenische Chronik* (TU 9.1, 1893). [ET by B. H. Cowper in *Journal of Sacred Literature* 5 (1864): 28 ff.]

27. Hallier, *Chronik*, p. 63.

12

is presented for the most part in short sentences or sections. According to the concluding remark, this flood account purports to be the authentic record that King Abgar—at this time it is Abgar IX, whom we already know (see above, 4 ff.)—had drawn up and incorporated into his archives. According to the account, everything that lay in the range of the river Daisan, which flowed through the city, had been flooded, including the king's palace and "the holy place of the church of the Christians."

Thus by the end of the second century, at the latest, there was already a special Christian cultic edifice in Edessa, and therefore certainly also an organized church group.

With respect to the course of argument being pursued, I do no now intend to withdraw from the field by insisting that the co-religionists of Bardesanes could have sung their hymns in the above-mentioned house of God. Nor will I maintain that the Marcionites, of whose tremendous importance for the establishment of Christianity in Edessa we shall hear more (below, 16 and 21 ff.), were the owners of the building, and thus rule out the orthodox church at Edessa around the year 200. Finally, it is also not my intention to seek cover behind the *Chronicle* of Dionysius of Tell Mahrê (from the year 776),[28] which contains the same account of the inundation, only briefer and without mentioning the church building. Something else arouses my suspicions. Could there already actually have been a Christian church in Edessa around the year 200 that a neutral observer would have singled out for mention from the general catastrophe as the only building besides the royal palace? Is it not far more likely that Christian interest is manifest here? "The holy place of the church of the Christians" is too emphatic. The pagan archivist who was commissioned to frame the report would, in my opinion, have spoken either of the "holy place" or of the 'church"—both in the sense of the cultic building. The redundance points to a Christian. For at this time simply the *one* word alone—the church—can designate the building; with the expression "holy place," on the other hand, the emphasis falls upon the concept implied therein, which is to be rendered adjectivally—"the holy church of the Christians." But this,

28. Ed. by J. B. Chabot, CSCO Script. Syri 3.1-2 (1927, 1933), with corresponding Latin translation in CSCO 121 (= Scr. Syri 3.1, 1949). German translation by T. Nöldeke in Gutschmid, *Osroëne*, p. 7.

it seems to me, is an impossible mode of expression for an unbeliever. [19]

In addition, something more is recorded, and that settles matters for me. The Christian *Chronicle* which follows the pagan archival account notes for the year 205/6: "Abgar built the palaces[29] in his city," but it says nothing about that which must above all else have been of interest to its readers, the rebuilding of the church. And to illumine the state of things even more clearly, even to the most remote corner, it is more than a century before the *Chronicle* declares, for the year 313: "Bishop Ḳûnê (= *Koinos*) laid the foundation for the church in Urhâi. His successor Scha'ad built and completed it." Thus it was not a rebuilding, even of a structure that had lain in ruins for more than a century, but an initial construction of *the* church of Urhâi. *This* church was actually destroyed by flooding in the year 525 and was restored by the Emperor Justinian in lavish splendor.[30] Therefore a Christian of the sixth century, to whom it was, of course, self-evident that the apostolic emissary Addai had already built the church of Edessa,[31] may have felt the impulse to include the destruction of the church with the account of an earlier inundation. At any rate, this much seems certain to me—in the year 201 there was still no "church of Edessa."

Nevertheless, the *Edessene Chronicle* offers us also some important positive insights. In it an Edessene Christian of the sixth century has listed the succession of events that are of particular significance for his countrymen and his fellow believers. At the beginning, he also brings forward matters from secular history, but later the secular recedes more into the background. If we count as number 1 the chronologically, materially, and formally different account of the flood,

29. The pural number is explained by the official report, which speaks of a temporary winter dwelling for the king, and of a new palace ready for occupation in the summer. Cf. Hallier, *Chronik*, p. 91. That also helps us to understand the chronological interval between 205 and the year of the catastrophe in 201.
30. Procopius *Buildings* 2.7 (ed. Dindorf, 3 [Bonn, 1838]: 228; ed. and ET by H. B. Dewing and G. Downey, LCL [1940]).
31. *Doctrina Addai* (ed. Phillips, p. 30). This is repeated by, among others, Solomon of al-Basra, *The Bee* (ed. with ET by E. A. W. Budge [Oxford, 1886]), p. 109; and Bar Hebraeus (see Haase, *Kirchengeschichte*, p. 74). According to the Syriac biography of Bardesanes by Michael the Syrian (ed. J. B. Chabot, *Chronique de Michel le Syrien*, 1 [Paris 1899]: 183 f.; reproduced in F. Nau [ed.], P Syr 1.2 [1907]: 523), in 169, Bardesanes passed by the church built by Addai; see below, 38.

which today stands at the beginning, the *Chronicle* proceeds as follows: [20]

2. In the year 180 (of the Seleucid era = 133/32 B.C.E.), kings began to reign in Urhâi.

3. In the year 266 (Sel. = 44/43 B.C.E.) Augustus Caesar (*qsr*) entered upon his reign.

4. In the year 309 (Sel. = 3/2 B.C.E.) our Lord was born.

5. In the year 400 (Sel. = 88/89 C.E.) King Abgar (VI, 71-91 C.E.) built his mausoleum.

6. In the year 449 (Sel. = 137/38 C.E.) Marcion departed (*npq mn* = to go out) from the catholic church.

7. Lucius Caesar, in company with his brother, brought the Parthians into subjection to the Romans in the fifth year of his reign (this would be in 165 C.E.). [See below, n. 33]

8. On the 11th of Tammuz in the year 465 (Sel. = 11 July, 154 C.E.) Bar Daisan was born.

9. In the year 517 (Sel. = 205/06 C.E.) Abgar built the palaces in his city (see above, 14).

10. In the year 551 (Sel. = 239/40 C.E.) Mani was born.

11. In the year 614 (Sel. = 303 C.E.), in the days of the Emperor (*mlka*) Diocletian, the walls of Urhâi collapsed for the second time.

12. In the year 624 (Sel. = 313 C.E.) Bishop Kûnè laid the foundation for the church in Urhâi. And Bishop Scha'ad, his successor, built it and completed the construction (see above, 14).

And now it proceeds along the lines of ecclesiastical reporting:

13. In the year 635 (Sel. = 324 C.E.) the cemetery (*koimētērion*) of Urhâi was built, in the days of Bishop Aithilaha,[32] one year before the great synod of Nicaea.

14. In the year 636 (Sel. = 325 C.E.) Aithilaha became bishop in Urhâi. And he built the cemetery and the east side of the church. (This does not agree at all with 13, and it does not fit very well with 12, according to which Bishop Scha'ad had *completed* construction of the church.)

32. In Greek, *Aeithilas*. Cf. H. Gelzer (et alii), *Patrum Nicaenorum nomina* (Liepzig, 1898), p. LXI no. 78; also pp. 102 f. and Index 1 (p. 216), under Aïthalas.

15. And in the next year the synod of 318 bishops was gathered in Nicaea. (This bypasses 14 and is connected with 13.) [21]
16. In the year 639 (Sel. = 328 c.e.) an expansion of the church building of Urhâi was undertaken. (This again relates back to 14, where construction on the east side of the church is mentioned.)
17. In the year 649 (Sel. = 338 c.e.) Mar Jacob, bishop of Nisibis, died.
18. In the year 657 (Sel. = 346 c.e.) Abraham became bishop of Urhâi. And he built the chapel of the confessors.

Here I break off; the form of the *Edessene Chronicle* probably has been adequately illustrated. One further word about its contents is indispensable. In its particular details, the *Chronicle* cannot have been composed entirely by the Christian of the sixth century who is responsible for the work as a whole. Otherwise we could not understand how Jesus, in his relation to Abgar, and the apostolic missionary after Jesus' death could have been completely overlooked. Abgar V is not referred to at all, a fact that is all the more significant since we hear of Abgar VI; we also hear that Abgar IX had rebuilt his ruined palace, but find nothing of what modern scholarship says about him, that he was converted. The *Chronicle* has grown up gradually, as is already indicated by its inorganic connection with the originally independent archive account; [33] and the material surrounding the Council of Nicaea, with its discrepancies, leaves the impression of a literary seam, in which new material is joined to the old tradition. The older portion of the *Chronicle* certainly comes from the time in which the Abgar legend had not yet taken root in Edessa, and from a person who was still aware that the earliest history of Christendom in Edessa had been determined by the names of Marcion, Bar Daisan, and Mani. The first and third of this trio probably never had been in Edessa; at any rate Marcion's departure from the church, referred to in the *Chronicle*, took place not in Edessa, but in Rome. The inclusion of these names in a *Chronicle* from Edessa thus must be due less to the relationship of their persons to this city than to that of the doctrines that they advocated. If these three, and *only* these—with no "ecclesiastical" "bishop" alongside of them—are specified by name in

33. Item seven also is open to suspicion of being a later interpolation, on both formal and chronological grounds.

a Christian *Chronicle* of Edessa, that indicates that *the* form of religion and of Christianity which they advocated [22] represents what was original for Edessa. Ecclesiastically organized Christianity, with cultic edifice, cemetery, and bishop, first appears at the beginning of the fourth century—the time of Eusebius and of the Emperor Constantine —and from then on, it unremittingly determines the course of things for the chronicler.

To be sure, the existence of three other predecessors of Kûnê can be verified historically—Palût, 'Abshelama, and Barsamya.[34] But the sources on which one must rely in this matter are quite questionable: the *Doctrina Addai* from the turn of the fifth century, with its expansion of the Abgar story which wanders into utter impossibilities, and martyr acts from the same time and of equal worth. Only Palût need occupy us here. The other two figures are much less certain than is he. The *Doctrina Addai* asserts that Palût, who was made a presbyter in Edessa by the apostle Addai (one of the seventy-two disciples), betook himself to Antioch after the death of the apostle and there was consecrated bishop of Edessa by Serapion of Antioch (in office *circa* 190-210), who for his own part had received consecration at the hands of Zephyrinus of Rome (198-217).[35] Simon Cephas, who for twenty-five years had occupied the Roman chair, had chosen Zephyrinus as his successor. Even a critic of the stature of R. A. Lipsius discovers in this rumor a historical kernel, that Palût actually was consecrated to the office of bishop of Edessa by Serapion of Antioch.[36] And yet, apart from the actual names Serapion, Zephyrinus, and Simon Cephas, the statement of the *Doctrina Addai* is devoid of all credibility. No one can force the apostle Addai and his presbyter into the same time period with Serapion. Simon Cephas was not bishop of Rome, least of all not for twenty-five years; he could not have selected Zephyrinus, who was active a century and a half after his own time, as his successor; and again Zephyrinus could not have ordained Serapion, who already had ascended the throne almost a decade earlier. And finally, an Edessene presbyter around

34. Cf., e.g. Hallier, *Chronik*, p. 52.1; H. Leclercq, DACL 4 (1921): 2082-2088. F. C. Burkitt, *Early Eastern Christianity* (London: Murray 1904), pp. 31-35 (cf. 18-21), goes even further.
35. Phillips, *Doctrine of Addai*, pp. 5 (Addai as one of the 72 in Luke 10.1), 39 (Palût as presbyter), and 50 (Palût made bishop) of the translation.
36. Lipsius, *Die edessenische Abgarsage* (Braunschweig, 1880), pp. 8 f. [See also Lietzmann, *History*, 2: 264.]

200 would not have the slightest reason for receiving a higher consecration from Antioch. [23]

It is indeed confidently asserted that such a necessity did exist for him. But with what justification? Konrad Lübeck argues that even in the middle of the third century no one troubled himself about Antioch and its bishop. In the Easter controversy (at the end of the second century) Antioch played no role. "The bishops of Palestine and Syria ignore it and are united into a synod under the presidency of the bishops of Caesarea and Jerusalem in Palestine. Or on the other hand, the provinces [that is, those in the vicinity of Antioch] act independently and for themselves. . . . Antioch is still without any leading hierarchical central position among the Oriental provinces." [37] We can appreciate this to some extent when we consider what intellectual mediocrity this church endured at this time in having Theophilus as its bishop.[38] Others may have been like him; we can at least evaluate him with the help of his books to Autolycus. It does not follow that we ought to deny him authorship of this well-attested work (EH 4.24), as Viktor Schultze recently has recommended on the grounds that it "seems impossible that an Antiochene bishop could have composed a writing filled with so much folly and so many errors." [39] We can only receive this opinion of Schultze as an acknowledgment of the state of affairs in Antioch, as to what sort of inferior personalities could at that time be called to the leadership of the "church" there. On the basis of such leadership, it is hard to avoid drawing an inference as to the kind and number of those subject to him.

Nor does Serapion of Antioch, in his helpless conduct with respect to the gospel of Peter (EH 6.12.2-6), make a particularly imposing impression. If we consider all this, in addition to what Lübeck has adduced (above, n. 37), we are all the more disconcerted when

---

37. K. Lübeck, *Reichseinteilung und kirchliche Hierarchie des Orients bis zum Ausgang des vierten Jahrhunderts* (Münster, 1901 = Kirchengeschichtliche Studien 5.4), p. 100.

38. I fully realize that F. Loofs, *Theophilus von Antiochien adversus Marcionem* (TU 46.2, 1930) thinks otherwise. He respects Theophilus more highly and concludes that Theophilus "was greater than Irenaeus both as a writer and as a theologian" (431). To me, there is no comparison between the superior theologian Irenaeus and the shallow babbler of the *Apology to Autolycus*. A. Ehrhard has also raised objections to Loofs' judgment; *Die Kirche der Märtyrer* (Munich: Kösel, 1932), pp. 217 f.

39. V. Schultze, *Antiocheia*, Altchristliche Städte und Landschaften 3 (Gütersloh, 1930), p. 57.

Lübeck continues: "On the other hand it [i.e. Antioch] exercises, even if only temporarily, jurisdiction [24] even in countries that later were never subject to it, such as Edessa, whose bishop received consecration from Antioch." As evidence he makes reference to two books by Tixeront and Duchesne. In sum, among Greeks of the immediate neighborhood Antioch has nothing to say; but it exercises jurisdiction over Syriac-speaking people in a city which lies nearly three hundred kilometers away, as the crow flies [= 186 miles.] In my opinion such an interpretation collapses of its own weakness without any refutation. The two Frenchmen do not frighten us. They base their argument on those sources whose usefulness we have already contested (above, 17 f.), the Syrian legends from around the year 400 and later.

Just how loose the connections between Antioch and Edessa still must have been in the second half of the fourth century is well illustrated by the fact that in a recently published two-volume work on John Chrysostom [40] Edessa is not even mentioned, in spite of the fact that the church father was born in Antioch, worked in his home city for some decades, and composed a large part of his writings there.

In agreement with this is the fact that in the following instance where we are able to grasp the facts, nothing is said of Antioch. In 379 Eulogius was consecrated as bishop of Edessa by Eusebius of Samosata (Theodoret *Eccl. Hist.* 5.4). And the famous Rabbula, according to his *Life* (below, n. 60), was indeed elevated to the office of bishop in Antioch. Nevertheless, along with this is contained the recollection that the one who actually brought him to the bishop's chair in Edessa had been Bishop Acacius of Aleppo.[41] Not until the fourth century do we note something of Antioch's extending its ecclesiastical influence beyond its own territory. The Council of Constantinople in 381 says in Canon 2: "The bishops of the Orient [42] are to limit themselves to the ecclesiastical administration of the Orient

40. C. Baur, *John Chrysostom and His Time* (ET by M. Gonzaga from 2nd German ed. [post 1947], Westminster [Md.]: Newman, 1959–69).
41. Cf. C. Brockelmann, *Geschichte der christlichen Literaturen des Orients²* (Leipzig, 1909), p. 34. Basil of Cappadocian Caesarea is supposed to have offered Ephraem the Edessene episcopate (see E. Nestle, RPTK³ 5 [1898]: 407.42 f.).
42. This means the bishops from the eastern diocese according to the divisions of the empire established by Diocletian in 292. Mesopotamia and the Osroëne are included. Cf. Lübeck, *Reichseinteilung*, pp. 106 ff.

with the preservation of the privileges which the Canons of Nicaea [what is meant here is Canon 6, which however does not [25] more precisely define the "privileges"] guarantee to the church of Antioch." An effort at expansion by Antioch is obvious here, which is met by the attempt of a part of those Syrian nationals to link up with the West. We need not investigate whether, how and when this led to the point where the Edessene bishop actually received consecration from Antioch. It suffices that we now recognize the basis upon which, for example, the legend could grow that the "*catholikos*" or primate of the East, the head of the Persian church (he resides in the Mesopotamian city of Seleucia-Ctesiphon) is to be consecrated in Antioch. The men who occupied this office are found listed in *The Bee* of Solomon of al-Basra (see above, n. 31) and in some *Patriarchal Chronicles*.[43] The list begins—and already the somewhat musty air of Edessa hits us—with the apostle Addai, the missionary of the East. He is followed by his pupil Mari, who serves the Oriental church as actual founder of the patriarchate of Seleucia-Ctesiphon.[44] After him comes Abris or Abrosis (= Ambrosius), a relative of Jesus who is elected in Jerusalem and consecrated in Antioch. Next comes Abraham—related to James the Just—who also is ordained in Antioch. It is clear that we are dealing here not with history, but with legend.[45] When the *Doctrina Addai* then asserts that Palût had received his episcopal consecration in Antioch, we immediately recognize the legendary thrust, and sense that we are not in the second century, but in the fourth, at the earliest. Thus even with reference to the figure of Palût, there is no confirmation of the claim that there was already a bishop deserving of the name in Edessa prior to the year 200, that is, a bishop consecrated in the context of the "great church." The *Edessene Chronicle* apparently is correct when it begins the series of bishops only in the fourth century.

43. Cf. Burkitt, *Eastern Christianity*, pp. 28 f. G. Westphal, *Untersuchungen über die Quellen und die Glaubwürdigkeit der Patriarchenchroniken des Māri ibn Sulaimān, 'Amr ibn Matai und Salība ibn Johannān* (Strassburg inaugural dissertation, Kirchhain, 1901), pp. 38, 40, 44, 46-48.
44. Westphal, *Patriarchenchroniken*, p. 30.
45. Seleucia-Ctesiphon had never been dependent on Antioch. At the place where the legend must be brought into relationship with the existing situation at the time of the chronicler, there is a section explaining why the patriarch no longer, as previously, is consecrated in Antioch (see Westphal, *Patriarchenchroniken*, pp. 47 f., 53). For Edessa, which was part of the Roman Empire, conditions may have been different—but certainly not in the second century.

Not that the figure of Palût himself dissolves under the acid test of criticism. [26] But we must remove from his hand the episcopal staff of the West. Ephraem of Edessa testifies to his existence, and that in a form which astonishes us. In his twenty-second *"Madrash"* [metrical homily] against false teachers the church father, after he has named and abused all kinds of heretics, says in verses 5 and 6:

> They [i.e. the heretics] again call us [i.e. the orthodox] 'Palûtians,' and this we quite decisively reject and disown. Cursed be those who let themselves be called by the name Palût instead of by the name Christ! . . . Even Palût would not wish that people call themselves by his name. And if he were still living, he would anathematize all disobedience. For he was a pupil of the Apostle, who was filled with pain and bitterness over the Corinthians because they had given up the name of Christ and called themselves after the name of men [see 1 Cor. 1.13].[46]

Thus at the end of the second century (or possibly a bit later), Palût was the leader of those people in Edessa who confessed what later developed into orthodoxy in the sense acceptable to Ephraem. It is quite possible that Palût's own group called him "bishop." Certainly no one will want to introduce modern conditions into the picture and suggest that for one to be a "bishop," there must be thousands upon thousands of people who are his spiritual subjects. He who was called "bishop" at that time certainly would, in many cases, have had room for his entire constituency in a private house. But much more important than clarity about the title that he enjoyed in his own circles is the insight that Palût was the leader of a minority that was of such limited significance that the *Edessene Chronicle* could completely forget him in favor of such significant personalities as Marcion, Bardesanes, and Mani.

In addition to this, another point is of great importance—the fact that Palût and those in agreement with him first appear after Christianity of another type already is in existence. They had to identify themselves, and to allow themselves to be identified, by the name

46. See below, n. 58. The Syriac text from the Roman edition (vol. 2, pp. 437 ff.) is reproduced in the *Chrestomathia syriaca, sive S. Ephraemi Carmina selecta* of A. Hahn and F. L. Sieffert (Leipzig, 1825), pp. 137 ff. Cf. also the Letter of Jacob of Edessa to John the Stylite (below, nn. 49 and 55), in W. Wright, *Catalogue of the Syriac MSS. in the British Museum acquired since the year 1838* (London, 1870–72), p. 300, and *Journal of Sacred Literature* 10 (1867): 430 ff. [H. E. W. Turner, *Pattern of Christian Truth* (see below, p. 297 n. 9), p. 44, gives an ET of this passage from Jacob of Edessa.]

of their leader. The name of "Christians" was denied them. Surely [27] this was because that name could in no way clearly distinguish them from the Marcionites and the Bardesanites, probably also because the name "Christians" already had been appropriated by another group—naturally those who had come first, and had introduced Christianity of their own brand into the city.

When we ask who that might have been, the chronological sequence favors the Marcionites. Already around the year 150, Justin says that their false teaching has spread to the whole human race, and in the same connection, he emphasizes that they placed great value in being called "Christians" (*Apol.* 26.5-6). Similarly, Tertullian states: "Marcion's heretical tradition has filled the whole world" (*Against Marcion* 5.19). One may also suggest in support of Marcionite priority that although the teaching of Bardesanes, at least in its earliest stages,[47] remained a local Edessene phenomenon in which the name of the great "local son" hardly could have failed to play a role,[48] the Christianity of Marcion had become even more international than that of the apologists. It is true that Ephraem, like Justin before him (*Dial.* 35.4,6), is of the opinion that only the representatives of the unadulterated apostolic teaching may be called "Christians." The heretics on the other hand should have had to call themselves after the current human leader of their sect (*Madrash* 22.7). This view is so firmly rooted in his circles that later on it was even found necessary to defend Palût against the belief that he had been a heretic or even a heresiarch.[49] But that with Ephraem it expresses more a wish than a reality is clearly seen by his vexed acknowledgment: "They call us 'Palûtians.'" This is how things still stood in the fourth century. Since the appearance of Palût, nothing had changed in this regard.

As for the other side of the question, whether the Marcionites designated themselves simply as "Christians," here, as is so often the case, the true state of affairs has become unclear because we are informed about the heretics primarily by men of the church for whom it is simply self-evident that the name Christian belongs only to people of their kind. That in the early period this had not been true,

47. His students seem to have been the first to enter Greek-speaking areas; see EH 4:30.1.
48. This is confirmed by the indignation of Ephraem; *Madrash* 23.5.
49. See the twelfth Letter of Jacob of Edessa (above, n. 46, and below, n. 55), page 27 of the Syriac text.

at least not everywhere, in my opinion follows from the account of the conversion of Mar Aba, [28] patriarch of the Orient who died in 552. I have no thought of accepting the "History of His Marvellous and Divine Struggles" [50] as a whole. But one passage, which does not seem to be tendentious—indeed it stands in contrast to the otherwise prevailing rule—may still prove to be useful.

Mar Aba, originally a fanatical pagan, during an attempt to cross the Tigris was brought to see the light through a miracle and an ensuing conversation with a Christian ascetic Joseph, whose surname was Moses. He was struck by the strangeness of Joseph's clothing (the Syriac uses the Greek loan-word *schēma*), and wishing to know whether Joseph might be an orthodox, a Marcionite or a Jew, he asked (chap. 3): "Are you a Jew?" The answer was "Yes." Then comes a second question: "Are you a Christian?" To this comes also an affirmative response. Finally: "Do you worship the Messiah?" Again agreement is expressed. Then Mar Aba becomes enraged and says: "How can you be a Jew, a Christian, and a worshipper of the Messiah all at the same time?" Here the narrator inserts by way of explanation: "Following the local custom he used the word Christian to designate a Marcionite." Joseph himself then gives his irate companion the following explanation: "I am a Jew secretly [cf. Rom. 2.29]; I still pray to the living God . . . and abhor the worship of idols. I am a Christian truly, not as the Marcionites, who falsely call themselves Christians. For Christian is a Greek word, which in Syriac means Messiah-worshipper (*m²šⁱʰhiā*).[51] And if you ask me 'Do you worship the Messiah?', I worship him truly." [29]

50. Syriac text in P. Bedjan (ed.), *Histoire de Mar Jabalaha, de trois autres patriarches, d'un pretre et deux laiques nestoriens²* (Paris, 1895), pp. 206-274. German translation by O. Braun, *Ausgewählte Akten persischer Märtyrer*, BKV² 22 (Munich, 1915). In chapter 7, Mar Aba comes to Edessa. [For a brief summary of the life of this Mar Aba (Mār-abhā, Marī-abha; "the Elder"), see W. Wright, *Short History of Syriac Literature* (London: Black, 1894), pp. 116-118.]
51. The same comparison is used to explain the (Syriac) proper name *Kristiāna*, applied to the believers on the basis of Acts 11.26, in Aphraates, *Demonstrations* 20.10 [ed. J. Parisot, PSyr 1.1 (1894)], and in Marutha (ed. Braun, p. 41; see below n. 64). *Kristiāna* was used especially in Edessa as a designation for Christian: *Book of the Laws of the Countries* 46 (see above, n. 12); *Edessene Chronicle,* (addition to) the flood report (ed. Guidi, p. 2.4; see above, n. 26); Ephraem *Syrische Schriften* 2 (above, n. 46), 490 E—cf. ed. Overbeck, p. 161.24 (above, n. 13); *Doctrina Addai,* Syriac p. 49 (ed. Phillips; above n. 7); *Martyrdom of Shamuna and Guria,* chaps. 1, 7, 8, and *passim* (in F. C. Burkitt, *Euphemia and the Goth with the Acts of Martyrdom of the Confessors of Edessa* [London: Williams and Norgate, 1913]); Syriac *Apology* of Aristides 2.6 [ed. and ET by J. R. Harris and J. A. Robinson (Cambridge, 1893²)].

This story reveals that even at a relatively late date, Marcionites designated themselves as *the* Christians—much to the offence of the orthodox, who must be content with misleading alternatives such as "Messiah-worshippers." Is it not reasonable to suggest that something similar was true with respect to the beginnings of Christianity in Edessa? [52] That would be an excellent explanation of why the orthodox call themselves Palûtians until far into the fourth century, or at least are known by that name to the public. [53]

How hard they must have had to struggle for their existence is indicated clearly in our sources. For centuries the theologians among them had no demand more pressing than to contend against Marcion, Bardesanes and Mani, precisely those three who appear in the *Edessene Chronicle* as bearers of Christian thought prior to Eusebius. The first native Syrian ecclesiastical author of any importance, Aphraates the "Persian" sage (that is, he lived in or came from the Sassanid kingdom) dealt with Marcion, Valentinus, and Mani in his third treatise, [54] which according to his own account was written in 336/37. The absence of the Edessene native son Bardesanes is easily explained and is balanced by the inclusion of the gnostic Valentinus, whose influence penetrated both East and West and whom Hippolytus (*Ref.* 6.35.7), Eusebius (EH 6.30.3), and Epiphanius (*Her.* 56.2), as well as Syrian authors [55] and even the Armenian Moses of [30] Chorene [56] described as the spiritual foster father of Bardesanes. What persisted as Valentinianism in the areas known to Aphraates,

52. Naturally, it is not my intention to suggest that the Marcionites have made a universal claim to the name Christian, as their own monopoly. Well known is the Greek inscription from the year 318/19 from the vicinity of Damascus, referring to a *synagōgē Markiōnistōn* (W. Dittenberger, *Orientis graeci inscriptiones selectae* [Leipzig, 1903-1905] 608.1). But in those places where Marcionites *introduced* Christianity, the designation "Christians" was quite simply used of them.
53. See also below, n. 82, on the question whether the Marcionites called themselves "Christians" in Edessa.
54. *On Fasting* 9 (ed. Parisot, p. 115; see above, n. 51).
55. Jacob of Edessa (d. 708), in his 12th *Letter* to John the Stylite (ed. Wright, above nn. 46 and 49, Syriac page 26, line 2 from below); Theodore bar Khoni (ninth century) in his scholion ed. by F. Nau PSyr 1.2 (1907): 517 f. (= H. Pognon, *Inscriptions mandaïtes des coupes de Khouabir* [Paris, 1898], pp. 122 f.). Biographical materials concerning Bardesanes from Syrian sources are contained in the *Chronicle* of Michael the Syrian (Jacobite patriarch in Antioch, 1166–1199), ed. J. B. Chabot 1 (above, n. 31), p. 184 = ed. Nau, p. 523. Cf. F. Nau, *Une biographie inédite de Bardesane l'astréopologue* (Paris, 1897). For the heresies according to Philoxenus of Mabbug (d. 523), see Nau, PO 13 (1919): 248.7.
56. *Historia Armenia* 2, chap. 63 (ca. 450 C.E.). The text is in A. von Harnack, *Geschichte der altchristlichen Literatur bis Eusebius* 1.1 (Leipzig, 1893; supplemented reprint ed. K. Aland, Leipzig: Hinrichs, 1958), p. 188.

apparently became absorbed in Edessa by the teaching and the community of faith of Bardesanes.[57]

Concerning the situation in Edessa in the middle of the fourth century we would do best to let Ephraem inform us. He indeed names still other heresies, and behind the "pedants" whom he attacks but does not describe more specifically, more than one kind may be concealed. In poetry and in prose he fights against the followers of Marcion, Bardesanes, and Mani, whose names again and again he exposes to hatred and scorn; and he attacks them so vigorously, so frequently, and so explicitly that one cannot escape the impression that there is a pressing, present danger.[58] Of what significance is an Arius in comparison to them? He does, in fact, appear. Still, compared to them—this is around the year 370—his appearance is almost infinitesimally rare, and he is not "the ravening wolf," "the filthy swine," "the dreadful blasphemer." These designations are reserved for the "raving Marcion," the "deceiver Bar Daisan," and the "deranged Mani." [59]

Despite all his efforts, Ephraem was not able to exorcise the danger. With great tenacity the heretics held firmly to what appeared to them to be true. Their suppression was finally accomplished—to a large extent only by expulsion—by the powerful personality of the Bishop

57. H. H. Schaeder, "Bardesanes von Edessa in der Überlieferung der griechischen und der syrischen Kirche," ZKG 51 (1932): 21-74, has disputed (41 ff.) that Bardesanes may have been a student of Valentinus. He maintains that only contacts of a general gnostic sort and origin exist between the two figures (43).
58. The second Syriac-Latin volume of the Roman edition of the works of Ephraem, by S. E. Assemani (1740), contains 56 *Madrashes* (learned discourses in poetic form) against the heretics, primarily against the three named above (pp. 437-560; selections are reprinted in Hahn-Sieffert [above, n. 46], and there is a German translation by A. Rücker in BKV² 61 [= *Ephraem* 2, 1928], pp. 80 ff.). [The material has now been reedited by E. Beck in CSCO 169-170 = Scriptores Syri 76/77 (1957); for an introduction and ET of a few selections, see H. Burgess, *Select Metrical Hymns and Homilies of Ephraem Syrus* (London, 1853), xxviii-xxxi (from *Madrashes* 2, 53, 1, 55), lxv f. (M. 46), 142-155 (M. 14, 27).] See also G. Bickell (ed.), *S. Ephraemi Syri Carmina Nisibena* (Leipzig, 1866), nos. 43-51 and 66-77 [reedited by E. Beck, CSCO, pp. 218-219 and 240-241 = Scr. Syri pp. 92-93 and pp. 102-103 (1961 and 1963); ET of nos. 66-68 by J. Gwynn, NPNF 13, series 2 (1898)]. For anti-heretical prose writings of Ephraem, see C. W. Mitchell, *St. Ephraim's Prose Refutations of Mani, Marcion and Bardaisan* (2 vols., London, 1912–1921). The *Madrashes* against the remaining unnamed "pedants" ["disputers"] are in vol. 3 (1743) of the Roman edition, pp. 1-150 [ET by J. B. Morris, *Rhythms of St. Ephrem the Syrian* (Oxford: Parker, 1847), pp. 106-361].
59. Of the close relationship between Marcion, Bar Daisan, and Mani in Edessa, John of Ephesus still speaks in the sixth century in his *Lives* [or, *History*] *of the Eastern Saints*, ed. E.-W. Brooks, PO 17.1 (1923): 138 f.

Rabbula of Edessa (411-435). [31] And here, indeed, we find ourselves in a period in which the power of the state also was already deliberately cooperating in the suppression of outspoken heresy. The "Life of Rabbula," [60] composed after his death by a colleague of the bishop, pictures the heresies of their time and the attitude of Rabbula in the following manner, in which panegyric judgments and exaggerations are evident enough: "Even with many words I could not show how great was his zeal with respect to the Marcionites. This putrefying malignancy of Marcionite false teaching he healed with the solicitude of the great physician [= Christ] . . . full of long-suffering toward them. For God sent into their hearts fear in the presence of the holy Rabbula and they faithfully accepted his truth, so that they renounced their false teaching" (193.17-25).

Bardesanes had already been treated previously, and this entire section about the heretics was introduced by a comparison of Rabbula with Joshua (192.3 ff.): as Joshua found the land of Canaan full of the thorny undergrowth of paganism, so Rabbula found the Edessene region completely overgrown by the thicket of sins. Particularly flourishing in Urhâi was the evil teaching of Bar Daisan (192.11 ff.), until it was uprooted by Rabbula. "For once, through his cunning and the sweetness of his songs, this accursed Bar Daisan had drawn all the leading people of the city to himself, so that by them as by strong walls he might be protected." That is, Bardesanes nourished the foolish hope of being able to secure the permanency of his false teaching through the transient power of influential patrons. Rabbula did not proceed against them as had Joshua, did not blow them down with frightening trumpets, but with his gentle and kind language (193.1 ff.) succeeded in having their meeting place torn down and all their property transferred to his church; in fact, even obtained their building stones to use for his own purposes. He gently persuaded the heretics themselves of the truth of the apostolic teaching so that they abjured their error. Then he baptized them into Christ and took them into his (i.e. Christ's) [32] service. In this manner through his

---

60. Syriac text in Overbeck (above, n. 13), pp. 159-209; also in P. Bedjan, *Acta martyrum et sanctorum*, 4 (Paris, 1894): 396-470. German translation in G. Bickell, *Ausgewählte Schriften der syrischen Kirchenväter Aphraates, Rabulas und Isaak von Ninive*, BKV 102-104 (Kempten, 1874), pp. 166-211. [The references that follow in the body of the text are to pages and lines in the Overbeck edition.]

teaching he converted many sects and brought them into subjection to the truth. And he baptized thousands of Jews and tens of thousands of heretics into Christ in all the years of his episcopate (193.10 f.).

"And likewise, through his divine wisdom, he brought the deluded Manichaeans to careful consideration of reasonable understanding. Therefore they made their confession as he desired. And they believed in the truth, allowing themselves to be baptized into Christ and to be joined to his people" (193.25 ff.).[61]

Even when we make considerable allowance for the tens of thousands of heretics whom the enthusiastic disciple pictures as pressing for baptism at the hands of Rabbula, there is still enough left over for us to recognize the abiding attraction of those "heretical" teachings. Only through rather coarse methods [62] [33] was the "tyrant of

61. The danger of the Manichaeans for the environs of Edessa, in both a narrow and a broad sense, is also attested by the *Acts of Archelaus* by Hegemonius (from the first half of the fourth century [ed. C. H. Beeson, GCS 16 (1906); ET by S. D. F. Salmond, ANF 6: 179-235]), in which (the setting is fictitious) Archelaus, Bishop of Charchar (= Carrhae-Harran, in Mesopotamia) disputes with Mani himself. A biographical sketch of Mani (see below, n. 93) in Syriac by a Christian author can be found in the *Chronicon Maroniticum* (MS of the 8/9 century) ed. by Brooks, *Chronica minora*, 1.2: 58-60 (above, n. 3; Chabot's Latin translation, 47 ff.); similar materials are found in Theodore bar Khoni (ed. Pognon, *Inscriptions mandaïtes*, pp. 125-127 and 181-184; see above, n. 55), in the *Chronicle* of Michael the Syrian (ed. Chabot, vol. 1: pp. 198-201; see above, n. 31), and already in Epiphanius *Her.* 66.1 ff.

62. Cf. also Rabbula's *Rules for Priests and Clerics* (ed. Overbeck, pp. 215-222; see above, n. 13), where arraignment in chains before the municipal judge is prescribed as a means of ecclesiastical discipline (218.16 [ET in Burkitt, *Eastern Christianity*, p. 146 #27]); similarly 219.11 f. Moreover, pressure is brought to bear on ascetics and consecrated virgins who withdraw from monastic life that not only they, but also their parents be cut off from communion (218.22 [ET in Burkitt, p. 147 #28]). This harsh step was later considered too severe. To the words "their parents" is added the phrase "if they agree with them" in Bar Hebraeus ("Book of Directions" or *Nomocanon* for the Syrian church of Antioch, a Latin translation of which, by J. A. Assemani, appears in A. Mai, *Scriptorum veterum nova collectio e vaticanus codicibus* 10.2 [Rome, 1838]), p. 58.

In general, Rabbula was neither the only one nor the first to employ such unscrupulously callow and violent measures in the struggle with heresy. Emperor Julian writes to the Bostrians, who had been persecuted by his imperial predecessor, how "many multitudes of the so-called heretics had even been executed" (*polla de hēde kai sphagēnai plēthē ton legomenōn hairetikōn*) in Samosata, which is near Edessa, and various regions of Asia Minor. Entire villages had been completely depopulated and destroyed (*Epistle* 41 [ed. and ET W. C. Wright, LCL 3 (1923)] = 141 ed. Bidez = 52 ed. Hertlein). This is the context to which belongs the cry of triumph that Theodoret strikes in his letters—eight whole Marcionite villages he has "converted" in his bishopric, a thousand, yea ten thousand Marcionites (A. von Harnack, *Marcion: das Evangelium vom fremden Gott*[2] [TU 45, 1924; repr. Darmstadt, 1960], pp. 158, 341° f., and 369° ff. (cf. 454° f.).

Edessa" [63] able to alienate the heretics, at least outwardly, from their former faith. That makes it easy to imagine how strong an appeal these beliefs might have had in the freshness of their youth, before any pressure was exerted against subscribing to them. What was achieved in Edessa—to be honest about it—was at best only the outward submission of people whose buildings had been torn down, whose scriptures had been burned, whose community goods had been confiscated, and who found themselves subjected to the worst kind of harassment, including danger to life and limb. Thus it would be illegitimate for one to reason back from the situation which Rabbula had brought about by force, and to use this as a corrective to the picture that we have discovered for the time of Ephraem, when orthodoxy in Edessa still occupied a quite secondary place.

Our case is supported by still another consideration. The situation in Edessa during the fourth century would hardly have been much different from that in the southwest part of Greater Armenia, a region not far from Edessa and part of the Roman Empire. Here an older colleague of Rabbula, Bishop Marutha of Maiperkat (= Martyropolis), who died prior to the year 420 and like Rabbula, spoke Syriac, describes the situation as follows: [64] Satan brings a profusion of heresies to the church, and things go so far that there are as many heresies as there are bishops—an instructive use of the superlative from both points of view. "The orthodox decreased and became like *one single* stalk of wheat in the great field of tares. . . . Thus the heresies flourished." Of course, this too is an exaggeration of pious anxiety. But it certainly strengthens the impression that even far into the fourth century orthodoxy simply had not prevailed against heresy in its various forms. [34]

In the picture that the representatives of the church sketch, it is precisely the detail about a great apostasy from the true faith that is seen to be incorrect—in any event, it is not true of Edessa. Here it

---

63. This is what the presbyter Ibas calls his bishop, Rabbula; cf. his letter to bishop Mari [or Maris] of Hardashēr in Persia (probably from the year 433), in J. D. Mansi, *Sacrorum Conciliorum nova collectio,* 7 (Florence, 1762): 245—*ho tēs hēmeteras poleōs tyrannos.*
64. German translation by O. Braun, *De Sancta Nicaena Synodo* (Kirchengeschichtliche Studien 4.3 [1898]). See also A. von Harnack, *Der Ketzerkatalog des Bishofs Maruta von Maipherkat* (TU 19.1[b], 1899). The Syriac text is edited by I. E. Raḥmani in *Studia Syriaca* 4: *Documenta de antiquis haeresibus* (Mt. Libano, 1909), pp. 76-80 and Syriac pp. 43-98.

was by no means orthodoxy, but rather heresy, that was present at the beginning. Christianity was first established in the form of Marcionism, probably imported from the West and certainly not much later than the year 150.

After some time, probably considerably before 200, a dangerous rival to Marcionism developed in the person and doctrine of the native son Bardesanes. The differences became obvious to everyone and demanded a decision. "Bar Daisan adorns himself," [65] so Ephraem orates, "with fine clothes and precious stones; Marcion is clothed with the garb of a penitent. In the grottoes of Bar Daisan are heard hymns and songs—amusements for the youth; Marcion fasts like a serpent" (*Madrash* 1.12 and 17). Elegance, education, artistic sense, culture, in a word openness to the world collided with ascetic fanaticism and the most extreme world-rejection. With respect to Christology, Bardesanes would have been able more easily to come to an agreement with Marcion than with the orthodoxy of the "great church." Here it is instructive to observe that Bardesanes did not dispute with orthodoxy, in spite of the fact that, even apart from Christology, sufficient sources of irritation would have been present in Bardesanes' astrology, belief in fate, and rejection of the resurrection. Instead, he engaged in a feud with the Marcionites, noise of which echoed for a long time.[66] Orthodoxy, embodied in the handful of Palûtians who perhaps already were in existence, apparently presented no threat for people like him in Edessa at that time. But Marcion had to be eliminated, or at least repressed, in order to gain room for the new development.

This was achieved by forming his own community with its own meeting place and its own order of worship, in which the splendid psalms of the accursed "new David" [67] played such a great role, and also by using his own "scripture," since the Marcionite Bible was unsuitable both in terms of content and for personal reasons. [35] Perhaps Bardesanes acknowledged no Old Testament, if his 150 psalms were intended to take the place of the Davidic corpus and if the statement by Ephraem can be taken literally: "He [= Barde-

---

65. Schaeder, "Bardesanes," 30.12, renders it "he [= the devil] adorns Bardesanes."
66. Cf. EH 4.30.1, Bardesanes writes *dialogoi* against the Marcionites; Theodoret *Her.* 1.22; Hippolytus *Ref.* 7.31.1, refers to a polemical writing against Bardesanes by the Syrian Marcionite Prepon.
67. This is what Ephraem calls Bardesanes in *Madrash* 53.5 f.

sanes] did not read the prophets but the books of the Zodiac" (*Madrash* 1.18). But certainly he possessed a New Testament. It is not simply our idea to equip the rival of Marcion in such a way, but Ephraem refers expressly to Bardesanes' *Apostolos*.[68] And an *Apostolos* without a corresponding "Gospel" to precede it never existed anywhere. Thus we are confronted with the question: what did the gospel of Bardesanes look like? As has been said, it is out of the question that Bardesanes could have adopted the gospel used by the Marcionites; but it is equally unlikely that there was a special "Gospel of Bardesanes," of which we scarcely hear anything, and never anything of value.[69] Likewise, it could not have been the so-called Gospel of the Separated [*Evangelion da-Mepharreshe*]—i.e. the four canonical gospels arranged one after another but regarded as a unit. At a time in which Irenaeus strives rather laboriously to establish the fourfold gospel in the "great church," it cannot already have been in use in Edessa. Furthermore, if that had been the case, it is inconceivable how the fourfold gospel then could have disappeared once more from this city for a quarter of a millennium, or at least have receded so completely into the background for Edessene Christianity. The view that one or another of the four constituted the gospel of Bardesanes—perhaps the Gospel of John, which the western Valentinians Heracleon and Ptolemy treasured so highly—is purely a hypothetical possibility, the further pursuit of which is unrewarding.

Thus there remains, it seems to me, only the so-called *Diatessaron,* the [36] harmony of the gospels which Tatian, shortly before the appearance of Bardesanes, offered to the Syriac speaking Christians as the first written gospel in their native language. In favor of the *Diatessaron* as the gospel of Bardesanes is first of all the general observation that for a Syrian living among Syrians, the most obvious

68. *Commentary on the Pauline Epistles;* see T. Zahn, *Geschichte des neutestamentlichen Kanons,* 2.2 (Leipzig, 1892): 598.
69. A collection of Nestorian narratives, preserved in Arabic and published in PO 5 (1910), contains a "History of Ephraem" in which it is reported on the basis of ancient authorities that Bardesanes used a gospel different from the canonical gospels (p. 298). But this evidence cannot be used. Bardesanes and Ephraem supposedly are contemporaries here. The manner in which Ephraem obtains a copy of the book is completely unbelievable, all the more so since it is quite similar to what is related in the panegyric on Ephraem by ps. = Gregory of Nyssa, only there the story refers to Apollinaris and his blasphemous writing (cf. also Haase, *Kirchengeschichte,* p. 334). Even if, in spite of this, there is some validity to the report, it is not difficult to bring it into harmony with the view that I have suggested above.

thing to do would be to obtain that Syriac book, the recent appearance of which in Mesopotamia could not have been unknown to Bardesanes because of his connections and his sophistication. It was much more comprehensive than the scanty [70] gospel booklet of the Marcionites that had been used previously in Edessa. And even though Tatian himself had not done so, a member of his school by the name of Rhodon composed writings in opposition to the sect of Marcion just at the time Bardesanes flourished (EH 5.13.1), and thus established himself as a desirable ally. Under such circumstances there would have been hesitation only if the contents were felt to be objectionable, thus precluding it from acceptance as the true gospel.

Clearly this was not the case. On the contrary, it contains certain similarities to Bardesanes' teaching that are all the more comprehensible if, as Irenaeus had already claimed, Tatian also had come under the influence of Valentinus.[71] While the Syriac gospel-harmony excluded Marcion's view that Jesus had come directly from heaven to the synagogue at Capernaum by eliminating the genealogies of Jesus as well as everything that was connected with the birth of Jesus from the seed of David according to the flesh,[72] it could accommodate the interpretation of Bardesanes concerning the heavenly body of the Lord, which had only passed through Mary but had not been formed in her.[73]

If Bardesanes already had introduced the *Diatessaron* in Edessa and [37] had made it popular there, it becomes easier to understand how that later, among the orthodox Edessenes, the gospel edition of a person whose heretical position the church had never been able to overlook [74] could gain canonical status. The numerically weak

70. This peculiarity requires little demonstration. That Marcion's opponents clearly perceived this is intrinsically self-evident. According to Irenaeus, the Marcionites had a "circumcised little Gospel"; H. Jordan, *Armenische Irenaeusfragmente* (TU 36.3, 1913), 135, no. 10.16 f.

71. Irenaeus, AH 1.28.1 (= 26.1) = Hippolytus *Ref.* 8.16 = *Eusebius* EH 4.29.3. Cf. Clement of Alexandria *Strom.* 3.(13.)92; *Chronicle* of Michael the Syrian (ed. Chabot, vol. 1: p. 181; see above, n. 31).

72. Theodoret *Her.* 1.20.

73. See the Bardesanite Marinus, in Adamantius *On the True Faith* 5.9 (ed. van de Sande Bakhuyzen, GCS 4 [1911], 190.24 ff); Ephraem in his interpretation of *3 Corinthians* (Zahn, *Geschichte*, 2.2; 597 f.; see above, n. 68). Cf. also the eastern Valentinian *"Ardēsianēs"* in Hippolytus *Ref.* 6.35.7.

74. Irenaeus AH 1.28.1 (= 26.1), 3.23.8 (= 37)—*Tatianus connexio quidem factus omnium haereticorum;* Rhodon, once a student of Tatian; Clement of Alexandria; Origen; Tertullian; Hippolytus; *Acts of Archelaus;* and later witnesses. The passages are listed and the most significant reproduced by Harnack, *Geschichte*, 1.1: 486 ff.

group of Palûtians, composed of poor people—the wealthy Christians in Edessa adhered to the prominent Bardesanes (see above, 26, 29)— were probably not in any position to provide their own Syriac gospel. Of the two books available, that of Marcion and the *Diatessaron*, the latter was decidedly more orthodox in orientation—indeed, under a not very penetrating examination, it was simply orthodox. It would have had very little to fear from a comparison with the gospels used in the "great church" as books of instruction. There was scarcely a single instance in which Tatian had expressed his particular views by means of additions, but to a much greater degree had expressed them by means of omission. But such omissions are so characteristic of the style of a harmony that in a particular case one can almost never determine for certain whether the omission was due to literary considerations, or whether it reflects the malicious wickedness of the false teacher.

"Not only Tatian's group have used this book," says Theodoret of Cyrus as late as the fifth century (*Her.* 1.20), "but the adherents of the apostolic teaching also have innocently employed the book as a convenient compendium, since they did not recognize the deception of the compilation. I myself found more than two hundred such books which were being held in honor in the congregations of our region; I collected and destroyed them and in their place introduced the gospels of the four evangelists." This is the way in which the Palûtians also may have come into contact with the *Diatessaron*, and without prejudice, had put it to use. It was much better than having no gospel at all in the language of the people, in spite of its being tainted with the approval of Bardesanes—possibly the Palûtians knew nothing of Tatian, since the name of a human author seldom remains attached to such gospel compilations, by their very nature.

As for the letters of Paul, it is first of all indisputable that a collection [38] of writings of the Apostle to the Gentiles was used by the Christians of Edessa from the very beginning. For if Marcion stands at the beginning of Edessene Christianity, with him stands also the apostle Paul. It was only in the contents and order of this corpus that a difference existed between Marcionites,[75] Bardesa-

75. Mention of Marcion's particular textual recension, which obviously was not, as a whole, used beyond the bounds of his own community, will suffice at this point. [See Harnack, *Marcion²*.]

nites,[76] and the orthodox. To be sure, it is not entirely certain when this difference became obvious. The fact that both Ephraem and an orthodox Syrian canonical list from around the year 400 agree with Marcion in the arrangement of the letters of Paul at important points [77] encourages the suggestion that in Edessa, with reference to the Pauline canon, Marcion's influence was not limited to his immediate adherents. We observe how "heretical," or better "original" conditions effect later epochs and how even the ecclesiastical structure cannot avoid this. That strengthens our belief in the correctness of the view presented above, that Edessene orthodoxy received the *Diatessaron* through Bardesanes and his community, just as it received the letters of Paul ultimately from Marcion.

But at what point did the orthodox actually become something of a power factor—we do not mean for Edessa as a whole, but rather, within the Christianity of that city? It makes sense to pose the problem in this more modest form, for at the beginning of the third century the totality of those baptized, including all kinds, constitute only a small minority by comparison to the [non-Christian] Edessenes with their customs (*Laws of the Countries* 32 and 40; see above, n. 12). Perhaps the wisest thing to do would be to refrain from offering a more detailed answer to the above question on the grounds that it is impossible to do so. In spite of this, however, I will seek to give an answer, although with full awareness that I am thereby treading on uncertain ground to a greater degree than previously.

I should like to ascribe the decisive influence to *that* person whom the *Edessene Chronicle* names as the first bishop, Kûnê (*Koinos* in Greek). He was the one, if I am correct, who organized orthodoxy [39] in Edessa in an ecclesiastical manner and gave to it significant impetus—with the assistance of favorable times, yet not without merit of his own. At the beginning of such a development, especially in a region in which one must prevail against strong rivals by his own power, must stand a person of energy, ability, and determination, who also has time to expand. That Kûnê was a man of exceptional

76. It is uncertain whether Bardesanes had been influenced by Tatian also with respect to his "Apostolos"; cf. EH 4.29.6, and the comments of Zahn, *Geschichte* 1.1 (1887): 423 ff.
77. Cf. T. Zahn, *Grundriss der Geschichte des neutestamentlichen Kanons*[2] (Leipzig, 1904), pp. 48-50. W. Bauer, *Der Apostolos der Syrer in der Zeit von der Mitte des 4. Jahrhunderts bis zum Spaltung der syrischen Kirche* (Giessen, 1903), pp. 32 ff.

importance is confirmed by the fact that among the sacred buildings of Edessene Christianity a "house" (Syr. *beit*) of Mar Ķûnê later was displayed,[78] probably a chapel dedicated to him. At any rate this is evidence that grateful recollection distinguished him from the multitude of bishops, although he had not suffered a martyr's death.

As to his length of time in office, I would prefer to appeal to Leclercq, who has Ķûnê active from before 289 until 313.[79] Unfortunately, however, only the year of his death is unquestionably established by the *Edessene Chronicle* (above, 15, item 12). A *terminus ad quem* for his entrance into office is provided by the *History of the Martyrs Shamuna and Guria*, which can be trusted as far as the externals are concerned because they are two of the three Edessene marytrs who are named already in the ancient Syrian martyrology contained in a manuscript written in Edessa in 411/12, the contents of which certainly go far back into the fourth century.[80] They suffered in the days of Ķûnê,[81] but perhaps not until the year 309. This in no way rules out a more lengthy episcopate for Ķûnê, but neither does it champion that possibility with the desired vigor. Only a period of some half-dozen years is a firm necessity. [40]

In any event, in that which the *Edessene Chronicle* lists as his achievement, the building of the church, Ķûnê waited until the end of his days, when he had to be content only with laying the foundation. Too much should not be ascribed here to accident. If Ķûnê allowed the year 313 to arrive before remedying a deficiency that he surely had already been aware of for a long while, this demonstrates the powerful purposefulness of a person who knows how to interpret the signs of the times and to take advantage of favorable circumstances without hesitation. For it is certainly significant that 313 is the very year in which, on the 13th of June, after the victory over Maximinus in Nicomedia, Licinius issued an edict of toleration that

78. *Chronicle* of Joshua the Stylite 43 (ed. W. Wright [Cambridge, 1882 repr. Amsterdam, 1968], p. 39.8). The context indicates that this does not refer to the church founded by Ķûnê [mentioned above, 15 item 12].

79. Leclercq, DACL 4: 2088 f.

80. See H. Achelis, *Die Martyrologien*, Abhandlung der Gesellschaft der Wissenschaften zu Göttingen, 3.3 (1900), pp. 30-71, with extensive reference to the work of L. Duchesne. A German translation is given by H. Lietzmann, *Die drei ältesten Martyrologien*, Kleine Texte, 2^2 (1911), pp. 7-15.

81. So chap. 1 of the *History*; the text is found in Burkitt, *Euphemia*, Syriac p. 3.8 f. (see also pp. 90 and 29 ff.). [Burkitt, *Eastern Christianity*, 22 and 131, dates their martyrdom in 297.]

now guaranteed Christians the free exercise of religion even in the East and explicitly decreed that the confiscated meeting houses and all possessions should be returned to the church without cost to them. Kûnê took advantage of the favorable situation immediately, and certainly did not hesitate to present the claims of his community. There was no meeting house to be returned to them, but there were all sorts of possessions, which facilitated the construction of a new building.

Just as I have refused to view as coincidental the contemporaneity of the church building and the edict of toleration, I now wish to go a step further and to oppose the assumption that it happened by chance that Eusebius prepared and issued his *Ecclesiastical History* precisely in the same years that Kûnê was in office. In this, we turn back to the question as to who had been the *spiritus rector* [guiding light] in the fabrication of the Abgar legend (see above, 10-12). I would suggest that it was Kûnê, who surely did not intend to give expression to his parochialism thereby, but wished to strike a powerful blow against the false beliefs. It has already been established that only Edessene Christians had an interest in the falsification (above, 10). But we can describe these Christians with even more precision; they were solely the orthodox. Marcionites and Bardesanites could not trace their origins back beyond the founders of their sects. Or, if they attempted to do so, the story that served such a purpose must take a turn that shows how the revelation of Jesus has come down unadulterated through the generations to Marcion or Bardesanes—something like what is reported by Hippolytus (*Ref.* 7.20.1), that Basilides was said to have been in contact with the apostle Matthias, to whom Jesus in secret instruction had communicated the Basilidian teaching. Yet in our case nothing of this sort occurs. On the contrary, from the very beginning it is one of the anti-heretical [41] devices of orthodoxy to demonstrate how the church, in contrast to the heresies which stem from men and are named for them, establishes through the apostles a sure line of contact with the Lord himself, which it never needed to break. If Jesus in person already has ordered the gospel to be preached in Edessa by his apostle, then the teaching of Marcion, Bardesanes, or even Mani immediately is unmasked and condemned as a human work by way of imitation. They have belatedly stolen their sheep from someone else's flock. Ephraem says: "Bar Daisan designated and called his flock by *his* name. Moreover, the flock of Mani is called by *his* name.[82] Like stolen sheep they are marked with the detestable brand of the thief. It is Christ who has gathered them; [thus] the sheep are [to be called] Christians" (*Madrash* 56.1). Then the apostles, the "sons of truth," are described as *the* ones who as the wedding attendants of Christ have secured for him the bride who is to be called by his name (*Madrash* 56.2; cf. 22.3).

Thus, with the tentativeness that limits all such conjectures, it was Kûnê who gave the impetus for the establishment of the Abgar saga and secured for it the widest conceivable distribution and credibility by slipping the "Syrian records" into the hands of Eusebius, who was collecting materials for his *Ecclesiastical History*. If the latter had been inclined at all to examine his materials critically, such thoughts must have been further from his mind than ever in this case.

We need not make excuses for the Edessene bishop to whom we attribute such a deed. He lived in an epoch in which the growth of Christian legends flourished, and which accepted a remarkable number of them to help oppose the heretics. So as not to go too far from Edessa, we need think only of the Syriac *Didascalia* as an apostolic writing, of the *Apostolic Constitutions* and the expansion and reworking of the collection of Ignatius' letters, and of the *Testament of Our Lord Jesus Christ*.[83] [42] It is not necessary to point to examples such as Juvenalis of Jerusalem in order to establish the probability that even bishops were associated with "forgeries."[84] It was simply self-evident that they would look after the interests of the true faith in the most effective manner. What other authority stands behind the church orders mentioned above, if not the bishops?[85]

Even the apostles had not viewed things differently and had not shrunk from using methods that a lesser mind perhaps would have

---

82. Here only Bardesanes and Mani are lumped together, whereas in the wider context of the hymn, Marcion again fills out the trilogy of leading heretics in the usual way. Could this be additional evidence that such a rebuke would not apply to the contemporary Edessene Marcionites because they call themselves simply "Christians?" See above, 24.

83. The numerous legends of martyrs and saints can be left aside. [On *Didascalia*, see below, 244-257 (244 n. 7 also provides material on *Apostolic Constitutions*); the *Testamentum Domini* was edited by I. E. Raḥmani (Mainz, 1899).]

84. Cf. Schultze, *Antiocheia*, p. 231.

85. Concerning such forgeries in the first half of the fourth century, see A. von Harnack, *Die Briefsammlung des Apostels Paulus und die anderen vorkonstantinischen christlichen Briefsammlungen* (Leipzig: Hinrichs, 1926), pp. 31 f.

called questionable. Possibly Kûnê was acquainted with the story that found its way into a metric homily of Jacob of Sarug (d. after 519), and tells of the conversion of Antioch by the apostles Peter, John, and Paul.[86] At first the former two begin to preach in Antioch. But Aëtius, the high priest of the city, stirs up the populace against them and, instead of having success, they are beaten and their heads are shaved as a mark of disgrace. Paul meets the men thus humiliated, and explains to them that one cannot proceed in such an innocent and simple manner—purely as a preacher of the gospel. He proposes the following crafty procedure, which meets with their approval. He pretends to be a pagan and becomes an associate of Aëtius. As the chief defender of the religion then dominant in Antioch, he demands a miracle of the newcomers as proof of the correctness of their faith. Thereupon Peter heals a blind man. But Paul proceeds to do the same, seemingly with the help of the pagan gods, but in truth by means of a secret invocation of the name Jesus. Thus the scales are evenly balanced. So as to bring about a decision, Paul demands that his alleged opponent raise a dead person. If he can do this, Paul would then accept the faith in the God of the Christians. So, in the theater in the presence of all the people, Peter calls back to life the dead son of a prominent Antiochene. Now Paul enacts his conversion, and great masses of people follow his apparent example. In the house of Cassian, the father of the resuscitated young man, a church is established, and in it the new converts are baptized. [43]

If the apostles themselves proceed in such a fashion,[87] who would blame the bishop for his actions on behalf of the correct faith? To wish to apply here the categories of "honest" and "dishonest" is to employ a standard that is simply out of place. Moreover, to the extent that Kûnê also shares the firm conviction of his circle that heresy is conceivable only as a departure from the true (i.e. his own) faith, he is operating in good faith. The orthodox Christian was not able to understand that at the beginning the heresies often were nothing

---

86. A. Baumstark, *Die Petrus- und Paulusacten in der litterarischen Überlieferung der syrischen Kirche* (Leipzig: Harrasowitz, 1902), pp. 27-29.
87. Cf. also the recently published *Apocalypse of Peter;* A. Mingana, Woodbrooke Studies, 3.2 (Manchester, 1931), p. 93 ff. Here the Apostle to the Gentiles, and Peter with him, plays almost a double role (132 ff., 396 ff.). He behaves like an idolater before the "King of Antioch" and then before the emperor, and by this clever, obliging conduct, which Peter supports with great miracles, secures the conversion of the rulers and of their people.

but mixtures, produced in the soil of syncretism, in which elements of the most diverse kinds, including some Christian, were bound together into a new unity. He interpreted Christian elements as indications of original adherence to the *one* church, the protectress of all genuine Christian possessions. And if the originator or the representative of the divergent approach actually stood outside the "church," this was either because he himself had withdrawn from it, usually for impure motives, or because he had been expelled from the church as being unworthy.

That the apostolic teaching, which is identical with the conception of orthodoxy of all times and places, had been present long before there was heresy is also the view of Edessene orthodoxy of the fourth century. As Ephraem explains (*Madrash* 24.20 f.): "For years the apostles preached, and others after them, and still there were no tares." They first emerge with Marcion.[88] And, in fact, they emerge in such a way that Marcion withdrew from the orthodox church, a point that the *Edessene Chronicle* also explicitly noted.

With Bardesanes it is no different. The *Edessene Chronicle*, it is true, does not claim that he withdrew from the church, or that Mani did so. And in Eusebius the correct information is still preserved that Bardesanes originally was a Valentinian of sorts (see above, 24 f.) and [44] had never shared the faith of the church (EH 4.30.3). However, already in Epiphanius he is depicted as having withdrawn from the church (*Her.* 56.1.2). Jacob of Edessa clearly pictures him as having been removed by force.[89] But alongside this, the Syrians tell the following edifying story, which has been transmitted in various forms.[90] Bardesanes had grown up somewhere outside Edessa as the adopted son of an idolatrous priest, who taught him pagan hymns. When he was twenty-five years old, his father sent him to Edessa to make some purchases. There he passed the church built by Addai and heard Bishop Hystaspes explaining the scriptures to the people. The discourse pleased Bardesanes so much that he wished to be

88. Cf. also *Madrash* 23.10: "Let us go back even before Bar Daisan and Marcion to the earlier ones, who are more ancient than Marcion."
89. In his twelfth epistle (see above, n. 55), Syriac page 27 (ed. Wright): "The adherents of Bar Daisan . . . got their start from him. When he was expelled from the church of the orthodox of Urhâi, many adherents of his wickedness followed him and founded a heresy and a sect for themselves."
90. Theodore bar Khoni (above, n. 55), ed. Nau, 517 = ed. Pognon, pp. 122 f. Michael the Syrian (above, n. 31), ed. Chabot, vol. 1: pp. 183 f. = ed. Nau, 523.

initiated into the secrets of Christianity. Hystaspes taught him, baptized him, and ordained him as a deacon or presbyter. Now he would have liked to become bishop. But when he was not able to do this, he left the church [91] and became a Valentinian; and when even in this setting his ambition was not completely fulfilled, he founded his own sect.[92]

From the same sort of viewpoint, Mani is said to have become a Christian presbyter who fought against Jews and pagans, but then he turned his back upon the church because his pupils were not accepted with their message.[93] Thus for Bishop Kûnê, the Abgar legend is only a concrete expression of his bedrock [45] conviction that *his* faith is older than all heresy and therefore also must have made its appearance in Edessa, with a clearly apostolic seal, earlier than heresy.

But the Abgar legend is perhaps not the only example of the way in which Kûnê attacked the heretics through literature, and summoned Jesus with the apostles against them. If with some confidence we may conjecture such efforts on his part, then surely it is also permissible to explore this approach still further, and to explain a peculiarity of the Edessene Bible that is particularly striking along with the presence of the *Diatessaron*. The Pauline canon also had a peculiar shape in Edessa, since it contained a third letter to the Corinthians, or more correctly, an exchange of letters between Paul and the

91. This is yet another recurrent device in the struggle against heresy: frustrated ambition drives the one in question out of the church and causes him to become a heresiarch. Tertullian already says this of Valentinus (*Against Valentinus* 4; cf. *Prescription against Heretics* 30). Epiphanius reports a similar story about Marcion, who is supposed to have wanted to be bishop of Rome (*Her.* 42.1).
92. Burkitt (*Eastern Christianity*, pp. 30 f., 156 ff., 187 ff.) agrees with this presentation to the extent that he pictures Bardesanes as having first belonged to the orthodox church, after which he turned to "gnosis" and was excommunicated. [But Burkitt is himself quite sympathetic to Bardaisan, whom he calls "the best scientific intellect of his time," and is saddened that Syrian orthodoxy rejected him through "intellectual cowardice" (189; see also 34 f.). It is not clear that *Burkitt* would want to call him "gnostic."]
93. See above, 27 n. 61, for the relevant materials from *Chronicon Maroniticum* and Michael the Syrian. According to Epiphanius *Her.* 66.5 ff., Mani deceitfully passes himself off as a Christian. [For other similar references, see K. Kessler in RPTK[3] 12 (1903), 202.20 ff., and the recently published Arabic material in S. Pines, "Jewish Christians" (below, p. 314 n. 31), pp. 66 ff.—Mani was first a priest, then bishop/metropolitan in Christian Persia, before proclaiming his objectionable message. By way of contrast, Eusebius has nothing of the sort in his vituperative paragraph on Mani (EH 7.31); see also Cyril of Jerusalem *Catecheses* 6.21 (on the Unity of God)—"Mani was not a Christian. Far be it. He was not thrown out of the church like Simon" (for text, see Migne, PG 33; ET by E. H. Gifford, NPNF 7, series 2 [1894]).]

Corinthians with a connecting passage in between. At the time of Ephraem, this material had a firm spot in the New Testament, and in Ephraem's commentary on Paul it is dealt with after 2 Corinthians. Since Aphraates already cites two passages of "3 Corinthians" as the words "of the apostle," the letter must have been accepted as canonical in Syriac-speaking areas, and above all in Edessa, around the year 330. Neither the Syriac *Didascalia* nor Agathangelos' notice about Gregory the Illuminator, the apostle of the Armenians,[94] provide any evidence that this would have been the case earlier.

Indeed, Ephraem asserts that the Bardesanites had not admitted "3 Corinthians" into their Bible because it contradicted their teaching.[95] And if he were correct, we would have to conclude that the letter was already regarded by the Palûtians as sacred by the time Bardesanes' false teaching arose; and that would guarantee for the Palûtians greater antiquity than has been conceded to them. However, the discovery and deciphering of the Coptic version of the *Acts of Paul* by Carl Schmidt [96] has established that the correspondence originally formed a part of the *Acts of Paul,* and that makes the assertion of Ephraem impossible. For, [46] as we learn from Tertullian, the apocryphal story of Paul had been composed only about the year 180 or even later, after Bardesanes was fully active, by a presbyter in Asia Minor, "as though he could add something on his own authority to the reputation of Paul" (*On Baptism* 17). The author himself confessed that he had acted out of love for the Apostle to the Gentiles. Thus we see here quite clearly an officer of the "great church" perpetrating a "forgery" that focuses upon an apostle. In view of these considerations, a Syriac translation of the correspondence and its use in Edessa before the third century is quite inconceivable. And it is not the patrons of "3 Corinthians" but rather Bardesanes and his people who bear witness to the earlier situation by their silence concerning the letter.

But Ephraem was correct at one point. In a life devoted to fighting

94. See E. Rolffs, "Paulusakten," in Hennecke[2], p. 195.
95. In the Armenian works of Ephraem, ed. by the Mekhitarists in Venice, vol. 3 (1836), p. 118. German translation in Zahn, *Geschichte,* 2.2: 598; J. Vetter, *Der apocryphe dritte Korintherbrief* (Vienna, 1894), p. 72.
96. C. Schmidt, *Acta Pauli aus der Heidelberger koptischen Papyrushandschrift Nr. 1* (Leipzig, 1904, 1905[2]). [This material was reedited by Schmidt and W. Schubart (Hamburg: Augustin, 1936); for more recent developments, see W. Schneemelcher in Hennecke-Schneemelcher, 2: 322 ff.]

heretics he had learned by experience that the Bardesanites rejected "3 Corinthians" as non-apostolic because it conflicted with their viewpoint; they had become acquainted with this material at a later period through its incorporation into the Bible of their orthodox fellow citizens, and from their disputes with them. This makes sense, since the correspondence was intended, in the context of the work of its orthodox inventor, as part of the anti-gnostic polemic. Once again the question arises: who was interested in introducing such literature in Edessa? And again comes the only possible answer: only the orthodox —with their farsighted and industrious bishop Kûnê leading the way. For it was in the century in which his tenure falls, from the beginning of the third to the beginning of the fourth century, that the exchange of letters must have been incorporated into the canon of the orthodox in Edessa.

Even in this case, the integrity of Kûnê is to a large extent maintained. He certainly never doubted for a moment the authenticity of this Pauline correspondence. To him it was only a new confirmation of his unshakable confidence that he, rather than the heretics, was in agreement with the apostles. We can perhaps infer from a remark made by Ephraem in his commentary on "3 Corinthians" how the *Acts of Paul* came to Edessa. According to this, the Bardesanites have written apocryphal Acts of the apostles in which the miraculous deeds of the apostles are told, but at the same time the teachings of the Bardesanites also had been put into the mouths of the apostles— [47] perhaps the *Acts of Thomas* is the main target here.[97] We know how the "church" met the efforts of the heretics to influence the common man through such popular books—partly by reworking the heretical works in an orthodox fashion, and partly by using their own newly created works containing barbed thrusts against the enemy, where such works existed. In the latter category, we may include the *Acts of Paul;* which Eusebius values much more highly than the gnostic *Acts of Peter*—the latter he simply rejects (EH 3.3.2), while he counts the former among those writings whose canonical worth is not sufficiently firm (EH 3.3.5, 25.4). By using a little imagination, we might picture Kûnê's emissaries to Eusebius returning home to their bishop and bringing the Pauline material in exchange for the

97. See G. Bornkamm, *Mythos und Legende in den apokryphen Thomasakten* (Göttingen, 1933), pp. 86 f., [and more recently, Bornkamm's treatment of the *Acts of Thomas* in Hennecke-Schneemelcher, 2: 425 ff.].

"Syriac records," as an instrument for combatting the apostolic books of the Bardesanites.

We will disregard such possibilities. But I would consider it certain that the *Acts of Paul* came to Edessa *as a whole*,[98] for the correspondence probably became separated from the body of the work in an area in which the former actually came to have a separate existence, which up to the present time is not demonstrable for the Greek-speaking world.[99] I do not wish to dwell upon hypotheses as to why Kûnê, or whoever it was, did not incorporate into his New Testament the entire document, but only the correspondence most immediately connected with the apostle, with its clearly discernible anti-heretical attitude. (I have already had to assume much more than I would like, but unfortunately, in this area, there is very little that one can know for sure.) Perhaps this was decided for him by the fact that the Lukan Acts of the Apostles, which was exegeted as holy scripture by Ephraem some decades after Kûnê's tenure, already occupied a place in the Edessene Bible. Possibly the *Acts of Paul* also was too extensive for him and was still not sufficiently authenticated as a whole. Or he was offended, as were other churchmen, by the role played there by Thecla—especially since in the Marcionite communities women possessed the right to administer baptism.[100] [48] Furthermore, there certainly would be much less resistance to the innovation if only the correspondence were added, and thus it would become all the more difficult for the heretics to parry the thrust. One could easily turn the figure of Thecla into something ridiculous. Perhaps Kûnê was on his guard because he could observe an actual example such as the Sabbatians,[101] who later were opposed by Ephraem. "A woman," scoffs Ephraem, "brings the Sab-

---

98. On the use of the *Acts of Paul* among the Syrians, see Baumstark, *Petrus-und Paulusacten*, and W. Bauer, *Apostolos*, pp. 19-21.

99. [Discoveries subsequent to 1934 necessitate some readjustments in this argument, for a Greek text of "3 Corinthians" has appeared among the Bodmer papyri (several Latin fragments also are known)—see M. Testuz, *Papyrus Bodmer X-XIII* (Cologne-Geneva: Bibliotheca Bodmeriana, 1959), and W. Schneemelcher in Hennecke-Schneemelcher, 2: 326 f. For the Latin text, see A. Harnack, *Die apokryphen Briefe des Paulus an die Laodicer und Korinther*[2], KT 12 (1912): 8 ff.]

100. Cf. Harnack, *Marcion*[2], pp. 147 and 365°, n. 2.

101. In the heresy-catalogue of Marutha (above, n. 64), they are treated first. More precise information concerning them is found in the 12th letter of Jacob of Edessa (above, n. 55). The text is on Syriac p. 25, line 13 from below (ed. Wright). See also Rücker, *Ephraem*, 2: 12 f. (above, n. 58).

batians under her power, so that they bow their heads beneath her hand. Sitting on the teacher's chair in the chancel,[102] she rants at them and derides their beards. Is that not a reproach and a shame to nature itself?" (*Madrash* 2.6). Thus there are reasons that could make it seem advisable to an Edessene churchman to limit the addition to the exchange of letters between Paul and the Corinthians.

We need not tarry longer on this point. These closing comments about Kûnê are intended only to bring into some kind of focus various lines of the investigation that we had to pursue. The time of Kûnê itself lies far beyond the boundaries of the period which we have in view. We are concerned with the beginnings. And the investigation of these beginnings for the history of Christianity in Edessa has made us aware of a foundation that rests on an unmistakably heretical basis. In relation to it, orthodoxy comes to prevail only very gradually and with great difficulty, becoming externally victorious only in the days of Rabbula, and then through means the use of which leaves behind a bitter taste—means that no one had dared to use in the pre-Constantinian era.

102. Jacob of Edessa stresses explicitly that at that time, there had been a church of the Sabbatians in Urhâi (Syriac p. 26.5 ff., ed. Wright). Jacob knows from personal experience (lines 13 ff.) that the place where they gathered was still called by his contemporaries "church of the Sabbatians."

2

Egypt

Let us now turn our attention to another region, which resembles Edessa in its physical proximity to the cradle of Christianity and possesses an even greater significance for the intellectual as well as the ecclesiastical history of Christianity, namely Egypt, and the origins of Christianity there. What we have observed with respect to Edessa makes it difficult for us to accept the attitude with which even the most competent investigators approach this subject. For example, Adolf von Harnack says:

> The most serious gap in our knowledge of primitive church history is our almost total ignorance of the history of Christianity in Alexandria and Egypt . . . until about the year 180 (the episcopate of Demetrius). It is only at that time that the Alexandrian church really emerges for us into the light of history. . . . Eusebius found nothing in his sources about the primitive history of Christianity in Alexandria. We can with more or less probability suppose that certain very ancient Christian writings (e.g. the *Epistle of Barnabas* . . . [*et alia*]) are of Egyptian or Alexandrian origin, but strictly speaking, this can hardly be demonstrated for any one of them.[1]

This implies simply that there is nothing in the sources. But they are too uncommunicative. *Something* ought to be found in them!

1. Harnack, *The Mission and Expansion of Christianity in the First Three Centuries*[2], 2 (ET by J. Moffatt from the 2nd German edition of 1906; London: Williams and Norgate, 1908): 158 f. The material of this second edition is revised and extensively supplemented in the 4th German edition (Leipzig, 1924); thus reference to both ET and the more recent German ed. are included below (see German[4] 2: 706 f., for the above quotation).

44

Now these sources were certainly seen and inspected, if not written, by churchmen. What reason could they have had for being silent about the origins of Christianity in such an important center as Alexandria if there had been something favorable to report?

Eusebius, who "found nothing in his sources about the primitive history of Christianity in Alexandria," had in any event [50] searched very diligently in them. He repeats various items from pagan reporters concerning the Jewish revolt in Egypt under Trajan (EH 4.2), quotes excerpts from Philo and in his desperation even allows Philo's Therapeutae (below, n. 14) to appear as the oldest Christians of Egypt and to be converted by Mark, the first bishop of Alexandria, after Philo previously had been in touch with Peter in Rome (EH 2.16-17). He traces a succession of ten bishops from Mark down to the reign of the Emperor Commodus (180-192).[2] But this list, which he owes to Sextus Julius Africanus, serves only to make the profound silence that hangs over the origins even more disconcerting. "There is absolutely no accompanying tradition"—since this is so, what may be gathered at best is still almost less than nothing.[3] And the timid notation of that copyist of the *Ecclesiastical History* of Eusebius who calls Annianus, the immediate successor of Mark, "a man beloved by God and admirable in all things,"[4] does not raise the tradition above the zero point. The first ten names (after Mark, the companion of the apostles) are and remain for us a mere echo and a puff of smoke; and they scarcely could ever have been anything but that. At least, here and there, the Roman succession list to the time of the Emperor Commodus offers us a living personality. And even in the defective catalogue of Antioch (see below, 63-64), with its half dozen names for the same span of time, we already meet a familiar face in Ignatius, quite apart from the sixth figure, Theophilus. There is simply nothing comparable that can be established for Alexandria. Yet we can hardly suppose that some inexplicable misfortune overtook the account of the earliest period of Egyptian church history, and in this way explain the deathly silence.

In the same vein as those remarks from Harnack quoted above

2. EH 2.24, 3.14, 3.21, 4.1, 4.4, 4.5.5, 4.11.6, 4.19, 5.9. For the various names, see the GCS edition by Schwartz, vol. 3: p. 9.
3. Harnack, *Geschichte* 2 (*Chronologie*) .1 (1897): 205 f.
4. *Anēr theophilēs kai ta panta thaumasios.* See the apparatus to EH 2.24 in the GCS edition.

(cf. to n. 1) are the brief lines which Karl Müller has recently devoted to our subject: [5]

> It is precisely because of the strength of the Jewish community in Alexandria [51] that Christianity cannot long have been absent from Egypt.[6] Yet we have no actual reports about it: it is unknown whether Apollos of Alexandria (Acts 18.24) already had become a Christian in his native city, and the literary vestiges (the *Epistle of Barnabas*), like the beginnings of gnosticism in Alexandria, first appear in the time of Hadrian. But in any event, this evidence permits the inference that Christianity was present in the country at the latest by the turn of the century,[7] a conclusion that, on other grounds, also could hardly be doubted.

The question whether Apollos already was a Christian in Alexandria is answered in the affirmative by codex D at Acts 18.25, where he is said to have preached already "in his homeland."[8] Be that as it may, it is perhaps no accident that here also, as in Eusebius' *Ecclesiastical History* (see above, 45 n. 4), an amplification of the original text insists on knowing something about the most primitive period of Christian Egypt. But even supposing codex D were correct, surely no one would care to label as in any sense "ecclesiastically oriented faith" that mixture made up of Alexandrian Judaism and scriptural learning, of discipleship to John which knows only the baptism of the Baptist and of Christian ingredients—Apollos himself does not at first proclaim more than this at Ephesus. Also of quite uncertain value is the letter of the Emperor Hadrian to the Consul Servianus quoted by Flavius Vopiscus, *Vita Saturini* 8, though a historian of the stature of H. Gelzer regards it as authentic, and Harnack is also willing to give it consideration.[9] According to the context (7.6), this letter comes from the writings of Phlegon,[10] the

---

5. K. Müller, *Kirchengeschichte*[2], 1 (Tübingen: Mohr, 1929): 121. Cf. also Lietzmann, *History*, 1: 132 f.

6. Is it possible to demonstrate, not as an occasional occurrence, but as a general rule, that a large population of Jews would immediately attract Christianity?

7. Notice that here, too, we have the good ecclesiastical view that "the beginnings of gnosticism" must presuppose the prior existence of "Christianity" in the same locality.

8. [Strictly speaking, the Greek of codex D says only that Apollos was *instructed* in Christianity at Alexandria: *hos ēn katēchēmenos en tē patridi ton logon tou kuriou*.]

9. Gelzer, *Sextus Julius Africanus und die byzantinische Chronographie*, 1 (Leipzig, 1880): 16; Harnack, *Mission*[2], 2: 159 f. n. 4 (= German[4] 2: 707, n. 3).

10. See W. Weber, *Untersuchungen zur Geschichte des Kaisers Hadrianus* (Leipzig: Tuebner, 1907), pp. 97 ff.

freedman of Hadrian. In the letter, the emperor remarks that he is well acquainted with the Egyptians as frivolous and avid for novelties: "Here those who worship Serapis are [at the same time] Christians, and those who call themselves bishops of Christ are also devotees of Serapis. Here there is no synagogue leader of the Jews, no [52] Samaritan, no Christian presbyter who is not also an astrologer, a haruspex, and an *aliptes*" (8.2 ff.).[11] That the document is spurious seems to me readily demonstrable; nevertheless, that one could falsify in such fashion is not without significance.

Certainly neither Philo, when he complains of the distress of the Jews under Caligula,[12] nor the Emperor Claudius, in the letter to the Egyptian prefect L. Aemilius Rectus in which he demands the cessation of strife between pagans and Jews,[13] gives the slightest hint that there were also Christians in Alexandria. Likewise, no one today would dare to suppose with Eusebius (EH 2.16-17) that Philo's "Therapeutae" were Christians.[14]

When K. Müller deals with the *Epistle of Barnabas* prior to his discussion of gnosticism, perhaps he views it as a representative of some sort of orthodoxy in Alexandria. But quite apart from the fact that its origin in Egypt is no more than a possibility, its orthodoxy must also be viewed as suspect. The basic thesis of the *Epistle,* that Judaism is an aberration with which Christianity can have nothing to do, but which deserves only rejection, remains gnostic—even if, by means of a thoroughly grotesque allegorization, which turns the Old Testament topsy-turvy with respect to its literal meaning, a condemnation of Jewish scripture ostensibly still is avoided. Actually, the Valentinian Ptolemy has retained more of the Old Testament than

11. *Scriptores historiae Augustae,* ed. E. Hohl (2 vols, Leipzig 1927): *Aegyptum . . . totam didici levem pendulam et ad omnia famae momenta volitantem, illic qui Serapem colunt Christiani sunt et devoti sunt Serapi qui se Christi episcopas dicunt, nemo illic archisynagogus Iudaeorum, nemo Samarites, nemo Christianorum presbyter non mathematicus, non haruspex, non aliptes.* The final word is from the Greek *aleiphein,* to anoint. [The haruspex performs divination by interpreting the entrails of sacrificial victims.]
12. [Philo *Embassy to Gaius* 162 ff. and *passim.*]
13. Papyrus London 1912, dated 41 c.e. [10 November]. [For the text, ET, and an up-to-date discussion of the document, see V. A. Tcherikover and A. Fuks, *Corpus Papyrorum Judaicarum,* 2 (Cambridge: Harvard University, 1960), no. 153, pp. 36-55.]
14. See above, p. 45 [Philo describes the Therapeutae in his *On the Contemplative Life.* In connection with the theory that the "Dead Sea Scrolls" are of Jewish-Christian origin, J. L. Teicher recently has argued for the Christian origin of this allegedly Philonic treatise; cf. e.g. his article on "The Essenes" in *Studia Patristica,* 1 (TU 63, 1957): 540-545.]

has *Barnabas*. And quite similar to the latter may have been the approach of the Valentinian Theotimus, who took such pains with the "ideas of the law." [15] Quite significant is the high esteem enjoyed by the concept "knowledge" and the term "gnosis" in Barnabas. [16] We find the progression repeated: "wisdom, insight, knowledge, gnosis" (2.3, 21.5). Christians are to add "perfect gnosis" to their faith (1.5). And repeatedly, it is "gnosis" that perverts the real sense of the Old Testament (9.8, 10.10, 13.7). A passage from scripture is adduced and then the question raised: "but what does gnosis say about this?" (6.9). If we add that the Christology of *Barnabas* contains nothing which can be interpreted as *anti*-heretical—but on the contrary, it seems docetic—then the document has, to my mind, forfeited any claim to represent the ecclesiastically orthodox faith in Alexandria. [53]

Again, we are hardly brought into the realm of orthodoxy by that story which Justin tells concerning "one of our people" in Alexandria, as a proof of the high level of Christian morality (*Apol.* 29.2-3). This individual is stated to have lodged a *biblidion* with the prefect Felix [17]—a petition requesting that a physician be permitted to emasculate him. The physicians refused to fulfill his wish without the governor's authorization. Although the prefect refused permission, the young man led a moral life even without the physical operation.

Certainly there were Christians in Egypt in the middle and at the beginning of the second century—this story proves nothing more than that. But the burning question is, of what sort were they? Everything that we know of this Christianity, apart from what has been mentioned already, clearly has grown up apart from all ecclesiastically structured Christendom until far into the second century. Its personal representatives of whom we hear are the gnostics [18]—Basilides, with his son Isidore, Carpocrates and Valentinus, with various of his dis-

---

15. Tertullian *Against Valentinus* 4: *multum circa imagines legis Theotimus operatus est.*
16. [See the material collected by R. A. Kraft, *Barnabas and the Didache* (= Grant, AF 3, 1965), pp. 22-27.]
17. The person meant is L. Munatius Felix, who held office around the year 150. See A. Ehrhard, *Die altchristliche Literatur und ihre Erforschung von 1884–1900, 1: Die vornicänische Literatur* (Freiburg im B., 1900), p. 220.
18. According to the ps.-Clementine *Hom.* 2.22, Simon Magus already is supposed to have acquired all his gnostic knowledge and skill in Alexandria (cf. 2.24). [Actually, the texts speak of "Egypt" in general as the source of Simon's "magic."]

ciples,[19] Theodotus and Julius Cassianus—the overwhelming majority of whom demonstrably come from the land of the Nile.[20] Apelles, the independent pupil of Marcion, also was active here,[21] and according to Hippolytus, Cerinthus had been trained in Egypt.[22] The Barbelo-Gnostics also flourished here under the influence of Valentinus and produced a work which is preserved in Coptic under the title *Apocryphon of John* and which served Irenaeus as a source for his presentation of those [54] gnostics.[23] It must therefore have originated prior to 180, and that type of Egyptian gnosticism must be older still.

There are also other writings which, like the one just mentioned, betray their homeland by their language: Coptic-gnostic gospels and other apocryphal materials,[24] including the *Pistis Sophia* (which in turn presupposes the use of the gnostic *Odes of Solomon* in Egypt), and the *Books of Jeû*—gnosticism of the first water. We have also recently learned of a very copious Manichean literature in Coptic.[25]

19. The Valentinians still had communities in Egypt in the second half of the fourth century, as well as elsewhere in the East. Cf. Harnack, *Geschichte,* 1. 1: 174.
20. Cf. Harnack, *Mission*[2], 2: 159-162 (= German[4] 2: 707-710). J. P. Kirsch, *Die Kirche in der antiken griechisch-römischen Kulturwelt* (1930), pp. 185-195. I mention here only persons and movements that can be *proved* to belong to Egypt. The fact that the widely travelled and very well read collector, Clement of Alexandria, knows and fights them is not in itself sufficient evidence (cf. *Strom.* 7.[17.]108). Nevertheless, it is more than likely that other such heretics also flourished in Egypt, without leaving behind any express witness.
21. Tertullian *Prescription against the Heretics* 30; Harnack, *Marcion*[2], pp. 177 and 179 f.
22. *Ref.* 7.7.33 and 10.21. [According to the corresponding Latin material preserved in Irenaeus AH 1.26.1 (= 21), "in Asia" not "Egypt."]
23. AH 1.29 (= 27); C. Schmidt, "Irenäus und seine Quelle in adv. haer. I, 29." in *Philotesia* (Festschrift for Paul Kleinert; Berlin, 1907), pp. 315-336. [The text has now been edited by W. Till, *Die gnostichen Schriften des koptischen Papyrus Berolinensis 8502* (TU 60, 1955), pp. 33-51, 79-195. For other recently discovered Coptic forms of the text, see M. Krause and P. Labib (eds.), *Die drei Versionen des Apokryphon Johannes im koptischen Museum zu Alt-Kairo* (Abhandlung der Deutsche Akad. I, Koptische Reihe 1; Berlin, 1962). An ET of Till's text may be found in R. M. Grant, *Gnosticism: an Anthology* (London: Collins, 1961), 69-85, and further discussion of the document by H. C. Puech in Hennecke-Schneemelcher, 1: 314-331.]
24. C. Schmidt, "Ein vorirenäisches gnostisches Originalwerk in koptischer Sprache," Sb Berlin for 1896, pp. 839-847. Cf. Hennecke, "Bruchstücke gnostischer und verwandter Evangelien," Hennecke[2], pp. 69 ff. [A more up-to-date survey of these materials by H. C. Puech is now available in ET in Hennecke-Schneemelcher, 1: 231-362 (see also pp. 511-531).]
25. C. Schmidt and H. J. Polotsky, "Ein Mani-Fund in Ägypten," Sb Berlin 1 for 1933. [More recently, cf. H. Ibscher, *Manichaean Manuscripts in the Chester*

Although some of this literature certainly must be dated subsequent to the year 200, there still belongs to the beginning of the second century that book which Clement of Alexandria, the earliest possible witness for such things, already knows by the title *The Gospel of the Egyptians.*[26] The construction with *kata* is here, as in the similarly formed superscriptions to the canonical gospels (e.g. *to kata Matthaion euaggelion*) a good Greek substitute for the genitive. Since there surely never had been a heretical group called "the Egyptians," the designation *Gospel of the Egyptians* points back to a time in which the Christians of Egypt used this gospel, and only this gospel, as their "life of Jesus." And the pronounced heretical viewpoint of the *Gospel of the Egyptians*[27] accords well with what we have had to conjecture about the earliest state of Egyptian Christianity. For several of the gnostics enumerated above, the use of the *Gospel of the Egyptians* is demonstrable on good authority.[28] The Salome with whom the apocryphal gospel depicts Jesus in conversation is also a popular figure in subsequent extra-canonical [55] Egyptian gospel literature.[29] Moreover, the followers of the Egyptian gnostic Carpocrates derived the origin of their teaching from Salome.[30]

It may seem remarkable that the name *Gospel of the Egyptians* should arise in Egypt itself and be used by Christians there. They would have had no occasion to speak of their *lone* gospel as the gospel "of the Egyptians." It would simply be *the* gospel. The special designation presupposes a plurality of gospels which makes a distinction necessary. Quite right! It is only in this context that the expression

Beatty Collection, 2: A Manichaean Psalm-Book, 2 (Stuttgart, 1938), and *Manichäische Handschriften der staatlichen Museen Berlin, 1: Kephalaia,* 1 (Stuttgart, 1940). See also below, 315 n. 35.]

26. *To kat' Aigptious Euaggelion, Strom.* 3.(9.)63, 3.(13.)93.

27. Cf. Bauer, RGG², 1 (1927): 114; Hennecke in Hennecke², pp. 55-59. [More recently, O. Cullmann in RGG³, 1 (1957): 126 f.; W. Schneemelcher in Hennecke-Schneemelcher, 1: 166-78.]

28. Theodotus, in Clement of Alexandria *Excerpts from Theodotus* 67 (cf. *Strom.* 3.[6.]45.3, 3.[9.]63-64 and 66); Julius Cassianus, in *Strom.* 3.(13.)92-93. The gnostic Naassenes also made use of it according to Hippolytus *Ref.* 5.7.

29. Cf. *Pistis Sophia,* ed. by C. Schmidt in his *Koptisch-gnostische Schriften,* 1 (GCS 13, 1905): 401, col. 2 (name and subject index) [revised by W. Till (GCS 45, 1954²), p. 417, col. 2]. The Coptic text was published by Schmidt in *Coptica,* 2 (Copenhagen 1925), with the name index on p. 450. [For ET of *Pistis Sophia* see G. R. S. Mead (London, 1921²) or G. Horner (London, 1924).]

30. So Celsus according to Origen *Against Celsus* 5.62. Surely it is they who are concealed behind the name *"Harpocratianoi"* that is transmitted in the text.

"of the Egyptians" can be correctly appreciated. The phrase would be completely incomprehensible if one supposes that only a heretical minority of the Egyptian Christians used this book while, on the contrary, the majority employed the canonical gospel, or at least some of them. The gospel of a minority could never have been called simply the Gospel of the Egyptians.[31] And neither the Gospel of Matthew, nor that of Luke, really constitutes a plausible (i.e. a natural) antithesis to the Gospel of the Egyptians.

Now it is instructive that the same Alexandrians who speak of the Gospel of the Egyptians refer to another gospel with the title The Gospel of the Hebrews.[32] From the beginning, an unlucky star has hovered over the Gospel of the Hebrews and its investigation, in that Jerome used this name to designate a Jewish-Christian revision of the Gospel of Matthew which he found among the Nazarenes in Beroea (a work we would do better to call the Gospel of the Nazarenes), and Epiphanius confused the Gospel of the Hebrews with the Gospel of the Ebionites. What we know of both these Jewish Christian gospels [56] clearly has nothing to do with that Gospel of the Hebrews that was known in Egypt.[33] The latter probably was composed during the first half of the second century, in Greek, and I should suppose, in Egypt. It is there that it makes its first appearance,[34] and to that country belong the Jesus-logia of the Oxyrhynchus papyri with which it has affinities in content. Note that we also find among the "logia" of Oxyrhynchus papyrus 654 a dominical saying which Clement of Alexandria cites from the Gospel of the He-

---

31. Cf. (L. Mitteis and) U. Wilcken, Grundzüge und Crestomathie der Papyrusurkunde, 1.2 (Chrestomathie) (Leipzig: Teubner, 1912), 22.17 (p. 38 f.), where the "true Egyptians" (alēthinoi Aiguptioi) are distinguished from the grecianized Alexandrians (= Papyrus Giessen 40, dated 215 c.e.).
32. To kath' Hebraious Euaggelion. Clement of Alexandria Strom. 2.[9.]45.5; Origen Commentary on John 2.(12.)87 [and elsewhere]. Origen also refers to the Gospel of the Egyptians in his first Homily on Luke (ed. M. Rauer, GCS 35 = Origenes 9, 1930). The texts are collected in E. Klostermann (ed.), Apocrypha 2: Evangelien (Kleine Texte 8, 1929³), p. 4. [For ET, see Hennecke-Schneemelcher, 1: 120, 164, 166 (and 55).]
33. Cf. Bauer, RGG², 2 (1928): 1673; A. Schmidtke, Neue Fragmente und Untersuchungen zu den juden-christlichen Evangelien (TU 37.1, 1911); H. Waitz in Hennecke², pp. 10-32, 39-55. [See now H. W. Surkau in RGG³, 3 (1959): 109; and P. Vielhauer in Hennecke-Schneemelcher, 1: 117-165.]
34. When Eusebius (EH 4.22.8) states that Hegesippus quoted from the Gospel of the Hebrews and from the Syriac (Gospel), we should probably refer the former to the Gospel of the Nazarenes (cf. Jerome Illustrious Men 3) and the latter to the Gospel of the Ebionites (cf. EH 3.27.4 and 6.17).

brews: "He who seeks will not rest until he has found, and when he has found he will marvel, and when he has marvelled he will reign, and when he has reigned he will rest." [35]

If I am not mistaken, the *Gospel of the Hebrews* was the "life of Jesus" used by the Jewish Christians of Alexandria. "Hebrews" can also mean Greek-speaking Jews when it is a matter of designating their nationality. Paul, a hellenistic Jew, spoke of himself in this way (Phil. 3.5, 2 Cor. 11.22), and Eusebius applies the same term to Philo of Alexandria, a Jew of Greek culture (EH 2.4.2). The recently discovered door superscription in Corinth reads "Synagogue of the Hebrews." The ancient title of the *Epistle to the Hebrews* means by *Hebraioi* Jewish (-Christian) recipients who spoke Greek. Indeed, the words of an Egyptian magical text, "I adjure you by the God of the Hebrews, Jesus," [36] sound almost like an echo of those persons who oriented themselves around the *Gospel of the Hebrews.* In contrast to it, the *Gospel of the Egyptians* was the gospel of the "real" Egyptians (see n. 31 above) who had become Christian—the gentile Christians of Egypt. In such circumstances, the genesis of the name and its use in Egypt become intelligible.

It is quite in harmony with our conception of the original situation in Christian Egypt that the *Gospel of the Hebrews* clearly displays the heretical trademark. In the fragment preserved by Origen, Jesus declares (on an occasion that we can no longer recover with certainty): "Just now [57] my mother, the Holy Spirit, seized me by one of my hairs and carried me away to the high mountain Tabor." [37]

---

35. Clement of Alexandria *Strom.* 2.(9.)45.5 and 5.(14.)96.3. [For the text of P. Ox. 654, see B. P. Grenfell and A. S. Hunt, *The Oxyrhynchus Papyri,* 4 (London, 1903), with reproductions (also Klostermann's ed. mentioned above, n. 32). This papyrus has now been identified as part of the *Gospel of Thomas* (see Schneemelcher and Puech in Hennecke-Schneemelcher, 1: 97 ff., 278-307), and there are some recent commentators who would argue for a Syrian rather than Egyptian origin of the Gospel (e.g. H. Koester in HarvTR 58 (1965): 293; see below, p. 310).]

36. Paris Magical Papyrus [Bibl. Nat. suppl. gr. 574], line 3019. [For the text, see K. Preisendanz, *Papyri Graecae Magicae: die griechischen Zauberpapyri,* 1 (Leipzig: Teubner, 1928): 170. An ET may be found in C. K. Barrett, *The New Testament Background: Selected Documents* (London: SPCK, 1956; reprint Harper Torchbooks), no. 27 lines 13 ff. This section of the Paris papyrus also closes with the words "the sentence is Hebrew and kept by men that are pure" (3084 f.).]

37. *Commentary on John* 2.(12.)87, *Homily in Jeremiah* 15.4 [The passage is also cited by Jerome; see the references by Vielhauer in Hennecke-Schneemelcher, 1: 164.]

According to Cyril of Jerusalem, the following also stood in the *Gospel of the Hebrews:* "When Christ desired to come to earth to men, the good Father chose a mighty Power in heaven named Michael, and entrusted Christ to its care. And the Power entered the world and was called Mary, and Christ was in her womb seven months." [38] The great importance which Michael has in the Egyptian magical texts—Greek [39] as well as Coptic [40]—and in the *Pistis Sophia* [41] is well known.

Thus in Egypt at the beginning of the second century—how long before that we cannot say—there were gentile Christians alongside Jewish Christians, with both movements resting on syncretistic-gnostic foundations. But apparently they were not both united in a single community, but each group congregated around a distinctive gospel, with the Jewish Christians at the same time also being influenced by the synagogue with regard to worship and organization. That these people, whose primary religious books were differentiated as the *Gospel of the Egyptians* and that *of the Hebrews,* called themselves simply "Christian" seems to me self-evident. For them, the situation was no different from that of the Marcionites in Edessa (above, 22-24).

We first catch sight of something like "ecclesiastical" Christianity in Demetrius, the bishop of Alexandria from 189 to 231. Certainly there had already been orthodox believers there prior to that time, and their community possessed a leader. But we can see how small their number must have been from the fact that when Demetrius assumed his office he was the *only* Egyptian "bishop." Apart from him there were a limited number of presbyters, who when need arose elected a new leader.[42] Demetrius was the first to begin to develop the organization systematically by appointing three other

38. See V. Burch, *Journal of Theological Studies* 21 (1920): 310-315. [The Coptic text was edited by E. A. W. Budge, *Miscellaneous Coptic Texts* (London, 1915), p. 60 (ET on p. 637). See also Vielhauer in Hennecke-Schneemelcher, 1: 163, and M. R. James, *The Apocryphal New Testament* (Oxford: Clarendon, 1924, 1953²), p. 8 (with a larger context). "The good Father" seems preferable to Bauer's German version "der Vatergott" (the Father God).]
39. See Preisendanz, *Papyri Magicae* (above, n. 36), vols. 1 (1928) and 2 (1931); e.g. numbers 1 (line 301), 2 (158), 3 (148), 4 (1815, 2356, 2769), 7 (257), 13 (928), and 22b (29—to the great father, Osiris Michael).
40. A. M. Kropp, *Ausgewählte koptische Zaubertexte*, 2 (Brussels, 1931): 267 (index).
41. Cf. the indices to the eds. of Schmidt (above, n. 29): German (GCS), 397 col. 2 [= 413 col. 2 in Till's revision]; Coptic, 450.
42. E. Preuschen, RPTK³, 14 (1904): 474 (lines 30 ff.).

bishops. He played [58] approximately the same role for Egyptian orthodoxy as that which we have thought should be ascribed to Bishop Kûnê, who lived a century later, in Edessa (above, 33-43). Demetrius lived long enough to achieve success and possessed a consciousness of his own power that was sufficient to take disciplinary action against even an Origen, when the latter crossed his organizational policies (which aimed at concentrating all power in the hands of the leader of the Alexandrian church) by accepting elevation to the status of presbyter at the hands of Palestinian bishops.

The fact of presbyterial ordination by itself would hardly suffice to explain the extraordinarily violent behavior of Demetrius toward a man of Origen's importance and reputation. Such a dangerous game must have offered a correspondingly desirable prize. Obviously Demetrius felt powerful enough in the years 230-231 to press the Alexandrian catechetical school into service for himself. Here Origen, whom he had earlier actually implored not to give up his work (EH 6.14.11) stood in his way. For this reason he now unleashed, as Origen himself puts it, all the storms of wickedness against him and attacked him through writings which plainly contradicted the gospel (*Commentary on John* 6.[2.]9). Among these undoubtedly belongs the circular letter [43] by means of which Demetrius apprized Christendom of the decisions which he directed his Egyptian bishops and presbyters to reach in two synods—namely, Origen is to be banished from the city, and further teaching activity is forbidden him as a representative of unecclesiastical views. His ordination as priest is invalid.[44] In order to justify his action, Demetrius made an issue of Origen's act of self-castration which had taken place long since (EH 6.8.5).

In 231, Heraclas became director of the catechetical school in place of the banished Origen. He was indebted to Origen for the best of what he was and knew; nevertheless, he abandoned him and took sides against him. Indeed, when Origen later returned once more to Egypt, Heraclas excommunicated him anew and repeated the charge of unecclesiastical teaching. His decisive support for Demetrius had

43. Eusebius EH 6.8.4; Jerome *Illustrious Men* 54.
44. O. Bardenhewer, *Geschichte der altkirchlichen Literatur*², 2 (Freiburg: Herder, 1914; repr. Darmstadt, 1962): 109.

borne fruit also in that he had become his successor in the bishop's chair at Alexandria.[45] [59]

When Julius Africanus takes the opportunity in his *Chronicles* to report that he travelled to Alexandria because he was attracted by Heraclas' great reputation for learning (EH 6.31.2), we can see how quickly after Origen's removal the catechetical school entered the service of decidedly "ecclesiastical" efforts with obvious publicity. Eusebius took his list of Alexandrian bishops from the *Chronicle* of Africanus.[46] And from what source can the latter have obtained it except from the very learned head of the school, Heraclas, and his bishop, Demetrius? [47] Thus there was being cultivated at that time in Alexandria that branch of theological endeavor which fought and tried to discredit the heretics by appealing to an unbroken succession of orthodox bishops. We also suspect whence this new incentive to scholarly studies derived. We learn from Jerome that while in the nearby regions of Palestine, Arabia, Phoenicia, and even Achaia, nobody was concerned about Demetrius' circular letter, Rome hastened to support it.[48] Origen had been at Rome during the episcopate of Zephyrinus (198-217), but departed after a short time (EH 6.14.10). It would seem that little goodwill existed between them. Certainly, as Jerome rightly remarks (*Epistle* 33.5), what was of decisive importance for the attitude of Rome as well as for that of Demetrius was their jealous fear lest they be eclipsed by the incomparable eloquence and erudition of Origen and forced into the background. But this state of mind surely also opened their eyes to those aspects of Origen's teaching [60] which must have seemed to them to be inade-

45. EH 6.26. Cf. A. Harnack, *RPTK*[3] 7 (1899): 693.
46. Cf. Harnack, *Geschichte* 2 (*Chronologie*).1: 123; Schwartz, GCS eds. of Eusebius' EH, vol. 3, ccxxi.
47. The journey of Africanus to Alexandria is usually dated earlier, around the year 215 (Harnack, RPTK[3], 9 [1901]: 627), probably because the date 221 is held with absolute certainty as the year in which the *Chronicle* was published. I can see no really convincing evidence for thus fixing either date. That the *Chronicle* of Africanus was intended to run only up to the year 221 does not exclude the possibility that at a somewhat later time he could have procured material for the period before 221 and incorporated it. In any event, Eusebius seems to think that Heraclas was already bishop at the time of the visit (EH 6.31.2). And even if Africanus obtained the Alexandrian list before 221, it unquestionably came from the circle of Demetrius.
48. *Epistle* 33 (*ad Paulum*).5. Concerning the relations between Rome and "ecclesiastical" Alexandria, see also below, p. 60.

quate. At all events, Origen took advantage of an opportunity to make a positive defence of his orthodoxy before the Roman bishop Fabianus (236-250; EH 6.36.4).

But what sort of Christianity existed in Alexandria-Egypt in the half century that preceded the victory, backed by Rome, of Demetrius and his policy? At the end of his life, Demetrius fought Origen most vehemently and drove him out of his sphere of activity where he had accomplished enormous things, and even out of his native city. In contrast, at the beginning of his tenure Demetrius had no ear for Rome's wishes in the matter of the Easter controversy; [49] nor had he molested Origen's predecessor, Clement, although the latter deviated from the teaching of the church far more than did his successor. It may here suffice to recall the harsh judgment which Photius passed regarding the *Outlines* (*Hypotyposeis*) of Clement: [50]

> In some passages [51] he appears to teach quite correctly, but in others he allows himself to be carried away entirely into impious and fictitious assertions. For he holds that matter is eternal, and he seeks to derive something like a doctrine of ideas from certain passages of scripture, and he reduces the Son to the status of a creation. Moreover, he drivels on about transmigrations of souls and many worlds before Adam. And with reference to the origin of Eve from Adam, he does not agree with the teaching of the church, but expresses his opinion in disgraceful and outrageous fashion. The angels, he fancies, interbred with women and begot children by them, and the Logos did not really become flesh but only appeared so. He also lets himself be trapped by the fact that he fabricates stories about two Logoi of the Father, of which only the lesser appeared to men, or rather not even that one. . . . And all this he seeks to support from certain passages of scripture. . . . And on and on endlessly he prattles and blasphemes. . . .

Photius is inclined to express his opinion here rather pointedly; nonetheless, his hostility must have been provoked to a large extent

49. Obviously Egypt, which is not even mentioned by Eusebius in this connection (EH 5.23.3-4), did not allow itself to be drawn into this quarrel. That is all the clearer since it had no reason for denying support to Rome on this point (EH 5.25).
50. *Library*, codex 109. The text is also included in the GCS edition of Clement by O. Stählin, vol. 3 (GCS 17, 1909), p. 202 [now being re-edited by L. Früchtel. For a convenient ET, see J. H. Freese, *The Library of Photius* (London: SPCK, 1920), p. 200.]
51. That is, passages dealing with the Old and New Testaments, which are interpreted and discussed in the *Outlines*.

by the work which he thus discusses. [61] His orthodoxy detected an abundance of heresy alongside isolated ecclesiastical statements. Clement never lost his enthusiasm for "gnosis." To be sure, he makes a distinction between genuine and heretical gnosis, and feels himself to be separated from the latter and linked with the former through the holy apostles Peter, James, John, and Paul (*Strom.* 1.[1.]11.3). But this does not keep him from having some central points in common with heretical gnosticism; and this is even more true of the earlier work, the *Outlines,* than of the later *Miscellanies* (*Stromateis*).[52] We can clearly discern at Alexandria the stages of a development that steadily leads away from gnosticism: the Clement of the *Outlines,* the Clement of the *Miscellanies,* Origen, Demetrius. If we trace the line backward behind the *Outlines* to the origins, we obviously arrive very quickly at gnosticism proper. One need not be surprised that even the Clement of the first stage already exhibits characteristics of ecclesiastical orientation, as Photius himself does not deny. From the very outset, Clement distinguished himself in a conscious and not inconsiderable way from what we have delineated as Egyptian Christianity prior to his time. After all, he came to Egypt from abroad in order to place himself under the influence of Pantaenus (who was himself from Sicily; *Strom.* 1.[1.]11.2). Perhaps Clement was born in Athens;[53] in any event, as a Christian he had been in southern Italy, Syria, and Palestine. Probably Clement first became acquainted with the *Gospel of the Egyptians* in his new home. And it is very characteristic of the intellectual outlook that he brings with him and cultivates further, that he no more rejects its contents as false than he rejects the contents of the *Gospel of the Hebrews,* although he himself personally prefers our four gospels which he learned to value in the world abroad, and which he regards as, strictly speaking, the gospels of the church.

Now if Demetrius allowed a man who thought and taught as Clement did to operate undisturbed in a most influential position, and first lashed out against Origen, who was far less offensive from the viewpoint of the church, it seems to me that the most obvious

---

52. On the relation of the *Miscellanies* to the *Outlines,* see Harnack, *Geschichte* 2 (*Chronologie*) .2 (1904): 19 f.

53. According to the tradition in Epiphanius *Her.* 32.6. See further T. Zahn, *Forschungen zur Geschichte des neutestamentlichen Kanons und der altkirchlichen Literatur* 3 (Leipzig, 1884), pp. 161 ff.

explanation is that there existed no prospect [62] of successfully assailing ideas like these and the personalities who supported them one generation earlier in Alexandria. No possibility—and perhaps not even any serious inclination.

There is every reason at least to raise the question whether distinct boundaries between heretical and ecclesiastical Christendom had been developed at all in Egypt by the end of the second century. So as to set aside less certain evidence, I will disregard the *Epistle of the Apostles,* preserved in Coptic and Ethiopic, which C. Schmidt published with full commentary and supplementary materials in 1919 [54] and which he dated shortly before 180, although I am inclined to accept the opinion of Lietzmann [55] that it belongs not to Asia Minor but rather, to Egypt. With its peculiar mixture of gnosticism and anti-gnosticism, it would relate well to the situation of Clement of Alexandria. Similarly, we shall leave undecided to what extent the *Preaching (Kerygma) of Peter,*[56] which was particularly suspect to Origen (*Commentary on John* 13.[17.]104) but was used unhesitatingly prior to him by Clement of Alexandria and the gnostic Heracleon, is relevant here.

But the following observations and considerations can surely teach us something. When Origen had to find lodging after the martyrdom of his father and the loss of the confiscated family property, a distinguished and wealthy Christian woman offered him accommodations in her household. Now Eusebius informs us that this woman also had living in her house a very famous man from among the number of heretics (*hairesiotai*) in Alexandria at that time, and that she treated him like her son. He was named Paul and had come from Antioch, and in consequence of his great reputation there flocked to him a "countless host of persons, heretics as well as orthodox believers" (EH 6.2.13-14). If we leave aside the conviction of the later

---

54. *Gespräche Jesu mit seinen Jüngern* (TU 43, 1919). [ET by R. E. Taylor in Hennecke-Schneemelcher, 1: 189 ff.]
55. ZNW 20 (1921): 175 f.
56. Cf. E. Dobschütz, *Das Kerygma Petri kritisch untersucht* (TU 11.1, 1893). The fragments are conveniently collected by E. Klostermann in *Apocrypha,* 1[2] (KT 3, 1908), 13-16. Cf. Hennecke, "Missions predigt des Petrus," in Hennecke[2], pp. 143-146, although with regard to p. 145 one may question whether it would not be more accurate to speak of "certain ecclesiastical forms" rather than of "certain gnostical forms." [For ET, see G. Ogg in Hennecke-Schneemelcher, 2: 94-102.]

churchman Eusebius that heretical Christendom and orthodoxy always must have been clearly distinguished from one another, we obtain the picture [63] of a Christianity which sees nothing amiss in entrusting at a most impressionable age so valuable a member as the seventeen-year-old Origen, already widely recognized because of his extraordinary gifts, to a woman whose house is the center of a wide-ranging religious movement that definitely cannot be characterized as orthodox. In that event we have before us a community whose intellectually fastidious members do not hesitate to satisfy their hunger by means of an Antiochene-Alexandrian "heretic."

A few pages later, Eusebius reports something very similar of Origen, who for him naturally was a representative of orthodoxy. To Origen also there flocked "countless heretics" (EH 6.18.2) as well as orthodox, in order to be instructed by him in all areas of learning, including the secular. Yet even more instructive than this general statement about the great popularity that his well-known erudition enjoyed even among the heretics is the specific notice that his famous friend and patron, Ambrose, to whom he dedicated many of his writings, had been a Valentinian who was subsequently converted by Origen.[57] He too, incidentally, came from Antioch.[58]

Thus even into the third century, no separation between orthodoxy and heresy was accomplished in Egypt and the two types of Christianity were not yet at all clearly differentiated from each other.[59] Moreover, until late in the second century, Christianity in this area is decidedly unorthodox. I avoid for the moment the term "heretics" for the Egyptian Christians of the early period (and the same holds for the beginnings at Edessa) because, strictly speaking, there can be heretics only where orthodox Christians stand in contrast to them or serve as a background for them, but not where such a situation does not exist because all Christendom, when viewed from a particular later vantage point, is colored "heretical." The idea that orthodoxy had been present in Egypt from the very first can as little be proven

57. EH 6.18.1 (cf. also 6.23.1). According to Jerome, *Illustrious Men* 56, Ambrose had been a Marcionite. Origen also indicates that Ambrose was later persuaded of the correctness of Origen's position: *Commentary on John* 5.8 (GCS ed. Preuschen, p. 105, lines 16 ff.). The passages in our sources concerning Ambrose are conveniently collected in Harnack, *Geschichte*, 1.1: 328 ff.
58. E. Preuschen, *RPTK*[3], 14 (1904): 473 (line 30).
59. Cf. also S. Morenz, *Die Geschichte von Joseph dem Zimmermann* (TU 56, 1951), p. 123.

by the church legend of Mark as the [64] founder and first occupant of the Alexandrian episcopal see [60] as can the corresponding proposition for Edessa by the Abgar legend. Rather, the fact that one has to rely on legends is a fresh and clear indication that historical recollection did not support, and never was the basis of, such a view. There is some reason to suppose that Rome placed at the disposal of orthodox Alexandria the figure of Mark as founder of the church and apostolic initiator of the traditional succession of bishops.[61] At all events, it is not easy to imagine from what other source he could have come.

60. Cf. A. Jülicher, RPTK[3], 12 (1903): 290 (lines 16 ff.). [To the older material should now be added the allusion to this tradition in a newly discovered letter attributed to Clement of Alexandria, which is being published by its discoverer, Morton Smith. See the brief reference by A. A. Ehrhardt in HarvTR 55 (1962): 97, n. 16 (reprinted with corrections in his *The Framework of the New Testament Stories* [Manchester, 1964], p. 175 n. 3); see also below, p. 315 n. 34.]
61. Regarding the relation of Rome to Alexandria and to its orthodoxy, see also above, p. 55, and below, pp. 97 and 117.

3

Ignatius of Antioch
and Polycarp of Smyrna;
Macedonia and Crete

Ignatius, the martyr of Antioch, is regarded as the most important and most successful ecclesiastical representative in the second-century struggle against heresy prior to Justin. He is an organization man whose significance H. Lietzmann recently characterized thus: "In Ignatius we already find that the monarchial episcopate is an accomplished fact and is applicable to both Syria and western Asia Minor." [1] I think that with a man like Ignatius who, in his exuberance, time and again loses all sense of proportion, one must be especially careful in evaluating the accuracy of his statements. Indeed, he even speaks of communities such as Magnesia and Tralles, whose situation he knows primarily from the descriptions of their "bishops," who had no reason to place themselves and their influence in an unfavorable light. That Ignatius is less concerned with depicting the actual situation than with portraying the ideal is already suggested by the fact that, for the most part, his approach takes the form of admonition rather than of description.

What is it that makes the monarchial episcopacy seem so attractive to a man like Ignatius? First of all, he does not begin from a position in which he sees a plurality of ecclesiastical bodies of officials who for practical reasons may be governed by one particular office which, nevertheless, is not necessarily superior. No, for him the first and foremost figure is the bishop, who is like God or Christ in whose place he stands. [2] And [66] just as there can be no second, even

1. Lietzmann, *History*, 1: 248.
2. See W. Bauer, excursus to Ignatius *Eph.* 2.2, in *Die Briefe des Ignatius von Antiochia und der Polykarpbrief*, HbNT, Ergänzungsband: *Die apostolischen Väter*, 2 (1920): 201 f.

approximately similar position beside them, neither can there be such beside the bishop. At a suitably respectable distance behind him come the presbyters and deacons, attentive to his beck and call and obliged to render him due reverence. The administration of the particular community should rest completely in the hands of this *one* bishop who sets in motion and supervises all its activities, without whom no ecclesiastical function has validity and who, by virtue of his office, is immune to any criticism no matter how young in years or deficient in character he might be. At what point has the historical development become ripe for such extremely high esteem for a single official? It would hardly arise in peaceful times when there is no need for such an approach. As long as a harmonious spirit pervades the community, a council of those with similar status can take care of it without difficulty—one does this and another does something else, according to the abilities of each. Only when opposition arises and conflicting interests confront one another does the picture change. Even then there is little danger for the one who sides with the majority, since the majority opinion is, as a rule, reflected in the composition of the governing board. But the situation would become precarious for the one who identifies himself with the minority and who now finds that his wishes no longer, or only seldom, gain a hearing with the governing powers. Such a man easily arrives at the conclusion that his legitimate claims are being neglected by the circle of leaders and then the desire stirs in him for a dictatorship that would establish the supremacy of his own party.

Demands like these are typical of minorities which, through their own strong man who is clothed with a special aura and equipped with unusual power, endeavor to obtain that overriding importance which they are unable to gain by virtue of the number of their members. But if they can supply one who is in absolute control of the whole group, then the possibility emerges either of bringing those who differ to heel within the community, or else, if there is no alternative, of crowding them out. So long as a council is in control of the church, it is unavoidable that it will be composed of Christians of various sorts and that—to move from generalities back to the specific case of Ignatius—alongside members holding views like those of Ignatius there would also be representatives of the gnostics and

62

of acknowledged Jewish Christians in it. [67] If, however, the leadership of the community responds to the command of the *one* bishop, then orthodoxy can hope to take the helm even where it constitutes only a minority of the whole group—provided that the others are disunited. Of course, there is the possibility that Ignatius' group actually represented the majority in certain cities. However, in view of Ignatius' frantic concern, it hardly seems likely that this was the general rule. Any conclusion of a more comprehensive sort must be preceded by a more detailed investigation into this subject.

What is the situation with reference to the monarchial bishop in those churches with which we are acquainted through the story of Ignatius? First, what about Antioch itself? Was Ignatius really "bishop" there, or even in Syria (*Rom.* 2.2), in his own sense of a monarchial ruler over all the baptized of that region? For him, orthodoxy and heresy are not yet so neatly divided that it would be sufficient to rule over the "church" people because the heretics, however numerous they might be, are "outside" the church. What was the complexion of Christianity in Antioch at the time of Ignatius? The last thing that the sources had reported concerning it prior to Ignatius was the awkward scene which centered around Peter and Paul (Gal. 2.11 ff.), and which, it appears, led to a division within the community—most certainly it greatly disturbed its life. In no other context did Paul ever speak of Antioch. And the book of Acts limits itself to noting that later, Paul once again stayed in Antioch "for some time" (18.22 f.), without recording anything in particular about that visit —not even that he "strengthened all the disciples," as is related with reference to his trip through the "region of Galatia and Phrygia" that is mentioned next. Quite in harmony with this is the fact, noticed above (17-20), that during the second part of the second century, and even long afterward, Antioch played no significant role in the history of the church. The "ecclesiastical" tradition here is so scanty that Eusebius, and before him Julius Africanus,[3] were unable to produce a credible list of bishops from the apostles to the end of the second century—credible at least because of its uninterrupted comprehensiveness.[4] Eusebius can only make Theophilus, his sixth An-

3. Harnack, *Geschichte* 2 (*Chronologie*).1: 208-213.
4. Cf. the GCS Schwartz edition of EH, vol. 3: p. CCXXI.

tiochian bishop, [68] contemporary with the eleventh Roman and the ninth Alexandrian bishop,[5] in spite of dating him inadmissibly early.[6] If one realizes that the actual floruit of Theophilus was around 180, then in Antioch six bishops must cover the same span of time that is covered by twelve in Rome and ten in Alexandria (cf. EH 5.pref.1 and 5.9).

This lack of ecclesiastical tradition does not encourage the view that there was already a bishop worthy of the name in Antioch at the beginning of the second century. Alexandria and Rome, with their much richer stock of episcopal personnel, have such a figure only at a much later time.[7] What is concealed behind this title for Ignatius is, corresponding to the situation of Palût in Edessa, the leadership of a group that is engaged in a life and death struggle against an almost overwhelming adversary. Certainly this title itself implies the claim to be the authoritative interpreter of the faith for all Christians of Syria, or at least of Antioch. But the question remains to what extent this self evaluation was acknowledged by others. It appears to me that large segments of Antiochian Christianity flatly rejected it, in view of the almost frantic efforts of Ignatius to push his home church in the direction he desired by dispatching to Antioch delegations of eminent coreligionists from every congregation accessible to him (cf. *Philad.* 10—bishops, presbyters, deacons) or at least by sending written messages.[8] The apparently quite local and rather brief persecution in the Syrian capital can hardly be the real reason for his efforts. After all, the news that the church in Antioch had regained its peace in no way prompted Ignatius to discontinue his efforts (*Philad.* 10; *Smyr.* 11; *Polyc.* 7). Polycarp is to exert influence upon those Asian churches which Ignatius himself had been unable to reach.[9] And the necessity of such a task was impressed upon Polycarp to such an extent that, regardless of the precarious position of orthodoxy in Smyrna itself (see below, 69 f.), he would have preferred [69] to undertake the journey to Antioch in person (Polycarp *Phil.* 13.1). In fact, there is even concern to draw the community

5. At the time of the accession of Soter in Rome, in 166 (EH 4.19-20).
6. The GCS Schwartz edition of EH, vol. 3: p. 26.
7. On Alexandria, see above, 53; on Rome, see the GCS Schwartz edition of EH, vol. 3: p. CCXXV.
8. R. Knopf, *Das nachapostolische Zeitalter* (Tübingen, 1905), p. 51.
9. See Bauer, *Ignatius*, to *Polyc.* 8.1.

at Philippi in far off Macedonia into the circle of those who send their good wishes to Syria (Polycarp *Phil.* 13.1).

This display, which deprived a number of churches that were themselves experiencing a difficult situation of their leading figures even to the rank of "bishop"—and which, as far as I know, is unparalleled in the history of the ancient church—is only explicable to me if there is a great deal at stake; that is to say, if orthodoxy in Antioch, deprived of its champion Ignatius, was in danger of being driven back, if not routed from the field, by heresy. Indeed, all his letters to the Asiatic Christians bear eloquent testimony to this acute danger of heresy. In his homeland, Ignatius learned to know, to hate, and to fear the "mad dogs," the "beasts in human form," as he calls them (cf. *Eph.* 7.1, *Smyr.* 4.1).

It is not necessary to investigate in great detail the religious situation of non-Christian Antioch in order to discover the soil into which Christianity was planted there.[10] Libanius, in his *Antiochikos*,[11] extols the religious richness of his native city: The foreign gods aspire to be represented there—thus, during the reign of Seleucius II (246-226 B.C.E.), Isis forced her image to be transferred from Memphis to Antioch (§ 114)—and the native *daimones* do not wish to roam in foreign lands (§ 117). The impression of a pronounced syncretism is further deepened when we observe the presence of magic and star worship, mysteries and alchemy, combined with gross superstition and a tendency toward Indian gymnosophistry, which makes Ignatius' fanatical desire for martyrdom somewhat more explicable to us.[12] The observation that in Antioch, Jewish Christianity existed side by side with gentile Christianity contributes little to an understanding of the early form of Christianity in that city. We also found that in Christian [70] Alexandria both groups coexisted at the outset. But if our impression is accurate, both the gentile and the Jewish were conditioned by the syncretistic-gnostic setting (above, 53).

---

10. Treatments of this subject include: O. Müller, *Antiquitates Antiochenae* (Göttingen, 1839); R. Förster, "Antiochia am Orontes," *Jahrbuch des Archaeologischen Instituts des Deutschen Reiches*, 12 (1897): 103-149; H. Leclercq, "Antioche," DACL 1 (1924): 2359-2427; K. Bauer, *Antiochia in der ältesten Kirchengeschichte* (Tübingen: Mohr, 1919); V. Schultze, *Antiocheia*; C. H. Kraeling, "The Jewish Community at Antioch," JBL 51 (1932): 130-160.
11. *Oration* 11, ed. R. Förster, vol. 1 (Leipzig: Teubner, 1903), pp. 437-535.
12. See Müller, *Antiquitates Antiochenae*, pp. 32 ff., and Schultze, *Antiocheia*, pp. 167 ff.

In Antioch, no doubt, the situation was different as long as genuine apostolic influence prevailed. But had not such influence cancelled itself out to a large extent? [13] And must that situation which probably existed in the period until 70 also hold good for a subsequent time? At any rate, already prior to Ignatius, gnosticism made itself felt in Antioch in a serious way. Menander, a countryman and pupil of Simon Magus (Irenaeus AH 1.23.5 [= 1.17], 3.4.3), already was teaching there in the first century,[14] and, according to Justin (who was also a Samaritan and was informed about conditions in the East), was winning *many* followers (*Apol.* 26.4). One of those, who worked successfully after him in the same areas, was Saturninus.[15] His contemporary and coreligionist in these regions was the Syrian gnostic Cerdo,[16] whom we later encounter in Rome as a man of such importance that he was even able to exercise some influence over the already mature Marcion. Another pupil of Menander, Basilides, is the first of whom we hear that he brought gnostic ideas from Antioch to Alexandria,[17] and thereby took up, from the Christian side, the religious interchange between Egypt and Syria that we were able to observe already in the migration of Isis to Antioch. This exchange of religious ideas was then continued in a manner that concerns us through those Antiochian heretics who still played such an important role in the leading city of Egypt at the time of Origen (see above, 58 f.). We may leave aside at this point the very clear traces of heresy that can be found in Antioch during the period between Basilides and Origen. But it should be recalled in this connection that Syrian-Antiochian heretics also had access to a gospel which suited their own approach and for which they claimed the authority of Peter,[18] [71] just as Basilides asserted that he had received revelations through Glaukias, an interpreter of Peter (Clement of Alexandria *Strom.* 7.[17.]106.4).

13. See Lietzmann, *History*, 1: 108-111.
14. See Harnack, *Geschichte* 2 (*Chronologie*).1: 533.
15. Irenaeus AH 1.24.1 (= 1.18); Eusebius EH 4.7.3, claims that he founded schools of godless heresy throughout Syria.
16. Hippolytus *Syntagma* (in Epiphanius *Her.* 41.1; ps.-Tertullian *Her.* 6; Filaster *Her.* 44). See Harnack, *Marcion*², 38° [these and other texts on 31°-34°].
17. Epiphanius *Her.* 23.1; cf. Irenaeus AH 1.24.1 (= 1.18).
18. The *Gospel of Peter* probably originated in Syria. See A. Stülcken in Hennecke², p. 60 [and more recently, C. Maurer in Hennecke-Schneemelcher, 1: 180].

It should not be objected that gnosticism is much too scantily attested at the beginning of the second century as an influential factor in the development of Antiochian Christianity. After all, who is it that actually bears witness to the presence of the ecclesiastical faith in that region during the same period? Almost exclusively Ignatius; [19] and he does so in a way that, not simply because of the type of defense, proves the strength of his opponents. It seems to me that H. Schlier is correct in his judgment that "in terms of their value for this history of religions, the seven Ignatian letters display a type of Christianity localized in Syria and closely related in concepts and ideas to Syrian gnosticism." [20] In spite of Ignatius' conscious polemic against this abominable heresy, he was no more able to free himself from gnosticism than was Clement of Alexandria in a similar situation. Even to a greater degree than for Alexandria, we gain insight at Antioch into a process of painstaking disengagement from a religiosity that in important points can no longer be shared. By no means, however, do we gain the impression that Ignatius felt he had already won the victory. His episcopate, to which each baptized person must submit, is still seed sown in hope. It is also highly significant that precisely his gnostic contemporaries and countrymen can without hindrance call themselves "Christians," as Eusebius twice complains in utter disgust (EH 3.26.3 f. 4.7.2 f.; cf. below 109 f. and above, 22-24).

And the situation is not any different with respect to those "bishops" of the communities in Asia Minor whom we encounter through Ignatius. To be sure, he designates as *episkopos* each of the leaders of those groups in sympathy with him in the particular Christian communities: Onesimus of Ephesus (*Eph.* 1.3), Damas of Magnesia (*Magn.* 2), Polybius of Tralles (*Trall.* 1.1), Polycarp of Smyrna (*Magn.* 15; *Polyc.* salutation)—and he also knows the bishop of Philadelphia (*Philad.*, salutation, 1.1, 3.2, 4). But this does not prove that these men exercised unlimited power over the shaping of Christian faith and life in those cities. The inherent contradiction [72] of a monarchial bishop with only partial recognition is no greater than

19. Even if we were to include the Johannine Epistles here, the picture would not change; see below, 91 f.
20. Heinrich Schlier, *Religionsgeschichtliche Untersuchungen zu den Ignatiusbriefen* (ZNW Beiheft 8, 1929), p. 175.

the contradiction of a community which is praised for having rejected the false teachers (*Eph.* 9.1) and yet still receives most explicit warnings against heresy (*Eph.* 7-9, 13-19) and has to be told that whoever corrupts the faith with false teaching is on the path to unquenchable fire together with anyone who listens to such a person (*Eph.* 16.2). In both instances the ideal and the actual are far removed from each other.

An even clearer indication of the existence of at least a minority that does not care about the bishop and his teaching is given when Ignatius charges the Ephesians: "Do not let yourselves be anointed with the evil odor of the teaching of the prince of this age, lest he lead you captive from the life that is set before you. Why are we *not all* prudent, since we have received the knowledge of God—that is, Jesus Christ? Why are we perishing in foolishness, ignoring the gracious gift that the Lord has truly sent?" (*Eph.* 17). In his letter to the Magnesians, Ignatius rejoices that he has beheld the *whole* community in the person of the officers delegated to meet him, with the bishop at the head (6.1; cf. 2.1 and *Trall.* 1.1). But immediately thereafter, he utters a warning to maintain the unity and to avoid false teaching (*Magn.* 6-11). He knows "certain people" who pay lip service to the bishop, yet never work in cooperation with him but hold their own meetings (*Magn.* 4). And the danger is all the more pressing in Magnesia since its bishop is still young, and because of his inexperience is able neither to enforce obedience nor to see through hypocrisy (*Magn.* 3).

Also with regard to the community at Tralles, praise of her blamelessness (*Trall.* 1) immediately is cancelled by a summons to submit to the bishop and to the other church officials (*Trall.* 2-3) as well as by reference to all sorts of imperfections, which make her seem to be particularly susceptible to false teaching (*Trall.* 6). Notice how Ignatius exhorts the believers: "Continue in your harmony and in prayer with one another. For it is fitting for every single one of you, and particularly for the presbyters, to refresh the bishop, to the honor of the Father, of Jesus Christ, and of the Apostles. I beseech you to listen to me in love that I by my writing may not become a witness against you" (12.2-3). Clearly the closing words of this admonition stand in tension with its beginning and indicate that actually it is not at all a matter of "continuing" but rather of eliminating a situation in which even presbyters are neglecting to "refresh" the bishop. [73]

The situation appears to be even more critical in Philadelphia where *many* wolves lie in wait for the sheep (*Philad.* 2). The assertion that everything is in good order (2.2, 3.1) alternates in this letter in an almost embarrassing fashion with the summons to make it better. Ignatius himself must have been convinced that the power of the bishop there was decidedly limited. On his trip through Philadelphia he had a discussion with dissenters in the community gathering, without succeeding to persuade them (*Philad.* 7 f.); on the contrary, he had experiences that caused him to complain anxiously that there were people who consciously avoid the leadership of the bishop (3.2 f., 8.1). His own co-workers Philo and Rheus Agathopus had been treated with disrespect in Philadelphia, and the bishop had been unable to protect them against it (11.1).

In Ephesus, Magnesia, Tralles, and Philadelphia (only those four cities come under consideration at this point, not Asia Minor nor even its western part as a whole, concerning which see below, 77 ff.), those persons whom Ignatius addresses as bishops and treats as monarchs, who thus were the leaders of the ecclesiastically oriented people, may have gathered larger or smaller majorities of the local Christians around them. Undoubtedly Ignatius himself did not have as secure a position in Antioch. And it seems to me that the same can be said of his friend Polycarp, who also provides us with relevant material for ascertaining more precisely what the concept of "monarchial bishop" involved in that epoch. His situation was burdened with difficulties resulting from the fact that heretics occupied high offices within Christianity. Ignatius, in his letter to the church at Smyrna and in the center of a detailed and vehement attack on those who dismiss the life and work of the Lord as mere appearance (*Smyr.* 4-7), also turns against a particular person who, by virtue of his high position (*topos*), is puffed up (*Smyr.* 6.1). *Topos* is the same word used by Ignatius in his letter to Polycarp to denote the latter's rank as bishop (*Polyc.* 1.2). Evidently this is the same person who in Smyrna performs "behind the bishop's back" cultic acts which are of the devil (*Smyr.* 9.1). Thus we have here, I believe, something like a gnostic anti-bishop in Smyrna. Of course, the title itself is unimportant; what matters is the phenomenon.

In his letter to the Philippians, Polycarp himself confirms this situation [74] insofar as he can be expected to do so. He begins: *Polykarpos kai hoi syn autō presbyteroi tē ekklēsia*, etc. This does not mean, as I had innacurately translated it in the *Handbuch*, "Polycarp and the presbyters with him"—as though it included all presbyters [21] —but rather, "Polycarp and those presbyters who are with him"— that is, who are on his side.[22] Here the fervor of the demand that there be but *one* bishop becomes especially evident to us. But again, doubts arise as to whether the situation is correctly described in words such as those of R. Knopf: "The monarchial episcopate is firmly established in the communities of Asia to which Ignatius writes." [23] Not at all! In this respect, his letters bear witness to his fervent desire, but not to existing reality. At best they attest reality insofar as the desire to organize themselves along monarchial lines may have arisen in orthodox circles of particular Christian groups in Asia. Still, a community-wide separation of the orthodox under their bishop from the false believers under their leaders has by no means taken place as yet, but is envisioned at best as a last resort, a final expedient if the efforts to unite all of the baptized under the *one* orthodox bishop should fail.

On the basis of this understanding of the situation, I must disagree with Harnack's statement that "Phrygia and Asia were closed to Marcion" because Papias and Polycarp would have nothing to do with him.[24] I find here only an impossible exaggeration of the influence of both men upon the formation of Christianity in their provinces. Polycarp, who previously had not even been able to rise to a monarchial position in Smyrna, certainly does not hold the key to Asia in his hand. And even if in his home town he really had reviled Marcion as the "firstborn of Satan" (Irenaeus AH 3.3.4; Eusebius EH 4.14.7), this deterred Marcion just as little there as the same phrase, which this foe of heretics apparently used quite freely, obstructed those people in Philippi to whom it was applied (Polycarp

21. That would be something like *Polykarpos syn tois presbyterois*. Cf. Luke 20.1, 23.11; Acts 2.14, 14.5; Eph. 3.18; and especially Phil. 1.1.
22. Corresponding to the limited circle of "the brethren who are with them" (*hoi syn autois adelphoi*) in Rom. 16.14. Cf. also Rom. 16.15, Gal. 1.2, Phil. 4.21, *Martyrdom of Polycarp* 12.3.
23. Knopf, *Zeitalter*, p. 210.
24. Harnack, "Die ältesten Evangelien-Prologe und die Bildung des Neuen Testaments," Sb Berlin 24 for 1928, p. 16 (= 335).

Phil. 7.1). Surely as soon as Marcion [75] really wanted to, he could find in Smyrna a suitable point of contact for his teaching among the docetics.

The reason why Marcion departed from Asia and pressed on to Rome is not that there was an impregnable wall of defense erected by the orthodox bishops of Asia for the protection of believers, but rather, it lies solely in the fact that Marcion's farsighted, world-encompassing plans called him, like so many others, to the capital of the world. Only from that place could he hope to realize his plans. And if, even there, he could hold his own for years within the church, then certainly he could have done so even more easily at an earlier time in Smyrna. In spite of his long life, Polycarp evidently did not see the day in which heresy ceased in Smyrna, or in which the separation between ecclesiastical Christianity and heresy took place. How little he was able to restrain the heretics can probably be inferred from the letter of Irenaeus to Florinus (EH 5.20.4-8). For even though Irenaeus need not have seen or heard that Polycarp vacated his place and fled with his ears stopped upon the appearance of heretics at community gatherings (EH 5.20.6-7), he still hands down the customary sigh of Polycarp on such an occasion: "Good God, to what sort of times have you kept me that I must endure such things?" (EH 5.20.7). The powerful self-understanding of a monarchial bishop hardly confronts us in such words.

It is therefore not surprising to notice that shortly after Polycarp's death, Noëtus developed his patripassian doctrine here, causing unrest in the community.[25] Even a century later, after the "ecclesiastical" position should have become considerably consolidated, heresy still is flourishing in Smyrna—especially the spirit of Marcion. The martyrdom of Pionius,[26] a presbyter of the church of Smyrna at the time of Decius (249-251), is clearly catholic and pays careful attention to the fact that after an accused person confessed that he was a Christian, the presiding official Polemon would confirm that he was dealing with a catholic Christian by asking the question "To which church do you belong?" (9.2, 6, 8; 19.4 f.). This makes it all the more significant that *none* of the like-minded companions of Pionius,

25. [Cf. Hippolytus *Ref.* 9.7 = 10.27 and *Against Noëtus* 1, but Epiphanius calls him an Asian from Ephesus (*Her.* 57.1).] A. Hilgenfeld, *Die Ketzergeschichte des Urchristentums* (Leipzig, 1884; reprint Darmstadt, 1963), p. 616.
26. O. von Gebhardt (ed.), *Acta martyrum selecta* (Berlin: Duncker, 1902), pp. 96-114.

not even Limnus, "a presbyter of the catholic [76] church" (2.1, 11.2), go to their death at the very side of this great champion of the faith and in such a distinguished manner as he; rather, this place if filled by Metrodorus, "a presbyter of the heresy of the Marcionites" who appears quite unexpectedly (21.5 f.). Evidently, as far as the pagan authorities are concerned, Metrodorus stands together with Pionius in the foreground of the Christian movement. Euctemon, on the other hand, the catholic bishop of Smyrna, has committed disgraceful apostasy and has ensnared most of the community in his downfall.[27] But among the few fellow-sufferers in prison we also find Eutychianus, "an adherent of the heresy of the Phrygians" (11.2).

In the reference to the "Phrygians" the key word occurs that must suffice at this point to substantiate my doubts also with respect to the other ecclesiastical authority mentioned by Harnack (above, 70 n. 24). Of course, Papias could reject Marcion for himself and for those like him.[28] But this represents neither the view of Christian Hierapolis, nor that of the whole of Phrygia. Papias was as unable to stop uncatholic trends and movements in this region, which was inundated by Montanism immediately after his death, at the latest, as was Polycarp in Asia.

But to return to Polycarp, it would seem to me that his letter to the Philippians, a writing contemporaneous with the Ignatian epistles, is instructive for understanding the situation with respect to the Christianity of that city, for it suggests that the ecclesiastical influence is even more restricted there, as compared with Asia. In 7.1, Polycarp fights against a docetic gnosticism: "Everyone who does not confess that Jesus Christ has come in the flesh is an antichrist . . . and whoever perverts the words of the Lord . . . and says that there is neither a resurrection nor a judgment, that man is the firstborn of Satan." Immediately after this he adds: "Therefore let us abandon the foolishness of the great majority (*mataiotēs tōn pollōn*) and the false teachings, and let us return to the word which was transmitted to us from the beginning" (7.2). Apart from the conviction, which is also expressed here, that a heretic must *return* since he has for-

27. [15.2, 16.1, 18.12.] See H. Achelis, *Das Christentum in den ersten drei Jahrhunderten*, 2 (Leipzig, 1912): 270 f.
28. See the "anti-Marcionite" prologue to John connected with Papias' name: Harnack, *Evangelien-Prologe*, 6 and 15 [= 325 and 334]. [For ET and commentary, see W. R. Schoedel, *Polycarp, Martyrdom of Polycarp, Fragments of Papias* (= Grant, AF 5, 1967), pp. 121 f.]

saken the true teaching that was present from the beginning, there still remains the admission which certainly can be trusted that the majority [77] rejects the ecclesiastical faith. Already in 2.1, Polycarp had repudiated "the error of the great masses (*hē tōn pollōn planē*)." It is not enough to gather from this, as does Knopf, that "twice he expressly mentions 'many' (*polloi*) who are the preservers and adherents" of heresy.[29] The text does not read merely *polloi*, but both times has *hoi polloi*; and this does not signify simply an indefinitely large quantity,[30] but with the definite article it means "the overwhelming majority," "the great mass"—usually with the distinct connotation of contempt for "the many," to whom intelligence normally is denied.[31]

It has often been noted that in his letter to the Philippians, Polycarp does not make any reference to a bishop of that community, although he is a "bishop" himself and he knows Paul's letter to the Philippians with its reference to Philippian *episcopoi* (1.1). In this he also is in sharp contrast to Ignatius, whom he regarded most highly along with his letters (Polycarp *Phil.* 13.2). Neither does Polycarp prescribe the office of bishop as a remedy to the problems at Philippi, nor does he advise them to organize along monarchial lines. And yet it is precisely in this city that such an overseer would have been appropriate for more reasons than one. There was a presbyter by the name of Valens, who apparently was unassailable doctrinally, but who, with his wife, had gone astray in a serious ethical matter and because of their conduct had severely damaged the cause of

29. Knopf, *Zeitalter*, p. 317.
30. As is true with the indefinite use of *polloi* in EH 6.14.6—"those present, who were many (*tous parontas, pollous ontas*)."
31. Cf. W. Dittenberger (ed.), *Sylloge inscriptionum Graecarum*[3], 2 (Leipzig, 1917), no. 672.21 (162/60 B.C.E.), where *hoi polloi* refers to the common people, in contrast to the senators; Epictetus 1.2.18, 1.3.4, and *passim* (see index in H. Schenkl's edition, Leipzig, 1894; cf. also LCL ed. and ET by W. A. Oldfather [1926–28]); Plutarch, *How to Study Poetry*, 12 (= 33 A; LCL *Moralia* 1, ed. F. C. Babbitt [1927], p. 172) and *Tranquility of Mind* 10 (= 470 B; LCL *Moralia* 6, ed. W. C. Hembold [1939], p. 196); Plotinus *Enneads* 2.9.9 (ed. and ET by A. H. Armstrong, LCL 2 [1966]); 2 *Macc.* 2.27; Philo *Who Is the Heir* 42; Josephus *Antiquities* 3.8.8; Papias according to EH 3.39.3 speaks of the inferior tastes of the great multitudes; the report of Eusebius on the letter of Dionysus of Corinth to Pinytus of Cnossos refers to "the weakness of the many" (*hē tōn pollōn astheneia*, EH 4.23.7); Justin *App.* (= 2 *Apol.*) 3.2, accuses Crescens of playing upon the tastes of the multitudes (*hēdonē tōn pollōn*) in his accusations against the Christians; Eusebius EH 2.2.2 claims that immediately after his resurrection, Christ was considered to be a God *para tois pollois*—that is, by the great majority (of believers).

their party (11.1-4). Might not Polycarp's peculiar approach stem from the fact that there was, indeed, a "bishop" in Philippi, but in accord with the majority situation in the community, he was a heretic? Because of his aversion to heresy, Polycarp cannot turn to such a bishop for support of his own interests, which coincide with those of orthodoxy, [78] and thus is restricted to making contact with those presbyters and deacons (5.3) whom he regards as his allies, so that through them he can approach the main body of Christianity there. He challenges them to "bring back those who have erred" (6.1).

Were I not fearful of misusing the argument from silence, I would now have to raise the question as to why we hear nothing at all about the community in neighboring Thessalonica in this connection? One would suppose that this community found itself in a very similar situation to that of Philippi. It also had been established by Paul, in a Macedonian city through which Ignatius had passed on his triumphal procession of suffering. It also had received instructions from the Apostle to the Gentiles, not only orally, but also by letter. Nevertheless, as far as we know, Polycarp never wrote to Thessalonica in spite of the fact that in addition to his letter to the Philippians he seems also to have sent letters containing instructions to other communities (EH 5.20.8). This contrasting treatment is not satisfactorily explained even by pointing out that believers from Philippi had appealed to Polycarp for help (Polycarp *Phil.* 3.1 and 13.1-2), while apparently those of Thessalonica had not. For even in the case of Philippi, the actual impetus for writing cannot be attributed to the Christian group there or to its orthodox portion, but to Ignatius (13.1-2), who came through the city (1.1, 9.1) and invited the Philippians to participate in the demonstration of support for Antioch. We must therefore raise the question as to why Ignatius did not personally or by letter, or through a messenger, also approach the community at Thessalonica with the same request? The suggestion that, subsequent to the time of Paul, Christianity had disappeared once again from Thessalonica, although not intrinsically impossible, is in this instance excluded on the basis of the testimony of Melito of Sardis.[32]

Could it be that what we suspected in Philippi obtained to an even greater degree in Thessalonica and thus explains this reticence of

32. According to EH 4.26.10; see K. J. Neumann, *Der römische Staat und die allgemeine Kirche bis auf Diocletian* (Leipzig, 1890), p. 28.

Ignatius and silence of Polycarp?[33] "Demas has left me, being in love with this present world, and has gone to Thessalonica" (2 Tim. 4.10), says the ecclesiastically oriented "Paul" of the pastoral epistles. [79] To be sure, this is only a conjecture and nothing more! But 2 Thessalonians already shows, whether it is genuinely Pauline or not,[34] that prior to Ignatius the impression arises that certain people were operating in Thessalonica who, by various means, sought to alienate the Thessalonian Christians from the Apostle to the Gentiles and from his teaching (2.2, 3.17). And Dionysius of Corinth, who around the year 170 sent letters for the orthodox cause as far as Bithynia and Pontus (EH 4.23.4, 6) did not expend effort on any Macedonian community. Was his reason for not writing the fact that everything was in the best of order in Macedonia, in contrast to Lacedaemonia, Athens, and Crete—those neighboring regions in which he attempted to intervene by writing letters (EH 4.23.2, 5, 7)? Or was it that there was simply no possibility of gaining a hearing there? I am inclined to suspect the latter.[35] Accordingly, I would also include post-Pauline Macedonia among those districts reached by Christianity in which "heresy" predominated, along with Edessa and Egypt from their very earliest Christian beginnings, and Syria-Antioch from almost the outset. Is it accidental that all these regions were unaffected by the passover controversy[36] and saw no reason to express any opinion in this matter? Or is not their silence an indication, rather, of their lack of interest in questions which were of vital concern to "the church"?

Dionysius of Corinth views with apprehension another area, not

33. Nor is Thessalonica ever mentioned in the ancient apocryphal Acts.
34. See A. Jülicher, *Einleitung in das Neue Testament*[7] (Tübingen: Mohr, 1931, with E. Fascher), pp. 63-67, for whom the spuriousness of the letter seems highly probable [Jülicher's earlier, more positive attitude to Pauline authorship of 2 Thessalonians is reflected in the ET by J. P. Ward from the 1900 German 2d. ed. (New York: Putnam's, 1904), pp. 62-68]; also A. Oepke, in his commentary in *Das Neue Testament Deutsch*, 8 (Göttingen. Vandenhoeck, 1933): 111, is aware of many difficulties. [For a recent discussion of the problem, see Feine-Behm-Kümmel, *Introduction to the New Testament* (ET by A. J. Mattill from 1965 German ed. [New York: Abingdon, 1966]), pp. 187 ff.]
35. If Thessalonian Christianity became sharply divided around the year 100, considerations in favor of the authenticity of 2 Thessalonians, such as those raised by Harnack, lose their persuasiveness; see Harnack, "Briefsammlung," pp. 11 f., and even earlier, "Das Problem des zweiten Thessalonicherbriefs," Sb Berlin 31 for 1910, pp. 560-578.
36. See the report about the churches affected by this dispute in EH 5.23.3, and compare above, p. 9 on the Osröene.

discussed above, in which Christianity had spread to various places, namely the island of Crete. He writes to the church in Gortyna together with the other communities in Crete, commends their bishop Philip, but at the same time he warns against the seductions of the heretics (EH 4.23.5). In another letter, to the Cretan Christians of Knossus, Dionysius exhorts their bishop, Pinytus, to consider the weakness of "the great mass" (above, 73 n. 31, to EH 4.23.7 f.). To be sure, this "majority" is characterized here as being deficient only [80] with respect to the demands of chastity. But in the letter to the church in Amastris in Pontus, which is summarized in the immediately preceding section of EH (4.23.6), Dionysius recommends that the same sort of welcome be extended to those who return after erring in the realm of chastity (*hagneia*) as to those who had been involved in heresy (*hairetikē planē*). At all events, Eusebius takes advantage of the opportunity expressly to confirm the *orthodoxia* of Pinytus, the bishop of Knossos (EH 4.23.8).

As we move back in time from Dionysius to the letter to Titus, let us remember that it is only for those who regard the latter as genuine that it is necessary to associate the establishment of Christianity in Crete with Paul. If that is not the case, it may be that here also there existed in the beginning a type of Christianity that completely lacked the "ecclesiastical" brand, despite all its other varieties. The letter to Titus would then be regarded as an attempt initially to open the path for ecclesiastical Christianity with the help of the authority of Paul (who was connected with Crete through a recollection that is still reflected in Acts 27.7 ff.), as well as through ecclesiastical organization in general. Even by the time of Dionysius of Corinth, this undertaking had succeeded only to a very limited extent. The "many" (*polloi*) whom the epistle of Titus reproaches for combining false teaching with unruliness (1.10) correspond to *hoi polloi* for whom Pinytus is urged to leave the way open for reconciliation.

4

Asia Minor Prior
to Ignatius

In the preceding chapter (p. 69), we found it to be probable that at the time of Ignatius, the majority of the faithful in the churches of Asia Minor at Ephesus, Magnesia, Tralles, and Philadelphia held to a form of Christianity that allowed Ignatius to consider them to be his special allies. But at the same time, we advised against hastily extending this judgment to cover the whole of Asia Minor, or even of only its western part. The surviving clues concerning Antioch, Philippi, and Polycarp's Smyrna should at least urge us to be cautious, if not frighten us away from such a generalization. It seems to me that this warning is reinforced and provided with even greater justification by the following considerations.

Approximately two decades prior to Ignatius another Christian had written to communities in Asia Minor—John, the apocalyptic seer (Rev. 1-3). It would not be easy to uncover significant common features that would permit us to group these two authors together as representatives of the same sort of Christian religious position. What distinguishes them from one another is, above all, the difference that separates a Syrian gentile Christian from a Palestinian, or at any rate an unmistakably Jewish Christian (cf. 84-87). Moreover, in this early period "orthodoxy" is just as much a sort of collective concept as is "heresy," and can clothe itself in quite different forms according to the circumstances. There is also room for doubt as to whether the apocalypticist, with his extremely confused religious outlook that peculiarly mixes Jewish, Christian, and mythological elements and ends in chiliasm, can be regarded in any sense as an intellectual and spiritual leader of an important band of Christians in western Asia Minor. To what extent was he really an influential figure in the region to which he addresses himself? [82] To what extent might this have been only wishful thinking? Did anything else meet with general approval, other than his stormy outburst, seething with hate, against the pagan empire, which perhaps found acceptance in those circles directly affected by the persecution? Unqualified confidence that his recipients would follow his lead is not exactly the impression left by the apocalyptic letters, at least when taken as a whole!

But a real connection between John and Ignatius does appear in the fact that John's letters find him in opposition to a false teaching of an umistakably gnostic brand [1]—a heresy which pursues its path within the churches themselves, and not alongside them.[2] There is no need here to enter into the lively controversy, connected especially with Ramsay's notions,[3] as to the reasons that prompted John to select precisely these seven cities. That the number is significant for Revelation, with its propensity for sevenfold divisions, requires no proof. The *Muratorian Canon* already recognized this and thought that a kind of "catholic" appearance had been achieved thereby (lines 48-59). But why did John select precisely these communities from the Christianity round about him? What, for example, gave Laodicea precedence over Colossae and Hierapolis? In view of our earlier explanations, I think that I am entitled to suppose that John selected the most prominent communities from those in his area which met the prerequisite of seeming to afford him the possibility of exerting a real influence. Subsequently, Ignatius apparently followed a similar procedure and in turn made a selection from among those seven communities. The necessity of retaining the number seven resulted less in pressuring the apocalypticist to exclude communities in great number, as in compelling him to include one church or another which only to a very limited degree belonged to the sphere of his influence.

Of the seven communities of Asia Minor mentioned in Revelation, Ignatius addresses only three—Ephesus, Smyrna, and Philadelphia;

1. Theophilus, a later successor to Ignatius as a leader of Antiochian orthodoxy, used the Apocalypse in his struggle against the gnostic, Hermogenes (EH 4.24).
2. Knopf, *Zeitalter*, pp. 291 f.
3. W. M. Ramsay, *The Letters to the Seven Churches of Asia* (London, 1904), pp. 171 ff.

[83] he does not address those of Pergamum, Thyatira, Sardis, and Laodicea. Can it be a coincidence that the churches of Smyrna and Philadelphia, to which Ignatius turns, are precisely those which fare best in the Apocalypse, appear also to be especially free of heresy,[4] and later produce the martyrs of the catholic church during the persecution connected with Polycarp (*Martyrdom of Polycarp* 19.1-2)? Is it by chance that the communities of Pergamum, Thyatira,[5] Sardis, and Laodicea [6] are missing from Ignatius' audience—communities that the seer vehemently rebukes, in which Balaamites and Nicolaitans (2.14 f.), the prophetess Jezebel and those who know "the deep things of Satan" (2.20, 24) live undisturbed and are allowed to mislead the servants of the Son of God (2.20), or which from the viewpoint of the author are utterly indifferent and lukewarm (3.15 ff.)? On his final journey, Ignatius passed through Laodicea and Sardis as well as Philadelphia and Smyrna, and yet neither of the former names is even mentioned by him, much less are the communities of the respective cities addressed in a letter. In Sardis, however, there were also a few who had not soiled their garments, according to Revelation 3.4. Similarly in Thyatira, which for the travelling Ignatius was no more difficult to reach nor more remote than Ephesus, Magnesia, and Tralles (which likewise had not seen him within their walls), already in the view of John (Rev. 2.24) the heretics are opposed by "the rest" (*hoi loipoi*) in such a way that the latter also is branded as a minority.

Is it too much to claim if, on the basis of what Ignatius both says and does not say, and considering the evidence of the Apocalypse, one concludes that in his attempt to stretch the circle of his influence as widely as possible for the sake of his constituency there was nothing Ignatius could hope for from the Christian groups represented at Pergamum, Thyatira, Sardis, and Laodicea, because no points of contact existed for him there—no "bishop" was present whom he

4. Cf. Knopf, *Zeitalter*, p. 290.
5. A few decades after Ignatius, Thyatira was completely lost to Montanism (Epiphanius *Her.* 51.33). Cf. Zahn, *Forschungen*, 5 (1893): 35 f.
6. Cf. the Christian *Sibylline Oracle* 7.22 f.:

> Woe Laodicea, you who not once did see God,
> You will deceive yourself, insolent one!
> The surge of the Lycus will wash you away.

[For other ETs, see R. McL. Wilson in Hennecke-Schneemelcher, 2: 721; also M. S. Terry, *The Sibylline Oracles*[2] (New York: Eaton and Mains, 1899), p. 150.]

could press into service, because the heretics had maintained, or had come to exercise, leadership there? Even Smyrna no longer left Ignatius [84] with the same favorable impression as it had the apocalypticist (see above, 69). It is unfortunate that no gnostic revelation is extant in answer to the seer, that no heretical community leader describes the conditions in Asia Minor from his point of view! In light of the early and abundant literary activity of the heretics in diverse regions, I do not doubt for a moment that those concerned would neither meekly swallow the attacks of a John or of Ignatius and Polycarp, nor limit themselves to oral defense. Surely they sent out letters and written works of various sorts. But unfortunately the tradition has been prejudiced against them, and their literary protests have perished just like the heretical gospels of Egypt and Antioch, to which reference already has been made (see 50-53, 66 f.).

One further point should not be overlooked in this connection. While the community of Laodicea to which Paul once had written (Col. 4.16) makes a very unfavorable impression on the apocalypticist but still can serve to round out the number seven, two other churches from the immediate vicinity, well known to the Apostle to the Gentiles, are completely neglected. The community of Hierapolis (Col. 4.13) and that of Colossae are bypassed in icy silence by both John and Ignatius.[7] The latter went right through Hierapolis, and as for Colossae, if he did not also go through it, he at least passed very close by. Furthermore, a figure like that of Papias prevents us from even toying with the idea that there might not have been Christians at least in Hierapolis at the time of Revelation and of Ignatius. Indeed, Paul already had testified of his friend Epaphras, that he had labored much with the people of Colossae, Laodicea, and Hierapolis (Col. 4.13).

In Asia Minor, Ignatius appears in approximately the same small region as does the apocalypticist. This fact, and the way in which they both conduct themselves, furthers our insight into the extent of orthodoxy's authority at the end of the first and the beginning of the second century. We might learn even more from Ignatius if we [85] were informed in greater detail about the route of his journey. Unfortunately, however, we do not know for sure whether he covered

7. Geographical considerations provide no satisfactory explanation. Whoever treats Laodicea as part of Asia (Rev. 1.4) cannot consider Hierapolis and Colossae as Phrygian, and thus exclude them.

the whole distance from Antioch to Smyrna by the land route, or whether, as has been conjectured and is surely possible, he made use of a ship as far as, say, Attalia.[8] If he had not done the latter,[9] then the yawning gap between Antioch in the east and Philadelphia in the west in which Ignatius left behind no traces [10] would surprise us even more than his bypassing of Hierapolis, Laodicea, and Colossae. For in that case a district is completely omitted in which numerous Christian communities already must have existed prior to Ignatius. Paul traveled through Lycaonia and Pisidia during his first missionary journey, and later he revisited the communities founded at that time. Why is it that these regions also, like the Phrygian area reached by Paul, are so completely thrust aside, while Ignatius' concern and his attempt to exercise influence are first aroused as he draws near to the west coast?

Does it not provide further food for thought, that we miss here a reference to the very same sector in southern and eastern Asia Minor to which the opening words of 1 Peter fail to refer—a fact that, in the latter instance, has repeatedly caused astonishment and occasioned all sorts of attempts at explanation? Thus, for example, writes H. Windisch: "He [i.e. 1 Peter] apparently wanted to include all the provinces of Asia Minor. That he did not mention Lycia, Pamphylia, and Cilicia is indeed surprising; nevertheless, Lycia may still have been without any important congregations, Pamphylia may have been included in Galatia, and Cilicia may have been excluded as belonging to Syria." [11] I find this just as unpersuasive as the notion that the unnamed Phrygia is hidden away in the designation "Asia." No doubt that was true for the Roman administration. But the Romans also united Pontus with Bithynia,[12] which are as clearly separated as possible in 1 Peter, where the one district is mentioned at the

---

8. On this problem, cf. Eusebius EH 3.36.3-6, who in any event attests that Ignatius used a land route through Asia.
9. The land route is supported particularly by T. Zahn, among the older commentators—see his *Ignatius von Antioch* (Gotha, 1873), pp. 250-295 and especially 264 f. Cf. also J. B. Lightfoot, *Apostolic Fathers*[2], 2 (*S. Ignatius, S. Polycarp*).1 (London: Macmillan, 1889): 33 ff. [and W. M. Ramsay, *The Church in the Roman Empire* (London, 1893), p. 318].
10. Philo, the "deacon from Cilicia" (*Philad.* 11.1; cf. *Smyr.* 10.1), can scarcely be viewed as evidence for the land route, any more than can the "nearby (*eggista*) churches" (*Philad.* 10.2).
11. *Die katholischen Briefe*[2], HbNT 15 (1930): 51.
12. J. Weiss, RPTK[3] 10 (1901): 536.29 f.

start of the series, while the other, separated by three names, concludes it. The Christians who, in the year 177/78, composed the account of martyrdoms [86] that occurred in the churches of Vienne and Lyons still are able to distinguish accurately between Asia and Phrygia (EH 5.1.3, 5.3.4; cf. 5.14); and from the very beginning, the Montanists [13] are called Phrygians or Kataphrygians, which shows that even for a long time after 1 Peter, Phrygia has by no means been absorbed into Asia from the Christian perspective.[14] I should therefore prefer to explain the blank spot on the map of Asia Minor in 1 Peter by believing that there simply was nothing to be gained for "ecclesiastically" oriented Christianity in that area at that time. In southeastern Asia Minor, from the borders of Syria westward to Phrygia, "ecclesiastical" intervention was not tolerated at the end of the first century, and even Rome realized the futility of such an attempt—the same Rome which at about the same time acted in a quite different manner with respect to Corinth (see below, chap. 5).

The estimation of the situation in southern and eastern Asia Minor as proposed above appears to me to receive further support through an examination of the earliest history of that church which occupies the first place both for the apocalypticist and for Ignatius, and receives excellent treatment from both. Even *Ephesus* cannot be considered as a center of orthodoxy, but is rather a particularly instructive example of how the life of an ancient Christian community, even one of apostolic origin, could erode when caught in the turbulent crosscurrents of orthodoxy and heresy. Paul had laid the foundation in Ephesus and built up a church through several years of labor. If Romans 16 represents a letter to the Ephesians, then, on the basis of verses 17-20, we must conclude that already during the lifetime of the apostle, certain people had appeared there whose teaching caused offense and threatened divisions in the community. To this would correspond the complaint in 1 Corinthians 16.9, concerning "many adversaries" in Ephesus, if it refers to those who had been baptized. In any event, the book of Acts has Paul warning the Ephesian elders (*presbyteroi*) in his farewell to them at Miletus that *from their own midst* there will arise men speaking perverse things

13. N. Bonwetsch, RPTK[3] 13 (1903): 420.25 ff. Achelis, *Christentum* 2, 45, 420.49.
14. Cf. the references to "Phrygians" and "Asia" in the anti-Montanist writing quoted in EH 5.16.9-10.

to draw away the Christians for themselves (20.30). This prediction actually describes the situation in Ephesus at the time of the composition of Acts.

Ignatius also knows of difficulties in Ephesus. But the picture that [87] he sketches for us obviously is already rather blurred. In clear contrast to the earlier book of Acts, Ignatius praises the Ephesians for having stopped their ears against the strange teachers who had stealthily slipped into their midst *from elsewhere* (*Eph.* 9.1). And although the book of Acts presupposes that a presbyterate consisting of several members was leading the church of Ephesus, Ignatius, faithful to his interests, treats the monarchial episcopate as a deeply-rooted institution also in this city (see 1.3, 2.1, 6.2—Bishop Onesimus).

To what extent Ignatius was still conscious of the fact that Paul was the actual father of the community cannot be determined. To be sure, he calls the Ephesians "fellow initiates with Paul" (*Paulou symmystai, Eph.* 12.2). But not only can the *one* Apostle become "the apostles" with whom the Ephesians "always agree in the power of Jesus Christ" (11.2), but the expression in 12.2 is in no way based upon Paul's apostolic activity but rather on the fact that the road to martyrdom, which Paul also travelled, leads past this city, and thus on the claim that the Apostle mentions the Ephesians in every letter (12.2). Nevertheless, Ignatius knows 1 Corinthians (see below, chap. 9) and he could have learned from it that Paul actually had labored in Ephesus.

While this last point must remain open, we find as we turn to the Apocalypse that in this book the recollection of the Pauline establishment of the church of Ephesus appears to have been completely lost, or perhaps even deliberately suppressed. At most one finds a faint recollection that at an earlier time this community had been better off, in the statement about having "abandoned the love you had formerly" (Rev. 2.4). But now it is in danger of slipping into gnosticism; now it must strive against the false apostles and the Nicolaitans (2.2, 6). The threatening words of the Son of Man (2.5) surely do not sound as if the struggle were easy and the victory certain! And as far as Paul is concerned, in the Apocalypse only the names of the twelve apostles are found on the foundations of the new Jerusalem (21.14); there is no room for Paul. And at the very least, it will be but a short time before the Apostle to the Gentiles will have been totally displaced in the consciousness of the church of Ephesus in favor of one of the twelve apostles, John. [88] In Ephesus, Paul had turned out to be too weak to drive the enemies of the church from the battlefield.

The Apocalypse does not leave us with a particularly impressive idea of what sought to replace the Pauline gospel in the "ecclesiastically oriented" circles at Ephesus. Aside from Revelation's being a book of comfort and faith for threatened and persecuted Christians, features which are the result of the difficult contemporary situation and which thus to some degree transcend party lines, there remains for the most part a Jewish Christianity, presumably of Palestinian origin.[15] This was undoubtedly better suited for the anti-gnostic struggle than was the Pauline proclamation, but in other respects it is hardly comparable.

The pastoral Epistles (see below, chap. 9) are chronologically most recent, compared with Acts, Ignatius, and the Apocalypse. For the earliest history of Christianity in Ephesus they yield hardly anything that originated in actual recollection of the apostolic age. To the same extent that we are unwilling to concede that the epistle to Titus conveys actual knowledge about the relationship of Paul to Christianity in Crete (see above, 76), neither do we grant that 1-2 Timothy give us insight into the relations between the Apostle to the Gentiles and Ephesus. What they report to us concerning the apostolic period, namely that Paul himself already left one of his helpers there in order to check the danger of heresy which was already in full bloom (1 Tim. 1.3 ff.) is not correct, and is refuted by the future tense in Acts 20.30. This merely reveals to us the desire of orthodoxy to know that the Apostle to the Gentiles, whose activity in Ephesus is related by 1 Corinthians as well as Acts (which may also have provided the basis for the relationship between Paul and Crete), also stood on their side in the struggle against heresy. The Paul of the pastoral Epistles fights in union with "the church" *against* the heretics. Nevertheless, history categorically prohibits ascribing victory to him on the Ephesian front, from which he and his influence fade rapidly in the second century. Even the Pastorals, in agreement with Revelation, have to admit that in the second century, the Apostle [89] had

15. If the apocalypticist is to be identified with the "presbyter John, a disciple (*mathētēs*) of the Lord" mentioned by Papias (in Eusebius EH 3.39.4).

lost the contest in Ephesus. While 2 Timothy 1.18 heaps praise on Onesiphorus for special services performed at Ephesus, it is at the same time admitted that his labors had not borne fruit. All the brethren in Asia, laments the same passage (1.15), have turned their backs on Paul. And Onesiphorus himself has vacated this futile battlefield in order to visit the Apostle in Rome (1.17). If we inquire into the history of heresy in Ephesus as to whence this difficulty may have arisen, we encounter, without supposing thereby to have found a complete explanation, the person of Cerinthus,[16] whom we can introduce at this point with all the more justification since not only his gnostic teaching in general, but also his specific enmity toward Paul and his letters are clearly attested.[17]

I can understand this state of affairs, which I have sketched in bold strokes, only by supposing that in Ephesus a community of apostolic origin has, through its struggles with external enemies [18] and above all through internal discord and controversies (see above, 82-84), suffered such setbacks and transformations that for many, even the name of its founder became lost. Orthodox Christianity underwent reorganization and now found an apostolic patron in that member of the twelve who shared his name with the apocalypticist and who established close connection with Jesus more securely than had Paul, which was considered to be the highest trump in the struggle with heresy. Only the canonization of the book of Acts and of the Pauline letters, including the Pastorals, once again provided clear insight into the real situation with respect to Paul.[19]

I cannot agree with K. Holl and E. Schwartz in describing what took place in Ephesus in postapostolic times and resulted in the transfer of leadership from Paul to John [90] as a taking over of the province of Asia by the primitive (Palestinian) community.[20] Prob-

16. See Polycarp's story about John and Cerinthus at the bathhouse in Ephesus (Irenaeus AH 3.3.4 = EH 4.14.6). Cf. Knopf, *Zeitalter*, pp. 328-330.
17. See Filaster *Her.* 36 and Epiphanius *Her.* 28.5.3, which probably reflect the lost *Syntagma* of Hippolytus [Hilgenfeld, *Ketzergeschichte*, pp. 411 ff.; see also below, 280-282].
18. Even prior to the writing of the Apocalypse, Paul could speak of such problems —1 Cor. 15.31, 2 Cor. 1.8 ff.; perhaps also Rom. 16.3 f.
19. See Irenaeus AH 3.3.4 (end), and the *Acts of Paul*.
20. K. Holl, *Gesammelte Aufsätze zur Kirchengeschichte, 2: Der Osten* (Tübingen: Mohr, 1928; repr. Darmstadt, 1964), p. 66; E. Schwartz, ZNW 31 (1932): 191. Cf. also Lietzmann, *History*, 1: 189 f.

ably a better explanation for what seems to have happened may be found in the fact that in the wake of the devastating blow that at first threatened, and then actually struck Jerusalem and Palestine in the war with the Romans, but under the pressure of other influences, something occurred that was similar to what had already taken place after the persecution of Stephen. Just as at that time the primitive (Palestinian) community did not "take over" Antioch (Acts 11.19 ff.), neither did it now bring under its dominion the province of Asia. Rather, now Jewish *Christians*, who no longer felt safe and secure in the Holy Land and east of the Jordan, sought a new home in more distant territory. Philip the evangelist, who had already left Jerusalem at the occasion of the persecution of Stephen (Acts 8.1 ff.) and had come to live in the coastal city of Caesarea where we still find him around the year 60 (Acts 21.8 f.), emigrated to Hierapolis together with his prophesying daughters.[21] John the "elder," the disciple of the Lord (above, 84 n. 15), probably also exchanged Jerusalem for Ephesus.

On the other hand, I cannot pass over in silence the fact that, as far as we can tell, no such migration took place either to Egypt or to Syria and the adjacent southeastern portion of Asia Minor.[22] Perhaps Christianity did not yet exist in Egypt at that time. And we may presume that in the other regions just mentioned things had become a bit too hot for a Jewish Christian version of the new religion. Here gnosticism predominated, with its explicitly anti-Jewish attitude. Even in not overtly gnostic circles of Christianity located closer to Palestine, there was little sympathy for Jews and their associates, as seems to me to be clear from the Gospel of John and the letters of Ignatius (see below, 88), not to mention writings which are later in time and cannot be localized with certainty.

In the western part of Asia Minor, the conditions apparently were more favorable. Here the Jewish Christian element, which from the very beginning was no more absent than it was in Corinth (see below, 99 f.), gained [91] impetus through the immigration of outstanding members of Palestinian Christianity, of whom John and Philip are

21. See Polycrates of Ephesus in EH 3.31.3 = 5.24.2; also Papias in EH 3.39.9.
22. I am quite aware of how scanty the material on this matter is, and I do not want to make any fuss about it if this idea does not fit naturally into what to me is becoming an increasingly clearer picture.

examples; an impetus that must have been all the more effective since, at the very latest, the catastrophe in Palestine forever erased the demand that the gentile Christians of the diaspora should be circumcised and should to some extent observe the ceremonial law. Thus the fence of the law had been pulled down and fellowship between Jewish and gentile Christians in the outside world became really possible. The line of demarcation henceforth no longer runs between Jewish and gentile Christianity, but rather, between orthodoxy and heresy. And in Ephesus we find the former embodied in the alliance between a type of Jewish Christianity which has no commitment to the ceremonial law and gentile Christians of similar orientation. Here orthodoxy and heresy struggle over the Pauline heritage, and in the process something is lost; certainly it is not the entire Pauline inheritance, but something that once existed—the consciousness of him to whom they were indebted.

The Jewish Christianity that had outgrown its legalistic narrowness and the "church" found themselves, where they existed, to be united against gnosticism with respect to their high esteem for the Old Testament and their mutual preference for a concrete (historical) interpretation of religious situations and events, especially as they relate to the life of Jesus and the age to come. The heresy fighter, Justin, a gentile by birth, who received the decisive stimuli for his conversion in the city of John and later lived there for some years as a Christian,[23] based his Christian faith upon the Old Testament, the synoptic gospels, and the book of Revelation (utilizing also certain suggestions from the hellenistic world of ideas).[24] And Papias, who lived in the city where Philip settled and who also struggled against heretics, wants to ground himself primarily on the apostolic tradition concerning the life of Jesus; along with it, he taught an eschatology that is also dependent on the Apocalypse, the coarseness of which certainly would not have been judged more leniently by the gnostics than it was by Eusebius![25] In exchange for having sacrificed the law for their orthodox gentile Christian brethren, Asian Jewish Christianity [92] received in turn the knowledge that hence-

23. See Zahn, *Forschungen*, 6 (1900): 8, 192.
24. Cf. EH 4.18 and the writings of Justin.
25. EH 3.39.13, "a man of exceedingly small intelligence." For general information on Papias, see EH 3.39, based in part on Irenaeus AH 5.33.3 f.

forth the "church" would be open without hesitation to the Jewish influence mediated by Christians, coming not only from the apocalyptic traditions, but also from the synagogue with its practices concerning worship, which led to the appropriation of the Jewish passover observance.[26]

Even the observance of the sabbath by Christians appears to have found some favor in Asia.[27] And the aversion of Ignatius, in Magnesia (8-11) and Philadelphia (5-9), toward a Jewish Christianity that apparently had abandoned its most offensive demands [28] is less characteristic of ecclesiastically oriented circles in Asia than of that Syrian gentile Christian for whom the Old Testament itself meant very little, at least in practice. For him, all such things belong to the realm of the heretics. Thus the existence of gnosticism side by side with Jewish Christianity in Ignatius' picture of the heretics he opposed in those two cities is, in my opinion, due less to the complicated nature of the heresy there than to the complex personality of Ignatius, who as an ecclesiastical leader rejects gnosticism, and as a gentile Syrian Christian opposes the Jewish falsification of the gospel wherever he thinks he finds it.

The fact that 1 Timothy also opposes a gnosticism containing Jewish features could be regarded as an indication that in Ephesus and Asia there actually existed a gnosticizing Jewish Christianity large and powerful enough to evoke opposition, so that one could not simply classify the Jewish Christianity of this region as being on the side of ecclesiastical orthodoxy without further examination. Thus Jewish Christianity would be divided, just as gentile Christianity was divided, into orthodox and heretical types. But since with reference to Crete also, the author of the Pastorals opposes the same admixture of Jewish Christianity and gnosticism, which is hardly natural and

---

26. Of course, this did not take place without difficulty. Melito of Sardis wrote a treatise concerning the Passover after the martyrdom of Sagaris, bishop of Laodicea (ca. 164/166; Neumann, *Römische Staat*, p. 66), because a great discussion on this matter had arisen in the bereaved community (EH 4.26.3). [This is not the "Pascal Homily" of Melito that has come to light in several manuscripts and versions since 1940; see below, p. 315 n. 37.] Shortly thereafter, Apollinaris, bishop of Hierapolis in Phrygia, wrote a work on the same situation (cited in the "Easter Chronicle" or *Chronicon paschale*, pp. 13 f., ed. L. Dindorf [Bonn, 1832]).
27. Ignatius *Magn.* 9.1; cf. Bauer, *Ignatius*, ad loc.
28. According to *Philad.* 6.1, it can even include the uncircumcised.

certainly not frequent, it appears to me to be more convincing to understand the peculiar heresy combatted in the Pastorals from the perspective of the mentality of the pseudonymous letter writer—as "Paul" [93] he must deal with the "teachers of the law" (1 Tim. 1.7) and the "circumcision party" (Titus 1.10), but as a second century churchman, he opposes gnosticism.

At Paul's time those communities that he had established or which developed under his influence and which were situated either in Asia or in adjacent Phrygia were almost totally of a gentile Christian type. Evidence of this is the letter to the Colossians, in the case of Phrygia.[29] Unfortunately, we do not possess a reliable witness from Paul himself that would reveal the conditions in Ephesus. But everything we know of other communities founded by Paul permits us to conclude that the congregations of Asia (1 Cor. 16.19) also were composed mainly of gentile Christians. Why do we find that in postapostolic times, in the period of the formation of the ecclesiastical structure, the Jewish Christians in these regions come into prominence as described above? It would seem to me that the easiest explanation for this is found in the assumption already suggested by the Apocalypse and by Ignatius, that a large segment of the gentile Christians became less and less suited for "ecclesiastical" fellowship, so that in the developing church the emphasis would automatically shift sharply in favor of the Jewish Christian element.

We will now briefly survey those New Testament writings of the postapostolic age which, in addition to the Apocalypse, are engaged in the struggle with heretics, even though we cannot claim their origin in Asia Minor with certainty. The *epistle of Jude*, the polemic of which is taken up in 2 Peter, shows us that the heretical gnostic teachers and their followers have not yet withdrawn from the orthodox group, but still participate in the common love feasts (Jude 12). Their influence is important and therefore the tone of their orthodox opponent is quite vehement. He makes the concession to the Christian group that he addresses that the deception has been brought into the community from the outside (Jude 4). Yet when we recall that, contrary to Acts 20.30 (above, 82 f.), Ignatius made the same concession to the Ephesian church, it is difficult to suppress the suspicion that in Jude also the reference merely represents a device of the

29. Jülicher(-Fascher), *Einleitung*[7], p. 129.

letter writer, or better, an attempt to prove the absolute correctness of his own group. The faith for which his fellow believers must fight [94] has been delivered once and for all to the saints (Jude 3); therefore that which troubles the faith must come "from without." For the church members addressed in Jude, such a view may bring some consolation, but it does not satisfy the historian. Rather, he sees a problem in the convenient expression "they secretly sneaked in," and asks the question "whence did they come?" Then, if he wants to attribute credibility to the letter of Jude for the congregations to which it first came, the historian must assume that the heresy had its home somewhere else in Christendom, and that it successfully sallied forth from there in conquest.

The *pastoral Epistles* have already been of assistance in our invesgitation and description of the earliest history of the church of Crete (above, 75 f.) and of Ephesus (above, 84 f.). Thus I can bypass them here without examining them anew from different perspectives. With regard to the Pastorals and the other primitive Christian writings under discussion here, I am not interested in renewing the oft-repeated attempt of describing the false teachings that are presupposed, interpreting exactly their meaning, testing their uniformity, and connecting them with names from the history of heresy—or else denying such a relationship. All this may be presupposed as already known (see above, xxv). For us, it suffices to observe that the Pastorals also deal with a situation in which there existed the antithesis between ecclesiastically oriented faith of some sort and a many headed heresy (Titus 1.10, *polloi*) in one form or another. But when we speak of orthodoxy and heresy in this way, we must once more guard ourselves against simply equating these words with the notions of majority and minority, of original form and deviation (see above, xxii f.). The confession of Jesus as Lord and heavenly redeemer is a common foundation for both tendencies, and for a long time sufficed to hold the differently oriented spirits together in *one* fellowship.

When it is reported—and that by a non-Christian gentile [30]—that a Christian group like the one in Bithynia sang hymns to Christ as God, pledged itself to live a holy life, and observed cultic meals, it

30. Pliny the Younger *Epistles* 10.96.7 [ed. and ET by W. Melmoth, LCL 2 (1915); ET also in Stevenson, *New Eusebius*, pp. 13-15, and in similar source books].

is by no means clear from such a description whether it refers to heretics or whether it was a mixed community of heretics and ecclesiastically oriented Christians, or finally, whether orthodox belief predominated there. All too [95] quickly, in my opinion, the final option is accepted as self-evident.[31] But Marcion of Sinope in Pontus [32] proves that at least very soon after Pliny's term of office, heresy was present in that region and the ground must have been somewhat suitable for the spread of heresy. Already in his homeland, Marcion had achieved a special status, and when he left he received letters of recommendation from his followers and friends in Pontus.[33] A couple of decades later, Dionysius of Corinth wrote to Nicomedia against Marcion (EH 4.23.4) and in another letter to the church of Amastris in Pontus, he advised them not to make the readmission of penitent heretics too difficult (EH 4.23.6). There were, moreover, more martyrs from among the Marcionites,[34] the Montanists,[35] and other heretical groups than orthodoxy would like to admit, and the church took great pains to divest this fact of its significance and seductive splendor.[36] Even from this point of view, we have no reason to conclude that Pliny was opposing a Christianity of an indubitably ecclesiastical orientation.

Just as Titus 1.10 f. laments about the many deceivers who are successful in winning whole families and household churches and therefore counsels to have as little as possible to do with them (3.10 f.), so also in the *Johannine Epistles* we find that there are many seducers (1 John 2.18, 2 John 7) and the danger is increasing at such an alarming rate that the antichrist himself appears to have taken shape in them (1 John 2.18). Boasting of their possession of the spirit, they deny the identity of the man Jesus with Christ, the Son of God (1 John 2.22; 4.2 f.; 5.1, 5, 6 ff., 20). "This is the one form of docetism

31. E.g. by Harnack, *Marcion²*, p. 23.
32. Epiphanius *Her.* 42.1; cf. Justin *Apol.* 26.5 and 58.1, Irenaeus AH 1.27.2 (= 25.1), Tertullian *Against Marcion* 1.1.
33. This information is found in an ancient Latin prologue to the Gospel of John: cf. Harnack, *Evangelien-Prologe* pp. 6, 15 f. [= 325 and 334 f.]. Also his *Marcion²*, pp. 24, 11° ff.
34. See the material in Harnack, *Marcion²*, pp. 150 (esp. n. 4), 154, n. 1, 315° f., 340°, 348°.
35. See the treatment in K. J. Neumann, *Römische Staat*, pp. 66-69.
36. See especially the anonymous anti-Montanist from Asia Minor quoted in EH 5.16.20-22: even though there are a great number (*pleistoi*) of martyrs from the various sects, and particularly from Marcionites, we still do not admit that they possess the truth and confess Christ truly (21).

that is attested and is conceivable only within gnostic [96] circles; apparently those in question have boasted that with their new and perfect knowledge (2.3 f.) of the true God (e.g. 5.20 f.), which excludes the idea of an incarnation of the divine, they themselves are the true bearers of the spirit (4.1-6, "pneumatics") and promise eternal life only to their followers (2.25-28)." [37]

How this particular form of gnosticism is related to that of Ignatius' opponents is open to question. But the author of 1 John resembles his ally against heresy (see above, 88) in that he also makes practically no use of the Old Testament, except for borrowing from it the figure of Cain as the monstrous prototype of the heretics (3.12). This attitude toward "scripture" is not really characteristic of the ecclesiastical approach of Asia, but would, in my judgment, fit better in the east, perhaps in Syria, where as I still hold to be extremely probable, the longer Johannine Epistle and the Gospel of John originated, around the time of Ignatius.

But be that as it may, it is certain that the separation of the two parties has already taken place in the Christian situation to which the author of 1 John carefully addresses himself. We hear that it took place in such a way that the heretics left the community and made themselves independent so that they now viewed their orthodox fellow Christians with hellish, fratricidal hatred: "If they really had belonged to our group, they would have remained with us" (2.19). The author of 1 John celebrates this as a victory (4.4). But when in the very next verse we hear his strained admission that "the world" listens to the others, our confidence that here the "church" represents the majority and is actually setting the pace evaporates. And it is hardly a sign of strength when we read the anxious instruction in 2 John, which originated in similar conditions, that heretics should not be received into one's house, nor even be greeted (10 f.). Only by strictest separation from the heretics can salvation be expected; orthodoxy here appears to have been pushed completely onto the defensive, and to be severely restricted in its development. And perhaps we do more justice to the actual historical situation if we suppose that it was not the heretics who withdrew, but rather the orthodox who had retreated [97] in order to preserve what could be protected from entanglement with "the world."

37. Jülicher(-Fascher), *Einleitung*[7], p. 227.

92

Insofar as we can hardly ascribe 3 John to a different author from, at least, 2 John, we ought to interpret the former in terms of the same background, as an attempt of the "elder" to carry forward the offensive—an offensive, however, that runs aground on the resistance of the heretical leader Diotrephes. The latter pays back the elder in kind [38] and sees to it that the elder's emissaries find no reception in his group (10). To be sure, 3 John does not contain an explicit warning against false teachers. Nevertheless, its close connection with 2 John is a sufficient indication of its thrust. And the assurance repeated no less than five times in this brief writing that the brethren who support the elder possess the "truth"—that entity which in 2 John and also in 1 John distinguishes the orthodox believer from the heretic —renders it very unlikely, to my way of thinking, that we are here dealing merely with personal frictions between the elder and Diotrephes. This situation would seem to be similar to that in Philippi, where the letter of Polycarp suggests the presence of a heretical community leader (above, 73 f.). Diotrephes holds the place of leadership (3 John 9)—according to the elder's opinion he presumptuously assumed it, but his opinion cannot be decisive for us—rejects the approaches of the elder, who feels himself unjustly suspected (10), and summarily excludes from the community those of his members who are sympathetic to the elder. Since 2 John shows the elder to be a determined opponent of a docetic interpretation of Christ, we need not spend time in searching for the real reasons that time and again prompt him to renew his efforts to maintain contact with the beloved Gaius through letters like 3 John, and with the church of Diotrephes through emissaries.

Third John thus becomes especially valuable and instructive for us in that it represents the attempt of an ecclesiastical leader to gain influence in other communities in order to give assistance to like-minded persons within those communities, and if possible, to gain the upper hand. Polycarp of Smyrna had attempted the very same thing in Philippi, and Ignatius also tried it in Asia by encouraging those churches that were accessible to him to join in an effort in behalf of the orthodox [98] in his home city in Syria (above, chap. 3). Later, Dionysius of Corinth wrote his letters for the same purpose,[39] and

---

38. That is, corresponding to 2 John 10 f. [See further below, pp. 289, 308.]
39. Cf. Harnack, *Briefsammlung* pp. 36-40.

the letters of recommendation for Marcion by the brethren in Pontus probably should not be regarded as being much different (see above, 91). Also the writer of the Apocalypse endeavored to influence a larger circle of communities in his vicinity to exhibit a clearly anti-heretical position. Contemporary with the Apocalypticist is *1 Clement*, and I am of he opinion that this famous letter of the Roman community to Corinth can only be understood correctly if it is considered in this sort of context, even though many particulars concerning *1 Clement* may remain obscure.

With *1 Clement* we have reached Rome, and have thereby come to an arena which is to be of unique significance for reaching a decision in the struggle between orthodoxy and heresy. This is indicated already in that, while the above-mentioned attempts to reach beyond one's own community either were completely unsuccessful or had no noticeable success, Rome was able to achieve a great and lasting result.

5

Rome and Christianity
outside of Rome

If we take *1 Clement* as our starting point for determining the position of Rome in the struggle between these outlooks, we immediately encounter a twofold difficulty. First, we must corroborate for ourselves the frequent claim that the main body of the letter has little or nothing to do with its clearly defined purpose. This is certainly the initial impression. R. Knopf states:

> The Romans are extremely verbose in giving a great number of admonitions about the main issues of Christian conduct and life above and beyond the immediate occasion for the writing, so that one cannot see precisely what relationship these admonitions have to the real purpose of the letter; cf. especially the extensive first main section of the writing (4-38) and the summary in 62.1 f. . . . Over and above the immediate needs, he has produced a literary work of art which goes beyond the form of an actual letter and sketches the ideal of true Christian conduct for life in broad homiletical arguments and expositions.[1]

Indeed, it is easy to get the impression that by far the greater part of the letter serves only to increase its size, in order thereby to enhance its importance and forcefulness.

For the person who keeps the question "why?" in view, the admission that, at least at first glance, he is faced with so much that is quite unexpected seems to me to make it imperative that he proceed with special care in attempting to determine the letter's purpose,

1. R. Knopf, *Die Lehre der zwölf Apostel. Die zwei Clemensbriefe*, HbNT, Ergänzungsband: Die apostolischen Väter 1 (1920): 42, 43.

and not limit himself to considering [100] only what appears on the surface. An author who admittedly presents such a quantity of material for which the reader is not prepared, and thereby consciously or unconsciously obscures his position, correspondingly could have been incomplete in what he actually says concerning the matter at hand. Such a suspicion should not be lightly dismissed. It is precisely with such a person that we have the least assurance that he reveals exhaustively and plainly his purposes and goals, particularly his basic motives.

This uncertainty in the evaluation of *1 Clement* as a source is all the more significant since, unfortunately, here again only *one* of the sides of the discussion is represented. (This is, for me, the second matter for concern.) We do not hear what the *altera pars* has to say (see above, xxi); and yet, in the interests of fairness, we really need to know what the members of the Corinthian community who were so severely attacked could adduce, and no doubt did present, in support of their position. However, the picture that faces us of the conditions in Corinth is sketched from the perspective of Rome, which was doubtless one-sided and based on self-interest—to say the very least, a biased picture. Just as the modern interpreter would no longer dare to adopt, without hesitation, Paul's point of view in evaluating Paul's relationship to a community or to a person whom he has rebuked, since in such cases the Apostle to the Gentiles surely is partisan, such a procedure would seem to me to be equally illegitimate in the case of one postapostolic church interfering in the life of another.

What is it, then, that actually happened in Corinth? Youth, it is said, rebelled against age. "The point in question was solely a matter of cliques, not of principles." [2] "The motive that precipitated the whole situation must therefore have been simply the desire for a realignment of the power structure"; and "at this point the Roman community, in full consciousness of the unity of the church, felt itself obliged to render a service of love, and thus intervened." [3] The ecclesiastical "office" was in danger and Rome assumed the position

2. A. von Harnack, *Einführung in die alte Kirchengeschichte* (Leipzig: Hinrichs, 1929), p. 92.
3. Lietzmann, *History* 1: 192.

of a protective shield. But just as surely as Rome felt it important to appear in an utterly unselfish light, as fulfilling a divine responsibility, I am all the less inclined to believe [101] that we have fully grasped the real situation by means of that approach. To acknowledge and accept such a picture, it seems to me, is to forgo an explanation. And it is just the sort of person who, as Lietzmann recently has done,[4] correctly views this action of Rome as of extreme importance, who should not treat the cause of the action so relatively lightly. Also, at least in later times, Rome shows itself to be controlled and motivated more by a strong desire for power than by the sense of brotherly love and by a selfless sense of duty. Rome knows how to take advantage of the right moment to transform minutiae into major issues in order to make other churches spiritually subject to Rome and then to incorporate them organizationally into Rome's own sphere of influence.

Consider, for example, the Easter dispute that was conjured up by Rome less than a century after *Clement,* and which "was occasioned by an insignificant difference in cultic practice"[5]—not that we judge it to be so minor by our standards, but it is evaluated by Irenaeus in just this way (in Eusebius EH 5.24.12 ff.). By the middle of the second century Rome had made an attempt to impose its will upon Asia, but held back from taking the final steps when the elderly Polycarp came to Rome in person. In 190 Victor, believing that Asia is isolated and regarding that fortress as easily assailable, advances with the heavy artillery of exclusion from church fellowship (EH 5.24.9). A little later we see Rome busy with measures designed to establish its influence in Egypt (see above, 55 f., 60). Then, in the middle of the third century, North Africa was the scene of a similarly motivated activity—"the occasion appears to be even more insignificant and petty than in the case of the Easter disputes."[6]

It seems to me, therefore, that Rome takes action not when it is overflowing with love or when the great concerns of the faith are really in jeopardy, but when there is at least the opportunity of en-

4. Lietzmann, *History* 1: 194 f.
5. So as not to fall victim to the danger of arbitrarily coloring the facts in favor of my arguments as the occasion demands, I follow here the presentation of Achelis, *Christentum* 2: 217-19.
6. Achelis, *Christentum* 2: 220.

larging its own sphere of influence. In this connection it certainly may be granted that, as far as Rome is concerned, its own interests coincide with the interests of the true faith and of genuine [102] brotherly love. The earliest such opportunity presented itself to Rome, in my judgment, toward the end of the first century in Corinth. But what exactly was it in this congregation that called Rome into action? No doubt it was the fact that the internal discord greatly reduced the power of resistance of the Corinthian church, so that it seemed to be easy prey. But what were the factors that indicated to Rome what position to take in the Corinthian arena, in favor of one party and against the others?

Certainly it was not moral indignation over the irreverence of the young people and their lack of a brotherly and Christian community spirit that induced Rome to intervene and produced the voluminous writing of sixty-five chapters. In that case, Rome's expenditure of effort would be disproportionate to the occasion. Even the ecclesiastical "office" as such is not of a decisive significance for Rome. If the change in Corinth had turned things in a direction acceptable to Rome, then *1 Clement* also would have embraced the wisdom of the orthodox Ignatius (see above, 62 f., 68) that the bishop must be obeyed even if he is young and inexperienced since what matters is not his age but only that he functions in the place of God and of Christ. It is not the office that is in danger, but apparently the officers whom Rome desires, and that is why Rome intervenes in favor of the principle that the church officer cannot be removed. In such a situation, one cannot very well intercede for particular persons; it is much better and more convincing to argue for principles. It appears to me, therefore, that we ought to search for the specific occasion that prejudiced Rome so strongly against the turn of events in Corinth; events that recently received rather clear expression when the ecclesiastical offices were restaffed. Unfortunately, our letter does not express itself on this point with the desired clarity.

With reference to *1 Clement* 44.6 and the removal of the Corinthian presbyters mentioned there, Knopf states: "Unfortunately we are not told why." [7] And Harnack is quite correct when he dismisses without further ado many things that *1 Clement* says in its characterization of the situation:

7. Knopf, *Clemensbriefe,* p. 120.

To determine what the occasion and the nature of the quarrel and the purposes of the troublemakers were, one must disregard Clement's moralizing criticism and condemnation.[8] [103] When he warns against contentiousness and pride, against ambition, conceit and self-glory, when he characterizes the troublemakers as 'rash and self-willed individuals' (*prōsopa propetē kai authadē*, 1.1) and calls the schism 'abominable and unholy' (*miara kai anosios*, 1.1), that need not be taken into consideration, for such reproaches are quite natural in the face of a definite schism.[9]

Such a statement acknowledges that we here encounter the all too familiar tune of the fighter against heresy (*hairesis*). When jealousy and envy are designated as the motivating forces, one would think that he were hearing Tertullian or some other champion in the battle with heresy. And when *1 Clement* bases his position upon the strong and unshakable foundation of tradition—God, Christ, the apostles, the leaders of the church [10]—he is employing a weapon that belongs to the favorite equipment in the same workshop.

In view of the insufficient reasons supplied by the letter itself, it seems to me not inappropriate also to take into account differences of doctrine and life, if we wish to understand the origin of the new order in Corinth which was so painful to Rome. But in order to do this, it is necessary to pay attention also to the church history of Corinth during the period before and after Clement. In the capital city of Achaia, there had been diverse patterns of Christianity from the very beginning. Alongside the personal disciples of Paul, who endeavored to preserve with fidelity the characteristic features of the proclamation of the Apostle to the Gentiles, stand the followers of Apollos and two kinds of Jewish Christians: (1) those who identify themselves with Cephas and, like their hero, hold fast to Jewish practice for themselves but do not demand the same from their uncircumcised brethren; and (2) the "Christ" group, who had the same requirements even for gentile Christians. Doubtless the latter group disappeared from Corinth in the postapostolic age (see above, 86 f.). But as far as the other parties are concerned, a change comparable to that which we have suspected for the Asia of the postapostolic

8. And thereby also the reasons that could be inferred therefrom.
9. Harnack, *Einführung*, p. 91.
10. [See *1 Clem.* 42-44.] Lietzmann, *History* 1: 193 f.

age (see above, 87 f.) probably took place in Corinth, conditioned by similar circumstances.

We have all the more reason to assume this, since such a change makes its appearance already in apostolic times. Already in 1 Corinthians, alongside the division which is identified by the names of the leaders, [104] there appears also another division that coincides only partly with the first and that bears within itself the seeds of further development. From the very beginning, there existed in Corinth conflict between the strong and the weak, a conflict in which "gnostic" ideas and attitudes play a role.[11] The strong proudly believe that since they possess gnosis and are pneumatics, "everything" is permissible, including the eating of food sacrificed to idols (1 Cor. 8. 1 ff.; 10. 23 f.) and the unhesitating satisfaction of sexual desires (1 Cor. 6. 12 ff.). The Apocalypticist resisted the very same view of Christian freedom in heretical circles in Pergamum (Rev. 2.14) and Thyatira (2.20)—the heretics teach the slaves of the Son of Man "to practice immorality and to enjoy food that has been sacrificed to idols." The same thing is characteristic of the Basilidians, according to Irenaeus (AH 1.24.5 [= 19.3]), and of the gnostics in general, according to Justin (*Dial.* 35. 1-6).

With the observation that there were gnostics in Corinth whom the Apostle time and again rebukes with the argument that although everything may be permitted, not everything that is permitted is beneficial, I would now like to establish a connection between this and a doctrinal deviation that we also encounter in Corinth and for which Paul assumed just as little responsibility. Certain people there were maintaining that there is no resurrection of the dead (1 Cor. 15. 12, 16, 29, 32). This too, is a trait which the churchmen of post-apostolic times never grow tired of branding as a heretical, and especially a gnostic degeneration: Polycarp (*Phil.* 7.1), Justin (*Dial.* 80.4; *Resurr.* 2) [12] 2 Timothy 2.18, 2 *Clement* 9.1. In the opinion of many, 2 *Clement* comes from the area of Rome-Corinth. The apocryphal correspondence between Paul and the Corinthians in the *Acts*

11. Cf. H. Lietzmann, *An die Korinther I/II*, 4³, HbNT 9 (1931): 38, 46.
12. [The authenticity of the preserved fragments of Justin's treatise "On The Resurrection" (see K. Holl, *Fragmente vornicänischer Kirchenväter aus den Sacra Parallela* [TU 20.2, 1899], pp. 36-49) has been widely disputed. For a recent, favorable treatment of the question, see P. Prigent, *Justin et l'Ancien Testament* (Paris: Gabalda, 1964), esp. pp. 50 ff.

of Paul [13] portrays the Apostle to the Gentiles fighting two gnostic teachers in Corinth, whose preaching included the statement that there was no resurrection of the flesh. The detailed discussion of the question in *1 Clement* 23.1-27.7 proves to me that the same aberration also must have come to the attention of the author of that document as a shortcoming of the Corinthian Christians.

If Paul already had rejected the "strong," with whose approach (food sacrificed to idols, immorality, denial of the resurrection) the Jewish Christians in question could sympathize even less than he, [105] the subsequent development (once again, compare the analogous situation in Asia; above 86 f.) must have taken place in such a way that the genuine successors of the original Paul and Cephas parties gradually drew closer to each other, so that finally they would merge to produce "orthodoxy," in opposition to the gnosticizing Christians in whom perhaps the spirit of the syncretistic Alexandrian Apollos continued to flourish. It seems quite natural to me that the former group, which could regard itself as the embodiment of the apostolic past of the Corinthian church, and which could lay claim to the reputations of Paul and Peter, took charge from the very outset. However, it is equally clear that the longer time went on, the less it could rely upon the majority of the faithful. Already at the time of Paul, the "strong" had become an extremely noteworthy factor. And it can hardly be doubted that they won a much greater number of adherents from the hellenistic world than the other groups, whose Jewish Christian wing would increasingly be pushed into the background. Thus it appears to be a natural consequence of the changed state of affairs that eventually the minority rule of the "old" became intolerable to the "young," so that they, inspired and led by particularly determined and ambitious persons (*1 Clem.* 47.6), brought about a fundamental change and instituted a unified take-over of the church offices in accord with their own point of view.

This development, however, touched a sensitive spot with reference to the interests of Rome. Now the community in the metropolis nearest to Rome—indeed, that important body of Christians with which, in general, Rome had the closest communications—was about to break away from Rome completely. But for Rome, this involved

13. ET by R. McL. Wilson in Hennecke-Schneemelcher 2:374 ff.; for the text, see above 42 n. 99.

the danger of total isolation, because the farther one travelled toward the East, the less Christianity conformed to Rome's approach. As far as we can tell, during the first century the Christian religion had developed in the world capital without any noticeable absorption of "gnostic" material; for even if the ascetic ideal which was so highly regarded by the "weak" of Rome (Rom. 14.1 ff.) [14] belongs to this category, that was and remained the way of life only of a minority. The course of events was gradually moving Corinth farther and farther from Rome, and when with the removal of the older generation of presbyters,[15] the gulf [106] threatened to become unbridgeable, Rome risked making the attempt to turn back the wheel—an action that held all the more promise of success since there was a powerful minority in Corinth upon which Rome could rely because their religious and ecclesiastical aims, and in several cases their personal desires as well, were completely in line with the Roman efforts.

To some extent, then, *1 Clement* describes the situation satisfactorily, as seen from Rome's perspective. Presbyters of venerable age, rooted in the apostolic past of their church, actually have been forced to retire and have been replaced by younger counterparts. Ambition and other human weaknesses doubtless also played a role. But this alone would not have caused Rome to intervene. Rather, we must search after the actual causes of the disturbances in Corinth, for these also constitute the real grounds for Rome's position. And I cannot find a more satisfactory answer to this question than the one we attempted above, based on the history of Christianity in Corinth. If marked traits of gnosis are passed over in silence by *1 Clement,* one should take into consideration that we are in the extreme Christian West and in the first century. Another warning that was issued abroad by Christian Rome around the same time, namely 1 Peter, does not show any knowledge of a distinct type of false belief in the sense of a later time—this is in marked contrast to 2 Peter. But that does not make it any easier for Rome to accept the change in

---

14. See H. Lietzmann, *An die Römer*[4], HbNT 8 (1933), pp. 114 ff.

15. According to *1 Clem.* 44.6 only "some" elders had been removed. Apparently, then, the flow [106] of events already had reached the point where representatives of the new line were being inducted into office. These, of course, would not be affected by the reorganization, and probably should be regarded as the leaders of the "young."

Corinth. Rome feels that Corinth now will orient itself officially toward the East, and in so doing will dissociate itself from the West.

The attempt to use the opposition between orthodoxy and heresy as a means of understanding *1 Clement* and its background finds support from the earliest users of this document of whom we are aware. Polycarp, who is thoroughly familiar with *1 Clement*,[16] is an anti-heretically oriented church leader whose life finds its main fulfillment in the struggle against the heretics. The same can be said about Dionysius of Corinth who refers to *1 Clement* in tones of highest respect (in Eusebius EH 4.23.11). [107] And his contemporary, Hegesippus, a churchman and foe of gnosis like the two already mentioned, after some remarks about *1 Clement* declares happily on the basis of personal impressions in Corinth and in Rome: "The church of the Corinthians continued in the true doctrine up to the time when Primus was bishop of Corinth.[17] When I traveled by ship to Rome I stayed with them, and had conversations with them for several days during which we rejoiced together over the true doctrine" (in Eusebius EH 4.22.1 f.). Here *1 Clement* is interpreted as a call to orthodoxy with which the Corinthians complied for a long time.

Finally, we have Irenaeus (AH 3.3.3 [= 3.3.2]), who first reports that Clement had seen the apostles and heard their preaching with his own ears. Irenaeus continues:

When during his [Clement's] time of office a not insignificant discord arose among the brethren in Corinth, the church in Rome sent a very lengthy letter to the Corinthians urgently admonishing them to be at peace with each other, to renew their faith, and to proclaim the tradition which they recently received from the apostles: that there is one almighty God, maker of heaven and earth, creator of man, the one who brought about the deluge and called Abraham; the one who brought the people out of the land of Egypt; the one who spoke with Moses, who ordained the law, and who sent the prophets; and who has prepared fire for the devil and his angels. Those who so desire can learn from this writing [i.e. *1 Clement*] that this is the God proclaimed by

16. Cf. Lightfoot, *Apostolic Fathers*[2] 1 (*S. Clement of Rome*).1 (1890): 149-52.
17. This refers to the time at which Hegesippus writes. Concerning subsequent developments he can say nothing. Thus "abiding in the true doctrine" stands in contrast to the unpleasant condition of earlier circumstances, in which *1 Clement* successfully intervened.

the churches as the father of our Lord Jesus Christ, and thus can gain insight into the apostolic tradition of the church, for the letter is older than those present false teachers who deceitfully claim that there is another God superior to the Demiurge and creator of all things.

Thus the situation with respect to the schism in Corinth has been corrected through a "renewal of the faith" and reference to the tradition of apostolic teaching of which Rome claims to be the guardian. Irenaeus sees the anti-heretical thrust of *1 Clement* especially in the frequent use of the Old Testament and in the praise of the almighty creator God. [108]

If we take to heart the hint which is given here and which comes from a man who had good Roman connections, then it seems to me that we can understand the essential content of *1 Clement* much better than before, because we can see it in its proper context. In its positive exposition of the common faith of the church, markedly moralistic in approach and based on the Old Testament and the sayings of the Lord, *1 Clement* offers the best refutation of any gnostic-tainted Christianity—soberly objective and free of the temptation to probe into the "depths of the godhead." In any event, Rome's intervention had a decisive effect. Rome succeeded in imposing its will on Corinth. How completely Rome cast its spell over the capital of Achaia is shown by the letter of bishop Dionysius of Corinth to the Roman Bishop Soter (175-182), in which Dionysius mentions *1 Clement* as well as a letter which was sent by Soter to the Corinthians, as follows: "Today we celebrated a holy Lord's day in which we read your [i.e. Soter's] letter, which we shall always read for our admonition just as we read the earlier one which came to us through Clement" (EH 4.23.11). We have no reason to question that this advantageous turn of events in favor of Rome was brought about by that action of the Roman church which is connected with the name of Clement. Not only is Corinth, in the time of Dionysius, conscious of this; Clement also lives on in the grateful memory of the Romans as the one who knows how to conduct successful correspondence with the churches abroad (*Hermas* 8 [= Vis.2.4].3). For them he is to such a great extent the churchman who is also respected abroad that we meet the still markedly Roman figure of Clement also in the Orient where "the church" later receives her orders. The *Apostolic Constitutions*, which were produced in the East in the fourth century, based on older writings, claim to be composed by "Clement, bishop and citizen of the Romans." [18] Probably this esteem was ultimately based in what Clement actually achieved for his church. We can also explain the old story about Peter and Clement, known already to Origen,[19] [109] in the light of Rome's endeavor also to send eastward that leader who had been victorious in the conquest of Corinth.[20] At any rate, his image was powerful enough that anonymous literary productions became attached to it. The so-called *Second Letter of Clement* is already considered to be a product of Clement by the first Christian who mentions it (Eusebius EH 3.38.4).

Just as one should not underestimate the success of Rome which at that time established toward the dangerous Orient a bulwark that has never been taken away, neither should one suppose it to have been greater than it really was. If we have already refused to permit our conclusions about Smyrna to be applied directly to Asia, or those concerning Hierapolis to Phrygia (above, 70 f. and 72), we must know resist the temptation to consider Corinth to be representative of Achaia. On the contrary, we need to recognize that apart from its capital city of Corinth, Christian Greece remained hostile toward Rome. The very proximity of Macedonia (see above, 72-75) should make this suggestion seem all the more reasonable. Dionysius of Corinth tries to gain a foothold in the churches of Lacedaemonia and Athens by means of letters whose subject matter is instruction in the orthodox doctrine or encouragement to faith and gospel-centered conduct (EH 4.23.2-3)—and one can imagine what these conceptions mean in the mouth of the devoted servant of Rome. But the results can not have been particularly significant. For although very soon afterward, as a result of the paschal controversies, synods and assemblies of bishops convened in Pontus and Gaul, which agreed with the assembly of bishops which met for the same reason in Rome

---

18. On Clement as a writer and author of church orders, see Harnack, *Geschichte* 1.2, 942 f., and Hennecke in Hennecke[2], pp. 554 f. and p. 143. [See also Lightfoot, *Apostolic Fathers*[2] 1 (*S. Clement of Rome*). 1, chap. 2 on *Apostolic Constitutions*, see below 244 n. 7.]
19. *Commentary on Genesis* = *Philocalia* 23 [at the end; J. A. Robinson expresses doubt that this material from the ps. Clementine tradition actually was quoted by Origen—see p. 1 of his ed. of the Philocalia (Cambridge University Press, 1893)]; *Commentary on Matthew*, series 77 (to 26.6-13); cf. Harnack, *Geschichte* 1.1, 219-221.
20. On Rome's desire to gain influence in the East, see below, 106-109.

(EH 5.23.3; see above, 75), we hear of nothing similar for Achaia. Not that the local bishop, Bacchyllus, had not taken great pains to bring about a common declaration in favor of Rome; but he was not successful. At least this is what I must conclude is meant when Eusebius, after enumerating the provinces which supported Rome, goes on to say that there is also a personal letter from Bacchyllus, bishop of Corinth, concerning this matter (EH 5.23.4). Eusebius, who like his native land Palestine is favorable to Rome, certainly did not eliminate materials from the tradition to the detriment of that church. [110]

Furthermore, we know that Achaia, in contrast to Rome, did not support Demetrius in his action against Origen. Jerome states this explicitly (see above, 55). Origen had been in Greece shortly before this (EH 6.23.4), but he did not visit the capital, which was under Roman influence; instead, he went to Athens (Jerome *Illustrious Men* 54) where he received a more favorable reception than earlier in Rome (see above, 55). Although Jerome makes no other claim except that Origen used this opportunity to fight against many heresies, Eusebius knows only of "urgent ecclesiastical affairs" that brought him there. And that can be taken in quite another sense than pro-Roman or anti-heretical.

The fact that in Greece Rome found its influence limited to Corinth does not at all mean that it had not made any efforts to gain more new territory for itself and for its interpretation of Christianity. To be sure, around the middle of the second century many serious difficulties arose for Rome in its own house. It is enough to refer to the names of Marcion and Valentinus to indicate what it was that soon restricted considerably Rome's outward expansion, limited its powers, and kept Rome within rather definite bounds. Nevertheless, behind Dionysius of Corinth with his efforts for Greece, Crete and certain northern areas of Asia Minor, stands ecclesiastical Rome. Generally speaking, whenever we see fighters of heresy at work in the time between Clement and Dionysius of Corinth, their connections with Rome are quite clear and quite close. Papias is perhaps the only one concerning whom we have no direct evidence from the sources that he had personal contact with the world capital. In the highly fragmentary tradition about him and his life, nothing is said about him ever having left his Phrygian homeland.[21] Of course, it would be hard to imagine that the energetic collector of old traditions who has consciously evaluated book wisdom as less valuable than living communication with the bearers of tradition (in Eusebius, EH 3.39.4) would have been permanently fettered to one spot. And even if he had not personally been in Rome, he had a clear connection with Rome in another way. His friend Polycarp (Irenaeus AH 5.33.4) stood near enough to the world capital; and both churchmen held in high regard 1 Peter, that proclamation with which [111] Rome had made inroads into the major part of Asia Minor.[22] Furthermore, we find among the traditions concerning the gospels collected by Papias some that are clearly of Roman origin. Although the name of Rome does not occur in the report of Eusebius about what Papias relates concerning the "elder's" account of the origin of Mark's gospel (EH 3.39.15), it does appear quite soon in this context in Irenaeus (AH 3.1.1 [= 3.1.2]), a theologian dependent upon Papias, and even more unmistakably in Clement of Alexandria (in his lost "Outlines", see EH 6.14.6 f.). Elsewhere, Eusebius makes it clear that in his judgement Clement of Alexandria is only repeating the opinion of Papias (EH 2.15, esp. 2). In accord with this is the fact that the old gospel prologues also claim that Mark, the interpreter of Peter, wrote his gospel in Italy.[23] Not only is the presence of Mark (Col. 4:10; Philem, 24; cf. 2 Tim. 4:11), like that of Peter,[24] already attested in Rome during the apostolic age, but both personalities appear to be so closely associated in Rome already in the first century that I can hardly doubt that it was here that the origin of Mark's gospel was first attributed to the influence of Peter, and that the "elder" derived from this source what he passed on to Papias.

Hegesippus, who dedicated his life to the fight against heresy, travelled by way of Corinth to Rome in order to take up residence there for an extended period of time (EH 4.22.1-3; see above, 103). Justin spent the major portion of his Christian life in Rome, whence he attacked the heretics, both at home and abroad, orally and in

21. Cf. Zahn, *Forschungen* 6: 109.
22. Papias' use of the document is described in EH 3.39.17; for Polycarp's use, see his *letter to the Philippians*, as Eusebius also noted in EH 4.14.9.
23. Harnack, *Evangelien-Prologe*, pp. 5 f. [= 324 f.].
24. H. Lietzmann, *Petrus und Paulus in Rom: Liturgische und archäologische Studien*[2] (Berlin/Leipzig, 1927).

writing. Rhodon of Asia Minor, who fought Marcion, Apelles, and Tatian, had been a pupil of Tatian in Rome when the latter was still considered orthodox (EH 5.13.1,8).[25] Perhaps Miltiades also, the enemy of the Valentinians and Montanists, whom the so-called *Little Labyrinth* lists between Justin and Tatian (EH 5.28.4), [112] and Tertullian places after Justin and before Irenaeus (*Against the Valentians* 5),[26] belonged to the same circle.

As we see here the lines running from Rome to the East and from the main representatives of orthodoxy back again to Rome, the case of Corinth becomes all the more instructive in showing that the Roman church took a special interest in gaining influence over communities located in the great metropolitan centers. In Corinth, Rome was able to do this in an extensive and conclusive way as early as the year 100; in Alexandria, this only happened in a more limited manner more than one hundred years later (see above, 55 f., 60), which is highly significant in relation to the situation in Christian Egypt at an earlier period. Rome did not wait for such a long time voluntarily and gladly. In another metropolis of the ancient world she apparently intervened much sooner, in spite of the fact that heresy had the upper hand there. Nevertheless, the situation in Antioch (see above, 63-67) was different and more favorable, insofar as here there was an orthodox minority with which cooperation seemed to be possible. In the capital of Syria the attempt to refute and to defeat the heretics becomes apparent to us with Ignatius. But at once, it seems to me, we also sense the desire of Rome to strengthen the forces of orthodoxy and ecclesiastical Christianity. A particularly fortunate circumstance shows it is also at work here, about twenty years after the Corinthian campaign. We can hardly value highly enough the fact that in addition to his letters to the Asians, we also possess from the pen of the Antiochene martyr-bishop a letter to the church of Rome from which a great deal can be learned for our purposes. It gives us some insight into the methods used by Rome to open Antioch to Rome's influence.

This is why the writings of Ignatius are of such extreme importance

---

25. I will refrain from attempting to infer from the names of particular heresy fighters such as Agrippa Castor, Modestus, or Musanus, that they had Roman connections.
26. O. Bardenhewer, *Geschichte*[2] 1: 284.

to us, because the ecclesiastical history of a later time leaves us almost completely in the dark with regard to the early period at Antioch. What, strictly speaking, has been included in the work of Eusebius from the life of the Antiochian church up to the time of Theophilus, who held office toward the end of the second century? We must admit that there is practically nothing. And the reserve which borders on silence on the part of the ecclesiastical historian [113] in this case is perhaps even more shocking than it was with regard to Mesopotamia (see above, 8 f.) and Egypt (see above, 45 f.). One should think that when the bishop of Caesarea undertook to write a church history he would have had the greatest interest in the past of the church of Antioch, which was founded in earliest apostolic times and situated in the nearby metropolis. In fact his interest does appear in the form of his attempt to provide a list of bishops also for this church, as had been done for Rome, Alexandria and Jerusalem. Unfortunately, however, his interest in Antioch's earliest history is practically exhausted in this sort of attempt, as far as we can tell; and if his interest was not exhausted, the material which he possessed or found worthy of relating was.

We have already discussed what an examination of the bishop lists reveals—little enough and all quite uncertain (see above, 63 f.). All we need to add here is that the mention of bishop Ignatius leads to an account about him, his fate and his letters, with quotations from the latter (EH 3.36). Nevertheless that yields almost nothing about Antioch itself, and nothing at all that we could not also gather from the Ignatian writings, which evidently are Eusebius' only source in spite of the fact that he calls their author "still highly esteemed by a great many" (EH 3.36.2). If we take the added assertion that Ignatius was second in the succession from Peter to hold the bishop's chair (see below, 115 f.) for what it really is—an untrustworthy feature in the growth of ecclesiastical tradition—then we have dealt with everything that Eusebius has to report about that period of the earliest church history of Antioch which he examines with the greatest detail. Apart from this, we find that Acts 11.20-30 is utilized (EH 2.3.3), a passage that is also echoed a couple of other times; we hear that Luke came from Antioch (EH 3.4.6); [27] and we can read

27. The ancient prologues to the gospels also know this; see Harnack, *Evangelien-Prologe*, pp. 5 f. [= 324 f.].

a small section from Justin's longer *Apology* (26.4) that refers to Menander as a successful heretic in Antioch (EH 3.26.3). Then when we hear that Saturninus had been an Antiochean (EH 4.7.3), we have compiled everything that relates to the time before Theophilus—that is, the first 150 years of Christianity there.

In what other way is it possible to explain this sort of reporting, except to suppose that the recollections concerning the beginning [114] have been forced through a narrow sieve which held back the main item? One need not speak directly of ecclesiastical censorship, for even before censorship became unilaterally effective the decay of tradition already had set in and had progressed rapidly. In the conflict between the two hostile parties, orthodoxy and heresy, the witnesses to the earliest history often were ground down and have disappeared. Each movement tried to blot from public memory that which was unfavorable to itself, to check its further distribution and propagation; this tendency became a most successful ally to those circumstances which in themselves already threatened the survival of a literature that was issued in such very small quantities and in such a perishable form. We know something of Ignatius because he wrote his letters in Asia and for (Rome and) Asia, where they were soon taken over by the faithful hands of Polycarp who supervised their reproduction and circulation (Polycarp *Phil.* 13.2). These were extraordinarily favorable circumstances. If Ignatius had fought the heretics in Antioch itself by means of some sort of polemical treatise, I am convinced that this would have perished just as surely as did so many other documents of antiquity which were issued in the struggle with heresy.

The fortunate circumstances mentioned above have rescued this informant for us, and thus a solitary light flashes forth in the darkness and illuminates a limited area. Within this area we are seeking to obtain information about those things that we can still more or less clearly recognize concerning the methods used by Rome to draw other churches into its sphere of influence. What we are still in a position to discover concerning the attitude of Rome toward Antioch is by no means limited to this particular case, but has a general significance. We would do well, therefore, to incorporate this piece of information from the primitive Christian history of Antioch into a larger context (see below, 113 f.).

6

Rome's Persuasive and Polemical Tactics

In her struggle with the heretics, a struggle which was also a contest for the extension of her own influence, Rome employed various tactics which can even better illuminate for us the whole nature of this controversy and Rome's significance in it. But the importance of the controversy must be assessed correctly, and again a great deal hinges upon our acquiring a true-to-life picture from indications in the sources, even if some degree of imagination should be necessary in order that this picture be brought into focus. Concerning Rome's achievement with respect to Corinth at the time of Clement, one could scarcely accord a higher estimate to it than has been given above. Nevertheless, the words of Dionysius of Corinth in his letter to Soter (above, 104) would in my opinion be incorrectly interpreted if one were to deduce from them that Rome had attained and had permanently insured its goal through the repeated public reading of *1 Clement* in the meetings of the Corinthian community. That portentous document hardly crushed and converted the members of a type of Christianity in which no serious attention was paid even to Pauline utterances. The "young Turks" of Corinth and their leaders would more likely feel irritated than put to shame by this act of foreign intervention. The undoubted Roman success was surely achieved by the employment of tactics which *1 Clement* rather more conceals from us than reveals. Regrettably we also do not know what made the influence of Titus in his time so effective that the community, once almost lost, found its way back to Paul. We can no longer say with certainty who played the role of Titus at the time of Clement; most probably the three bearers of the letter did—Claudius Ephebus, Valerius Biton, and Fortunatus (*1 Clem.* 65.1). I should be inclined to suppose that they [116] presented the basic ideas of the Roman position to the Corinthians in a much more comprehensible and effective form than did the long-winded letter. Relying upon the authority of those who had sent them, and supported by the minority at Corinth, they may also have been successful in forcing upon the unreliable, plural presbyterate an energetic bishop from the circle of elders. For Hegesippus, in any event, it is a foregone conclusion that *one* bishop has long stood at the head of the Corinthian church and has made its orthodoxy his business.

It is clearer that Rome appealed to the apostles for justification of her action, and did this with all the more reason if our view has commended itself that the deposed presbyters in Corinth were the continuators of the apostolic line in that community. Precisely in those chapters which most clearly touch upon the controversy does the discussion turn repeatedly to the apostles (42.1-2) or to our apostles (44.1), as those who have been instructed by Christ and through him establish the only possible contact with God. As early as the fifth chapter, the worthy apostles Peter and Paul are presented as examples—victims of envy, strife, and jealousy (5.2-7), as now most recently are the elders of Corinth. Peter and Paul are the only apostles whom the West has at its disposal. Both had suffered as martyrs in Rome, and the Roman church was conscious of this distinction from the outset and also knew from the beginning how to invest this asset to advantage. When Ignatius, who in all his letters to the churches again and again refers to "*the* apostles," refers only to "Peter and Paul" as apostles in the letter to Rome (4.3), it is because this association is of Roman origin. An Antiochian would have been the very last to gain the impression from the history of his own church that precisely these two apostles belong in close connection.

Likewise, Dionysius of Corinth is not looking back to the past of his own church but rather over to Rome when he writes: "By such a forceful admonition, you [Romans] now have united the communities of Romans and Corinthians planted by Peter and Paul. For both planted also in our city of Corinth and instructed us in like manner, and in like manner also taught together in Italy and suffered martyrdom

[117] at the same time" (EH 2.25.8). For even if Peter personally had been in Corinth,[1] a supposition which admittedly I consider to be almost impossible, certainly Dionysius 120 years later does not have at his disposal a tradition to this effect that is in any way defensible. I am skeptical not only because the details that he adduces are incorrect, insofar as the two apostles cannot possibly have appeared together in Corinth, thence to continue their work in close association at Rome. But I am even more dubious for another reason. Dionysius does not learn from history the only thing that history could teach him, namely, that Paul and Peter visited Corinth and Rome; rather he has Peter and Paul (in that order) sowing the undivided planting which consists of the Romans and then only secondarily of the Corinthians. He pays homage in submissive manner to the Romans and to their "blessed bishop" Soter (*makarios episkopos*, EH 4.23.10); is happy that the Romans, by their intervention at the time of Clement, have, as he expresses it, bound Rome and Corinth inseparably together; and suns himself in the splendor of the apostolic celebrities of Rome, who, as he delights to show, belong also to Corinth.

The basis for the supposition that in Dionysius' view Peter came from Rome to Corinth is strengthened for me by a corresponding observation concerning Antioch. We believe that the slogan "Peter and Paul" in Ignatius' letter to the Romans should be understood as a Roman contribution (above, 112). This becomes even clearer in view of the further development for which Rome sets the pace, which is characterized by the harmonization of opposing interests. Harnack has demonstrated,[2] with documentary evidence which need not here be reproduced, how toward the end of the second century "that momentous transformation of tradition took place in Rome, by virtue of which Paul was eliminated from any connection with the Roman episcopate and the office was attached to Peter" (703). The latter alone continues to play a role, first as founder of the Roman episcopate, later as first bishop (704). There is already an intimation here of what it was that prompted Rome to cut in half the apostolic foundation of its own church. Until far into the second century there

1. This is the opinion of E. Schwartz, *Charakterköpfe aus der griechischen Literatur, 2. Reihe*[3] (Leipzig: Teubner, 1919), p. 137; E. Meyer, *Ursprung und Anfänge des Christentums* 3 (Stuttgart: Cotta, 1923 repr. 1962), p. 441.1; H. Lietzmann, "Zwei Notizen zu Paulus" Sb Berlin 8 for 1930, 7 [= 155].
2. Harnack, *Geschichte*, 2 (*Chronologie*).1: 703-707.

has developed here [118], almost undisturbed, a consolidation of "orthodoxy," and accordingly Hermas, who has no heresies in view,[3] still presupposes a number of leaders at the head of the church.[4] But eventually not even Rome was spared controversy with the heretics, above all with Marcion and Valentinus, and this made even Rome recognize the advantages of her own use of the monarchical episcopate, an institution which in Rome is first embodied in Soter (166-174), according to a historical view of the matter.[5] But if an apostolic founder of the monarchical episcopate was still required, an exigency which the struggle with heresy did indeed produce, then a decision had to be made, which, as we have seen, did in fact take place a bit later.

If one asks why the decision went in favor of Peter, I find no answer in Matthew 16.17-19. But I also do not believe that any important role in the decision was played by the recollection that Paul actually had been in Rome only as a prisoner and therefore can hardly have held the chief office. The real reasons are not forthcoming from history, but rather must be grounded in the period of time and in the momentum which saw the introduction of the monarchical episcopate in Rome, and thus made the one apostle dispensable—which is to say in the controversy with heresy. Only Peter provides the close tie to Jesus which alone guarantees the purity of church teaching.[6] And Paul, who had indeed been eminently serviceable against the schismatics in Corinth (1 Clement 47.1), was no longer of any help in the battle against Marcion. [119]

At a slightly later date than in Rome, Peter also emerges in Antioch as the first of the monarchical bishops. Here too it was certainly not historical memory that elevated him to the cathedra. Our oldest tradition, Galatians 2.11 ff., knows of Peter in Antioch only in a situa-

---

3. See Kirsch, Kirche, p. 218.
4. Cf., e.g., Knopf, Zeitalter, pp. 182-86.
5. Cf. Schwartz, in his GCS edition of EH, vol. 3: p. CCXXV.
6. This point is acknowledged by the Paul who in the Acts of Paul (an ecclesiastical and anti-gnostic work coming from the time of Dionysius of Corinth) writes to the Corinthians: "For I delivered to you in the beginning what I received from the holy apostles who were before me, who at all times were together with the Lord Jesus Christ" ("3 Corinthians" 3.4; ET by R. McL. Wilson in Hennecke-Schneemelcher 2: 375; see above, 42 n. 99). In the Epistola Apostolorum 31-33, a work coming perhaps from the same time and having a similiar purpose, the twelve initiate Paul into the teachings which they have received from the Lord (ET by R. E. Taylor in Hennecke-Schneemelcher 1: 213 f.; text ed. by C. Schmidt in TU 43, pp. 96-102).

tion that would hardly have qualified him to become leader of the community; thus one would have to claim that Peter's position as leader was confined to the period before the clash with Paul. This opinion is, in fact, to be found in John Malalas (ca. 540), and there with reference to "the most learned *Chronicles* of Clement and Tatian." [7] But precisely the reference to Clement, who can be none other than Clement of Alexandria,[8] deprives the Byzantine author's notice of even that meager weight it might claim in view of both its contents and the trustworthiness of Malalas. It is to be remembered that in the opinion of Clement, the Cephas who had the famous confrontation with Paul was someone other than the apostle Peter (*Outlines* 5, in EH 1.12.2). The book of Acts knows nothing at all of Peter in Antioch and in fact really excludes such a possibility. That he did not found the Christian community there is clear from Acts 11.19 ff. Nor is he sent, in contrast to the case of Samaria (8.14), from Jerusalem to Antioch for the purpose of inspecting the newly founded community. This task falls rather to Barnabas (11.22). And in view of 13.1, the "other place" to which Peter went after being set free (12.17) really seems more likely to refer to any city but the one city Antioch.

In the following period, it is true, one or another thread of evidence leads from Antioch to Peter. Ignatius makes reference to an apocryphal gospel story in which Peter and his companions figure (*Smyr.* 3.2). A group of Christians in Greek Syria a bit later tried through Peter to establish their line of contact with the life of Jesus (above, 66) and thereby gave occasion for the Antiochian bishop Serapion to speak about "Peter and the other apostles" (EH 6.12.3). But certainly the *Gospel of Peter* did not provide grounds for, of all people, the "ecclesiastical" circles of Antioch to choose Peter as their first bishop. How long had this notion been present there? Julius Africanus plainly does not yet know anything of it, but [120] designates Euodius as the first Antiochian bishop,[9] as does Eusebius in dependence upon him (EH 3.22). In another place, to be sure,

---

7. *Hoi sophōtatoi Klēmēs kai Tatianos hoi chronographoi*, ed. L. Dindorf, *Chronographie* 10 (Bonn, 1831): 242. The passage is also cited in Stählin's GCS edition of Clement of Alexandria, vol. 3: pp. 229 f. and p. LXX.
8. See Zahn, *Forschungen* 3: 56-59.
9. Harnack, *Geschichte*, 2 (*Chronologie*).1: 119 ff., 123 ff;, 208 ff.

Eusebius says the illustrious Ignatius had been the second bishop in the succession from Peter at Antioch (EH 3.36.2). We hardly have the right forcibly to insert Euodius here, with the result that Peter would now not be bishop himself but would be viewed only as having established the episcopal office at Antioch. In both passages Ignatius is numbered as "second" (*deuteros*), and both passages place only one name before him. Each passage in itself seems to me unequivocal, and a collector such as Eusebius gives us the very least reason for forcibly harmonizing contradictory statements. We have all the more reason for keeping Euodius out of the picture in EH 3.36.2 insofar as the succession Peter-Ignatius is found also in Origen, the spiritual father of Eusebius. Origen calls Ignatius "the second bishop of Antioch after the blessed Peter." [10] Chrysostom and Theodoret also fail to include Euodius.[11]

The chronological impossibility of this arrangement is obvious. No proof at all is needed for the thesis that for Antioch that form of the list which places Euodius at the beginning is just as certainly the earlier as is that for Rome which commences with Linus.[12] Not until later was the attempt made to free Euodius' place in favor of Peter. Therefore it is not historical memory that is operative here, but a specific ecclesiastical requirement. The only question is, who is the "interested party" here, Rome or Antioch? Harnack supposes it to be the latter. He speaks of the "Antiochian *cathedra Petri*" and the "Alexandrian *cathedra Marci*" as "oriental imitative products," and of the "oriental imitations of the tendentious legend" which "followed hard on the heels of the original fiction." Although these constructions frequently were to become irksome to Rome at a later time, Rome nonetheless put up with them "because there was no way to control these fictions." [13]

Here, it strikes me, Rome is credited with a reserve and moderation in the use of effective tactics that has little relationship to its genius

---

10. Origen, *Homily on Luke*, 6.1: *ton meta ton makarion Petron tēs Antiocheias deuteron episkopon*. Cf. Harnack, *Geschichte* 2 (*Chronologie*).1: 209. [For a different interpretation, see A. A. T. Ehrhardt, *The Apostolic Succession in the First Two Centuries of the Church* (London: Lutterworth, 1953), p. 137 and n. 2.]
11. John Chrysostom *Ecomium on Eustathius of Antioch* (PG 50: 597 ff.); Theodoret *Epist.* 151 (PG 83: 1440).
12. Cf. Harnack, *Geschichte*, 2 (*Chronologie*).1: 191 f., 703.
13. Harnack, *Geschichte*, 2 (*Chronologie*).1: 707.

and circumstances. I can well imagine that Antioch and Alexandria could take over the method, proven in the battle with heresy, [121] of forming a succession of bishops which derives from the circle of the twelve. But it is more difficult to understand why they should latch on to Peter, and still more, if they could not get Peter, why they should be content with a figure of the second rank [Mark] instead of choosing someone else from that illustrious band of Jesus' closest friends. Actually, the party enthusiastic for Mark is not Alexandria but Rome; traces of Rome's influence on his behalf are discernible there (see above, 60). Through Mark his son and interpreter the Roman Peter (see above, 107) announces his claims, since he himself is much too busy in Jerusalem, Antioch, Corinth, and Rome to be able to go personally in quest of Alexandria also, which is off the beaten track for him.[14]

And so, just as I was of the opinion that I should view "Peter and Paul" in Ignatius as a sign of Roman influence (above, 112), I should be inclined also to find Roman influence in the assertion of a later period that Peter originally had been in the position of leadership at Antioch, an assertion which flies completely in the face of Antiochian history. Origen, who has confronted us as the first clear witness for Peter in his office as Antiochene bishop, also was acquainted with the original document underlying the pseudo-Clementines [15] and in his commentary on Genesis (see above, 105 n. 19) introduced an excerpt from it with the words: "Clement the Roman, a disciple of the apostle Peter . . . in Loadicea, says in the 'Journeys' (*en tais Periodois*), . . . he says. . . ." If Syrian Laodicea played a role in the ancient document, then in all probability so did neighboring Antioch, which is closely tied to Laodicea in the fully developed form of the pseudo-Clementines. The *Homilies*, we remem-

14. The Roman, and not Alexandrian, origin of the legend of Mark as founder of the church at Alexandria would stand out still more clearly if it were still possible today to accept such a judgment as Harnack's on the so-called Monarchian prologues to the Latin gospels (ed. H. Lietzmann, *Kleine Texte* 1[2] [1908]: 12-16; cf. 16.16f.: [*Marcus*] *Alexandriae episcopus fuit*): "But they originated in Rome. . . . The time . . . is the time of Victor and Zephyrinus (ca. 190-217)" (*Geschichte* 2 [*Chronologie*].2: 204 f.). But more recent research, with which Harnack has also agreed (*Evangelien-Prologe*, p. 3) places the Monarchian prologues in the fourth century and later than Eusebius, so that the latter becomes the earliest known witness for that legend.
15. On this point see E. Schwartz, "Unzeitgemässe Beobachtungen zu den Clementinen," ZNW 31 (1932): 151-199, esp. 159 ff.

ber, close with the notice that Peter set out from [122] Laodicea for Antioch (20.23), where Simon Magus, after some initial and very large successes, had suffered his decisive defeat (20.11-22).[16] And the *Recognitions* are in agreement, especially in the concluding narrative (10.53-72), which is only spun out a bit further and concludes with a description of the founding of the church at Antioch: a certain Theophilus places his basilica at the disposal of the community for use as a church, and in it is erected a cathedra for Peter (*Rec.* 10.71-72).[17]

How many of these details relative to Antioch already stood in the original "Journeys" (*Periodoi*) eludes precise determination. But it seems certain to me that the close connection with the quite explicitly Roman figure of Clement, whom the original Clementine document already calls "Clement the Roman" (*Klēmēs ho Rōmaios*), also stamps the Peter of the *Periodoi* as the *Roman* Peter. He, and not the head of the primitive community at Jerusalem (Jerusalem plays no role at all in this literature), claims the leading position in the founding of the Antiochian church. Of Paul working along with him, there is just as little said here as is being said in Rome at the same time. And when Peter ascends the cathedra in the basilica-turned-church belonging to "a certain Theophilus," it is not at all easy to suppress the following suspicion: here is a memory alluding to the way in which ecclesiastical Antioch under her bishop Theophilus (d. after 181), well known as an opponent of Marcion and other heretics (EH 4.24), marches up to the anti-heretical front led by Rome, a front which then later gains even firmer unanimity and stability in the shared conviction that it was established by Peter.

At Antioch, as at Rome and Alexandria, a first step in this direction was the attempt to build up an unbroken succession of orthodox bishops reaching back into the time of the church's founding. That also on this point Rome led the way is proven by the fact that the symptomatic efforts toward this end begin at Antioch later than at Rome and lead to less useful results (see above, 63 f.). As the Lord delayed his return and the necessity arose to preserve contact with him, [123] Christians had at first tried to avail themselves of simple

16. On Laodicea and Antioch in the ps.-Clementines see also *Hom.* 12.1, 2; 13.1; 14.12; *Rec.* 7.2, 24; 10.53 ff. and 58.
17. One branch of the tradition has Peter before his departure ordain another bishop and several presbyters.

means of assistance. They possessed the apostles, and later at least the disciples of the apostles; and when these died out, certain "elders" (*presbyteroi*) continued the succession, men who still personally remembered the apostles' disciples and perhaps even remembered one or another real apostle. Or there lay at hand in the community an "ancient one" (*archaios anēr*) [18] a man deriving from the very primitive period—in whom was honored the connective link to the beginning. It is obvious that the terms "apostle's disciple," "presbyter-elder," and "man of the primitive period" were not subject to sharp definition nor were clearly distinguished from one another.[19] But it is just as clear that precisely for this reason they were useful only for a transitional period. Irenaeus believed that he was linked to Jesus himself with the help of only two intermediaries, Polycarp and John. And Clement of Alexandria was certain that by such a route he came quite close to the first successors of the apostles.[20] His teachers, he says, received the "blessed teaching" personally from the apostles Peter, James, John, and Paul (*Strom.* 1.[1.]11). But these long drawn out lines, which after all could not be established without a darkening of historical memory—how were they to withstand a serious attack of the enemy? And were not the opponents likewise able to come up with apostolic traditions? Did not Basilides derive his wisdom directly from Glaukias, Peter's interpreter (*Strom.* 7.[17.]106.4), or even from Matthias,[21] **[124]** and Valentinus his

18. So Papias is called in Irenaeus AH 5.33.4. But Eusebius can rank Irenaeus himself with the band of the *archaioi* (EH 4.22.9). And he even gives the same value to Dionysius of Corinth (EH 3.4.10).
19. Occasionally even the apostles are separated into ranks: the Lord gives gnosis to James, John, and Peter; these impart it to the remaining apostles, who in turn give it to the seventy, to whom Barnabas belongs—Clement of Alexandria, *Outlines* 7/13 (GCS ed. Stählin, 3: 199) = EH 2.1.4. Or there occurs the combination of terms *hoi archaioi presbyteroi*—Clement of Alexandria *On the Passover* (ed. Stählin 3: 216.5) = EH 6.13.9. Or there appear classifications such as *hoi anekathen presbyteroi* = the original presbyters—Clement of Alex., *Outlines* 6/8 (ed. Stählin, 3: 197) = EH 6.14.5. Or an apostolic tradition is designated in Clement as *paradosis tōn pro autou phaskōn* = tradition of his predecessors—*Outlines* 7/14 (ed. Stählin, 3: 200) = EH 2.9.2. Elsewhere Clement speaks of *ho makarios presbyteros*—*Outlines* ?/22 (ed. Stählin, 3: 201.26) = EH 6.14.4. *Hoi presbyteroi* appear in Clement's *Prophetic Excerpts* 11.1 and in 27.1, *ouk egraphon hoi presbyteroi.*
20. In Eusebius EH 6.13.8: *peri heautou dēloi hōs eggista tēs tōn apostolōn genomenou diadoxēs.*
21. *Strom.* 7.[17.]108.1. Also Hippolytus, *Ref.* 7.20: Matthias **[124]** dispenses secret teaching which he received through special instruction from Jesus.

from Theodas the disciple of Paul (*Strom.* 7.[17.]106.4)? Indeed Ptolemy the Valentinian hopes that Flora will "be worthy of the apostolic tradition which *we also* have received in unbroken succession, together with the authentication of all our theses by the teaching of our Saviour." [22]

In Rome, where the whole environment spurred the Christians on toward the creation of stable forms for life in the community, there was evidently a refusal at first to rely on a couple of more or less doubtful personages for the most important position there was and for its continuation—personages, moreover, whose brittle chain of succession offered no security for the immediate future. Then, too, the apostolic period in Rome had been much too short and had been broken off too early for there to have grown up any significant or numerically extensive group of apostles' disciples and "very ancient men." With Mark one did not get very far. And one can only guess how extensively the ranks of this very circle were thinned out by the Neronian and later the Domitian persecutions, and by whatever else may have occurred in between. The individuals of whose activity we hear, a Linus or a Clement (Irenaeus AH 3.3.3), were in any case already dead by the end of the first century. Irenaeus made no belated attempt to bring a successor of Clement into personal acquaintance with the apostles, whereas in Asia Minor "John" outlived Clement, to say nothing of Papias and Polycarp,[23] by means of whom one was brought up almost to the middle of the second century and even beyond. Hegesippus, belonging to the company of those who followed immediately upon the apostles,[24] reached even farther. The prerequisites for securing the tradition in another manner probably were already present in Rome well at the beginning of the second century. That a few decades passed before these measures began to come into effect is to be explained by the fact that the

---

22. *Epistle to Flora* 5.10 (= Epiphanius, *Her.* 33.3-7; ed. A. von Harnack, *Kleine Texte* 9² [1912]: 9 f.; [see also Völker, *Quellen*, pp. 87-93]): *axioumenē tēs apostolikēs paradoseōs hēn ek diadochēs kai hēmeis pareilēphamen meta kai tou kanonisai pantas tous logous tē tou sōter hēmōn didaskalia.* [ET in Grant, *Gnosticism Anthology*, pp. 184-190.]
23. Irenaeus, in Eusebius EH 5.20.7 calls Polycarp "the apostolic presbyter" (*ho apostolikos presbyteros*).
24. Eusebius EH 2.23.3: "Hegesippus, who belonged to the generation of the first successors to the apostles" (*ho Hēgēsippos epi tēs prōtēs tōn apostolōn genomenos diadochēs*).

danger of heresy, and thereby the necessity for such measures, was not experienced in Rome until a comparatively late date (see above, 113 f.). [125] But precisely this fact shows us again that those localities which experienced the tension between heresy and orthodoxy much earlier and more incisively than did Rome, but which came to employ that particular defensive tactic only later and less thoroughly than Rome, were not acting independently but rather were under outside, i.e. Roman, influence.

This influence makes itself noticeable also in other ways. Ignatius praises the Romans as those who have been teachers to other Christians—"you taught others" (allous edidaxate, Rom. 3.1). The past tense of the verb prevents us from regarding these words as only a polite turn of phrase, an interpretation which may well be applicable to the present tense of Paul's statement in his letter to the Romans (15.14). Ignatius is evidently aware of attempts of the Roman community to exercise a teaching influence upon Christians in other places. And we know already that his contemporary and coreligionist Polycarp was thoroughly familiar with 1 Clement (above, 103) and with 1 Peter (above, 107), those two Roman manifestos addressed to other Christian churches (see above, 104 on Hermas). In like manner, Ignatius also may have heard of these letters, although the ascertainable echoes do not suffice to demonstrate this. Indeed one need not exclude the possibility that Rome, spurred and encouraged by its success at Corinth turned its attention to the Christians of Antioch itself, in which case the latter also would belong to those "others" whom Ignatius has in mind in the passage cited above.

This supposition would gain probability if we may venture to interpret the formula which Ignatius applies to the Roman church, prokathēmenē tēs agapēs (Rom. salutation), in the light of later statements. The words mean, "endowed with preeminence in love." [25] And this phrase calls to mind almost involuntarily the oft-mentioned letter of Dionysius of Corinth to the Roman church and its bishop Soter (EH 4.23.10). Full of the highest praise, the letter speaks of the way in which the Romans from the beginning (ex archēs) had been accustomed to shower benefits in many ways upon all Christians and to offer aid to many communities in whatever city (kata pasan

25. See Bauer, Ignatius, pp. 242 f.

polin). Thus the Romans from the earliest origins occupied themselves with preserving their ancestral customs (*archēthen patroparadoton ethos Rōmaiōn Rōmaioi phylattontes*). Indeed the activity of their present bishop, the *makarios* Soter, represents even an intensifying of the old practice. This is certainly [126] to be seen as exaggeration, the exaggerated style of a churchman subservient to Rome in the extreme degree. But these accents gain their peculiar quality and strength surely from the recollection that Corinth, already at an earlier time, has been the recipient of such assistance from Rome. Rome hardly supported the "young Turks" whom *1 Clement* attacks. It seems to me all the more probable that among the tactics used to break their rebellion and their hegemony, even monetary gifts were placed at the disposal of their opponents, and that such gifts were not the least reason why their opponents emerged victorious. In the grateful memory of ecclesiastical Corinth at a later time, Rome's assistance appears as a work of love for the benefit of the entire Corinthian church.

Since we have already become acquainted with Roman influence at Antioch, which was oriented similarly to Rome's successful undertaking at Corinth (see above, 114 ff.), I should like to interpret the words quoted above from the preface of Ignatius' letter to the Romans as signifying that even Antioch—meaning, of course, ecclesiastical Antioch—had been privileged to enjoy material support from Rome. And so as not to leave Alexandria out of the picture, alongside Corinth and Antioch, on the matter of relations with Rome, let us now recall the letter of Dionysius of Alexandria to the Roman bishop Stephen I (254-57; EH 7.5.2). The letter even includes "the whole of Syria" among the regions privileged to benefit from Roman sacrificial unselfishness, and reveals that Rome's shipments of aid are accompanied by letters. Likewise in the letter of Dionysius of Corinth the donations for the saints and the instructions to the brethren coming to Rome are mentioned alongside of one another (EH 4.23.10 end). In similar fashion is it likewise probable that the orthodoxy of Ignatian Antioch is the orthodoxy not only of those who have been privileged to experience the charity of Rome, but also of those "others" whom Rome was accustomed to teach (see above, 121).

If we ask to what degree donations of money could be of importance in the warfare of the spirits, our imagination would have no difficulty in suggesting all kinds of ways. In this context it is to the point to adduce further statements of Ignatius revealing to us needs and desires on the part of Christians which could be met by material gifts. In the letter to Polycarp, he turns his attention with pacifying intent to slaves who wish their freedom to be purchased at the church's expense (4.3). [127] If, as is certainly the case, many a slave joined the church because he hoped for the fulfillment of such a wish on the basis of the celebrated mutual solidarity of the "brethren," one can also imagine how within the Christian world that group which had at its disposal the more ample resources would draw many slaves to itself—and indeed, how many others from the poorer classes, who from anxiety were often scarcely able to contemplate the coming day! Certainly Dionysius, the outspoken enemy of heresy, cannot intend that his words, "You relieve the poverty of the needy" (EH 4.23.10), be understood to mean that Roman abundance indiscriminately blessed all poverty-stricken souls, provided only they were baptized.

Moreover the Christian communities were at an early date already making the attempt, often with success, to buy fellow believers free from prison and from the claws of the judiciary.[26] And Ignatius' letter to the Romans is filled with expressions of his worry lest such an eventuality befall him from the side of the Romans. The encomium of Eusebius upon the Emperor Constantine (3.58) teaches us that Rome viewed it as an altogether legitimate practice in religious controversy to tip the scales with golden weights: "In his beneficient concern that as many as possible be won for the teaching of the gospel, the emperor also made rich donations there [in Phoenician Heliopolis] for the support of the poor, with the aim of rousing them even in this way to the acceptance of saving truth. He too could almost have said with the Apostle: 'In every way, whether in pretense or in truth, Christ is to be proclaimed' [Phil. 1.18]."

He who has sufficient funds at his disposal is in a position to recruit assistants who can devote themselves without distraction to the tasks for which they are paid. And again it is Rome, so far as I know, where a Christian official first appears on the scene with a

26. Cf. the anti-Montanist Apollonius (ca. 197) in Eusebius EH 5.18.9 and also 5; *Didascalia* 18 (ed. Connolly, 160; see below, 244 n. 7); Cyprian *Ep.* 62; *Apostolic Constitutions* 4.9 [see also the story of Peregrinus in Lucian's treatise by that name 12-13; ET in Loeb edition of Lucian].

fixed salary. The *Little Labyrinth* relates how the Monarchians in Rome, when they were obliged to form their own community, induced the Roman confessor Natalius to become their bishop for a monthly stipend of 150 denarii (EH 5.28.10). Here the accent falls upon the word "fixed," for the principle that the laborer deserves his wages was familiar to Christians from the beginning [cf. Matt. 10.10||Luke 10.7, 1 Tim. 5.18]. On this there was no substantial difference between orthodox and heretics. [128] Apollonius, the opponent of the Montanists, reports already of Montanus himself that he offered *salaria* to those who preached Christianity according to his interpretation, and thus paid them for their activity (EH 5.18.2). Very perceptible here is the annoyance of the churchman Apollonius that the necessary funds flow in to the heresiarch in such ample supply. It also follows from what he says immediately thereafter about the heretic Themiso (EH 5.18.5) that he does not need to be enlightened as to the great importance that money possesses in the conflict of religions as everywhere else.

Finally, if we want to know in what way the Roman church raised the funds necessary for her purposes, even in this regard the sources are not entirely silent. From Tertullian we hear that Marcion, on the occasion of his joining the Roman Christian community, handed his fortune over to the church (*Against Marcion* 4.4). It was a matter of the very considerable sum of 200,000 sesterces (*Prescription against Heretics* 30). The amount of the gift and the person of the donor explain the fact that this case was entered into recorded history, but it will not have been unique. It is much more likely that the Roman church, for the well being of all, assessed her members according to each individual's resources and ability to give. And that among their ranks were to be found well-to-do people in larger measure than elsewhere is shown by the writings produced at Rome—1 Peter, *1 Clement*, and *Hermas* [27]—and by personalities such as the consul Titus Flavius Clemens together with his wife Flavia Domitilla the emperor's niece, and Manius Acilius Glabrio the consul of the year 91.[28]

If Rome is astute in the use of tactics, it knows also how to take advantage of every kind of situation. Again I should like to point

27. Knopf, *Zeitalter*, pp. 74-83.
28. Achelis, *Christentum* 2: 258.

to Dionysius, who as the occupant of the Roman outpost of Corinth is at least as much an informant concerning Roman ecclesiastical Christianity as a witness to the history of Christian Corinth. Among the letters by which he seeks to be of influence on behalf of orthodoxy is to be found one "to the church of Amastris together with the other churches throughout Pontus" (EH 4.23.6). The final words *hama tais kata Ponton* belong of course to those expressions in Eusebius which are to be accepted only with caution in that they are regularly introduced at those places where the intention is to emphasize the expanse of the church (see below, 190 f.). [129] Here the phrase, which unites the entire province with the city to which the letter is sent, is all the more suspect in that immediately before this, Dionysius is said to have written "to the church of Gortyna together with the other churches throughout Crete" (EH 4.23.5). But this can hardly be accurate, since Eusebius himself knows and states that in the Cretan area, Dionysius wrote not only to Gortyna but also to the Knossians (EH 4.23.7), who therefore fall outside the circle of the "other churches." I am of the opinion, therefore, that in regard to Pontus we can be assured only that Dionysius was writing to Amastris. But at this very point no ground must be yielded to a recent twist of interpretation which even outclasses Eusebius and impedes our access to reality. Harnack characterizes the person and influence of Dionysius as follows: "Dionysius then was of such high repute *in the churches* that advice and edification were solicited of him from far and wide. I know of no other such example from the whole of the second century. . . . The area encompassed by the pastoral and ecclesiastical influence of Dionysius *reached from Pontus to Rome*." [29] In my opinion, these words do not give an accurate picture. In Amastris it is by no means "the church" and its bishop Palmas who request his advice; rather, he explains that he has written at the instigation of two Christian brothers, Bacchylides and Elpistos. The bishop Palmas remains in the background. It is mentioned that his name occurred in the letter, but unfortunately, we do not know in what context (EH 4.23.6). For the rest, the letter contains exhortations to chastity and allusions to heretical error. I should like then to suppose a state of affairs in which personal contacts have resulted from the sea traffic between Corinth and Amastris, contacts which

29. Harnack, *Briefsammlung*, p. 37. The italics are mine.

Dionysius seeks to exploit in the interests of orthodoxy. Whether and to what degree the newly founded relations extended into the province, remains almost completely uncertain.

It was argued earlier (above, 75 f.) that also in Crete Dionysius was dealing not with "the churches" but at best with orthodox elements in a Christianity heavily permeated with heresy. That one certainly cannot speak in superlatives of the success he achieved there has been intimated [130] and will become even more evident below. Although in the spirit of Eusebius, who praises "the inspired diligence" of the bishop (EH 4.23.1), one can say with Harnack that "advice and edification were solicited of him from far and wide," Dionysius himself allows us to surmise what really happened when he complains: "At the request of some brethren, I wrote letters. But the apostles of the devil crammed them full of weeds, deleting one thing and adding another" (EH 4.23.12). Dionysius, then, writes to other areas when orthodox brethren request him to do so. But when they arrive, his letters are exposed to severe hazards on the part of other Christians, and are by no means treated in "the churches" with the esteem that, under his leadership, was accorded in Corinth to *1 Clement* and the letter of the Roman bishop Soter (EH 4.23.11).

Wherever Dionysius believes he has found points of contact and can hope for an audience, he tries to canvass on behalf of Roman-Corinthian orthodoxy. The results varied. At Amastris the undertaking was evidently a success. In any case, twenty years later we see Palmas, whose name appears in Dionysius' letter, as the senior bishop of Pontus and on the side of Rome in the Easter controversy (EH 5.23.3). The Roman-Corinthian influence had, accordingly, also gained ground in Pontus outside of Amastris in the course of two decades. Dionysius accomplished much less at Knossos on Crete. On the subject of chastity, he had urged the local bishop Pinytus not to force upon the brethren a burden too severe but rather to consider the weakness of the great mass of people and had received an answer that represents a polite refusal (EH 4.23.7-8; see above, 75 f.). To be sure, Eusebius takes pains to detect in the answer from Knossos something like admiration for the great bishop of Corinth. In truth, however, there prevails in Knossos only astonishment at how easily the head of the Corinthian community acquiesces in the imperfection of the multitude. Pinytus then expresses candidly to his fellow bishop the expectation that "on another occasion he might offer more solid nourishment and feed the Christian flock with a letter of more mature substance, so that they do not, by remaining continually at the level of milkish teachings, imperceptibly grow old under instructions fit for children." At heart, Eusebius is obviously much more favorably disposed toward the answer than to the letter of Dionysius, [131] and in viewing the exchange of letters breaks into praise, not of the latter, but of Pinytus.

In his moderation Dionysius certainly did not feel himself to be in opposition to Rome. Rome also was not in favor of forcing the issue and demanding the impossible. It much more favored the gentler manner, with sinners as with heretics. Official Rome was prepared to make significant concessions just as much on the question of second repentence [30] as in the controversy over the baptism of heretics. And so Dionysius, with his advice not to make life too difficult for sinners within the Catholic church, was probably following a suggestion or even a directive issuing from Rome. Rome had only recently discovered that in the matter of the relentless demand for chastity one could not successfully compete with a Marcion. And so the preference was to stick by "the great multitude," whom to have on one's side was in the long run a guarantee of success.

Rome's astuteness displayed and proved itself in other respects also. Rome knows how to call suitable leaders to its helm. Hermas may be ever so effective in his activity as a prophet, but for leadership of the community his brother Pius is better suited. And without filling a church office, Justin turns his rich erudition to good account in the controversy with pagans, Jews, and heretics. Rome can wait, and does not hurry the development along, but just as little does it allow favorable opportunities to escape. Anicetus is a courteous opponent of Polycarp on the matter of the celebration of Easter (EH 5.24.16-17), whereas on the same issue Victor is extremely violent in his confrontation with Polycrates of Ephesus and those in agreement with him (EH 5.24.7 and 9; see also above 97).

---

30. Knopf, *Zeitalter*, p. 433: "Hermas' preaching of repentence made extraordinary, even extreme concessions to the folk of the community." "Originally the preaching of repentence was unconditional: to all shall all sins be forgiven." The brother of the "bishop" Pius hardly supported views on this point which would not have been approved in high places. [According to the "Muratorian Canon," "Hermas" was the brother of Pius.]

Roman Christianity, so far as we know, was from the beginning under the heaviest pressure from external enemies. The persecutions under Nero and Domitian, which in recorded church history are counted as the two earliest (EH 3.17 end), were exclusively or at least predominantly Roman affairs. And Hebrews and *1 Clement*, as also 1 Peter, [132] show us that toward the end of the first century the believers of the capital city could no longer feel safe. Even when the membership of their own community was not directly affected, arrivals such as Paul or Ignatius, sent to Rome to pour out their blood there as Christians, made repeatedly clear to them how little they had to expect from the benevolence of the world outside. Such experiences forced them to develop attributes of shrewdness, energy, and communal unity. And since the integrity of Roman Christianity's faith seems to have been spared severe disturbances up to a point well into the second century (see above, 113 f.), there grew up here the one church of dependable orthodoxy, whose sound health repulsed, after a short and violent attack, even the Marcionite contagion that had invaded.

Marcion presented the greatest danger to which Roman orthodoxy was exposed. That, of course, does not mean that apart from him the Christian faith at Rome in the generation from around 135 to about 170 assumed an entirely uniform shape. Besides Marcion we know also of personalities and movements that would have been able in this period to give the development of religious life at Rome a turn away from orthodoxy if the direction of orthodoxy had not been already so firmly set. Although it is not entirely certain that Marcion's disciple Lucanus was active at Rome,[31] Marcion's precursor Cerdo lived there under Hyginus (136-140), and according to the account of Irenaeus (AH 3.4.3), was not on good terms with the majority of Roman Christians. According to the same authority and passage, Valentinus also appeared in Rome at that time, flourished under Pius and continued until Anicetus, i.e. from about 136-160 in all. Tertullian, who of course allows no opportunity for maligning any heretic to escape him, reports of Valentinus that he seceded from the church because he had suffered a defeat in the episcopal election. Out of vengefulness he set himself henceforth to the task of battling against the truth (*Against Valentinus* 4, [*Prescription against Heretics* 30]). What measure of veracity there is in Tertullian's account evades

31. Harnack, *Marcion*[2], pp. 172 and 401°-403°.

precise determination.[32] If there should be something in it, it would indicate that Valentinus' assets of ability and eloquence, acknowledged even by Tertullian (*Against Valentinus* 4), were not able to make up for his lack of followers. [133] That does not exclude the possibility that the Valentinian movement sustained itself in Rome for a longer period of time. The "Italian" branch of the school in particular can certainly claim association with this city, and even at the end of the second century a presbyter named Florinus attracted unfavorable attention through writings which show that "he had allowed himself to become ensnared in the error of Valentinus." [33]

The "many" Valentinians and Marcionites whom Polycarp won over to the church in Rome under Anicetus (154-165) are no more significant than the "many" disciples who at the same time and place, and according to the same authority (Irenaeus, AH 3.3.4 and 1.25.6 [= 20.4]) were won over by the Carpocratian Marcellina—the former were no great gain, the latter no appreciable danger. Neither did any danger for Rome emanate from Tatian. After Roman Christianity had rid itself of the Marcionites (and Valentinians), there still remained, to be sure, the possibility of differing styles of belief within the church, but not of serious heresy. In his *Dialogue*, Justin distinguishes between the orthodox and the "godless and unrighteous *hairesiotai*" (80.3-5), in which characterization one detects with little difficulty the Marcionites. The orthodox, however, fall into two groups for Justin: those who only in a general way share the "pure and holy outlook (*gnōmē*) of the Christians" (80.2) and others who are *orthognōmones kata panta*, i.e. who possess in *all* particulars the right *gnōmē* (80.5). The latter share with Justin the belief in the closely allied ideas of the millennium and the resurrection of the flesh. This strikes me as characteristic of the situation in Rome as it begins to take form and to become established in the second half of the second century. Essentially unanimous in the faith and in the standards of Christian living, tightly organized and methodically governed by the monarchical bishop, the Roman church toward the close of the second century feels inclined and able to extend further the boundaries of her influence. In Asia, Syria, and Egypt we saw her aiming at conquests and replacing by a more resolute procedure the earlier, more cautious attempts to work her will at Corinth.

32. Cf. E. Preuschen, RPTK³, 20 (1908): 396 f.
33. Irenaeus, Syriac fragment 28 in Harvey's edition, vol. 2, p. 457.

7

The Confrontation Between
Orthodoxy and Heresy:
General Characteristics
and Operating Procedures

The essential object of our investigation and presentation in the preceding chapters has been the approximately one hundred years that follow the conclusion of the apostolic age. In those chapters, the arrangement of the material has, for the most part, followed geographical lines. There still remains the additional task of determining what there is in the association between true and false belief and in its manifestations that is not necessarily bound to one location, but has a more general validity—even if, naturally enough, it appears many times in our sources in connection with definite personalities and places. When, for example, in the following passage Eusebius describes the effectiveness of Theophilus of Antioch, as one church leader among others,[1] one notices no particularly Syrian coloration nor any marked peculiarity characterizing the bishop who is mentioned by name:

---

1. It appears as though Eusebius may have inserted the commonplace presentation of the consecrated activity of "the shepherds" into an already existing list of the writings of Theophilus. If the whole context were formed in this way by Eusebius, he would, indeed, not only regard the book against Marcion that stands at the end of the list as evidence that Theophilus also belongs in the category of these church leaders, but he would similarly regard the writing mentioned at the beginning, against the false belief of Hermogenes. On Eusebius' method of working, see also below, chap. 8, esp. 154 n. 14.

Since the heretics, no less at that time, were like tares despoiling the pure seed of apostolic teaching, the shepherds of the churches every-where, as though frightening away wild beasts from Christ's sheep, sought to hold them back, so that at one time they would resort to persuasion and exhortations to the brethren, at another they would oppose them openly and, partly through oral discussions [135] and refutations, partly through written efforts, expose their opinions as false by means of the most solid demonstrations (EH 4.24).

To a certain extent we perceive in this quotation the viewpoint of a fourth-century churchman. For him the churches are folds in which the shepherd guards and protects the sheep. The heretics roam about outside like wolves, intent on gaining prey. But the care-fully planned measures taken by the "shepherds" have made that very difficult for the heretics. Nevertheless, according to everything we have ascertained, the situation in the second century simply was not that way. It was by no means the rule at that time that heretics were located "outside." It is, however, completely credible that already at that time the leaders of the orthodox were using the tactics men-tioned by Eusebius, so as to safeguard their own people against con-tagion. But we must quickly add that the party opposing the orthodox worked in the same way and with corresponding goals. That the exhortations and repeated warnings were directed against the false belief of the opposing party is too self-evident to require special examples. Already in the second century we hear of direct discussions between the representatives of ecclesiastical Christianity and their opponents, and can easily find the bridge to an even earlier period.[2] The letter of Ignatius to the Philadelphians (chapters 5-8) allows us to take a look at the clash of opinions within the company of Christians at the beginning of the second century, when there is no clearly defined community boundary between opposing circles, but when all the baptized still remain, at least externally, bound together as a unity. There is debate pro and con over the right and wrong of this opinion and that. The opponents of Ignatius are preaching "Judaism," with reference to their use of scripture (6.1). Ignatius, who sees in this an apostasy from the gospel, even if his opponents wish to remain in the Christian community (7), declares to be impossible every understanding of scripture that finds in the "charters" some-

2. Cf. W. Bauer, *Der Wortgottesdienst der ältesten Christen* (1930), pp. 61 f.

thing other than that which, according to his view, stands in the "gospel" (8.2)—a teaching that rests on such a basis is a delusion. Apparently no agreement was reached on this issue; each party retained its own point of view.

The religious discussion that brought about the split in Rome between Marcion and orthodoxy was of a special sort. [136] At least at the outset, it was not thought of as a struggle for the souls of Roman Christians fought from already well established positions, but as an effort to ascertain what the true meaning and content of the Christian religion really is, and to that extent it was somewhat comparable to the apostolic council (Acts 15). After the orthodox and the Marcionites had separated from each other, to be sure, discussions aimed at persuading others of the truth of one's own faith also took place. So we hear from the anti-Marcionite, Rhodon (see above, 108), that the aged disciple of Marcion, Apelles, started up a discussion with him, but that Apelles was convicted of many errors and crushingly defeated.[3] Presumably, Apelles considered himself to be the victor. We do not feel called to act as arbitrator, but we simply have learned to recognize here one of the ways employed by each combatant to establish and disseminate his own position.

The Montanist movement also produced polemical discussions. Indeed, on this topic we are in a position to gain a colorful picture of the struggle between different tendencies in Christianity—even though this struggle is not consummated in actual debates—by the fortunate circumstance that Eusebius has preserved extensive fragments from the works of two anti-Montanists from the ninth decade of the second century. The first is an anonymous writer (EH 5.16-17) and the second, Apollonius of Asia Minor (EH 5.18). Of course, each heresy is open to attack in special areas unique to itself, while it, in turn, finds fault with a particular feature of the "church"—thus the Montanists differ from gnosis, and Marcion is not the same as the Jewish Christians—with the result that there are, within certain limits, differences in the respective polemic and apologetic approaches. And yet there are many aspects that do not resist the characterization of being generally valid, especially those that concern the external course of the controversies. But in dealing with this material, the pattern

---

3. EH 5.13.5-7. Concerning this discussion, see Harnack, *Marcion*[2], pp. 180 ff. He places it at the end of the reign of Marcus Aurelius.

exhibited in polemical literature must be taken into consideration in order to distinguish correctly between reality and appearance.[4]

The anonymous author begins his writing with the explanation that he had [137] first argued against the Montanists orally and refuted them (EH 5.16.2), but in spite of requests directed to him, he decided not to enter into literary combat with them. Then a visit to Ancyra in Galatia recently induced him to alter his decision. There he found the church completely deafened by the "new prophecy," which might more correctly be called false prophecy. He had first repulsed his opponents in discussions that lasted several days and went into every particular, and then he confirmed the church in the truth and filled it with joy. Nevertheless, since he himself had not been completely convinced of the permanence of his success,[5] he had promised to send the presbyters,[6] at their request, a written recapitulation of his expositions. The treatise that he composed for this purpose elaborates upon the origin of the new movement in the unmistakable style of an ecclesiastical polemic against heretics. Montanus, so we learn, in his boundless desire for preeminence,[7] allows the adversary to enter into him, whereupon he falls into a satanic ecstasy and begins suddenly to utter peculiar things that are not compatible with the tradition passed on in the church from the very beginning (EH 5.16.7). Some people are repelled by him; others are won over—and he delights the latter with his great promises and fills them with pride, but occasionally he also reproves them in order to show that he could also make demands (EH 5.16.8-9).

We have no reason to agree with the anonymous ecclesiastical author when he claims that the moral demands laid down by Montanus were a pretence. Tertullian shows us how seriously this teaching was taken by the Montanists. And when "the anonymous" claims that the "new prophecy" led only a few Phrygians astray (EH 5.16.9), we are inclined to believe him just as little—precisely on the basis

4. On what follows, see Zahn, *Forschungen* 5: 3-57 (concerning the chronological problem relating to Montanism); Harnack, *Geschichte* 2 (*Chronologie*), 1: 363-371.
5. EH 5.16.4—he checks the influence of the opposition "for the moment" (*pros to paron*).
6. There is no reference to a bishop (EH 5.16.5). Is there still no bishop in Ancyra around the year 190, or is he on the side of the opposition?
7. *Philoprōteia;* cf. 3 John 9 concerning Diotrephes, "who loves preeminence" (*ho philoprōteuōn*).

of what he himself reports. On the contrary, one has the impression that the "new prophecy" must have gained a strong hold in its native land. When "the anonymous," with unmistakable aim and purpose, continues immediately with an account of how the faithful came together "frequently" (*pollakis*) and "in many places" (*pollachē*) in order to investigate the Montanist teaching, which they then [138] branded as heresy and forbade its adherents to remain in the ecclesiastical community (EH 5.16.10), he is no longer speaking of Phrygia or of Ancyra in Galatia, but of Asia, and he shows that even there, where ecclesiastically oriented orthodoxy had sunk stronger and deeper roots, the danger was not minor (see also below, 135).

Eusebius passes over the detailed refutation of the error, which the first part of the treatise is supposed to have offered next, in order to turn his attention to the second part. This second part, in the style of presentations *de mortibus persecutorum* [on the death of persecutors], discoursed *de mortibus haeresiarcharum* [on the death of heretical leaders], and indeed, in a form that clearly betrays that the particular details have been derived from the gossip of the "right-minded," and have no historical value of any kind. A widely disseminated rumor reports that Montanus and his assistant, Maximilla, driven by a deceiving spirit, had hanged themselves, each acting independently and under different circumstances (EH 5.16.13). In the same way, "a frequent report" (*polus logos*) asserted of Theodotus, another originator of the false prophecy, that he had wanted to ascend to heaven in reliance on the deceitful spirit and had thereby perished in a wretched manner (EH 5.16.14). Just as in the former instance "the anonymous" is reminded of the end of the traitor Judas (EH 5.16.13), so may we, with respect to Theodotus, think of the legend of the death of Simon Magus. The author concludes the descriptions of the demise of the heretics with the words: "At any rate, that is how it is supposed to have happened. But not having seen it ourselves, we do not claim to know anything for sure about it. . . . Perhaps Montanus and Theodotus and the above mentioned woman died in this way, but perhaps they did not" (EH 5.16.14ᵇ-15). This section is important chiefly because it permits us to evaluate correctly a considerable portion of the ever recurring polemical material, especially to the extent that this material relates to the person and life of the men who stand in an exposed place within a religious movement. Indeed, one can scarcely handle the maxim *semper aliquid haeret* ["something always sticks" (when mud is being thrown about)] more cynically than does this ecclesiastical protagonist, who really does not himself believe the truth of the rumors that he repeats. As we shall see, Apollonius, his comrade at arms, is in no way inferior to him in the defamation of opponents.

First of all, however, let us examine further the report of Eusebius about the work of "the anonymous," which, as we now learn, [139] also incorporates references to Montanist literature.[8] Venerable bishops and other approved men—the names of Zotikos from the village of Cumana[9] and Julian of Apamea are dropped in passing—try to "refute" the spirit of error in Maximilla, but are "prevented" by her followers, among whom Themiso especially distinguishes himself.[10] The account of the incident is not wholly clear. An intellectual exchange with a woman who pours herself forth in an ecstatic frenzy is, indeed, not really thinkable, and a "refutation" in that sense hardly possible. It seems that the Montanists have prevented the representatives of orthodoxy from disturbing the sacred event at all with their profane words, or perhaps they called a halt to an attempt from the orthodox side to drive the evil spirit out of the prophetess (see below, 143). But be that as it may, the defeat of the churchman is unmistakable, and the scene that takes place in Phrygia (Apollonius even tells us the name of the place—Pepuza; EH 5.18.13) shows anew how little truth there is to the assertion that only a few Phrygians were ensnared in the false illusion of Montanism (see above, 133 f.).

After Eusebius has even given an example of how "the anonymous," still in the second book, unmasked the prophecies of Maximilla as false (EH 5.16.18-19), he moves quickly to the third book, from which he reproduces the rebuttal of the attempt to argue from the large number of Montanist martyrs that the divine power of the living prophetic spirit resides in Montanism (EH 5.16.20-22). He

8. It mentions the book of an Asterios Orbanos (= Urbanus), in which the sayings of Montanist prophets have been gathered (EH 5.16.17), and uses, in addition, a Montanist polemical writing against Miltiades (EH 5.17.1). See below, 136.
9. A Phrygian village—Harnack, *Mission*[2], 2: 95 (in the expanded German 4th edition, p. 627).
10. EH 5.16.16-17. The two words *dielegchein* (refute) and *kōluein* (prevent) reappear in the abstract by Eusebius from the report of Apollonius concerning the same matter (EH 5.18.13). See also below, 143 n. 27.

does not contest the initial claim, but rejects the conclusion which other heretics as well (as, for example, the Marcionites) could draw to their own advantage. That an ecclesiastical blood-witness never recognizes a false believer as a fellow believer is demonstrated by a reference to a story of martyrdom from the very recent past.[11]

Eusebius cites additional material from the work of this unknown opponent of the Montanists in EH 5.17. "The anonymous" relies here on the [140] work of his coreligionist, Miltiades, in which the latter argues that a genuine prophet ought not speak in ecstasy. To be sure, "the anonymous" seems to know the polemical treatise of Miltiades only from a Montanist reply to it, from which he made an abridgement of what concerned him (EH 5.17.1). According to this material, Miltiades—for obviously he is the speaker in the passage from "the anonymous" (EH 5.17.2-4)—objected against the Montanists that their kind of inspired speech could not possibly be of divine origin, because in the whole range of the old and of the new covenant, no prophet can be named whom the spirit seized in a similar way in an ecstatic frenzy. Old Testament prophets are not adduced. But the figures of Agabus, Judas, Silas, and the daughters of Philip, familiar from Acts (11.28, 15.32, 21.9 f.), appear, and this series is continued without a break into a later period [12] with the names of Ammia in Philadelphia and of Quadratus (EH 5.17.3). The subsequent section shows that the last two served the Montanists in the capacity of "elders" (see above, 119) for the purpose of bridging the gap between apostolic times and the appearance of Montanus (EH 5.17.4). The churchman Miltiades lets that pass, but he expresses the conviction that the prophetic chain had been decisively broken for Montanus and his women, the last of whom, Maximilla, had died fourteen years previously. Since "the Apostle" [13] guarantees

11. Cf. Neumann, *Römische Staat,* p. 68.
12. On this feature, cf. the open-textured use of the concept "the word of the new covenant of the gospel" (*ho tēs tou euaggeliou kainēs diathēkēs logos*) by "the anonymous" in EH 5.16.3.
13. If we take this as referring to Paul (for Eusebius, use of "the Apostle" to refer to Paul is certain in EH 4.29.6, see below, 149 and 177 n. 61; indeed, it is already attested in Ptolemy's letter to Flora 4.5) and to a definite passage in his letters, we are reminded of Eph. 4.11 ff., and perhaps also of 1 Cor. 1.7 f. In the anti-Montanist writing of Apollonius (EH 5.18.5) "the Apostle" admittedly is not Paul, but probably the author of 1 John. Alternatively, "the anonymous" may be thinking of the apocalypticist John, whose work plays a helpful role in the refutation of the Montanists (cf. Rev. 22.6 and 9) according to EH 5.18.14.

that the charismatic gift of prophecy would remain in the entire church until the Lord's return, what Montanism exhibits by way of that sort of phenomena cannot be acknowledged as a genuine gift of God.

To a still greater degree than "the anonymous," the somewhat younger Apollonius marshalls everything in order to make his opponents appear contemptible. He is not only intent on branding their prophecies collectively as lies, but he also wants to expose the life story of the sect's leaders in [141] all its wretchedness (EH 5.18.1). "But his works and teachings show who this recent teacher is," he cries triumphantly. When it is asked what is so detestable in Montanus' teaching, we hear only the following: (1) He taught the dissolution of marriage—thus, if it ever occurred in this exaggerated form, he did something that the Christian notes with a high degree of edification as long as it confronts him as a result of the apostolic preaching in the apocryphal *Acts* literature. Furthermore, (2) Montanus issued laws about fasting and (3) he called two small Phrygian cities, Pepuza and Tymion, by the name "Jerusalem," in order thereby to make them the center of his community, which was gathered from every direction. It relates more to the life of Montanus than to his teachings when he appoints money collectors who, under the pretense of collecting an offering, cleverly organize the receipt of gifts and thus procure for Montanus the financial means to reimburse those who carry the Montanist message, "in order that its teaching might be established through gluttony" (EH 5.17.2). Thus, like the matter of the dissolution of marriages mentioned above, something is condemned with language that can scarcely be surpassed and is exhibited in an ugly caricature, although when it takes place in the context of orthodoxy, it is worthy of the highest praise (see above, 121-124). For me, the silence of the older anonymous author indicates that the management of money by Montanus and his adherents cannot have taken the unedifying forms scorned by Apollonius. Another indication is the fact that many times it was precisely the most serious minded people who devoted themselves to the prophetic movement. Obviously, Apollonius' language simply betrays his annoyance at the fact that men and resources have streamed to the leaders of Montanism at such a dangerously high rate (EH 5.17.4[b]). Thus it proves useful to him that in the forty years since the appearance of Montanus (156/157), the malicious gossip of his enemies has greatly enriched the genuine data that is remembered.

Indeed, one cannot take such an attack seriously, when it censures Montanus for issuing laws for fasting, and takes pleasure four lines later in the sarcastic observation that Montanus endows his messengers with goods gained in an underhanded manner [14] so that they serve the gospel through gluttony; or when it thinks it fraudulent that the Montanists called Priscilla a virgin, although [142] she really belonged to those women who under the influence of Montanus had left their husbands (EH 5.18.3). Then does the custom of the church in calling certain virgins "widows" (Ignatius *Smyr.* 13.1) also rest on insolent mendacity? Or what should one say about an attempt to offer scriptural proof that has the presumption to assert that "all scripture" (*pasa graphē*) forbids a prophet from taking gifts and money (EH 5.18.4)? Even to get a shaky foundation for this assertion, one would have to go to the *Didache* (11.12). But Apollonius probably is talking in vague generalities, unless he already has in mind a definite interpretation of Matthew 10.9 f. (EH 5.18.7). In any event, *pasa graphē* is in no way part of the picture. Our author continually takes pleasure in exaggeration. He offers "innumerable proofs" (*myrias apodeikseis*) that the Montanist prophets take gifts (EH 5.18.11; see below, n. 15).

His pronounced inability to admit anything good about the heretics is even more offensive. "The anonymous" had recognized the fact that there were Montanist martyrdoms, even if he had contested the idea that death as a martyr demonstrates that the faith of the heretic is approved. Apollonius knows only of "so-called" martyrs in the opposing party (see above, n. 14) whom he makes as ridiculous and contemptible as possible. Themiso, whom we know from the writings of "the anonymous" as an especially active and effective advocate of the new trend (see above, 135), appears in Apollonius in a different light (EH 5.18.5)—he is completely entangled in covetousness, and purchased his release from chains with a great sum of money, without bearing the sign of a confessor. Now, instead of being humble, Themiso boasts of himself as a martyr and

---

14. See also EH 5.18.7—the so-called prophets and martyrs fleece not only the rich, but also the poor, the orphans, and the widows.

even carries his impudence so far that he writes a kind of catholic epistle in imitation of the Apostle (see above, n. 13), so as to instruct people who have a better faith than he does, to defend his empty teachings, and to direct his blasphemies against the Lord, the apostles, and the holy church.

Themiso by no means stands alone as a pseudo-martyr. But rather than treating the "numerous" others,[15] Apollonius wishes to make explicit mention only of the case of Alexander (EH 5.18.6-9). Alexander had based his claim to the honored name of a martyr on his condemnation in Ephesus by Aemilius Frontinus, who had been the proconsul of Asia at the end of the reign of Marcus Aurelius or at the [143] beginning of the reign of Commodus.[16] Apollonius, however, asserts that Alexander was not condemned on account of his Christianity, but rather was condemned as a robber. Nevertheless, he succeeded in deceiving the Ephesian community about the true state of affairs, so that this community procured the release of the "transgressor" (parabatēs). But his own home church, which was better informed rejected him as a robber. In order to corroborate this interpretation, Apollonius appeals twice within the Eusebian excerpt to the public archives of Asia (EH 5.18.6[b] and 9[b]), which supposedly gave indisputable information about the crimes of Alexander. Apollonius expects his readers to imagine an Ephesian church that regards Alexander as an honorable man and is willing to make sacrifices for his freedom, in spite of the fact that the judicial authorities of the city are occupied with Alexander because of his numerous crimes and even his home congregation has been aware of the situation for a long time. The sarcastic claim that the prophetess was unaware of the character of her companion in spite of many years of association appears equally artificial. How could anyone who is so in the dark really be a "prophet,"[17] and know something about the future? Apollonius' presentation serves to awaken this insight.

In any event, the reference to the Asiatic archives will make no

---

15. "But not to speak of many (pleiontes). . . . We can show the same in the case of many (polloi) . . ."—EH 5.18.6 and 10.
16. Neumann, Römische Staat, p. 68.
17. It says "the prophet" (male, ho prophētēs—EH 5.18.9[b]), although the context speaks of a prophetess; possibly this is because the passage has to do with the concept "prophet."

impression on anyone who has investigated the situation with respect to similar appeals.[18] Furthermore, the older anonymous author not only admits that martyrdom has taken place even among the Montanists, but he even knows a martyr by the name of Alexander from Phrygian Eumenia (EH 5.16.22), whom one may in all probability equate with our Alexander.[19] It is also sufficiently attested how strong and how genuine the desire of the Montanists for martyrdom was.[20] Even though Apollonius cannot see all this, or has no desire to admit it, he cannot demand that one believe the injurious stories he circulates about his opponents. At best, a single case may once have been reported which is now transformed into an inadmissible generalization. [144] Scornfully he speaks about the relations between the prophetess Priscilla and Alexander, which even he does not attempt to extend from the table to the bed. Thereby Apollonius gives one to understand that Alexander stood in great honor in his circles—i.e. among people with a very strict and serious view of life. "Many paid him reverence" (*proskunousin autō polloi;* EH 5.18.6). To be sure, Apollonius sees in Alexander only the false martyr who feasts gluttonously with the prophetess, and concerning whose robberies and other crimes there is no need to speak since the court archives speak loudly enough. Mockingly, he inquires which of the two dispenses the forgiveness of sins to the other—a matter of great importance for Montanism; does the prophetess remit the robberies of the martyr, or does the martyr forgive the covetousness of the prophetess (EH 5.18.7[a])? And Apollonius believes that he has delivered a series of deadly blows with the following questions: "Does a prophet use makeup? Does he dye his eyebrows and eyelids? Does he love ornaments? Does he gamble and play dice? Does he lend money at interest?" (EH 5.18.11).

Furthermore, Apollonius calculates that Montanus embarked on his career forty years earlier with his "feigned" prophecy, without any of it having come true (EH 5.18.12). Since Apollonius plays off the Revelation of John against Montanus (EH 5.18.14), although it is a

18. Cf. the role that archives and public records play, at least since Justin, in defending the details of the life of Jesus; W. Bauer, *Das Leben Jesu im Zeitalter der neutestamentlichen Apokryphen* (Tübingen: Mohr, 1909; reprint Darmstadt 1967), pp. 26 f., 59, 195 f., 228, 536 f.
19. Neumann, *Römische Staat,* p. 68 n. 2, and pp. 283 f.
20. Neumann, *Römische Staat,* p. 69.

book which also tells what "is about to happen soon" (Rev. 1.1), he appears not to lay such harsh demands on it concerning fulfillment of prophecies. Rather, he finds its credibility demonstrated by means of a story, according to which John raised a dead man in Ephesus "through divine power." Thus John is a bearer of a genuine divine spirit, while the Phrygian prophets only have such at their disposal in their imagination. Besides the book of Revelation, Apollonius also appealed to a gospel story that concerns the risen Christ and reports of him that he commanded the apostles to remain at least twelve years in Jerusalem. The same tradition [21] is found in the "Preaching (*Kerygma*) of Peter," which is even older than Apollonius' story and perhaps gives us a hint as to how what was reported by Apollonius could take on an anti-Montanist thrust. In the *Preaching of Peter*, the risen Christ, in addition to ordering the disciples not to leave Jerusalem for twelve years (in Clement of Alexandria *Strom.* 6.[5.]43.3), also gives them the commission to preach to the world "what is about to happen" (*ta mellonta*) after the designated interval has expired (*Strom.* 6.[6.]48.1 f.). [145] Thus no concept of the coming things accords with Jesus unless it has its roots in the circle of the apostles and, at the latest, already had been in existence twelve years after the resurrection. Unfortunately, neither with respect to "the anonymous" nor to Apollonius do we hear whether, and if so, how they evaluated the gospel of John and its sayings concerning the paraclete. Nevertheless, Irenaeus apparently already had the anti-Montanists in mind who, in order not to be deceived by this false prophecy, throw the baby out with the bath water by rejecting prophecy altogether, and thereby expressly reject the gospel of John, in which the Lord promised the sending of the paraclete.[22]

Taken as a whole, both of the books with which we have become acquainted here are hardly anything more than abusive satires. That of Apollonius merits the title to a higher degree than that of "the anonymous." One must reject as biased all of the judgments found in these works, even if they are delivered in the costume of historical narrative, and let the facts speak for themselves. When such a procedure is followed, what is left over? Primarily this (in many cases

21. On this, cf. Bauer, *Leben Jesu*, pp. 266 f.
22. Irenaeus AH 3.11.9 (= 11.12). In addition, cf. N. Bonwetsch, *Geschichte des Montanismus* (Erlangen: Deichert, 1881), pp. 22 ff.

as an unintentional confession): the prophetic movement appears to have caught on strongly, especially in Phrygia, men and funds flowed into it, and the rigorousness of the view of life prevailing among the Montanists caused many of them to become martyrs, whose blood insured an even more magnetic power. The magnitude of the ecclesiastical defense corresponds to, and attests to, the amount of success realized by the movement. This defense produces discussions in which, to say the least, the church does not always emerge victorious. Alongside this there is the literary feud. Its prerequisite was already filled by the fact that Montanism gave rise to a body of literature. Just as the *logia* of Jesus once had been collected, so now one gathered together the sayings and predictions of the original Montanist prophecy [23] and equated them with older revelation (cf. Gaius in EH 6.20.3). Other writings followed: the "catholic epistle" of Themiso, the defense against Miltiades, to say nothing of Proclus (in EH 3.31.4) and Tertullian in the third century. The ecclesiastical perspective found literary representation in the second century through the persons already known to us—Miltiades, "the anonymous," and [146] Apollonius—and around the year 200 through the above-mentioned Gaius and through Serapion, who immediately followed him.

To the earliest ecclesiastical warriors on the battlefield belongs Claudius Apollinaris of Hierapolis, who lived in the reign of Marcus Aurelius (EH 4.21). Eusebius, who enumerated his writings already in EH 4.27, again mentions his effectiveness against the Montanists immediately after the section on Apollonius (EH 5.19), which is justified chronologically insofar as Eusebius takes his point of departure from the letter that Serapion of Antioch (190-210) wrote to Caricus and Pontius for the refutation of Montanism. What Eusebius extracts from or tells us about Serapion's letter can be of particular assistance in our attempt to achieve a suitable attitude toward general statements found in the polemical literature. Thus a word about that is in order here. To begin with, Euesbius quotes the following words from the letter of Serapion: "And in order that you may know that the working of this lying association called the new prophecy is detested

23. The claim of Hippolytus that there are "countless books" (*Ref.* 8.19) is more instructive for the language of the polemic than for its factuality. We do know of the collection of Asterios Orbanos (anonymous in EH 5.16.17; see above, 135 n. 8).

in the whole brotherhood throughout the world, I have sent you the writing [24] of the most blessed Claudius Apollinaris, the late bishop of Hierapolis in Asia" (EH 5.19.2). Eusebius further states (EH 5.19.3) that subscriptions by various bishops are found in this letter of Serapion.[25] He reproduces two of these subscriptions verbatim, and then continues: "The autograph subscriptions of many other bishops who agree with these are also preserved in the abovementioned writing" (EH 5.19.4). It seems that there is nothing more to be said about them except that they are *autographoi*—i.e. that the bishops concerned have placed their names (or marks) at the bottom of the letter in their own writing. That they were all of the same opinion is apparently only a conclusion drawn by Eusebius. Since this conclusion could be the product of an ecclesiastical disposition, it must be tested as to its justification. We have a fixed point of reference in the two subscriptions that are reproduced literally, with which, according to Eusebius, the others are in agreement. Of these two, the second is clearly directed against the Montanists: "Aelius Publius Julius, Bishop of Debeltum,[26] a colony of Thrace. As God lives in the heavens, the blessed Sotas of Anchialus [see n. 26] [147] desired to exorcise the demon from Priscilla but the hypocrites would not permit it." [27] The other signature, on the other hand, reads simply: "I, Aurelius Quirinius, a martyr, pray for your welfare." In this instance, as with the "many others" (*alloi pleiones*), it is apparently only from the fact that Serapion (or was it already Apollinaris? see above, n. 25) permitted them to attach their subscriptions that one

24. The plural *grammata* refers here, as is often the case, to only *one* written treatise, as is clearly evident from EH 5.19.4.
25. Whether they derived from the treatise of Apollinaris, I would not presume to decide.
26. Both Debeltum and Anchialus (mentioned below) are located on the west bank of the Black Sea.
27. We recall here what "the anonymous" had told us of Maximilla and of the attempt made by the church in Phrygia to refute her (above, 135). It is, of course, quite possible that clashes of a similar sort often occurred. But it seems to me just as likely that we are dealing here with a floating ecclesiastical story that originally referred to an actual incident, but then, with the names altered, it turns up here and there in order to show why the spirit of God was not successful in overcoming the spirit of the devil. The blame is laid on the hypocrisy and brutal use of force by the heretics, not on any lack of courage or incentive by the ecclesiastical warriors. The fact that this ecclesiastically oriented story turns up in various regions, appears to me useful for determining the degree of ecclesiastical success in combatting the Montanist movement.

can conclude that they agreed with him in a common anti-Montanist outlook. All but one of them have missed the opportunity for an express confession. And it is perhaps no accident that a martyr maintains neutrality. Even the martyrs of Lyons favored the prophetic movement. Yet even in view of the most favorable interpretation, what weight can a couple of names, which happen to appear in conjunction, carry in support of the sweeping statement that "the whole brotherhood throughout the world detests the new prophets"? On the whole, the witnesses invoked here contradict the above assertion by the paucity of their numbers and the insufficiency of their statements, even if we limit "the world" around the time of Apollinaris to Asia Minor and Thrace, leaving aside Gaul, Rome, and North Africa.

The statement obviously is not based on real experience, but was prompted by the apologetic need to offer proof *ex consensu omnium* [based on common consensus]. Thus we come to a consideration of the basic issues that fly back and forth, both orally and in written form, in the fight with Montanism. Once again our sources are more communicative with regard to the arguments of the church than with reference to the case of its opponents. The latter probably appealed primarily to the spirit, which has dwelt among favored Christians since the time of the apostles, as it becomes manifest in the words of the prophets and enables men [148] to meet the high requirements laid on them, including martyrdom. That such a spirit is actually still at work follows from the fact that still other forms of charismatic gifts have by no means disappeared from Christianity (EH 5.3.4). Furthermore, the Montanists have appealed to the imminent end of the world and the glory of the heavenly Jerusalem, and have demanded that one obtain these by means of a rigorous life in the spirit in conformity with the instructions of the paraclete. But we know scarcely anything at all about how the Montanists protected their faith against the attacks of the church and sought in turn to refute its preaching in the second century. And Tertullian is much too idiosyncratic a person for us to be able to attribute some sort of general validity to his polemic. Tertullian is only able to teach us that even "the church" has become the object of violent and unjust attacks. From an earlier time, we learn that the Montanists applied to themselves and to their rejection by the church such a saying of the

Lord as Matthew 23.34, concerning those who murder the prophets, and their victims (EH 5.16.12). Also Paul, the pneumatic, and the paraclete of the fourth gospel are appealed to for assistance.

With respect to this form of false belief, the church first of all had the desire to show that the spirit at work there is a spirit of error. Neither in the sphere of the old nor of the new covenant have prophets behaved the way its servants act (see above, 136). The vessels of this spirit are completely vessels of dishonor; the life and the death of the heretics are equally unedifying, and their moral pretensions are only a show (above, 133 f., 136-140). The spirit from hell, which has already seduced Montanus into apostasy (above, 133) could open neither his eyes nor the eyes of a single one of his disciples. They are blind, allow themselves to be duped, and make prophecies that never come true (above, 135 f., 140 f.). Experience teaches us this, as does a comparison with the genuine book of revelation, the Apocalypse, the content of which is beyond suspicion since the seer has demonstrated his godly connections by raising someone from the dead (above, 141). The gospel story also shows that a genuine look into the future is possible only in the circle of the apostles of Jesus (above, 141); thus there is no other alternative but to rely on the authorities of the church. [149] The unbreakable chain of all revelation is forged with the links Lord, apostles, holy church (above, 141). The way in which "history" came to be used in the service of orthodoxy is shown not only by the postcanonical stories about Jesus and the apostles, but also in a rather distressing manner by the way in which one speaks about the outstanding adherents of the new movement, about their life and death, without even excepting their martyrs from such treatment. Defamation of the enemy perhaps plays a greater role in these circles than proof from scripture. Later, when the New Testament was accepted as a collection of scriptural writings, when knowledge of the Old Testament was expanded, and when the antiheretical use of both was developed to some extent, the situation would become healthier. Then, with the increased production of Christian literature and the ever growing distance from the actual events, the controversy will also become more highly literary. The way is already being paved for that in the period under consideration. It seems that "the anonymous" knew the work of his coreligionist Miltiades only from the reply of their common opponents—i.e. from the literature (see above, 136). And Serapion relied on the work of the already deceased Claudius Apollinaris of Hierapolis. Evidently he was not successful in obtaining other literary works of a similar outlook. Otherwise he certainly would have used them also, in his ambition to demonstrate that aversion to the false prophecy permeated all of Christianity. And Eusebius, who is filled with the same desire, would hardly have withheld that information from his readers.

8

The Use of Literature in the Conflict

The Montanist controversy of the second century has, to a certain extent, given us a glimpse of the actual causes, the forces at work, the tactics employed and the forms used in the ideological conflict within Christendom at that time. This sketchy picture can now be filled in or even supplemented and enriched through material which other controversies supply, or through such materials as provide the answer to questions we must raise in the context of our present discussion.

Literary activity, as one would expect, has left the clearest traces in the sources. However, these traces, when compared with the impressions such activity originally made, have become very faint and blurred so that frequently they are hardly legible or cannot be read with any confidence. Of many of the books which arose at that time, whose titles we still know but which are otherwise lost, we are no longer in a position to say whether the subject matter treated in them was designed to oppose other Christians, or was intended for purposes of teaching unbelievers, or whether the author only had a general interest in the subject. We are quite aware that the question of the resurrection of the dead was often raised in controversies with heretics (see above, 100). But the apologist Athenagoras deals with resurrection in the eighth decade of the second century without any acknowledgement of that situation. Does that mark him as an Athenian (see above, 105 f.), or is it simply characteristic of his personal intellectual disposition? Or how else can this be understood?

Another favorite theme was the six days of creation ("Hexameron"). Yet we cannot tell to what extent its treatment in ecclesiastical circles was determined by an anti-heretical concern. One can only speculate about the matter. Even the predilection of *1 Clement* [151] for God the creator appears to us to have an anti-heretical thrust (above, 104). And around the year 180, Celsus expressly says in his *"True Word"* (*logos alēthēs*) that the members of the "great church" (i.e. other than Gnostics and Marcionites) took over the Jewish teaching about the origin of the world including the teaching about the six days of creation and the seventh day on which God drew back in order to take his rest (in Origen *Against Celsus* 5.59ᵃ). About the same time Rhodon of Asia Minor, whom we know as an active enemy of heretics, especially of Marcion and Apelles, wrote his *"Memoir on the Hexameron"* (*hypomnēma eis tēn hexaēmeron;* EH 5.13.8). The treatise of Melito *"On Creation"* (*peri plaseōs;* EH 4.26.2) may also be mentioned here. The church sensed that it had the task of validating its faith in the God and father of Jesus Christ as creator of the world not only against the demiurge or any other such angelic power, but also against the devil; in this context also belongs the question concerning the origin of man and his special character. Gnostics also treated this matter with specific reference to the beginning of the Old Testament—Valentinus in a letter [1]; *Preaching of the Naasenes* 1 ff.[2]; the *Book of Baruch* of the gnostic Justin.[3]

---

1. Clement of Alexandria *Strom.* 2.(8.)36.2-4; cf. also the references to a Valentinian "homily" in 4.(13.)89.1 and 4.(13.)90.2-4. [For an ET, see Grant, *Gnosticism Anthology,* pp. 143 f.; the Greek texts are collected in Völker, *Quellen,* pp. 57 ff.]

2. Ed. R. Reitzenstein (—H. H. Schaeder), *Studien zum antiken Syncretismus aus Iran und Griechenland* 1 (Leipzig, 1926; repr. Darmstadt, 1965): 161 ff. [from Hippolytus *Ref.* 5.7-9. Greek text also in Völker, *Quellen,* pp. 11-26; partial ET in Grant, *Gnosticism Anthology,* pp. 105-114].

3. In Hippolytus *Ref.* 5.25-27 [Greek text also in Völker, *Quellen,* pp. 27-33; ET in Grant, *Gnosticism Anthology,* pp. 94-100]. In a somewhat distorted way a passage out of Anastasius of Sinai's *Hexameron,* book 1 (J. B. Pitra, *Analecta sacra spicilegio salesmensi parata* 2 [Paris, 1884]: 160) gives evidence of the predilection of the ancient church to concern itself with the six days of creation: "Taking a cue [that is, the occasion for the opinion concerning the millennial kingdom] from Papias the illustrious one of Hierapolis, a disciple of the beloved disciple, and from Clement and Pantaenus, the priest of the Alexandrians, and Ammonius the most-wise—from the ancients and the expositors who lived prior to the councils (*tōn archaiōn kai pro ton sunodōn exēgetōn*) [or, "and earliest (*prōtōn*) expositors who were in agreement"] and understood that the entire Hexameron referred to Christ and the Church." For the Greek text, see K. Bihlmeyer, *Die apostolischen Väter* 1 (Tübingen: Mohr, 1924; ed. W. Schneemelcher, 1956²): 137, no. 6. [For a discussion of the text and its interpretation, with an ET, see Schoedel, *Polycarp,* pp. 114 f.]

For the end of the second century Eusebius enumerates some books by author and title—a small sampling out of a great wealth, if one may believe him [4]—which he characterizes as monuments of the devoted zeal of good churchmen (EH 5.27). Maximus deals with "the question which is discussed so extensively by heretics, the origin of evil, and that matter was created." Therefore, his writing is [152] clearly a witness to the battle against heresy. For this reason we can perhaps view the others listed here in a similar way. Directly after Maximus are mentioned Candidus "On the *Hexameron*" and Apion on the same topic. Then follows Sextus "On the Resurrection." First on the list is "The (Memoirs) of Heraclitus on the Apostle" (*ta Herakleitou eis ton apostolon*). One can hardly doubt that by "the apostle" Paul must be understood here (see above 136 n. 13), and thus we are possibly dealing with an apologetic writing in defence of the Apostle to the Gentiles, which attempts to defend him against misunderstanding or even abuse on the part of heretics.[5]

This list of literary works which gives us the painful impression of an exceptionally tiny body of information, is placed in the framework of some comments that indicate to us what attitude is supposed to be called forth or strengthened by each particular item. The passage (5.27) begins with these words: "A great many memoirs of admirable industry by churchmen of the ancient past are *still preserved by many to this day*. Among those, the writings of which we have personal knowledge (*diegnōmen*) are . . ." (the list follows). But how can we believe that Eusebius actually has read these books, in view of the fact that of the one mentioned last, by Arabianus, he only knows enough to report that he authored "a certain other work" (*allē tis hypothesis*), after which Eusebius continues: "And [there are books] of *countless* others, for whom our lack of any reference point leaves us in no position either to write about the times in which they lived or to provide a historical reminiscence. And *writings* of *very many others* of whom we cannot recount even the names, *have reached us*. They are orthodox, ecclesiastically oriented persons, as

4. This will be discussed in its proper context; see below, 158 ff.
5. One thinks perhaps of Marcion. The hatred of Paul by the Jewish Christians or by Cerinthus (see my discussion in Hennecke[2], 127 ff.) would hardly still have called for opposition at that time. Nevertheless, Eusebius mentions people with encratite tendencies from the time of Tatian who "slander" Paul and who reject his letters together with the Acts of the Apostles (EH 4.29.5, also 6).

their respective interpretations of the divine scripture show, but they are nevertheless unknown to us, because the works do not bear the names of their authors." What Eusebius intends by this piling up of superlatives is quite clear. It is a matter of concern to him to assert that there is in existence a [153] body of ecclesiastical literature, as old as possible and as extensive as possible, but also treasured as much as possible in the present, and just as widely dispersed. He wants to show that the general rejection of false belief can also be found from earliest times in Christian literature. For this reason the writings whose title and author are known to Eusebius and whose contents qualified for him as orthodox (one would like to know whether with justification) were dated as early as possible; in the two cases in 5.27 and 28 which we are able to check they were dated too early.[6] Thus we encounter here what we already noticed in the case of the Antiochian bishops (above, 63 f.). And the motivating factor on that occasion also had been the necessity of such a move for ecclesiastical historiography.

Even if, in his generalizations in 5.27, Eusebius was telling things as they actually were, the riddle still remains—wholly apart from his enormous lack of knowledge [7] concerning this literature—how is it possible that this abundant orthodox literature was preserved from the second to the fourth century (see below, 159 ff.) and circulated widely within Christendom in numerous fragments, only to disappear in the period after Eusebius when Christianity, mainly in its orthodox form, had established itself so that no danger existed any longer? Be that as it may, I fear that we have here the same kind of approach that Serapion used when he wanted to demonstrate the aversion of all Christianity to Montanism, but in his appeal to witnesses, he actually breaks off after the second name (see above, 142 f.). The statements in support and praise of orthodoxy that we meet in ecclesiastical authors without being able to test their contents and find verification, we do well to set aside and to distrust as tendentious.

6. Cf. Harnack, *Geschichte*, 1.2: 758.
7. It can hardly be more than a way of speaking when Eusebius claims that *all* these churchmen demonstrated their orthodoxy by their scriptural interpretation (above, 149 f.). At the time of Eusebius that may have been an important characteristic. But in the second century, scriptural interpretation was not so widely practiced (see below, 195 n. 1).

It is part of the style of the "ecclesiastical" historiography of Euse-bius, when he is adding one member after another to the episcopal lists, also to exercise concern for the orthodox theological tradition so that it flows in as rich as possible a stream, and not in a trickle. [154]

The conclusion of the fourth book of the *Ecclesiastical History* appears to me to be very characteristic, especially the order of the tiny excerpts in 4.19-21. There we read:

> (19) In the eighth year of the reign of which we are presently speak-ing [i.e. of Marcus Aurelius], Soter succeeded Anicetus, who had oc-cupied the episcopate of the Roman church for eleven years in all. After Celadion had presided over the church of Alexandria for fourteen years, Agrippinus became his successor. (20) And in the church of the Antiochians, Theophilus was the sixth bishop, numbered from the apostles. Cornelius, who succeeded Heron, had been the fourth there. After him, Eros followed as bishop in the fifth place. (21) Now there flourished in the church in those days Hegesippus, whom we know from the previous account [i.e. 4.8.1], Dionysius the bishop of the Corinthians, Pinytus, bishop of Crete, and besides them, Philip, Apolli-naris, Melito, Musanus and Modestus, and finally Irenaeus; *from whom the orthodoxy of the authentic teaching, as it was transmitted from the apostles, has come down in writing even to us.*

Then follow three longer chapters which have to do with the activity of various individuals among the persons mentioned—Hegesippus (22), Dionysius of Corinth (23), Theophilus of Antioch (24). The last of these sections call attention to the fact that, in addition to writing various other books, Theophilus also wrote an admirable work against Marcion which just happens, like his other works mentioned by name, *to have been preserved to the present time.*

After a brief remark at the end of section 24 concerning the epis-copal successor of Theophilus, EH 4.25 adds a fragment of the same scope and character as the series in 4.19-21, but also similar to the sections 22-24, since it reviews briefly the activity of some of the ecclesiastical theologians enumerated in 4.21. But Eusebius again wanders into generalizations. EH 4.25 reads: "Philip, who, as we learned from the letter of Dionysius [in 4.23.5] was bishop of the community at Gortyna, also composed a most weighty writing against Marcion, as did Irenaeus and Modestus, who was more successful than the others in unmasking the man's error with complete clarity, and *many others, whose works are still preserved to this day by a great many of the brethren.*" [155]

EH 4.26 is devoted to the Melito mentioned in 4.21. Eusebius refers to approximately [8] twenty titles of works by this theologian and indicates by the expression, they had "come to his attention" (4.26.2), that the list is not exhaustive. In fact there are still a few additional titles which appear in the tradition.[9] But, except for a few citations everything is lost.[10] If we ask of which of Melito's writings that had "come to his attention" does Eusebius actually divulge information beyond that given in the title, it seems to me that the following situation emerges. Immediately prior to the list itself we learn from 26.1 that "At this time [still the reign of Marcus Aurelius], Melito, bishop of the church of Sardis, and Apollinaris, bishop of the church of Hierapolis, flourished with distinction; and they addressed writings in defence of the faith to the aforesaid Roman emperor at that time, each respectively producing an Apology." Then 26.2 continues with the words already mentioned above—"Of these writers there have come to our attention the works [first] of Melito." Then follows an extensive enumeration of bare titles,[11] beginning with "two books on the Passover" (*ta peri tou pascha duo*) and concluding with "The Petition to Antoninus" (*to pros A. biblidion*). The beginning of 26.3 seems to hold greater promise. Eusebius begins to speak about the book mentioned first, that concerning the paschal observance, and we expect that he would briefly characterize its contents as well as at least some other writings from the catalogue and thus give proof that they actually were in his possession. But we find that we deceive ourselves. We hear almost exclusively about the book on Easter. This would be the one exception that we could understand, since we have already learned that Eusebius was interested in the Easter controversies (EH 5.23-25) and in treating

---

8. The titles are not all entirely clear, and thus the number cannot be established with full certainty; see also below, n. 11.

9. On Melito, see Harnack, *Geschichte*, 1.1: 246-255; E. Preuschen, RPTK[3] 12 (1903): 564-567.

10. [See below, p. 315 n. 37, on the more recently recovered *Paschal Homily* of Melito.]

11. According to the GCS edition of Schwartz, it includes fourteen items; Harnack, *Geschichte*, 1.1: 247 f., counts eighteen. [The ET of EH by H. J. Lawlor and J. E. Oulton has sixteen, while that of K. Lake in LCL has nineteen.]

them had mentioned Melito (5.24.5). While he observes in the present context that Clement of Alexandria referred to Melito's work in his book on the paschal observance (4.26.4), the point is repeated in 6.13.9 where he considers Clement again. [156] Otherwise Eusebius only shares with us the opening words of the book, in which Melito expresses himself as follows: "When Servilius Paulus was proconsul in Asia, at the time when Sagaris died as a martyr, there developed in Laodicea a vigorous dispute about the paschal festival, which fell in those days, and these things (*tauta*) were written" (4.26.3).

But here doubt arises, for I cannot hide the suspicion that in my opinion these words, especially their conclusion, could hardly have stood in Melito's work. Normally it is not the author himself, but a third person who reports concerning "these things" (*tauta*). Further, the portrayal of the situation strikes me as so artificial that I should at least regard it as greatly abridged. What is one supposed to think about such a situation, in which Christianity is subjected to such persecution that its bishop must become a blood offering, but because of the fact that his martyrdom fell at Easter time, becomes involved in a heated controversy over the proper celebration of the passover, instead of standing shoulder to shoulder against the common foe! In the writing by Melito, the contemporary of Sagaris, that probably would not have been expressed so crassly. Thus it seems to me that there is no certainty that Eusebius had actually seen Melito's work on the passover. And I would extend that judgment to almost all the other items on Eusebius' list (26.2). Not a single word remains from hardly any of them. Eusebius refers in detail only to the *Apology* (4.26.5-11) and mentions thereafter a writing which is not in the catalogue (26.12-14). He reproduces the opening of this work apparently without alteration: "Melito greets his brother Onesimus." So began the six books of *Eklogai*—i.e. excerpts from the writings of the Palestinian Old Testament.[12] The intention of the

12. Melito made no distinction between the Old Testament of Palestine and that of the Greek diaspora. Rather, he speaks about "the old books" whose crucial contents he wants to make available to his friends. In his opinion, one had to take a trip to Palestine in order to have access to more accurate (*akribōs*; 26.14) information about "the books of the old covenant" (*ta tēs palaias diathēkēs biblia*). This shows that neither the Church in Sardis, nor, as far as Melito was aware, any other Christian Church accessible to him had at its disposal a *complete* Old Testament. Apparently, in the area represented by Melito, one was still content with *Eklogai*. Cf. Bauer, *Wortgottesdienst*, 45 f.; also Josephus, *Life* (75)418, where Josephus receives the Old Testament as a gift from a prince (Titus).

work is to provide Onesimus with materials from the law and prophets that pertain to "our savior and our whole [157] faith" (4.26.13). Thus its purpose is to lay the foundation for the scriptural proof in support of the Christian proclamation.

Of the two books of Melito which Eusebius apparently has seen, the *Apology* (see also 4.13.8 and the *Chronicle* [13]) and the *Extracts*, the latter is missing from the list while the *Apology* instead of heading the list immediately after 26.1, stands at the end. This situation shows that he did not put the catalogue together on the basis of actual material from Melito which was available to him. He received the catalogue from tradition and it served the purpose of supplementing his own knowledge. He inserted it into his report on the *Apology*, which begins at 26.1 and resumes at 26.5, and appended two passages to it (26.3 and 4) which contain all that he has been able to learn about the only other writing on the list (apart from the *Apology*) about which he knew more than the title.[14] Harnack says: "Melito was very quickly forgotten in the Greek church, and this can be explained only by the fact that his writings were no longer suited to the later dogmatic taste." [15] I am more thoroughly convinced of Harnack's conclusion than of his reasons. I am not persuaded by Harnack's opinion that Eusebius "found in the library at Caesarea" a rich deposit of Melito's works, namely the specific items on the list.[16] I fear that Melito already had disappeared from the scene before the "later dogmatic taste" became dominant—it could hardly have done any more damage, even if Melito's corpus had been kept intact up to the time of Eusebius. What actually caused him difficulty was his outspoken position in the controversies of his time, whether in the paschal controversy or in the prophetic movement [17] or in his opposition to Marcion and other heretics.[18] That which served the general interest of Christendom and stood above the parties, as for

13. Cf. Harnack, *Geschichte*, 1.1: 247.
14. Eusebius' approach here is also similar to what we previously observed, 130 n. 1.
15. Harnack, *Geschichte*, 1.1: 248.
16. Harnack, *Geschichte*, 1.1: 247.
17. Tertullian ridiculed Melito, the "prophet" of the *psychikoi* (Jerome *Illustrious Men* 24).
18. Examples are given in Harnack, *Geschichte*, 1.1: 249 f.

example his apologetic writing and the collection of biblical proof texts, proved to be more capable of enduring opposition.[19] [158]

We have found that the book against the Montanists by Miltiades (ca. 160-170) was no longer available to his anonymous coreligionist writing only a couple of decades later (above, 136 and 145 f.). Harnack adds the observation: "Thus Eusebius did not actually have a copy of the anti-Gnostic work [of Miltiades]; but he did have [according to EH 5.17.5] 1. two books of Miltiades against the Greeks (*pros Hellēnas*), 2. two books against the Jews (*pros Ioudaious*), 3. an Apology to the emperor." [20]

Is it not striking to notice in this connection that also in the case of Justin, Theophilus, and Tatian, those books that were involved in the contemporary controversies within Christianity were lost, while the apologies directed to unbelievers were preserved? For a statement of what Eusebius still knew of Justin's literary activity, let me appeal briefly to Harnack: "Thus Eusebius here [i.e. EH 4.18.1 ff.] enumerates eight works of Justin known to him; a ninth, against Marcion (*pros Markiōna*), he knows only from Irenaeus; and a tenth, the *Syntagma* against all heresies, only from Justin's *Apology* (chap. 26; cf. EH 4.11.10). But he himself has only taken notes on the *Apology* [21] and the *Dialogue*; although it seems as if he is quoting from Justin's treatise against Marcion in EH 4.11.8, even here he is drawing from the *Apology*." [22] Harnack's closing words are a very gentle way of calling attention to the fact that Eusebius refers to Justin's book against Marcion, the title of which (but nothing more) he knows from Irenaeus, but after the introductory statement that "he wrote a treatise against Marcion . . . and expressed himself as follows," Eusebius reproduces material that could only come from Justin's *Apology* (*Apol.* 26.5-6 in EH 4.11.9). Even if one could persuade

---

19. That the author of the *Little Labyrinth* knew *dogmatic* writings [in contrast to apologetic or biblical excerpts] of Melito is hardly demonstrated by the exaggerated outburst in which he is mentioned: "For who does not know the books of Irenaeus and of Melito as well as the others, which proclaim Christ as God and man! And how many psalms and hymns have been written from the beginning," etc. (EH 5.28.5).
20. Harnack, *Geschichte*, 1.1: 256.
21. For Eusebius, the "Apology" includes what for us is divided into the "first" and the "second" *Apology* [or "Appendix"].
22. Harnack, *Geschichte*, 1.1: 102.

himself, with great effort, that the exact passage also could have been found in Justin's treatise against Marcion, this solution breaks down in light of the quotation's continuation, which is subjoined by means of the expression: "to these words he adds" (EH 4.11.10, citing *Apol.* 26.8). But since the emperor is addressed specifically in this material ("we will give you [the book] if you want to read it"), it is simply impossible that this quotation came from Justin's treatise against Marcion. [159]

What occurs here can easily rest upon a misunderstanding, such as an incorrect use of notices and excerpts; but one will have to admit that an author in whom such confusions occur—and that repeatedly [23]—elicits only our conditional confidence. Nor do we find any consolation in the fact that also with respect to Justin, Eusebius tosses off the kind of statement with which we are already familiar in one form or another—"*But many other writings from his hand are still found among many brethren*" (4.18.8); that he refers his contemporaries who are eager to learn to the "very many" books of Justin (4.18.1); and that as documentation for the claim that Justin's works already had enjoyed high esteem among the ancients, we are provided with only a reference to Irenaeus (EH 4.18.9). Does it not make us rather suspicious when we find again and again that a very slight acquaintance with the materials on the part of Eusebius is juxtaposed with the assurance that these literary works of the second century which are under discussion still enjoyed the widest circulation in his time?

As we turn to Theophilus of Antioch, we note that the *Apology to Autolycus* survived, while the writings against the heretics Hermogenes and Marcion have been lost. Indeed, Eusebius here claims once more that all these "*have been preserved until now*" (4.24b). Indeed, this time he also withholds any evidence for his assertion, except the quotation of a single line.

We have already discussed EH 4.25 and 26 (cf. 151-154). The next section (4.27) takes up Apollinaris, who was mentioned in 26.1 (see above, 152), and makes the characteristic claim, by now somewhat embarrassing and suspicious, that "*many writings of Apollinaris have*

23. See above, 153, the "citation" from Melito's book on the passover. From the beginning of this investigation (Abgar legend) we have had occasion to refer to other inadequacies in Eusebius' approach, and there will continue to be such occasions in what follows [e.g. below, n. 33].

been preserved by many." But in spite of the fact that Eusebius was in a better position than almost anyone else accurately to know the extent of available literature, in this instance also he knows only a few titles. He has the most to say about the last book he mentions, the one against the Montanists. But it is unlikely that he saw or read even that. Probably he is indebted for what he does know to the letter of Serapion [160] (EH 5.19; see above 142 f.), just as by his own admission he was acquainted with the work of Philip of Gortyna through reading the letter of Dionysius of Corinth (4.25).

In 4.28, Eusebius selects Musanus from the list of ecclesiastical authors presented in 4.21, so as to provide a transition to 4.29, which is concerned with Tatian. Musanus wrote a "very impressive book" against the heresy of the encratites, whose founder had been Tatian. Ths work also is *still in existence.* Chapters 29 and 30 bring book four of the *Ecclesiastical History* to a close with a treatment of Tatian and Bardesanes, neither of whom could lay any claim to orthodoxy. However, Tatian did have an orthodox past when he was under the influence of Justin (4.29.3) and gave favorable testimony about his teacher (4.16.7; 4.29.1). Tatian also bequeathed to Christendom "many memoirs in writing" (*pleista en suggrammasin mnēmeia,* 4.16.7), or "a very large number of writings" (*polu ti plēthos suggrammatōn,* 4.29.7). But again, apparently only the apology "Against the Greeks" (*pros Hellēnas*) reached Eusebius or lasted until his time, from which he quotes (EH 4.16.7-9). He did not know first hand the *Diatessaron* or Tatian's reworking of the Pauline texts, as he himself admits (4.29.6), nor did he mention any other books of Tatian in the section devoted to him. He had not yet worked through his own material well enough to have available the information that appears later in 5.13.8, in connection with Rhodon the disciple of Tatian, where Eusebius says that Tatian wrote a book called "Problems," in which he undertook to demonstrate the contradictions in the sacred Scriptures.

It may be added that Quadratus also, who concerned himself solely with apologetics (under Hadrian), survived, with his *Apology,* until the time of Eusebius. We would not give credence to Eusebius if he were only able to repeat once again that *"The writing still exists at present among very many brethren and among us as well"* (4.3.1). But fortunately he adds a quotation (4.3.2). The lack of such a quotation, however, justifies us in doubting somewhat the unqualified correctness of the subsequent claim that the apologetic work of Aristides, the contemporary of Quadratus, also *is still preserved among very many* (4.3.3).

The criticism in the preceding paragraphs is directed against the position which Eusebius deliberately cultivated for obvious reasons (above, 149, 151, 156 f.), [161] namely that during the first two centuries of our era an abundance of orthodox literature already existed in the Christian church (see also below, 171); that this literature enjoyed wide circulation, faithful preservation, and a long and flourishing life; and that it grew up and spread so vigorously that it was in a position to suppress the heretics and their approaches to life, or at least to push them into a corner.

Eusebius' phrase "still extant at the present time" is suspicious because of its monotonous repetition, and an expression which speaks of "being preserved" ([*dia-*]*sōzesthai*, 4.3.3, 4.24, 4.27, 5.27) or guarded (*diaphullattesthai*, 4.25) until today rather clearly suggests that it was more normal for books to perish. The papyrus book was a very unreliable tool for buttressing a position in the second and third century. And what is true of its deficiencies in general, applies two or three times as much to the Christian writings of that time. Certainly many pieces of early Christian literature found their way into libraries and there received competent treatment. And probably the most important of them were recopied when deterioration made that necessary, and thus were "saved" from destruction. Nevertheless in pre-Constantinian times there were, in every respect, definite limitations to such careful treatment.

What must the situation have been like in the library of Caesarea at the time of Eusebius! No sooner had he died than the library was carefully scrutinized so as to transcribe its most important treasures from papyrus to parchment in order to preserve them. It was high time. Of this library Jerome reports that *"as much of it as was in bad condition,* Acacius and then also Euzoius, priests of the same church, undertook to preserve on parchment."[24] Without further ado we believe Eusebius when he says that there were also books lying around in the library of his episcopal city of which no one knew the author,

24. Jerome *Epistle* 141 (to Marcellus): *quam ex parte corruptam Acacius dehinc et Euzoïus eiusdem ecclesiae sacerdotes in membranis instaurare conati sunt.*

audience, or purpose (see above, 149 f.). But we cannot agree with him in so quickly attributing these remains to the ecclesiastical literature of the second century, and thus increasing the scope of such literature.

Just what we may expect from this period can be learned from a particular case which fortunately has become known to us. [162] Sextus Julius Africanus wrote a work called *Kestoi* ("Embroiderings"), which can hardly be dated earlier than the year 225, since it is dedicated to the emperor Alexander Severus; but it could have been published as late as 235 (the year of the emperor's death) because Africanus did not die until 240, as his correspondence with Origen shows. On the front (recto) side of a recently discovered papyrus leaf (Oxyrhynchus Papyrus 412) we now are in possession of the conclusion of the eighteenth book of the *Kestoi*, in columns 35 and 36 of a scroll, whose contents are unmistakably identified by the subscription. What makes the papyrus so important for our purposes is the reverse side, on which there is a document dated from the reign of the emperor Claudius Tacitus, i.e. in 275-76. This use of the verso for different purposes presupposes that the final leaf of Africanus' work had been previously detached from the body of the original manuscript, thus making it available for reuse. From this we deduce that it was possible for a manuscript to be separated into its component parts within a generation of its original production, and so disappear. The process of disintegration also could have taken place much more quickly. Nothing compels us to accept the maximal limits required between the production of the *Kestoi* manuscript (= 225 at earliest) and the separation of the leaves (= 276 at latest) as representing the actual span of time. Even if the leaf had belonged to the autograph copy of the *Kestoi*, the interval between the time of issuance and the reuse of the leaf is short enough to cause us to wonder whether, at that time, the ink must not have been better than the glue.

Furthermore, it should be noted that in the case of Africanus we are not dealing with the literary product of some poor fellow who has to be satisfied with the very cheapest material, and is, in fact, happy to have his efforts published at all, but with the work of an eminent and prosperous man. How then can we imagine that the literary creations of the average Christians could have survived from the second to the fourth century in "many" or even "innumerable" copies, and in the private houses of the brethren at that? Furthermore, Africanus enjoyed an advantage over many other Christian authors in that his book, which had a rich content, free from religious bias, must have awakened considerable interest but would not have evoked any opposition or counter-measures to speak of. Its only enemy was the passage of time, but that took its toll quite rapidly. On the other hand, no one outside the circle of Christianity was interested in the anti-heretical writings of the ecclesiastical authors, [163] so that their editions suffered from the paucity of funds and remained extraordinarily limited. Worse still, the few available texts, in addition to being naturally frail, were threatened by such believers as would be aided if the texts disappeared as soon as possible and who thus helped them along, thereby repaying their opponents in kind. Christian writings which were useful in the discussion with the unbaptized were naturally in less danger, and the evidence from the literary history as presented above (see 154-158 on Melito, Miltiades, Justin, Theophilus, Tatian, Quadratus) tends to support this consideration.

The struggle between orthodox and heretics, insofar as it was fought in the literary arena, took the form of an effort to weaken the weaponry of the enemy as much as possible. What could not be completely eliminated was at least rendered useless, or was suitably altered and then put to one's own use. In plain language, the writings of the opponent were falsified. What could be done by way of "editing" existing writings in ancient Christianity can be seen from the aforementioned fragment of the eighteenth book of the *Kestoi* of Julius Africanus, even though it was not a part of intra-Christian polemics. Column one of the papyrus leaf (which was column thirty-five of the original scroll; see above, 159) begins in the middle of a passage from the *Odyssey* 11, on conjuring up the dead. It deals with *Odyssey* 11.34-50 but omits lines 44-47. This is no mistake. In the latter verses Odysseus calls upon his companions to pray to the gods of the underworld. But it is not that way in the *Kestoi;* rather Odysseus himself invokes the demons and then recites his conjuration verbatim. In preparation for this, the manuscript (lines 15-17) attaches *Iliad* 3.278-80 to *Odyssey* 11.50; for Homer, these lines from the *Iliad* contained a speech of Agamemnon, who calls certain divine beings as witnesses prior to the duel between Paris and Menelaus, but Africanus puts the words into the mouth of Odysseus, who is depicted as the speaker throughout. Then follow three verses made up of Homeric expressions (lines 18-20) which eventually refer to Odysseus' son Telemachus, and as an actual transition, have the father say: " 'My son'; for the conjuration was that powerful" (*teknon emon: toiē gar aristē ēn epaoidē*). These words are intended to mark what immediately follows as the strongest conceivable conjuration.

The train of thought in lines 15-20 offers no further difficulty. The souls of the dead will submit to human interrogation [164] only when they are under compulsion. Odysseus sees to this in the most thorough fashion. First he entreats some supernatural beings which the *Iliad*, and therefore Homer himself, supplied, but then he wanders off, in lines 22-36, into a completely different world. I give these lines according to the recent reconstruction of the text by Karl Preisendanz, and from his [German] translation: [25]

> Listen to me, propitious one, overseer, noble-born Anubis! [And you listen], wily one, secret consort, savior of Osiris! [Come] Hermes, rapacious one! Come, fair haired Zeus of the nether world! Give your decision and bring this spell to pass! [Come, Hades], and you Earth, imperishable fire, Helios Titan, come you also Iaa [26] and Phthas and Phre, preserver of the law, and you, highly honored Nephtho, and you, most wealthy Ablanatho, girt with fiery serpents, tearing up the earth, haughty goddess; [Abraxas], daemon, well known through your cosmic name, who hold sway over the world axis and the astral dance and the frosty light of the Bear constellations, come you also, Phren, most beloved of all to me for your restraint; I summon you, Briareus and Phrasios, and you, Ixion, you origin and decline, and you, beautifully flaming fire; and come, underworldly and heavenly, you guardian goddess of dreams, and Sirius, who [. . .].

With line 37 the manuscript returns to the context of *Odyssey* 11, although with spurious verses, and continues to line 43, where finally a link with *Odyssey* 11.51 is actually achieved.

In the second column Africanus claims that these verses were ancient and genuine, and had been either omitted subsequently by Homer himself or excised by the Pisistratidae as incompatible with

25. *Papyri Graecae Magicae*, 2: 150 f., which also includes bibliography. [The ET of this material has been made also with an eye to the Greek text.] Cf. also W. Kroll, "Julius Africanus," in Paulys *Realencyklopädie*, 11 (1917). F. Granger, "Julius Africanus and the Library of the Pantheon," *Journal of Theological Studies*, 34 (1933): 157-161, does not discuss the questions of interest to us. [For ed. and ET of Homer's *Iliad* and *Odyssey*, see the LCL volumes by A. T. Murray (1924-25 and 1919 respectively).]
26. *Iaa* = Yahweh, as Preisendanz renders it.

the structure of the poem. Nevertheless Africanus included them here as "a most noteworthy production" (*kyēma polytelesteron*). He felt that he was all the more justified in doing so because the archives of Jerusalem and of Nysa in Caria [southwestern Asia Minor] had them. The library of the Pantheon in Rome, by the baths of Alexander, also had them as far as "verse 13." He was well acquainted with this library because he himself had built and furnished it for the emperor Alexander Severus. [165] Of course, the "thirteen" verses preserved there cannot be reckoned on the basis of the quite accidental beginning of the Homeric text in our fragment. Nothing is more certain than that the preceding column of the original scroll (col. 34, now lost to us) also had contained a number of verses from Homer. The enumeration has to begin where the actual addition begins. Therefore the Roman copy also attested the expanded text, with little deviation.

How is this situation to be assessed? That is, who is responsible for the "enrichment" of Homer? Was it Africanus himself, or an earlier redactor by whom he was led astray? If one supposes that Africanus was deceived, the question immediately arises as to how he had such unsuspecting confidence in the falsified Homer, in view of the sharp critical sense he showed with respect to the story of Susanna.[27] In that case, (1) his linguistic sensivity led him to conclude that it must have been written originally in Greek, and could not be a translation; (2) a number of pertinent considerations suggested to him that the oppressed conditions of the Jews during the Babylonian exile hardly were consistent with the way that they appear in the Susanna pericope; (3) he referred back to the history of the tradition, which shows that the Susanna material did not originally belong to the book of Daniel.

The same sort of approach would have required him to raise decisive objections against attributing that syncretistic conjuration to Homer—assuming that it had come to Africanus from some earlier source. But instead he is completely blind to the problems and is satisfied to have come across that ancient and genuine passage in two or three libraries. Is this plausible, or is it suspicious? The li-

27. In his letter to Origen. Cf. W. Reichardt, *Die Briefe des Sextus Julius Africanus an Aristides und Origenes* (TU 34.3, 1909).

braries in Jerusalem [28] and Rome, in any event, were for him easily reached at will, while the one in Carian Nysa was hardly accessible for many. What makes the whole matter particularly suspect is the fact that no mention is made of the region in which such an addition to Homer most likely [166] would have appeared—a region, moreover, in which Africanus had demonstrably succumbed to syncretistic tendencies—namely, Alexandria-Egypt. Surely the process for which Africanus wants to gain recognition is nothing more than a parasitic enlargement of Homer by means of an Egyptian magical text. It reflects the desire to make Homer, like Hermes Trismegistos, Moses, and Democritus,[29] into a patron of the magical arts which flourished predominantly along the Nile. The markedly Egyptian color of the inserted passage must be obvious to everyone. What might seem to indicate a Greek orientation, such as the reference to "Helios," had general currency at that time—Helios is none other than the Egyptian Re. Or when we encounter the "fair haired Zeus of the nether world," we find that he is enthroned also in Alexandria.[30] But Osiris, Isis, Anubis, Phtha, Phre, and Nephto are expressly Egyptian; and in the land of the Nile again and again we meet in their society Jaa, as well as Abraxas and Ablanatho, and also the Bear constellations and the guardian of the world axis and ruler of the people, if it is permitted to refer to the so-called Mithras liturgy in the great Paris magical papyrus.[31]

And it all was supposed to have been preserved expressly and almost exclusively at Nysa in Caria! There was not much time for these interests to be transplanted from Egypt to the western part

28. W. Kroll (see above, n. 25) concluded from lines 58 ff. of the fragment that Jerusalem was the home of Africanus. At any rate, in later life he lived for some time in Emmaus on the Philistine plain, six hours from Jerusalem.
29. Manuscript 299 of the library of St. Mark in Venice (tenth century) includes Africanus as seventh in the list of "names of the philosophers of divine knowledge and art" (*onomata tōn philosophōn tēs theias epistēmēs kai technēs*), which begins with Moses and Democritus (M. Berthelot, *Collection des anciens alchemistes grecs* 1 [Paris, 1887]: 110). The content of the thirty-second chapter of this codex derives from Hermes, Zosimus, Nilus, and Africanus (Berthelot 1, 175 B).
30. Cf. R. Wünsch, "Deisidaimoniaka," *Archiv für Religionswissenschaft* 12 (1909): 19.
31. Cf. A. Dieterich, *Eine Mithrasliturgie* (Leipzig: Teubner, 1903; repr. of 1923³ ed., Darmstadt, 1966), pp. 12 f., 14 f., 70, 72 f. [See also the Greek text with German translation in Preisendanz, *Papyri Graecae Magicae*, 1: 94 ff. = no. IV.639 ff. (especially lines 681 and 700 f. for the above-mentioned titles).]

of Asia Minor. Africanus flourished at the beginning of the third century, while the magical texts of the kind we have described are characteristic of the second century C.E. Thus it seems to me that the question posed here points back to the two possibilities: (1) either Africanus himself revised Homer—Africanus, whose taste for Egyptian magic will be discussed shortly, and who undoubtedly had the libraries of Jerusalem and Rome at his disposal—(2) or someone else with essentially the same interests who was at home in the same libraries did it some fifty years earlier, and Africanus allowed himself to be completely hoodwinked, in spite of his capacity for literary criticism which was so well displayed in the handling of Susanna. [167] For my part, I see no reason to attribute to an unknown person the deed for which Africanus is such a prime suspect.

The connections of Africanus with Egypt and with magic remain to be demonstrated. The former is suggested already by his exchange of ideas with Origen (see above, 162 n. 27; Origen replied to the letter of Africanus), and is, moreover, clearly attested by Africanus himself since, as we have already noted (above, 55), he mentions a trip to Alexandria. He indicates some of the things he did there in his *Chronicle*. In one passage,[32] he gives an excerpt from Manetho, the Egyptian high priest in Heliopolis (ca. 300 B.C.E.) who in his work called *Aiguptiaka* ("Things pertaining to the Egyptians") undertook to instruct the Greeks about the history and religion of the Egyptians. Africanus, following Manetho, mentions King Suphis of the fourth dynasty, then adds that he had composed "the sacred book" (*tēn hieran biblon sunegrapse*) and comments further: "which I acquired for myself as a great treasure (*mega chrēma*) when I was in Egypt." Thus the Christian Africanus, who traveled to Egypt because of his interest in the Christian catechetical school, takes this opportunity to buy a sacred writing of the pagan Egyptians and values it highly as a cherished possession. We can see from the magical papyri in Greek—for the manuscripts purchased by Africanus must have been in that language—what usually was included in the "holy scriptures" in Egypt at the beginning of the third century. Evidently someone in Egypt had palmed off on him such a papyrus as an ancient book by Suphis. His critical acumen was inadequate to deal with this kind of situation. Here the mysterious and irrational be-

---

32. Quoted in George Syncellus *Chronicles,* 1: 105 f., where Africanus is mentioned expressly.

came the criterion of genuineness. This Egyptian acquisition, I believe, supplied Africanus with the material for his reworking of Homer.[33] [168]

In view of this lack of restraint by an educated Christian and intellectual leader as soon as certain interests are aroused, it is hardly surprising when Origen, writing at the same time, complains bit-

33. A book such as the present study, which is so critical of Eusebius (very much against the original inclination and intention of its author) may be allowed to justify its claim by referring to the wider context of the passage in which Africanus speaks of purchasing the Suphis book. The excerpt from Africanus quoted by George Syncellus literally reads as follows: "Suphis 63 years. He built the greatest pyramid, which Herodotus claims came from Cheops. But he was also one who scorned the gods (*hyperoptēs eis theous*). And he wrote the sacred book, which I acquired for myself in Egypt as a great treasure." [168] Shortly thereafter (106 f.), Syncellus repeats essentially the same thing, but this time depends on Eusebius as his source, just as he had previously used Africanus. This is not surprising in itself. Eusebius himself drew on Africanus in writing his *Chronicle.* Syncellus thus used Africanus, directly at first and then indirectly by way of Eusebius. This circumstance provides us with an insight into the way Eusebius evaluated and employed his sources. The quotation which Syncellus drew directly from Africanus, given above, is quite remarkable. It prompts the question, how did one who scorned the gods come to write a sacred book? Something seems out of line here. But if we go back to Herodotus, we find that the scorning of the gods was done by Cheops (Herodotus 2.124 says Cheops closed all the temples and prevented the people from sacrificing; [ed. and ET by A. D. Godley, LCL (1920)]). It is possible that Africanus understood it in the same way. If so, the words "he was one who scorned the gods" were a digression referring to Cheops, in connection with the allusion to Herodotus. But what follows concerning the sacred book applies to the person who is the subject of the paragraph as a whole, namely Suphis. Linguistically, however, it is also possible to refer it all to Suphis, except Herodotus' statement that Cheops, and not Suphis, was the builder of the greatest pyramid.

This latter interpretation is what Eusebius drew from the words of Africanus. Whereupon he felt obliged to offer an explanation of how Suphis, the scorner of the gods, came to occupy himself with sacred literature. He accomplished this by appending to the statement "he was a scorner of the gods" the clause "then however he repented" (*hos metanoēsanta auton*) and wrote the sacred book. But Eusebius had another problem. How could the learned and pious Christian Africanus, from whom he borrowed so much, have acquired the pagan book of magic by Suphis and have cherished it as a great treasure? Something also must have been wrong at this point with the text as transmitted. So Eusebius made an attempt to correct it; thus instead of "the sacred book which *I* acquired for myself as a great treasure" we now read in his text "the sacred book which the *Egyptians* guard (*Aigyptioi periepousi*) as a great treasure." Thus by inserting and changing only four words, Eusebius radically alters, indeed distorts, the sense in two directions, and all for reasons that could not be more clear. There is no doubt that Eusebius was operating here with a clean conscience; he unquestionably felt it was his duty to restore a corrupt text. But the urgent question must be raised as to how much one should accept from a historian found to be operating in such a manner? Is not one obligated to entertain reservations in all instances where there is no possibility of verification and where a purpose becomes clearly discernible on the other side?

terly about the Valentinian Candidus.[34] Origen had disputed with him before a large [169] audience, and a transcript of it was made. Candidus reworked this: "he added what he wished, and deleted what he wished, and changed whatever he wanted" (*quae voluit addidit et quae voluit abstulit et quod ei visum est permutavit*). In this process he did not limit himself to the opinions he himself had expressed, but tampered extensively with the statements of Origen. He secured a wide circulation among Christians for the record thus edited, and when Origen took him to task for it, he responded "I wanted to embellish the disputation more, and also to clean it up" (*quoniam magis ornare volui disputationem illam atque purgare*). Of course, both the *ornare* and the *purgare* worked to the disadvantage of the opponent. Indeed, another heretic prepared a report of a disputation with Origen which had never taken place.[35] Origen was aware of the existence of the forgery in Ephesus, Rome, and Antioch, and had no doubt that it was circulated even more widely.

When we move back into the second century, we find Irenaeus expressing the greatest apprehension that his writings against heretics would be altered—naturally, by the heretics (in EH 5.20.2). Likewise Dionysius of Corinth complained about the falsifying of his letters: "I have written letters at the request of the brethren. But the apostles of the devil have filled them with tares, removing many things and adding others. Woe is reserved for them. Since certain people have dared to tamper even with the dominical scriptures, it is not surprising that they have made attacks on less important writings" (in EH 4.23.12). If it was possible for the heretics to falsify writings of an orthodox "bishop" without having their project spoiled by opposition from the Christian public, then it must have been even easier for them to withdraw from circulation considerable amounts of "ecclesiastical" literature, which was disturbing and uncomfortable to them. As for the literature that remained, the heretics could optimistically rely on their good luck.

---

34. In a letter "to certain close acquaintances at Alexandria" (*ad quosdam caros suos Alexandriam*) preserved by Rufinus, "On the falsifying of the books of Origen" 7 (*De adulteratione librorum Origenis*, ed. M. Simonetti in CC 20 [1961]; ET by W. H. Freemantle in NPNF 3, series 2 [1892], 423 f.). The relevant passage is reproduced by Harnack, *Geschichte* 1.1, 182 (= Simonetti, lines 23-37).
35. In the same letter mentioned above (ed. Simonetti, lines 46 ff.; Harnack, p. 405 f.).

When we pursue the investigation back behind Dionysius to the beginnings of Christian literature, we find that the apocalypticist John had similar anxieties in his conflict with the heretics. He levelled a curse on anyone who would alter his prophetic book by additions or deletions (Rev. 22.18 f.). Although such language reflects to some degree stylistic conventions, it is nevertheless motivated by John's actual situation (see above, 77 ff.). He had no need to feel threatened by those whose positions were close to his, [170] but rather by those to whom he had so expressed his unblunted antipathy in the letters to the churches (Rev. 1-2) and who, as we have seen, commanded a majority in many communities. How easily they could there lay hands on his work and alter it to their liking. In that way they knocked a major weapon from their opponents' hand, or took away its cutting edge.

It was by no means always necessary to "falsify" in order to administer a telling blow to one's opponent. It was also effective, if there were some evidence of his weakness and inadequacy, not to conceal it behind a cloak of kindness and thus consign it to oblivion, but rather, to drag it into the public spotlight and proclaim it in the marketplace. Perhaps this provides an explanation for the peculiar situation relating to the collected letters of Dionysius of Corinth. We have already noted (above, 126 f.) that along with letters of the Corinthian bishop, the collection also included a reply by Pinytus of Cnossus, which amounted to a harsh rejection of Dionysius. Harnack thinks that Dionysius himself added this rejoinder to the collection of his letters which he had made—"otherwise, how could the letter of Pinytus been included?" [36] To me, that appears doubtful for more than one reason. First, because the contents are hardly complimentary. Further, if Dionysius himself had incorporated pronouncements from the other side along with his own letters, then he surely would have given primary consideration to what the Romans and their Bishop Soter wrote to Corinth, to which he replied by his letter to Rome. But that is not the case. [37] Thus Harnack's question, "Otherwise how could the letter of Pinytus have been included?" hardly decides the issue in his favor, for the letter of Pinytus was as little an actual

36. Harnack, *Briefsammlung*, p. 37.
37. See also Harnack, *Briefsammlung*, p. 79 n. 3.

private letter in the special possession of Dionysius, as was the writing to which Pinytus was responding, which admonished Bishop Pinytus but was addressed to the Knossians as a whole (EH 4.23.7). Similarly, the letter to Soter was directed to the Romans as well (EH 4.23.9).

It seems to me much more probable that Dionysius could not let the letter of Pinytus disappear, odious though it was to him, because its [171] contents were common knowledge. Not he, but his opponents were interested in circulating it more widely by including it in the collection—as a weapon against orthodoxy. How useful sharp rejection of a well-known ecclesiastical bishop and leader must have been to the Marcionites or encratites, even if Pinytus himself were not closely related to such circles. That heretical tampering actually constituted a threat to the collection of letters is proved by the complaint of Dionysius that his letters were falsified by them (see above, 166). Indeed, I can imagine that his cry of rage over the audacity of the heretics was evoked by the unhappy discovery that Pinytus' letter of reply had been inserted into the collection of his letters, strongly detracting from the beneficial effect it was intended to have.

If our view of the early Christian polemical literature and its vicissitudes is at all accurate, then one would have to say that the significance of literature in the ideological conflict of that early period was in some respects greater, and yet in other respects more limited than usually is supposed. Its significance was more weighty in so far as there were numerous writings of all sorts [38] which have disappeared without a trace; but it was also smaller in that the writings known to us led more of a defensive type of existence and were not capable of holding their own ground for very long. The theologian was aware of this writing or that; but, for example, what influence did the literary exchange between the church and Montanism have prior to the time of "the anonymous," or Serapion (see above, 133-137, 142 f.)? All this bypassed the average Christian. And what chanced to reach him by this or that route made little impression. These works hardly overflowed with persuasive power. I am firmly of the opinion that a Tatian had as little success in convincing Greeks that their religion and culture was inferior—his "Exhortation" served primarily as a form of easing his own tensions—as the libellous anti-Montanist

38. On this matter, cf. Bauer, *Wortgottesdienst*, p. 47 f.

writings (see above, 141 f.) succeeded in convicting the Montanists of their error. Basically, such literature was influential only in its own circle of sympathizers, and this effect was itself narrowly limited in time as well as in space. [172]

The use to which the literature of the century or so after the close of the apostolic age was put, in one way or another, in the disputes within Christianity, may still be subjected to an examination that will provide information in a different direction. Of course, we cannot treat the subject exhaustively. We must always remain conscious of the fact that a very important and instructive portion of the relevant writings of this period no doubt has disappeared without a trace, while of another portion we only know the titles—titles that no longer reveal to us whether, or to what extent, the works to which they belonged were *polemical*. Furthermore, the "church" is clearly in a privileged position insofar as it became authoritative bearer and custodian of the tradition. Although we are in a position to name a great number of pronouncedly anti-heretical writers—we are constantly encountering such—we can hardly demonstrate the fact (which cannot seriously be doubted) that heretics also took pen in hand to refute the ecclesiastical teaching, although their literary output also was quite prolific. At one point we do, indeed, hear of a Montanist writing against orthodoxy (see above, 136). But it was occasioned by a publication of the apologist Miltiades. And the ecclesiastical tradition in Eusebius saw to it that orthodoxy also had the last word. "The anonymous" promptly took care of the Montanists once again. We also hear of literary feuding between Bardesanes and the Marcionites (see above, 29). But in contrast to orthodoxy, according to its professional guardians, heresy always seems to be on the defensive, and capable of only a futile resistance at that. It is only occasionally that we are in the fortunate position of being able to read between the lines, such as in the struggle between ecclesiastical Christianity and the Montanist movement (see above, 141-146). Gnosticism, the tradition would have us believe, swallowed the rebukes and "refutations" of the church in silence and essentially confined itself to developing its own views. This attitude attributed to the heterodox is, indeed, not just a false illusion conveyed by the ecclesiastical reports, but has some truth to it insofar as for large areas during the period under investigation heresy constituted Christianity *to such a degree* that a confrontation with [173] the ecclesiastical faith was not necessary and was scarcely even possible. Had that not been the case, it would be impossible to explain the fact that among the rather numerous titles of gnostic writings of which we are still aware,[39] scarcely a single one arouses even a suspicion of an anti-ecclesiastical attitude.

What reason would someone like Basilides have had to fight against the "church" in Alexandria at the time of Hadrian (see above, 48-53)? It seems to have satisfied him to rally his believers around the *Gospel of Basilides;*[40] by means of a commentary to provide the firm foundation and the correct interpretation of this gospel,[41] in contrast to the other gospels current in Egypt—*Gospel of the Hebrews* and *Gospel of the Egyptians*—and to enrich the liturgical life of his communities through psalms and hymns.[42] Isidore, his "true son and disciple" (Hippolytus *Ref.* 7.20) added an ethical treatise as well as some other things.[43] It was up to orthodoxy to take the initiative in the struggle, because it needed first of all to gain a foothold in the area where Basilides was firmly entrenched. So Agrippa Castor composed a polemical writing against Basilides, which Eusebius calls a "devastating refutation by a highly renowned author" (EH 4.7.6). Whether he had personally seen it or had only heard of it in some roundabout way is an open question. He does not quote it verbatim,

39. Cf. Harnack, *Geschichte,* 1.1: 152 ff.; and 2.1: 536-541. [For a convenient and up-to-date catalogue of the "Coptic Gnostic Library" recently discovered near Nag Hammadi in Middle Egypt, see J. M. Robinson, "The Coptic Gnostic Library Today," NTS 14 (1967/68): 383 ff., and 16 (1969/70): 185-190. Thus far nothing in this collection, which is not yet fully published, seems to require modification of the above observation by Bauer; see also below, p. 314 n. 32, and p. 310.]
40. Mentioned by Origen *Homily 1 on Luke.* [For additional information, see the discussion by H.-C. Puech in Hennecke-Schneemelcher, 1: 346 ff.]
41. The so-called *Exēgētica* (in twenty-four books) mentioned by Agrippa Castor in EH 4.7.7 and by Clement of Alexandria *Strom.* 4.(12.)81-83; see also below, 190. [In addition, see Puech in Hennecke-Schneemelcher, 1: 347 f. The Greek text of this material is conveniently reproduced in Völker, *Quellen,* pp. 40 f.; for an ET, see Grant, *Gnosticism Anthology,* pp. 136 f.]
42. Origen *In Job* 21.11 f. (Pitra, *Analecta Sacra,* 2: 368). Cf. the *Muratorian Canon,* lines 83 f.; [and Irenaeus AH 1.24.5 (= 1.19.3), on Basilidean "*incantationes.*"]
43. Isidore's "*Ethics*" is quoted by Clement of Alexandria *Strom.* 3.(1.)1-3 (cf. Epiphanius *Her.* 32.2). [For a convenient collection of this and other fragments, see Völker, *Quellen,* pp. 42 f.; ET in Grant, *Gnosticism Anthology,* pp. 138 ff. See also below, 179.]

but uses the formula: Agrippa Castor says that Basilides did or taught such and such (EH 4.7.7). Thereby he deals with the subject in an extremely superficial manner and also damages his presentation by presuming to claim the following already for the reign of Hadrian: "Now at this time *very many* churchmen fought for the truth and triumphantly defended the apostolic and ecclesiastical teaching with great acumen . . ." (EH 4.7.5; see above, 149-158).

The orthodox tirade against Marcion was concentrated in the West.[44] Justin and the Muratorian fragment derive from Italy; east of there, Dionysius of Corinth [174] and Philip of Gortyna in Crete follow along. Orthodoxy was most fiercely locked in battle with this enemy in western Asia Minor—we know of Polycarp of Smyrna, of the Asiatic presbyter mentioned by Irenaeus as well as of Irenaeus himself (since this is the farthest east that he could be considered to represent), of Melito of Sardis and Rhodon from Asia. And Modestus also, because of his very name, should not be located any farther east; Eusebius (EH 4.25) lists him along with Philip of Gortyna and Irenaeus. Hierapolis (Papias), then, is the easternmost place where there was ecclesiastical opposition to Marcion in Asia Minor. Nicomedia (to which Dionysius of Corinth wrote; EH 4.23.4) takes us only to the northern coast and thus within range of Marcion's home territory.[45] The noise of strife dies away as soon as we turn to the regions of Asia Minor in which we have previously been unable to discover any active signs of "ecclesiastical" life (see above, 81 f.). Otherwise, we learn of (1) an attempt by Theophilus of Antioch, who was beleaguered by heretics and under the ecclesiastical influence of the West, to protect himself and his "ecclesiastical" group from this danger. This undertaking was hardly more skillful or successful than was his refutation of the heathen addressed to Autolycus (*Ad Autolycum*; see above, 18). (2) There are also statements by Clement, who at the end of the second century brought into play for the first time and in a subdued manner something like orthodoxy in Alexandria. (3) And finally, there is the attempt of Bardesanes at a somewhat later time to diminish the previous monop-

44. The material may be found in Harnack, *Marcion*², 314°-327° ("Die Polemiker vor Tertullian" = Beilage 6.1).
45. Hegesippus (in EH 4.22.4-7), with his polemic against the heretics, belongs thoroughly to the West, close to Justin, even though both were originally from the East.

oly of the Marcionites in Edessa, which was as yet quite devoid of all orthodoxy (see above, 29). One gets the impression that in the second century the church posed no real threat to the Marcionite movement from around Hierapolis eastward, while in the West, to the very gates of Rome, the church was its most dangerous enemy.

The Valentinians, whose founder had been active in Rome and Egypt, spread in various forms over the whole empire from the middle of the second century, and still had communities in the East and in Egypt after the middle of the fourth century.[46] [175] In the Marcosian sect, they advanced as far as Gaul already in the second century.[47] The western branch of the Valentinians settled there and in Italy, while the eastern branch was active particularly in Egypt and Syria, and even beyond.[48] The church vehemently opposed this heresy. But when we survey the situation in the second century, as far it can still be determined, we find the same situation with respect to anti-Valentinian writings [49] as was observed in the case of Marcion—such expressions of opposition are not found any farther east than western Asia Minor.[50]

The observations made above concerning the heresies of Marcion and Valentinus and the "ecclesiastical" confrontation with them permit a generalization. Apart from the tempest-tossed island of ecclesiastical orthodoxy within the Christianity of Antioch,[51] and the timid attempt to assist orthodoxy in Egypt to achieve a united existence (see above, 53 ff. and also 170 f.), the *Ecclesiastical History* of Eusebius shows no knowledge at all of "ecclesiastical" life and warfare east of Phrygian Hierapolis until the third century. The greater part of Asia Minor contributed as little to the refutation of the heretics as did Syria, Palestine,[52] and Mesopotamia. And we have seen above (160-165) how necessary it is to give a person like Sextus Julius Africanus every benefit of the doubt in order to certify his ecclesiasti-

46. See Harnack, *Geschichte*, 1.1: 174.
47. E. Preuschen, RPTK³, 20 (1908): 411.
48. Cf. C. Schmidt, RGG², 5 (1931): 1436.
49. Clement of Alexandria, of whose ideological life-setting in Egypt we are aware, can be omitted from consideration at present.
50. Cf. Harnack, *Geschichte*, 1.1: 174, where the opponents are enumerated.
51. On this situation, see above, 63-67, 75, 108-110, and *passim* (Ignatius, Theophilus, Serapion).
52. Whether the agreement of Palestinian church leaders with Roman Easter practice (EH 5.23.3) also extended to matters of doctrine, we do not know. In any event, we hear nothing of the participation of Palestine in the battle with the heretics.

cal orientation. It is just as illegitimate to suppose that in those regions where Christianity was not threatened by heresy it would have developed a unified orthodox position as it is to infer that no Christian communities had existed there at all at that time, thus providing a quite natural explanation for the silence. After all, this problem relates to the areas of Paul's missionary activity in Lycaonia, Pisidia, and Galatia, to his home province, Cilicia, and to the territories stretching from there to the cradle of Christianity, as well as to Palestine itself. The [176] relevant material in Harnack's *Mission and Expansion of Christianity* also suffices to render the above supposition completely impossible.[53]

But surely, if it is possible to deduce from something like the letter of Pliny as much as Harnack does concerning the spread of Christianity in Asia Minor (pp. 331 [= 737 f.]; cf. also p. 347 [= 754]), or if the material cited by Ramsay is assessed from a similar standpoint,[54] the silence of Eusebius about ecclesiastical life in central and eastern Asia Minor is doubly surprising. It is no longer satisfactory merely to express regret and say with Harnack, "our information about the history of the church in Cilicia until the council of Nicaea is quite limited" (p. 324 [= 730 in German [4]]). At the risk of tiring the reader, we must ask once again, why are things this way? Why do so many manifestations of ecclesiastical Christianity reach Eusebius from the western districts, while the East, his own home territory, is silent? In view of what has been ascertained about Edessa, Egypt, and other regions, only *one* answer is possible, namely, that there was no discernible "ecclesiastical" life in central and eastern Asia Minor in the second century. Christianity there was entirely, or predominately, of a different sort. The "heretics" kept to themselves for a long time. But since their own peaceful existence could not be the subject matter of an ecclesiastically oriented attempt at writing history, for which they would only be relevant as objects of rejection, we sense that the silence of Eusebius consistently represents the appropriate style for composing the *historia ecclesiastica*. He did not consider it to be his duty to transmit what he might have learned about the success of the missionary activity of the heretics if it was not repulsed immediately by some counter-attack of orthodoxy. It was not his busi-

53. Harnack, *Mission*[2], 2: 324 ff. (expanded discussion in 4th German edition, pp. 730 ff.)
54. Harnack, *Mission*[2], 2: 358 ff. (expanded in German[4], 766 ff.); the most pertinent works by Ramsay are listed on p. 766 n. 3 of 4th German edition.

ness to fix in the memory of Christianity reference to unchecked errors. And we cannot expect him to include in his account information from the heretical books to which he could not immediately attach the ecclesiastical refutation and rebuttal they deserved.

Consequently, there would be no other way of which I am aware to secure recognition throughout the whole of Christendom at that time for a point of view that was hemmed in by ecclesiastical Christianity, than to suppose that in the regions in which the battle raged, the "heretics" [177] used, to a considerable extent, the same offensive and defensive tactics as were also employed by the "church." Here and there such a hypothesis finds support in occasional references in the sources. I will not repeat what has already been stated in this regard (see above, 132-146, 166-169; cf. also chap. 6). But we should remind ourselves at this point that the books of the churchmen directed against heresy sometimes take the form of polemics against individual heresiarchs or heresies, and sometimes concentrate on certain particularly important controversial issues (see above, 147 f., 170-172). Alongside the doctrinal writing and the polemical writing was the letter. With the writings from churches or church leaders to other churches (see above, 77-81, 93 f., 95 ff., 121 f.) there is also the letter from one individual to another. Concerning the letter from Dionysius of Corinth to the Christian lady Chrysophora, Eusebius tells us nothing more than that he "presented her with the suitable spiritual food" (EH 4.23.13). And the more precise purposes of the letters of Valentinus [55] also elude our grasp because we are not sufficiently informed about their recipients. On the other hand, the aim of the Valentinian Ptolemy in his famous letter (see above, 120) is quite clear. He desired to win the distinguished Christian lady Flora to a gnostic view of Christianity and in so doing discloses how even in Italy toward the end of the second century Gnostics and "ecclesiastically" oriented Christians still could maintain a close personal relationship.[56]

Letters of recommendation, such as already plagued the life of the Apostle Paul (2 Cor. 3:1), play their role. "Take special care," says

55. Preserved by Clement of Alexandria *Strom.* 2.(8.)36, 2.(20.)114, 3.(7.)59 (to Agathopus). [For a convenient collection of the Greek texts, see Völker, *Quellen*, pp. 57 f.; for ET see Grant, *Gnosticism Anthology*, pp. 143 f.]
56. Cf. G. Heinrici, *Die valentinianische Gnosis und die heilige Schrift* (Berlin, 1871), pp. 76 f., 81 f.

the Peter of the pseudo-Clementine materials, "not to believe any teacher who does not bring a recommendation (*testimonium*) from Jerusalem, from James the brother of the Lord or from his successor. For whoever has not gone there and been endorsed there as a qualified and faithful teacher for the proclamation of the word of Christ—I mean, whoever has not obtained a recommendation (*testimonium*) from there—should not be accepted at all. You are not to hope for any prophet or apostle at this time other than us" (*Rec.* 4.35.1-2; similarly *Hom.* 11.35). [178] We have already noticed that Marcion also launched himself into the world equipped with letters of recommendation from his coreligionists in Pontus (see above, 91).

Apparently, a collection of the above-mentioned letters of Valentinus already existed by the time of Clement of Alexandria, who quotes from three of them in the passages listed. Valentinus' adherents chose this method to preserve the important pronouncements of the master and to exploit them to the full for strengthening the inner and outer life of their community. Ecclesiastically oriented groups acted no differently and for analogous purposes gathered the available letters of Ignatius, for example, or of Dionysius of Corinth.[57] Unfortunately we are no longer able to determine whether the collection of Valentinian writings stood in noticeable opposition to a Christianity of a divergent character, as was true of the two ecclesiastical collections. At Philippi, orthodoxy had requested the letters of Ignatius as a weapon in its struggle against docetism (Polycarp *Philippians* 13.2). The anti-heretical attitude of the letters of Dionysius is just as evident, but perhaps because of a counter-move by those under attack (see above, 167 f.) they did not realize their full potential.

Both orthodox and heretic alike seek, by means of literature of all kinds, by letters and collections of letters, and of course also by personal contacts, to extend their influence at home and abroad and to obstruct the path of their opponents wherever they meet. So also, both parties make use of the sermon and the homily, delivered orally as well as circulated in writing; both produce religious poetry,[58]

57. On this point, cf. Harnack, *Briefsammlung.*
58. In AH 1.15.6 (= 1.8.17), Irenaeus quotes the words of a "divinely favored elder" (*ho theophilēs presbytēs*), who polemicized against the gnostic Marcus in verse.

psalms, odes, and other songs; or by means of the apocryphal acts, both introduce an abundance of popular works so as to win the masses. If someone was lacking in creativity, he could always "edit" a work that originated with the other side, thus making it useful for his own cause. In the account of the communities of Vienne and Lyons we find a revelation of the martyr Attalus employed against encratitic tendencies. Alcibiades, another victim of the persecution, led an [179] austere life that allowed him to partake only of bread and water. Attalus, on the strength of divine instruction, forbade Alcibiades to continue this while he was imprisoned and thenceforth he partook of everything without distinction.[59] "The Holy Spirit was their counselor" (EH 5.3.1-3). In heretical gospels (*Gospel of the Egyptians*, Marcion, Tatian) and acts (*Acts of Thomas* 20 and 29), of course, abstinence with respect to food also is preached with reference to Jesus and his inner circle. Here "bread and water" is the motto of the Christian way of life.

It is not clear how the Holy Spirit manifested himself to Attalus. He felt that he was being instructed from heaven in some way thought to be supernatural. If he saw a vision, he was not alone in this, neither within orthodoxy nor with respect to the heretics. Valentinus attributed his teaching to a vision in which he saw a newborn child, which in answer to his question identified himself as the Logos (Hippolytus *Ref.* 6.43). Doubtless the "tragic myth" (*tragikon tina mython*) that was added and that forms the foundation and source for the religious concepts of Valentinus also derives from this vision. Similarly, the fragment of a Valentinian psalm displays a visionary nature.[60] The Valentinian Marcus likewise claimed direct heavenly illumination: "The supreme tetrad," he explained, "descended to him from the invisible and ineffable places in female form—since the world, he says, would not have been able to endure its male form— and revealed to him its own nature and explained the origin of the 'All' (*tēn tōn pantōn genesin*), which it had never before disclosed

---

59. Whether an ancient dungeon was really the best place to change one's diet from bread and water to elegant cuisine is, of course, open to question.
60. Hippolytus *Ref.* 6.37 [Völker, *Quellen*, pp. 59 f.; ET in Grant, *Gnosticism Anthology*, p. 145]. Cf. also Tertullian *Against the Valentinians* 4: "If they shall have added anything new, they immediately call their presumption a revelation and their ingenuity a gift of grace" (*si aliquid novi adstruxerint, revelationem statim appellant praesumptionem et charisma ingenium*).

to any of the gods or men, to him alone in the following words . . ."
(Irenaeus AH 1.14.1[= 1.8.1]).

Here, moreover, we have one of the isolated instances in which
we hear something to the effect that heretics responded to the re-
proofs of the church. Hippolytus, before his report of the vision of
Valentinus, says about Marcus that the blessed "elder" Irenaeus had
been [180] very frank in his refutation and described the baptisms and
other practices intended to bring salvation. When this came to the
attention of some of the adherents of Marcus, they denied that they
had any such practices at all—"they are always encouraged to deny."
For this reason Hippolytus went into everything with the greatest
care and even investigated the most carefully guarded secrets (*all'
oude to arrēton autōn elathen hēmas*). Hippolytus seized the opportunity to declare that the vision of Marcus was a deliberate
fraud—in order to make a name for himself Marcus imitated his
teacher Valentinus, and claimed that he himself also experienced in-
timate communication with heaven (*Ref.* 6.43[a]). Incidentally, from
what the churchman Hippolytus says in this passage it seems that
the Valentinians were not at all in agreement with what Hippolytus
thought he had uncovered as their most secret mysteries.

Outstanding personalities among the Montanists were likewise
granted divine visions and gained new knowledge or confirmation
of previous opinions therefrom. "The gospel is preached in such a
manner [61] by the holy prophetess Prisca [Priscilla]," says Tertullian,
"that only a holy servant would be qualified to serve holiness. 'For
purity,' she says, 'is the unifying bond; and *they* [i.e. the holy] *see
visions*, and when they incline their face downward, they then hear
distinct voices, which are as salutary as they are secret'" (*Exhortation to Chastity* 10). Epiphanius gives an account of the experience
of a prominent Montanist prophetess [62] in her own words: "In the
form of a woman, adorned with a shining garment, Christ came to
me and implanted wisdom within me and revealed to me that this
place [i.e. Pepuza] is holy and that it is here that the heavenly
Jerusalem will come down" (*Her.* 49.1). The Montanist acts of the

---

61. The "gospel" preaching of Prisca is intentionally joined to a "prophetic oracle
of the Old Testament" and a word "of the Apostle" (Paul = Rom. 8.6; see above,
136 n. 13) and is apparently considered to be equally valid.
62. He is not exactly sure whether it had been Quintilla or Priscilla, but in any
event she was *apatōmenē* (deceived).

martyr Perpetua from the time of Tertullian tell of several visions of Perpetua (chapters 4, 7, 8, 10) and of one of Saturus (chapters 11-13), through which the martyrs learned what lay ahead of them and what they could expect after their death.[63] [181] In these cases the divine communication was mediated by dreams, since we always hear that those who received it awoke later.

Finally, the attempt by the Montanist Tertullian to utilize the utterances of a "sister" with visionary powers as a source of knowledge is well known. He can present his view on the corporeality of the soul with such confidence because he knew that it had been confirmed by a revelation.[64] The gift of prophecy and the capacity for receiving supernatural visions had by no means ceased with John and his Apocalypse. There is, in fact, a woman endowed with the "gifts of revelation" (*charismata revelationum*) in Tertullian's own community. During the Sunday services she experiences Spirit-induced ecstasies. She converses with the angels and sometimes with the Lord himself, sees and hears mysteries, discerns what is in people's hearts, and leads the sick onto the path of healing. Whether there are scriptures being read, psalms sung, addresses delivered, or prayers offered, she obtains from them the material for her visions. "Once I happened to say something about the soul—I no longer recall what it was—when the Spirit came upon this sister." After the service she disclosed what she had seen; how the soul had appeared to her in bodily form, almost tangible, yet at the same time delicate, luminous, and the color of air, and thoroughly human in form (*forma per omnia humana*). Tertullian knows how difficult it is to gain credence for such a phenomenon. Thus he emphatically states that he has recorded everything with the utmost care so as to make verification possible. He invokes God as witness that he is telling the plain truth and appeals to the Apostle as surety for the fact that even in the church of later times there would still be *charismata* (see 1 Cor.

63. [For the text, see C. J. M. J. van Beek, *Passio Sanctarum Perpetuae et Felicitatis, latine et graece*, Florilegium Patristicum, 43 (Bonn, 1938). ET by W. H. Shewring, *The Passion of SS. Perpetua and Felicity: New edition and translation of the Latin text* . . . (London, 1931); partial ET also in H. A. Musurillo, *The Fathers of the Primitive Church* (New York: New American Library, Mentor-Omega paperback, 1966), pp. 161-172.]
64. *On the Soul* 9. [For a convenient ET of most of the passage referred to here, see Stevenson, *New Eusebius*, p. 187.]

12.1 ff.). Yet for all that he angrily goes on to say, "Do you actually refuse to believe, even though the fact itself speaks so convincingly!"

Since the mysteries of the supernal world were being disclosed to the heretic as well as to the orthodox at times of supremely heightened blessedness, we should not be surprised to find both sides cultivating that type of literature which depends on such visions and takes its departure from them, namely apocalyptic. There were revelations of both ecclesiastical as well as heretical orientation, and others that cannot be assigned to either side, if one feels compelled to make hard and fast distinctions.[65] [182]

Alongside the seer, but not always sharply distinguished from him, stood the prophet, who also was in direct contact with heaven and a mediator of divine knowledge, and thus was in a position to offer strong support for the accepted teaching by means of his prophetic declarations. We have already taken note of the orthodox seer and prophet John as he contended with heresy. He violently rejects his opponent Jezebel, who falsely called herself a prophetess (Rev. 2.20). The attitude of "Jezebel" toward John surely was no different.[66] The *Acts of Paul*, which stem from the same region, depict the Corinthians as complaining to the Apostle Paul about the false teachers Simon and Cleobius, who firmly repudiate the Old Testament prophets, but giving credence, on the other hand, to the revelations granted to Theonoe.[67] Basilides appealed to the prophets Barcabbas and Barcoph, as well as to some others who in the opinion of his ecclesiastical opponents Agrippa Castor and Eusebius never existed (EH 4.7.7). And Isidore, his "true son and disciple," wrote *Exēgētika* "of the prophet Parchor" (Clement of Alexandria *Strom.* 6.[6.]53.2; see also 170 n. 43, 190). The Ophite sect of Archontics boasted of the prophets Martiades and Marsianus (Epiphanius *Her.* 40.7) while the Gnostic Apelles placed great value in the revelations and prophecies of the prophetess Philumene, who furnished him with the material

---

65. In this connection, see H. Weinel, "Die Apokalyptik des Urchristentums," in Hennecke[2], pp. 298-302.
66. The distinction drawn by *Hermas* and the *Didache*, as well as earlier by Paul, between genuine and false prophets, does not fully coincide with that between true and deceitful doctrine.
67. Cf. Hennecke-Schneemelcher, 2: 374 (= "3 *Corinthians*" 1.8 ff.). For the Latin version and the recently discovered Greek text, see above, 42 n. 99.

for his work, "Phaneroseis." [68] Of course, the churchman Rhodon of Asia thought that this virgin was possessed by a demon (EH 5.13.2).

For Montanism, prophecy is something so characteristic that Tertullian calls the movement "the new prophecy," [69] and prophets of both sexes play an outstanding role in it. The Spirit, or Paraclete, governs life and teaching through these his instruments in such a way that human resistance is excluded. That is how the founder describes the overwhelming power of the Spirit on the basis of his own experience,[70] and Maximilla avers that [183] whether she wanted to or not, she was forced by the Lord to receive the knowledge of God (Epiphanius *Her.* 48.13). Under such influence, she predicted the coming of wars and revolts (according to the "anonymous" EH 5.16.18) and declared that with her the prophetic period was at an end, so that now all that remained to be expected was the end of the world (Epiphanius *Her.* 48.2). The Paraclete expressly forbade flight in time of persecution (Tertullian *On Flight During Persecution* 11) and limited marriage by prohibiting it a second time (Tertullian *Against Marcion* 1.29; cf. *On Monogamy* 104). Concerning the procession of the Logos from God (*Against Praxeas* 8), the mystery of the trinity (*Against Praxeas* 30), and the heavenly Jerusalem (*Against Marcion* 3.24), Tertullian felt that he was enlightened by the Paraclete or by sayings of the new prophecy. His work *On the Soul* concludes with the words: "And the Paraclete most frequently recommended this also, if one shall have received his words by recognizing them as promised spiritual gifts." [71] The book *On the Resurrection of the Flesh* ends much the same way (63). In the opinion of Tertullian certain ambiguous passages of Holy Scripture have provided a foothold for heretics. But that is no longer the case, and the heretics are in a hopeless position. For the Holy Spirit has now eliminated all the obscurities and alleged parables that previously

68. Cf. Harnack, *Marcion*[2], pp. 177 f., 321°, 371°.
69. *Against Praxeas* 30; *Against Marcion* 3.24; *On the Resurrection of the Flesh* 63.
70. Epiphanius *Her.* 48.4. [For ET of this and some other Montanist utterances, see Grant, *Second Century*, pp. 95 f., and Stevenson, *New Eusebius*, p. 113. The texts are conveniently collected by Bonwetsch, *Montanismus* (and later in KT 129 [1914]) and Hilgenfeld, *Ketzergeschichte*, pp. 591-595.] Cf. also the explanation of the Montanists, that the prophet has no control over himself [183] when the Spirit takes hold of him, in Didymus of Alexandria (fragments from his *Exposition on Acts*, PG 39, 1677.)
71. *On the Soul* 58.8: *hoc etiam paracletus frequentissime commendavit, si qui sermones eius ex agnitione promissorum charismatum admiserit.*

existed by means of a more clear and penetrating proclamation of the entire mystery in the new prophecy that flows forth from the Paraclete. "Draw from his spring, and you will never thirst for any other teaching."

Of course, Tertullian himself realized just how much this kind of argument depended on the receptivity of the person to be instructed. This is the reason for his angry cry, "Do you actually refuse to believe, even though the fact itself speaks so convincingly!" (above, 179). The Paraclete had come so much later than Jesus. His task is to secure the revelation of Jesus against misinterpretation, but also to complete it by supplementation, without thereby coming into contradiction with Jesus. This makes argumentation difficult and puts it at a disadvantage by comparison with the straight line which in the church runs from Jesus through the apostles to the present time. The Montanists [184] believe in the disclosures of their prophets. But the validity of such a conviction is not, like the validity of belief in the apostolic tradition for the others, self-evident; it needs support. The Montanists complained about their opponents: "You do not believe that there could still be prophets after the appearance of the Lord; but the Savior himself said, 'Behold, I am sending prophets to you' [Matthew 23.23]" (Didymus of Alexandria *On the Trinity* 3.41.3 = PG 39, 984).

The attempt to rely for support on contemporary prophetic phenomena or on a prophetism of the quite recent past was beset with many difficulties which made it impossible to conquer the scepticism of which Tertullian was so keenly aware. We know what the opponents replied. The prophets, to whom the heretics appeal, never existed or else they were victims of demonic possession (see above, 177 n. 62, 180). And it is impossible that a discourse delivered in a state of frenzy could be induced by the spirit of God (see above, 136). Thus it also follows that the predictions spoken by such persons are not fulfilled, and so disclose the putrid fount from which they come (see above, 139 f.). And if one adds to this their moral inferiority and the way in which God evidently turns his back on them by the type of death imposed upon them (see above, 134), then anyone with understanding is sufficiently informed.

The appeal to prophecy and the contention of the prophets and their associates concerning the source and reliability of the revelation

they proclaim is ancient. We have already spoken about the apocalypticist John and his prophetic adversaries (above, 179). Nearly
contemporary with him may be the "Paul" of 2 Thessalonians, who
enjoins his readers not to be shaken in their faith, "Either by spirit,
or by word, or by letter purporting to be from us" (2.2, *mēte dia
pneumatos mēte dia logou mēte di' epistolēs hōs di' hēmōn*). No
matter how one interprets the details of the passage, it is clear that
the author considers the teaching which he presents as Pauline-
apostolic to be threatened by a view that relies, among other things,
on manifestations of the Spirit (*pneuma*)—i.e. on utterances of a
prophetic nature. Moreover, he reckons with the possibility that someone might attack him by appealing to the authority of Pauline statements—indeed even bringing forth a letter which claims to be written
by the Apostle to the Gentiles. [185] We can thus observe how, alongside the utterances of Christian prophets, use is also made in the
conflict of ideas first of the recollection of Paul's oral preaching and
then of letters written by him which did not enjoy general acceptance
in Christendom. For the one side, both are taken to be authentic
and therefore decisive, but for the other they are considered forged
and therefore misleading.

We know that the anxiety over pseudo-apostolic writings and the
effects they produced was no chimera, but was thoroughly justified.
The Muratorian fragment (lines 63-67) mentions letters to the Laodiceans [72] and to the Alexandrians forged in the name of Paul in the
interest of the heresy of Marcion, and "many other" of the same
sort which the Catholic church rejects.[73] For its own part, orthodoxy
enriched the deposit of apostolic epistolary literature in the interest
of opposing heresy through the pastoral Epistles, the so-called third
epistle to the Corinthians, and the second epistle of Peter.[74] To this
category also belongs the attempt of those heretics who did not rely
on apostles for support, but appealed to their own spiritual fathers

72. In this connection see A. von Harnack, "Der apokryphe Brief des Apostels
Paulus an die Laodicener, eine marcionitische Fälschung aus der 2. Hälfte des 2.
Jahrhunderts," Sb Berlin 27 for 1923; also *Marcion²*, pp. 134* ff.
73. Since the fragment subsequently speaks about the Catholic Epistles, the "many
others" must have reference to pseudo-Pauline writings; of course, this hardly
proves that the author actually knew more than the two named. But his concern
about a brisk heretical activity in this area of pseudonymous literature is hardly
artificial.
74. Concerning literary works of apostles on the boundary line between correct
and false belief, see above, 58.

and attributed writings to the latter that were useful for their own interests. Thus Hippolytus knew and used a book with the title "*Great Proclamation*" (*Apophasis megalē*), which purports to be a work of Simon Magus, but doubtless is forged (*Ref. 6.9.4-6.18.7*).

Of course there were also genuine fragments of the primitive tradition which were zealously collected to use for support and confirmation of the teaching as well as for defense and offense in the ideological controversy. We have already spoken of the letters of Valentinus (above, 175). Similarly we already are aware of the Montanist collection of those prophetic utterances essential to their movement (above, 142). From the beginning, the Marcionites [186] treasured the *Antitheses* of their master as a basic confessional document and placed it alongside the gospel restored by him to its pristine splendor and the unadulterated Paul as the bases for all authentic Christianity. Of course, with respect to Marcion not only does his treatment of the transmitted text easily give the impression of being arbitrary, but the yawning chasm between the activity of the Apostle to the Gentiles and the appearance of his reviver also stands unbridged.

In this respect the "church" was in a better position. For it, there were no places at which the linkage back to the beginning appeared to be broken, whereby doubts could arise. Even before the church's tradition had achieved complete continuity and strength, the attempt had been made to reach back by means of the "elders" (see above, 119) into the apostolic period and even behind it to Jesus. Even so, not everything that could be desired was achieved thereby. For it was now no longer sufficient, as perhaps it had still been in the apostolic epoch, simply to guard and hand on, or by grouping the materials appropriately, to make useful for the life of the community what one learned either from written or oral sources of the life and teaching of Jesus—i.e. concerning the most important thing of all, that which is absolutely basic. In the course of time, the traditional material had not only swollen greatly, but it provided quite diverse pictures. Alongside the synoptic type of picture, there came John; alongside the canonical gospels were the many apocryphal gospels which were often pronouncedly heretical. One had to contend with error even with respect to the correct understanding of the earthly Lord and of the revelation provided by him.

Irenaeus is not the only one to say of the heretics in the introduction to his great polemical work that "they deal recklessly with the sayings of the Lord, becoming evil interpreters of the good things which have been spoken." [75] Dionysius of Corinth also complains about certain people who falsify the "dominical writings" (*kyriakai graphai;* EH 4.23.12), and his contemporary who expresses himself in the *Epistle of the Apostles* calls down eternal judgment on those who corrupt the teaching and falsify the word. [76] Polycarp already laments that heretics [187] twist the "sayings of the Lord" (*logia tou kuriou*) and draw from them what suits their own sinful desires. The Paul of the apocryphal correspondence with Corinth is thinking of the false teachers there when he writes: "My Lord Jesus Christ will come quickly, since he can no longer endure the error of those who falsify his word." [77] Similarly, the letter of Peter to James at the beginning of the pseudo-Clementine *Homilies* [78] unmistakably betrays concern for maintaining the purity of the apostolic memory of Jesus in opposition to heretical misinterpretation. Peter complains:

> Certain people have already during my lifetime attempted to alter my words to teach the dissolution of the law through all sorts of tricks of interpretation as though I held such a view but did not have the courage to proclaim it openly. Not in the least! This would be to work against the law of God, which was proclaimed through Moses and confirmed as eternally valid by our Lord. For he said, 'Heaven and earth will pass away, but not even a single jot or tittle of the law will ever pass away' [cf. Matt. 5.18 and 24.35] (2.4-5).

Thus it is an important task of the ecclesiastical teacher not only to collect and to classify the gospel material, but also to assist in the correct understanding of that which is approved so as to protect it against false interpretations. That was the goal that Papias set for himself and for which he strove in his five books of *Explanations of the Sayings of the Lord* (*Logiōn kuriakōn exēgēseōs suggrammata pente;* EH 3.39.1). He appears to have spoken so disapprovingly

75. AH 1. preface: *rhadiourgountes ta logia kuriou, exēgētai kakoi tōn kalōn eirēmenōn genomenoi.* Cf. also Tertullian *Prescription against Heretics* 38: the heretics practice falsification of the scriptures as well as of their interpretations.
76. *Epistula Apostolorum* 50 [ET by R. E. Taylor in Hennecke-Schneemelcher, 1: 227, from the German of H. Duensing (see also pp. 189-191 for introductory discussion by Duensing)].
77. "3 *Corinthians,*" verse 3 [= 3.3 in Hennecke-Schneemelcher, 2: 375].
78. [ET by G. Ogg in Hennecke-Schneemelcher, 2: 111 f. See further below, 198-199].

about Luke, the gospel of Marcion (if he took notice of it at all), that Eusebius hesitated to include his judgment in the *Ecclesiastical History*.[79] In fact the two other synoptics do not appear to have satisfied him completely either. Yet he sees their deficiencies only in certain gaps in the account and structural weakness in Mark, and in the way the Greek language is handled in Matthew (EH 3.39.15-16). He had no doubt about the apostolic origin [188] of the contents. Indeed, the Markan apostolic material, which derives from the teachings of Peter, stands forth all the more clearly when the outward form of Mark's gospel is abandoned. Objections of the opponents, who wish to argue that what is true of the form applies also to the content, can be countered successfully by this approach. In a similar way, the Alexandrians sought to rescue the *epistle to the Hebrews* for Paul (cf. EH 6.14.2, 6.25.11-14).

But if the criticism of Mark and Matthew has its basis in the controversy with heretics and the gospel writings they supported, we no longer need to explain it by appealing to the hypothesis that Papias evaluated the two synoptic gospels by using the Fourth Gospel as the standard [80] and thereby became aware of their inadequacies.[81] A standard gospel by which one evaluates apostolic gospels and traditions must without qualification derive from the same origin itself. That Papias had such an attitude toward the Fourth Gospel, however, is no longer as clear to me as when I prepared the third edition of my commentary on John.[82] The only evidence in support of the supposition that Papias considered the Fourth Gospel to be a work of the apostle John is provided by the ancient gospel prologues recently treated by D. de Bruyne and A. von Harnack, which may belong to the period around the year 180.[83] According to the prologue to John, Papias of Hierapolis, the beloved disciple of John, claimed

79. Cf. in this connection Jülicher-Fascher, *Einleitung*[7], p. 312. One should also keep in mind here the position of Papias with respect to Paul (see below, 214 f.). On the other hand, it should be noted that Eusebius also has suppressed the favorable judgment of Papias concerning the Johannine *Apocalypse* (cf. W. Bousset, *Die Offenbarung des Johannes*[2], Meyer *Kommentar* 16[6] [1906], pp. 19 f.).
80. Jülicher-Fascher, *Einleitung*[7], pp. 283, 396.
81. What Papias says about Matthew, especially as regards its content, can hardly be the result of a comparison with the gospel of John.
82. W. Bauer, *Das Johannesevangelium*[3], HbNT 6 (1933): 241 f.
83. Donatien de Bruyne, "Les plus anciens prologues latins des Évangiles," *Revue Bénédictine*, 40 (1928): 193-214, Harnack, *Evangelien-Prologe*. [For ET and discussion, see Schoedel, *Polycarp . . . Papias*, pp. 121-123.]

to have transcribed the Fourth Gospel correctly at the dictation of his teacher; and he appended to this the remark that the heretic Marcion had been rejected by him because of his false teaching and then also by John. But on chronological grounds alone, the latter claim cannot have come from the works of Papias. It assumes not that Papias, as a rather young man, put himself at the disposal of the aged apostle in Asia,[84] but that [189] he, as leader of the church in Hierapolis, can repudiate heretics just as John does in Ephesus. Thus the most that could be applied to Papias is the assertion that he had been a personal disciple of John, the son of Zebedee, and in turn, that this John was the author of the Fourth Gospel.

This, however, is nothing but the ecclesiastical point of view, as represented by Irenaeus at the time of the origin of the prologue when he defends the apostolic origin of the Fourth Gospel and also pictures Papias as a personal disciple of John of Zebedee (AH 5.33.4). It has been shown often enough that the latter is not true, on the basis of the criticism which Eusebius, relying on Papias himself, levels against Irenaeus with regard to this passage.[85] But then the other item claiming that the Fourth Gospel had been written by the apostle John,[86] which appears to be intimately bound to this in the Papias material of the prologue, hardly could have come from Papias himself. Only on the basis of such a hypothesis is it possible also to account for the attitude of Eusebius, who withholds from us any indication of Papias' opinion concerning the origin of the Fourth Gospel. The idea that Papias, the diligent collector of ancient traditions of the Lord, was unfamiliar with the Fourth Gospel is as unlikely as the suggestion that Eusebius, who was jubilant to have found 1 John used by Papias (EH 3.39.17), would have suppressed a viewpoint of Papias that was in agreement with the later outlook of orthodoxy. Thus the situation with regard to the Fourth Gospel must have been much the same as with the third. Either Papias expressed himself

---

84. According to the conclusion of the prologue to Luke, the Fourth Gospel is supposed to have been written "in Asia." [This reading appears in the Latin version, but not in the preserved Greek manuscript of the prologue to Luke; cf. e.g. K. Aland (ed.), *Synopsis Quattuor Evangeliorum* (Stuttgart: Württembergische Bibelanstalt, 1964), p. 533. For ET, see Grant, *Second Century*, p. 93: "John the apostle, one of the twelve, wrote the Apocalypse on the island of Patmos, and after that the gospel."]

85. EH 3.39.1-7. See for example, Bauer, *Johannesevangelium*[3], p. 242.

86. This John is clearly meant; see the end of the prologue to Luke (above, n. 84).

in an unfavorable manner, or he kept silent also with respect to this gospel, a silence sufficiently significant to one who has understanding. For Papias, the contents of the Fourth Gospel apparently belonged to the long-winded prattle in which the great masses took pleasure, to the "foreign commandments," but not to the truth as it was given by the Lord to the believers and is contained in the uniform tradition of the church and which is rooted in the circle of the twelve (EH 3.39.3-4).

As long as one is not bound to the dogma of the fourfold gospel, infallible because it is inspired, one can scarcely conceal the deviations of the last canonical gospel from the others. And whoever, with Papias, rediscovers the attitude of the twelve apostles concerning the life and teaching of Jesus in the books of [190] Matthew and Mark/Peter, will not easily free himself from serious reservations about the presentation in the Fourth Gospel. It is even more difficult for him to attribute this gospel, which like that of Luke is being used by heretics, to one of the closest friends of Jesus and even to value and treat it as Holy Scripture, especially when he is not forced to do so by any authority. In the gospels of Matthew and Mark Papias considered himself to be in contact with the apostolic-ecclesiastical tradition on the life and teaching of Jesus; the other two gospels are at least suspect to him—the gospel of Luke because of misuse, since the worst of the heretics of his day made use of it, and the Fourth Gospel, no doubt, because of its content, origin, and the friends it had made. After all, the preference of the Montanists and Valentinians for the Fourth Gospel shows us that ecclesiastical circles were not the first in which it was recognized as a canonical expression of a particular religious persuasion. And this deficiency was in no way compensated for by its particular suitability as a weapon in the battle against Marcion.[87]

It would seem to me, as we attempt to understand the place Papias occupies with respect to the gospels of Luke and of John, and within the history of early Christian literature in general,[88] that we do well to keep in mind that he found himself in a particularly exposed outpost. He was situated, so we have discovered, at the easternmost

---

87. See W. Bauer, review of Harnack's *Marcion*[1] (1921), in the *Göttinger Gelehrte Anzeigen* 183 (1923): 12 n. 1.
88. Concerning his relation to Paul and to the Apostle's letters, see below, 214 f.

point that the church in opposition to heretics succeeded in occupying in Asia Minor, or indeed anywhere (see above, 171 f.). He offered resistance there with the realization that he was dealing with a superior force. At least, he explains that his anti-heretically conditioned perspective with reference to the materials of the gospel tradition set before him the task of excising everything that delights the "great majority" (*hoi polloi*). He is convinced that to carry out this plan means to sacrifice the bulk (*ta polla*) of the material. But it is also clear to him that what he rejects has nothing to do with the truth, nor with the commandments which the Lord gave to the believers, but it is foreign in origin and nature (EH 3.39.3). Since he therefore knows that he is limited in his influence to the minority of Christians in Hierapolis, [191] he quite consciously withdraws to that which he, from his ecclesiastical standpoint, judges to be an authentic apostolic heritage.

In his literary endeavors on behalf of orthodoxy, moreover, Papias did not think that he had to limit himself in any way to the four gospels of the New Testament or to that material in them which he considered valid. He also collected all sorts of other material from written as well as oral sources (see EH 3.39.4,11). In addition to the highly treasured accounts stemming from the twelve, he also referred to an *Explanation of the Words of the Lord* (*tōn tou kuriou logōn diēgēseis*) by a certain Aristion of the postapostolic generation, and to certain "traditions" (*paradoseis*) by a contemporary of Aristion, "John the elder" (EH 3.39.14; cf. 3.39.4). In terms of content, the material dealt with "strange parables of the savior and teachings from him," and indeed with some matters that Eusebius would like to relegate immediately to the realm of the mythological, namely all sorts of phantasies concerning the millennial kingdom (EH 3.39.11-12a). Of course, even here Papias could appeal to the apostles, as Eusebius reluctantly admits; but Papias had not grasped the mystical symbolic sense of the expressions (EH 3.39.12b). Thus Papias, who wanted to smite the heretics by means of exegesis of the Lord's words, is himself opposed by the same means and judged to be in error.

The statements of Jesus concerning the glories of the new kingdom fit well into the context of a gospel and are found inserted into a conversation of Jesus with the unbelieving traitor Judas in an account of Irenaeus concerning Papias.[89] Nevertheless, other references could give rise to the supposition that Papias, in the only work he composed (so EH 3.39.1, depending on Irenaeus), did not confine himself to the life of Jesus but went beyond that into the subsequent period. He deals not only with the death of the traitor Judas—and that in a way which really denies the account a place in a written gospel—but also with the martyrdom of the Zebedees;[90] with a peculiar experience of Justus Barsabbas, who first gained significance for the community after the departure of Jesus (Acts 1.23); and with a resuscitation of a corpse, attested by the daughters of Philip (EH 3.39.3 f.). Nevertheless, it does not seem impossible that even this material could have been included in a collection and interpretation of gospel traditions; the account about the death of the Zebedees perhaps as an exegesis of Mark 10.38 f. = Matt. 20.22 f. [192]

The book of Hegesippus indeed bore the title "*Memoirs*" (*Hypomnēmata*, EH 4.22.1), but it summed up "the unadulterated tradition of the apostolic preaching in simplest form" (EH 4.8.2) in opposition to gnosticism. Thus, he also drew together for ecclesiastical use reminiscences from earliest times. Above all, Hegesippus appealed to primitive Christian history in support of the view that during the lifetime of the apostles there had as yet been no heretics. At that time the church had been a holy and unstained virgin, and if there were already any people who intended to falsify the life-giving proclamation, they kept themselves concealed in darkness. Only when the holy choir of apostles died and that generation passed away which was privileged to hear with its own ears the divine wisdom, did the conspiracy of godless error begin through seduction by the false teachers. Henceforth, the *gnosis* falsely so-called (cf. 1 Tim. 6.20) sought to rebel against the apostolic preaching of truth (EH 3.32.7-8). It can be imagined that such a reconstruction was possible only by means of thoroughgoing "exegesis." Among other things this sort of

---

89. Irenaeus AH 5.33.3 f. [ET and discussion in Schoedel, *Polycarp . . . Papias*, pp. 94-96.] Cf. Bauer, *Leben Jesu*, pp. 174 f.; also pp. 244 n. 1, 294 n. 1, 367, 403 f.

90. [The Judas story is from "Apollinaris" (probably of Laodicaea; fourth century), as preserved in catenae and commentaries; see Schoedel, *Polycarp . . . Papias*, pp. 111 f. for ET and discussion. Papias' accounts of the martyrdoms of James and John are referred to by Philip of Side (fifth century) and George Syncellus (ninth century); see Schoedel, pp. 117-121. In the same passage, Philip of Side also alludes to the next two accounts mentioned above.]

"exegesis" finds that the heretics had manifested their moral degeneration by causing Simeon to suffer martyrdom as a result of their informing against him (EH 3.32.6 and 2; cf. 3.19-20.1).

The heretics seized on the same means in order to give the primitive tradition a twist in their direction. Basilides not only made use of a gospel of his own, but he sought to secure its contents through a commentary in twenty-four books which bore the title "Interpretations" (Exēgētika; see above, 170 n. 41). The gnostic found justification for pursuing his own exegesis of the words of the Lord from the conviction that Jesus spoke to the general public only in parables, but that he unravelled these to his disciples in secret (Theodotus in Clement of Alexandria Excerpts from Theod. 66). Thus, the meaning of his proclamation was not at all self-evident. But the exegetical effort was in no way restricted to the gospel material. Wherever a source of revelation bubbled forth, it required a suitable container. Isidore interpreted the proclamations of Parchor, a Basilidean "prophet," in his "Interpretations of the prophet Parchor" (Exēgētika tou prophētou Parchor; see above, 179). The accepted approach to interpreting such prophets was also suitable for interpreting the Old Testament, where the latter was acknowledged and thus used. Julius Cassianus appears [193] to have dealt even with Old Testament material in his "Interpretations" (Exēgētika; Clement of Alexandria Strom. 1.[21.]101.2). And from the orthodox perspective, Dionysius of Corinth appended to his instructions "interpretations of divine scriptures" (Graphōn Theiōn Exēgēseis, EH 4.23.6). Similarly Irenaeus passed on the interpretations of divine Scriptures by an "apostolic elder" (EH 5.8.8). At this juncture we are faced with the question, what is the general significance of this literature which exegesis so energetically seeks to master?

Before we turn to this subject in the next chapter, however, we should attempt to add a word about the relative sizes of orthodoxy and heresy to what was said at the beginning of the section on the geographical distribution of the two outlooks (see, e.g. 172 f.). As a point of departure, let me refer back to what has been said earlier (173 f.) concerning Eusebius' silence about the success of heresy—a silence to which he is entitled from his perspective as an "ecclesiastical" historian. But although the tone with which he speaks of orthodoxy may be permissible from his point of view, it is no less in need of correction for a historical approach. He tries to make the best of everything, and manifests a tendency to move churchmen as close as possible to the generation of the apostles (see above, 63 f. and 150) and to push their writings as far back as he can into the apostolic age, while he obscures the chronology of the heretics so that they appear to be more recent.[91] He also shows, as we have already noticed (see above, e.g. 156-158 n. 2), an interest in displaying a very rich and universal anti-heretical literature already in the second century—a claim that immediately provokes scepticism. In the same vein Eusebius is guilty of a serious misuse of the superlative (*myrioi* = "countless," *pleistoi* = "very many," *pantes* = "all," etc.) when he deals with the church, its size, its influence, its success, its champions, its sacrifices, and the like, even in cases where the particular piece of evidence he reports actually should have made him more moderate in his claims.

What an incredible outburst of faith, worlds away from all reality, characterizes the situation in the apostolic era in this presentation! In connection with Psalm 18.5, EH 2.3.2 comments: "And truly in every city and village ("of the whole world" [194] according to 2.3.1), like a filled threshing floor, arose communities with countless members and a huge multitude crowded together."[92] The apostles endure "countless" (*myria*) mortal dangers in Judea (3.5.2), Paul knows "countless" (*myria*) mysteries (3.24.4), and he has "countless co-workers" (*myrioi synergoi*, 3.4.4). In the apostolic age the followers of Jesus consist of "twelve apostles, seventy disciples, and countless others as well" (*dōdeka men apostoloi, hebdomēkonta de mathētai, alloi te epi toutois myrioi*, 3.24.5). Even in the postapostolic period "very many marvelous wonders" (*pleistai paradoxoi dunameis*) are occurring and close-packed hordes of unbelievers come over to Christianity on the first hearing of the gospel (3.37.3). At the time of Basilides (around the year 130) "very many churchmen" (*pleistoi ekklēsiastikoi andres*) contend for the apostolic and ecclesiastical doctrine. But only "some" took pen in hand (4.7.5)—thus Eusebius

91. See the Schwartz (GCS) edition of EH, 3: 24 ff.
92. It is difficult to reproduce so much exuberance in a translation: *ana pasas poleis te kai kōmas . . . myriandroi kai pamplētheis athroōs ekklēsiai sunestēkesan.* Cf. also EH 2.13.1 [with its reference to how the faith was being spread abroad "among all men" at the time of Simon Magus].

restricts his treatment and thereby relegates the matter to an area no longer subject to verification. Then only a single one is named, Agrippa Castor (4.7.6). Hegesippus, who is associated with Agrippa Castor in 4.8.1 (a convenient arrangement for Eusebius' purposes), has been borrowed from the succeeding generation. This Hegesippus, so we hear, met with "very many bishops" *(pleistoi episkopoi)* on his trip to Rome, all of whom advocated the same teaching. But besides Rome, specific mention is limited to Corinth (4.22.1 ff.). Thus in no way can we consider Hegesippus as providing evidence for the presence of a widespread orthodox church which flourished even in the East. Dionysius of Corinth puts himself at the service of *all* the churches (4.23.1). Polycarp is snatched away through very great persecutions (*megistoi diōgmoi*, 4.15.1), but according to 4.15.45 the total of those martyred from Smyrna and Philadelphia is twelve. Myriads (*myriades*) of martyrs under Marcus Aurelius are mentioned in 5.preface.1. However this number is arrived at by treating the multitude of martyrs among *one* group (i.e. in Gaul) as though it represented a general average for the whole world (see also 5.2.1).

I will forego continuing this easy task of assembling even more evidence of this sort from Eusebius' *Ecclesiastical History*. The above is sufficient to remove any inclination I might have to take such assertions seriously. Except where he is quoting from earlier authors, only the individual pieces of information presented by Eusebius, examined with the necessary critical attitude, are of value. [195] If we cannot establish any firm foothold on the basis of what Eusebius himself contributes, we must proceed on the basis of what we have already been able to ascertain by inference. It seemed to us that orthodoxy, as seen from Rome's vantage point, in general reached only to western Asia Minor, approximately to Hierapolis, during the second century (above, 171-173). Beyond this there was an orthodox minority in Antioch (above, 172 and 91-93 on the Johannine Epistles). But this in no way means that orthodoxy gave its stamp to the Christianity that existed everywhere up to Hierapolis. On the contrary, even in Hierapolis orthodoxy evidently is a rear-guard movement (above, 187 f.). Similarly, certain of the letters in the Apocalypse indicate that heterodoxy is in the majority in their area—namely, those addressed to Pergamum, Thyatira, Sardis, and Laodicea (above, 79 f.)—while in Colossae, viewed from the perspective of the "church," the situation may be even more unfavorable (above, 80 f.). In Smyrna, the scales are evenly balanced (above, 69 f.). Possibly other locales in western Asia Minor allow a more favorable judgment (above, 69); besides Magnesia, Tralles, and Philadelphia, there is Ephesus—the defeat that Paul suffered there, even though heretics certainly were involved in it, in no way signifies the breakdown of orthodoxy as such (above, 82 ff.).

As in Pauline Phrygia, so also in Pauline Macedonia (above, 72-75), Christianity developed along the path leading to heresy, so that orthodoxy sees itself forced to take second place. *Hoi polloi*, "the great majority," were in the camp of the church's enemies in Hierapolis (above, 187 f.), as in Philippi (above, 72 f.), and finally also in Crete (above, 75 f.). Only in the case of Rome can we state confidently that orthodoxy possessed the upper hand. And the distinctive character that marked Rome from the outset passed over to Corinth around the year one hundred, where it remained.

A few observations may serve to confirm the conclusions we have reached in our assessment of the two opposing forces. Quite frequently we hear the churchmen bewail the extent of the danger from heresy, but nowhere do we find [196] them attempting to adduce numerical evidence of the success of their own position concerning the outcome. We would look in vain for phraseology such as: "only a couple of fools, beguiled by the devil, are in the opposition." To some extent, the quantity of literature found here and there also is indicative of the size of the group that it represents, although we must always keep in mind that we are undoubtedly better informed about ecclesiastical literature than about that of the heretics. It is impossible neatly to divide the Christian writings known to us down to the year 200 between orthodoxy and heresy. Too many uncertainties remain. Where should we classify Tatian (see below, 207) and his books? Or the productive Melito, and Clement of Alexandria? Or even the Fourth Gospel (see below, 204-212) and the apostle Paul (see below, 212-228 and 233)?

Nevertheless, no one can avoid the impression produced by the abundance of forms of heresy already evident in the second century and the mass of literary works produced by them. Hippolytus knows of "innumerable books" that Montanus and his prophetesses had authored (*Ref.* 8.19). In his section on the *Gnōstikoi*, Epiphanius speaks of "countless writings produced by them" (*alla myria par' autois plasthenta grapheia, Her.* 26.12) after mentioning their literary efforts in specific cases. Papias already considered the major part of the available traditional material to be suspicious (above, 187 f.), and thus consciously turned from literature to oral tradition. And whoever has to deal with heretics censures their fruitful literary activity —Hegesippus (EH 4.22.9), Gaius (EH 6.20.3); Irenaeus (AH 3.11.7 and 9, 3.12.12[= 3.11.10 and 12, 3.12.15]), and others. It is easy to see that we are not dealing here with the customary accusations of an established polemical pattern when we recall the number of heretical writings from that time, which we know mostly only by title and many not even that well. Harnack identifies fifty-five different writings from the Ophites (or "Gnostics" in the narrow sense of the term) alone, of which the overwhelming majority were written by them, while they appropriated others for their own use.[93] If one adds to this what else we know about heretical literature until around the year 200, of which one may also learn from Harnack (cf. also above, 170 n. 39), we are forced to conclude [197] that in this camp a far more extensive literary activity had been developed than in the ecclesiastical circles. And thereby a new foothold is established to substantiate the view that the heretics considerably outnumbered the orthodox.

One final point. The reckless speed with which, from the very beginning, the doctrine and ideology of Marcion spread [94] can only be explained if it had found the ground already prepared. Apparently a great number of the baptized, especially in the East, inclined toward this view of Christianity and joined Marcion without hesitation as soon as he appeared, finding in him the classic embodiment of their own belief. What had dwelt in their inner consciousness in a more or less undefined form until then, acquired through Marcion the definite form that satisfied head and heart. No one can call that a falling away from orthodoxy to heresy.

93. Harnack, *Geschichte*, 1.1: 171 and 2 (*Chronologie*).1: 538-540.
94. Cf. Harnack, *Marcion*[2], p. 28.

9

The Old Testament, the Lord, and the Apostles

It is one thing to use the Old Testament (and the same holds true for sayings of the Lord or writings of the apostles) for the purposes of supporting or even refuting a view which is already in existence, and thus to regard it as a weapon. It is quite another thing when those writings become contributing factors in the formation of a particular brand of Christianity, whether in a positive manner or because they arouse opposition. It is not always easy, however, to differentiate between these usages in the period of origins with which our investigation is concerned. The two can blend together and one can be transformed into the other. The possibility also exists of employing scripture in support of a doctrine, even though it had no special importance for the establishment of that position, at least in the consciousness of those who produced it and who represent it. As a point of departure, we move from the end of the second century, prior to the stage of development represented by Irenaeus, Clement of Alexandria, and Tertullian which shows the church to be in possession of the two testaments, willing and able to use them in every respect in support of orthodoxy, and proceed backward toward the beginnings. What significance does the Old Testament have in the interplay of forces within Christianity? [1] [199]

1. That is the only thing of concern to us here. We leave aside the question of that use of the Old Testament which does not clearly relate to the disagreement within Christianity. So far as we can tell, Christians had not written commentaries on Old Testament books in the period with which we are dealing. Such activity first commences in a modest way with the *Hypotyposes* ("Outlines") of Clement of Alexandria. The prior stage in the lectures of Pantaenus and other of Clement's "elders" who have not left behind any written traces (*Strom.* 1. [1.] 11; *Prophetic*

Perhaps Hegesippus could give us an impression of the ecclesiastical situation at the end of our period. But as a witness he is not fully satisfactory. He claims to have found, on his journey to Rome, that "in every succession and in every city,"[2] the basis of faith had been "the Law and the Prophets and the Lord" (EH 4.22.3)—that is, the Old Testament and the Lord.[3] Eusebius immediately draws the conclusion from the words of Hegesippus that the latter has had contact with a great many "bishops" (EH 4.22.1; see above 190 ff. on Eusebius' use of superlatives) in the course of his journey to Rome. Hegesippus himself, in the portion reported in Eusebius, speaks only of contact with the heads of the Christian communities in Corinth and in Rome (EH 4.22.2-3). And even when we take into consideration everything else reported about him, we hear nothing at all about orthodox bishops with whom he had been in accord apart from James and his successor in Jerusalem (EH 4.22.4). Even Polycarp and Papias, who usually like to appear on [200] such occasions, are not present in the account. But as far as Corinth and Rome are concerned,

---

Excerpts 27.1) is no longer available to us. [199] Perhaps at that time Theophilus of Antioch also wrote an interpretation of the Proverbs of Solomon, although the only evidence for it comes from Jerome *Illustrious Men* 25. This is by no means outside the realm of possibility. Indeed, Eusebius reports that Hegesippus, Irenaeus, "and the whole company of the ancients" (*kai ho pas tōn archaiōn choros;* EH 4.22.9) had called the Proverbs of Solomon a work of excellent wisdom, and Ignatius of Antioch really referred only to this Old Testament book in a clear manner [*Eph.* 5.3]. Nevertheless, we cannot appeal here to this commentary, assuming that it really existed, any more than we can to Melito's "Excerpts from the Law and the Prophets concerning our Savior and our Whole Faith" in six books (EH 4.26.12-14), because we do not know whether they were used in the battle of Christian against Christian. In the *Preaching of Peter*, the "books of the prophets," which contained material about the whole activity of the earthly Jesus, were used in instructing the gentiles (Clement of Alexandria *Strom.* 6.[15.]128; [ET by G. Ogg in Hennecke-Schneemelcher, 2: 101 f.]). The Old Testament served Ariston of Pella in winning Jews, and Justin used it in the same way in the *Dialogue.* We also refer only in passing here to the attempts of the epistles to the *Hebrews* and of *Barnabas* to find a positive significance for the Old Testament, despite everything that stands in the way; it is not clear whether and in what way they were used as instruments in a disputation within Christianity.
2. *En hekastē diadochē kai en hekastē polei. Diadochē* is a term used to designate official succession around the end of the second century. Ptolemy uses the word with reference to the apostolic tradition (*Epistle to Flora* 5.10 = Epiphanius 33.7.9; see above 120 n. 22). Ecclesiastical authors like to use it for the succession of bishops (Irenaeus AH 1.27.1 [= 1.24]). Thus Hegesippus wants what he describes to be regarded as the state of the apostolic, bishop-led churches, no doubt as opposed to heresy, in accord with his entire outlook. [See also below, 275 n. 95.]
3. *Ho nomos kai hoi prophētai kai ho kyrios.* According to Stephan Gobarus, Hegesippus refers to "the divine scriptures and the Lord" (below, 214 n. 33).

Hegesippus' formula is no longer adequate for the churches of his day since for them, the Apostle Paul with his collection of letters has undoubtedly already assumed a regular place alongside the Old Testament and the Lord around the year 180. The formula "Old Testament and the Lord" apparently applies more satisfactorily to the Jewish Christian communities of Palestine, whence Hegesippus came (EH 4.22.8), or preserves an expression which to some extent adequately described the ecclesiastical outlook of a Justin [4] and a Papias a generation earlier. What we learn from Hegesippus concerning the state of affairs in *all* orthodox churches of his time can therefore only to a very limited degree be regarded as a result of his investigations on a journey to the West in which the current situation was recorded impartially. But for our present purposes (see further below, 213 f.) it suffices to note that wherever Hegesippus went, he found the Old Testament acknowledged to be holy scripture in the ecclesiastical brotherhoods. That is certainly correct. That there were orthodox Christians at that time who denied the Old Testament is extremely unlikely since its rejection was one of the chief characteristics of abominable heresy.

According to the view of the Basilidians, the Old Testament derived from the creators of the world, and the law in particular came from their chief (*a principe ipsorum*) who had led the people out of Egypt (Irenaeus AH 1.24.5 [= 1.19.3]). Among the Valentinians, Ptolemy was the first [5] to go beyond the position of complete rejection of the Old Testament, a position held by the founder himself as well as by Heracleon, and which surely also characterized Marcus. Ptolemy differentiated between various parts of the law, and traced one of them back to God. The "pure legislation" was fulfilled, not destroyed, by the Savior although he did abolish the "law which was intertwined with evil." Finally, a third group of regulations, the actual ceremonial law, should be understood in a typological and symbolic way, as an image of the higher, spiritual world. Since the law as a whole is imperfect, it could not have come from God, but derives from the "demiurge." [6] [201] In this way, Ptolemy not only expressly

---

4. Cf. *Dial.* 48.4: "Christ has commanded us not to follow human teachings but rather the proclamation of the blessed prophets and the teaching of Christ himself."
5. Perhaps the same is true of the Valentinian Theotimus; cf. above, 48.
6. *Epistle to Flora* (in Epiphanius *Her.* 33.3-7); see above, 120 n. 22.

rejected the teaching of the church, according to which "the God and Father" had given the law, but also rejected a view which regarded the devil as the actual legislator (1.2 = Epiphanius 33.3.2). The people with whom the Paul of the *Acts of Paul* contends in "3 Corinthians" forbid appealing to the prophets (1.10; see above 42 n. 99), and the false teachers mentioned in the epistle of Jude similarly reject the Old Testament revelation.[7] The "elder" who was instructed by those who had seen and heard the apostles and their disciples, and from whom derive the examples of the correct use of scripture cited by Irenaeus (AH 4.27.1-32.1 [= 4.42-49]), strongly opposes a use of the Old Testament which separates it from God, connects it with that inferior being the demiurge (AH 4.27.4 [= 4.43.1]), and thus depreciates its content for the Christians. In this connection we need not even mention the name of Marcion, while Apelles, who was influenced by him, in many treatises uttered countless blasphemies against Moses and the divine words, according to Eusebius (EH 5.13.9).

The mode and manner by which the heretics discharged their obligations with regard to the Old Testament varied, and sometimes exegetical devices played a part. Such skills made possible the assertion that the prophets contradict themselves and thereby betray their complete unreliability (Apelles in EH 5.13.6; *mēden holōs alēthes eirēkenai*). Or the Lord is said to show that the ancient writings are wrong: "The followers of Valentinus and of certain other heresies suppose that the Savior said things that had not been said in the ancient writings," etc.[8] Even apostles, and by no means only Paul, are brought into play against the old covenant. In his letter to James (in the ps.-Clementine *Homilies;* see above, 184), Peter complains bitterly that certain of the gentiles have rejected the lawful proclamation which he preached and not only that, but they have twisted the meaning of his own words so as to make it seem as though he says the same thing as they do. "But those people who, I know not how, claim to understand my thoughts, attempt [202] to explain words they have heard from me more accurately than I who spoke

7. Jülicher-Fascher, *Einleitung*[7], p. 214.
8. *Hoi apo Oualentinou kai tinōn heterōn haireseōn, oiomenoi ton sōtēra legein ta mē eirēmena en tois palaiois grammasin.* . . . From the *Exposition of the Psalms* by Origen (Pitra, *Analecta Sacra*, 2: 335 ff., no. 3). Cf. Harnack, *Geschichte*, 1.1: 295.

them, and they tell their disciples that this is my opinion, although I had never thought of it at all. If they dare to produce such lies already during my lifetime, how much more will those who come after me dare to do it after I am gone!" (2.6-7).

With that, the line is already established along which the ecclesiastical valuation of the Old Testament proceeds. It contains no contradications, and neither Jesus nor the apostles stand in opposition to it. The cleft which, for example, Marcion in his *Antitheses,* or others in similar ways, opened between the God of the old and the God of the new covenants, is immediately filled in again by the presbyter of Irenaeus—whatever fault the heretics find with the God of the Old Testament holds true no less for the Lord (AH 4.28.3-32.1 [= 4.44.3-49.2ᵃ]). This section concludes with the triumphant assertion: "In this way the elder (*senior*), the disciple of the apostles, discoursed about both Testaments and showed that both derive from one and the same God" (4.32.1 [= 4.49.1]). And when Tatian was industriously at work on a writing entitled *Problems* in which he promised to show the obscure and hidden approach of the scriptures, the churchman Rhodon announced at once a refutation which would offer the *Solutions* for Tatian's problems (EH 5.13.8).

The Old Testament was only of limited usefulness in opposing the heretics. This was not simply because it is not possible to use it for convincing people who do not acknowledge it. It was not very much different with those who did accept it, since they read it also from their own perspective and did not allow themselves to be influenced by the opposing viewpoint; they had their "own interpretation" (*epilusis*, 2 Pet. 1.19-21). But in addition to that, a primary consideration was the fact that the controversy focused primarily on christological issues, and the Old Testament was not very productive for that. To be sure, occasionally someone disputed with the heretics even at that level. Thus, Hermogenes believed that he could use Psalm 19.4 f. (= 18.6 LXX) as a support for his position that Christ, at the time of his return to his home above, left his body behind in the sun. The orthodox interpreted the passage differently, and Pantaenus also challenged the interpretation of the heretic on linguistic grounds.[9]

9. Clement of Alexandria *Prophetic Excerpts* 56 [ET in Grant, *Second Century,* pp. 54 f.]. On Hermogenes and his ideas, see also Hippolytus *Ref.* 8.17.

Nevertheless, such instances are only sporadic in the period under discussion. [203] It seems to be more typical when Polycarp, who hates the heretics as much as he values scripture (*Phil.* 12.1), still does not attempt to use the latter polemically any more than does Ignatius. And it is not possible to determine whether Justin appealed to the Old Testament against the heretics to any significant degree. Certainly it could be employed in opposition to the immorality of the heretics, and also in opposition to the impossible notion of prophecy which Montanism cherished (see above, 136 and 145). Otherwise, with respect to error, we see the orthodox restricting themselves to the use of Old Testament threats of judgment (2 Tim. 4.14) or to the consolation that the Lord already knows his own (2 Tim. 2.19, following Num. 16.5). And this is done by a person who cherishes the conviction that it is precisely a knowledge of scripture that equips the leader of the community both in and for this struggle (2 Tim. 3.14-16). More than a few times, the assertion is made that the Old Testament had already alluded to the fact that heretics would arise. The wise man whom Clement of Alexandria had heard speaking, probably Pantaenus, discovered the heretics in those "who sit in the seat of the scornful" (Ps. 1.1 in *Strom.* 2.[15.]67.4). And where particularly grievous sinners appear in the Old Testament, they are viewed as types of the new godlessness, and comfort is derived from contemplating the fate which overtook them. The epistle of Jude, and likewise 2 Peter (2.1-22), which follows it for the most part, depicts the false believers as the counterparts of the unfaithful Israelites, of the fallen angels, of the men of Sodom and Gomorrah, of a Cain, Balaam, and Korah (Jude 5-13)—as the impious people of the last times who are announced by the prophet Enoch (Jude 14-16). Second Timothy complains that the heretics rebel against the truth as Jannes and Jambres did against Moses (3.8) and the only material that 1 John has taken from the Old Testament is the reference to Cain, as the opposite of the Christian that is genuine, because orthodox (3.12).

As we have already seen with respect to *1 Clement* (above, 104), the chief value of the Old Testament for the church, in its opposition to gnosticism, lay in the fact that by beginning with God as the creator, it made it more difficult to slip into a conceptual framework in which subordinate beings, or even the devil himself, had created the world. In that way, the connection between creation and redemption was preserved, and it was impossible to construe redemption as meaning redemption from creation. [204]

On this point (cf. Irenaeus AH 1.26.2 [= 1.22]), and on the whole in the acknowledgment of the Old Testament as the record of divine revelation, orthodoxy could easily come to an understanding with Jewish Christianity. But as soon as one began to deal with particular details, there became evident even here disagreement that separated the known Jewish Christians from that portion of the gentile Christians who had not renounced the old covenant. To be sure, both groups consciously subjected themselves to the guidance of the Old Testament and the gospel. But it made a great deal of difference whether one attempted to understand the latter on the basis of the former, or whether one approached the former from the viewpoint of a gentile Christian interpretation of faith in Christ. The inevitable controversy died out only with the demise of Jewish Christianity itself. As long as Jewish Christianity existed, gentile Christians who came into contact with it were offended by what they regarded as a Judaizing perversion of the Christian heritage, and were accused in return of having deprived the Old Testament—and therefore a major portion of the divine revelation—of its true meaning just as the arch-heretic Paul had done. We are no longer able to determine whether the lost writing of Clement of Alexandria entitled "Ecclesiastical Canon, or Against (or 'To') the Judaizers" (*kanōn ekklēsiastikos ē pros tous ioudaizontas*, EH 6.13.3) relates to this situation. After all, Egypt would have provided a particularly appropriate stage for that sort of conflict. Irenaeus accuses the "Ebionities" of supporting their peculiar and thoroughly heretical teaching with a most curious interpretation of the prophetic writings (AH 1.26.2 [= 1.22]). They regarded Jesus as merely human,[10] denied the virgin birth, and were not startled by the reference to Isa. 7:14 (Matt. 1.23). They simply followed Theodotion and Aquila, who found there a "young woman" (*neanis*) instead of the "virgin" (*parthenos*) of the Septuagint (Irenaeus, AH 3.21.1 [= 3.23]; cf. EH 5.8.10). Thus textual criticism and interpretation of the Old Testament go hand in hand, whether to provide the basis for a non-ecclesiastical opinion, or to help ecclesiastical doctrine to be victorious.

10. Cf. Bauer, *Leben Jesu*, pp. 30 f.

Justin plays off the orthodox understanding of the Old Testament and the gospel against the "human" convictions of the Jewish Christians (*Dial.* 48.4). Concerning Ignatius, we have already heard (above, 131 f.) that he acknowledges the law and the prophets (*Smyr.* 5.1)—the [205] "beloved prophets" (*Philad.* 9.2)—but wishes to understand them solely on the basis of the gospel, and he sharply rejects the representatives of the opinion he is opposing, who want to establish their perspective on the basis of the Old Testament. Indeed, the Judaizers in Philadelphia have proved themselves to be unenlightened, and to the assertion of Ignatius that the gospel, as he understands it, is written in the sacred "charters" (*archeioi*) they stubbornly answered: "That is just the question" (*Philad.* 8.2). Since the prophets had already gained entrance to the Father through Christ (*Philad.* 9.1) and had accordingly lived after the manner of Christ Jesus (*Magn.* 8.2), awaiting him in the spirit as his disciples awaiting their teacher (*Magn.* 9.2) and even having oriented their proclamation toward the gospel (*Philad.* 5.2), Ignatius could in no way conceive of any possibility that the prophets could have declared anything that was not also contained in the gospel. This gospel, together with the law and the prophets, constitutes a unity (*Smyr.* 5.1), but it is a unity in which the gospel takes the lead, and the others must follow. More than what is presented in the gospel, the chief content of which is outlined briefly in *Philad.* 8.2, cannot be found in the "charters"—thus Judaism loses all justification and the possibility is thereby opened for Ignatius to limit himself for all practical purposes to the gospel, and to be satisfied with a more theoretical appreciation of the prophets, whose statements are no longer put to use.

At the center of the gospel stands *the Lord*, the other authority for that Christianity of which we learned above—an authority superior to the "scriptures" not only because it dictates the way to understand them, but also because all the believers agree in respect for it. But even at this point there is great diversity. Each individual and each special group is fighting for its Christ and against the Christ of the others, and is endeavoring to enlist tradition and theological inference in his service. Here one attempts to produce what is considered to be the most authentic possible tradition of the life and teaching of Jesus—attributed to the eyewitnesses themselves—primarily by dressing up the tradition and supplying an appropriate interpretation. In my earlier work dealing with traditions about Jesus (*Leben Jesu*), I attempted to describe how the mode of viewing the Lord, both inside and outside the "church," takes the form of historical narrative, and as such demands unconditional belief, [206] and I will refer to that work for the postcanonical portion of the period we are discussing in the present book. At that time there probably was no version of Christianity worthy of note that did not have at its disposal at least *one* written gospel, in which Jesus appears as the bearer and guarantor of that particular view, and (if only with a silent gesture) repulses those who think differently. Each one found in the differing presentation of his opponent a falsification of the tradition concerning the Lord (see above, 183 ff.).

Jewish Christianity, in accord with the diversity it spawned, has at its disposal several gospels: the *Gospel of the Nazarenes* and of the *Ebionites*, as well as the *Gospel of the Hebrews* (see above, 51 f.). Alongside the last-named gospel, there appeared the *Gospel of the Egyptians* (above, 50-53) as the corresponding book of the Egyptian gentile-Christians. The *Gospel of Peter* of the Syrian heretics already has come to our attention also (above, 66, 115), as well as the *Gospel of Basilides* (above, 170) and the *Apocryphon of John* of the Barbelo Gnostics (above, 49). Also attested from this period are the *Gospel of Truth*, which the Valentinians used and which differed completely from the canonical gospels,[11] the *Gospel of Judas*,[12] and certain items from the Coptic gospel literature (see below, 314 n. 32). In order to prove that the peculiar content of these books was divine truth, the gnostics asserted that the Savior had communicated the truth to the common people only in an incomplete fashion, but reserved the most profound material for a few of his

11. Irenaeus AH 3.11.9 (= 3.11.12). [A Coptic version of a *Gospel of Truth* was found among the Nag Hammadi (Chenoboskion) materials (see above, 170 n. 39), and probably is to be identified with this Valentinian work. For ET with introduction and commentary, see K. Grobel, *The Gospel of Truth* (London: Black, 1960); the Coptic text may be found, with another ET, in M. Malinine, H.-C. Puech, G. Quispel, *Evangelium Veritatis* (Zürich: Rascher, 1956), and *Supplementum* (1961). See also Hennecke-Schneemelcher, 1: 523-531 (extracts); Grant, *Gnosticism Anthology*, pp. 146-161 (ET by W. W. Isenberg).]

12. Irenaeus AH 1.31.1 f. (= 1.28.9). [See Hennecke-Schneemelcher, 1: 313 f. Whether this gospel, attributed to the "traitor" Judas by Irenaeus, has any relation to the recently discovered (Coptic) *Gospel of (Judas) Thomas* can no longer be determined.]

disciples who were capable of comprehending it (Irenaeus AH 2.27.2 [= 2.40.3]). Sometimes it is the pre-crucifixion, sometimes the post-resurrection Christ who imparts this material; sometimes the recipients are identified simply as the apostles, sometimes individual disciples, male and female, are named.[13]

On this matter, it is scarcely possible to make any distinction between a Clement of Alexandria or an Origen and the heretical gnostics. The former also assume that in his teaching, Jesus acted differently toward those whom he trusted than toward the common people, and that [207] with reference to the apostles, he made a further distinction between the time before and the time after his resurrection (cf. *Leben Jesu,* pp. 376 f.). The *Epistle of the Apostles* (above, 184) also provides evidence that ecclesiastical circles by no means rejected the idea of extensive special instructions to the disciples by the Lord.[14] But where the "church" was in competition with heresy, the close agreement with heresy in this respect soon became distressing. Important as it was to secure the ecclesiastical interpretation of generally acknowledged tradition by means of exegetical effort, it was at least as important to establish firm boundaries between that which really could qualify as gospel tradition, and the great mass of heretical forgeries. We have already become acquainted with the efforts of Papias in this context, and have noted their hostility toward heresy (above, 185-188).

Papias' conclusion was that apostolic tradition about the life and teaching of Jesus is to be found in the Gospels of Mark/Peter and of Matthew, and also here and there where his perception and probably even more, his particular preference had come across material that was agreeable and thereby proved itself to be genuine. We have suspected that he ignored the Third and Fourth Gospels because their usefulness had been called into question by the esteem with which they were held by the heretics. To be sure, Matthew and

13. E.g. the Carpocratians and the "Gnostics" according to Irenaeus AH 1.25.5 [= 1.20.3] and 1.30.14 [= 1.28.7]; Ptolemy *To Flora* 4.15 [= Epiphanius 33.7.9; above, 120 n. 22]; *Pistis Sophia* and the *Books of Jeû* [see Hennecke-Scheemelcher, 1: 250-262]; *Acts of John* 88-102. [For a more detailed discussion of this material, see Bauer, *Leben Jesu,* pp. 374-376.] See also above, 119 f.; on John as the informant in the *Apocryphon of John,* see 49; on Salome, 50.
14. Cf. my detailed arguments in Hennecke[2], pp. 114 f.

Mark also were used by heretics,[15] but apparently not in so blatant a fashion as the other two. In addition, the place which Matthew and Mark occupied within the "church" was already so secure at the time of Papias, and the two gospels, especially the first, had become so indispensible, that there could no longer be any question of abandoning them. The encroachment by the heretics had to be countered in another way, namely, through *exēgēseis*. One example of such a procedure will suffice. The Montanists referred Matthew 23.34 to their prophets, and thus called the churchmen, by whom those prophets were rejected, "murderers of the prophets" (Matt. 23.31). [208] "Ecclesiastical" theology preferred, on the contrary, another interpretation, and emphasized that the prophets about whom Jesus was speaking had been persecuted by the Jews, something which did not apply at all to the Montanists (the anonymous anti-montanist in EH 5.16.12). Since exegesis offered almost unlimited possibilities, it would be a mistake if one were to conclude from the mere use of one of the gospels, concerning which the church subsequently made a favorable decision, that already in our period the orthodox position of the one who used it was established without further discussion. Such an argument is inadequate in itself, just as the later ecclesiastical view was in no position to give the last word on the origin and nature of the canonical gospels. For this reason alone we could not expect to receive conclusive information from these sources, since we know that the concept of what is "ecclesiastical" developed gradually and involved transformations that were not unaffected by stimuli and limitations from the side of the heretics.

Papias felt that he could acknowledge only two of our biblical gospels. Perhaps this was because his particularly vulnerable situation made it advisable for him to limit himself only to what was completely reliable. It was somewhat different for his contemporary and coreligionist Justin. Justin did not shrink from using Luke as a source for the earthly life of Jesus, in addition to the other synoptics, and because he considered all three of these gospels to be written by apostles or their companions (*Dial.* 103.8), he acknowledged for

---

15. Mark, for example, by Cerinthus (Irenaeus AH 3.11.7 [= 3.11.10]). We need not list the evidence for Matthew—it was used by Jewish Christians as well as by gnostics (e.g. Ptolemy, Heracleon) and Montanists.

them the same claim to credibility as for the Old Testament, with which they could alternate in the Sunday readings (*Apol.* 67.3). Thus sayings taken from the synoptic gospels are introduced with the solemn formula "it is written" (*Dial.* 49.5; 100.1; 101.3; 103.8; 104; 105.6; 106.4; 107.1).

Perhaps Justin knew the gospel of John, but even if he did, his outlook is intrinsically foreign to it.[16] It is basically so foreign that we can scarcely silence the voice that would bid us to give up altogether any thought of such an acquaintance. Justin completely follows the narrative sequence of the synoptics, even where they conflict with John. Like John, Justin is possessed with the idea of existence of Christ as the Logos prior to the creation of the world, but he does not derive his proof from the Fourth Gospel, neither from the prologue nor any other portion; moreover he does not even derive it from the letters of Paul, [209] but seeks laboriously to press the synoptics into the service of such ideas. The miraculous birth or the confession of Peter must bear the brunt of providing a proof which John could have given with no difficulty. Whenever we feel certain that John can no longer remain silent, we find ourselves disappointed.[17] That becomes all the more striking when we observe, in contrast, how Justin is able unreservedly to take advantage of his sympathies with the Apocalypse, where he has such. The least that we can say is that the gospel of John has left no noticeable impression on Justin. But in this respect, Justin represents the position of ecclesiastically oriented Rome in the middle of the second century. This is all the more evident insofar as the old Roman confession assumes the same stance toward the canonical gospels as does Justin, and like him follows the synoptic line.

Can it be a coincidence that immediately after Justin, the enemy of heretics who also took aim at the Valentinians (*Dial.* 35.6), we note the appearance in Italy-Rome of two representatives of this latter school who especially treasure the Fourth Gospel—namely Ptolemy and Heracleon (Hippolytus *Ref.* 6.35)? To be sure, Justin's

16. So Jülicher-Fascher, *Einleitung*[7], p. 474.
17. Cf. W. Bousset, *Die Evangeliencitate Justins des Märtyrers* (Göttingen, 1891), pp. 115-121. More recently W. v. Loewenich has dealt with this problem in *Das Johannes-Verständnis im zweiten Jahrhundert*, ZNW Beiheft 13 (1932): 39-50; [also A. J. Bellinzoni, *The Sayings of Jesus in the Writings of Justin Martyr*, Supplements to Novum Testamentum 17 (Leiden: Brill 1967): 134-138, 140].

disciple Tatian placed the gospel of John on the same level as the synoptics, but he also broke with the church on account of profound differences in faith—poisoned, so Irenaeus thought, by the Valentinians and Marcion (AH 1.28.1 [= 1.26.1])—and he left the world capital to move once again toward the East. Thus Tatian cannot provide us with a satisfactory testimony concerning the moods and conditions within the "church" at Rome. The silence of a Dionysius of Corinth, of a Hegesippus, of a Rhodon, and of others whose enmity toward heresy goes hand in hand with their alliance with Rome, as we have already heard (above, 106-108), is regrettable, and should not be used to draw inferences in either direction. When an ecclesiastically oriented Roman again expressed himself with respect to our problem, it is for the purpose of vigorously rejecting the Fourth Gospel.

I am convinced that the Roman presbyter Gaius, whom Hippolytus also thought he should refute explicitly, is closely connected with those people whom Epiphanius [210] opposes as "alogoi" on the basis of statements made against them by the Roman Hippolytus.[18] Their view concerning the Fourth Gospel is already present by the year 175, as the opposition of Irenaeus indicates (above, 141); and even if Gaius had not been active before the end of the century, he nevertheless appropriated for himself many of the views of that group. But he did not thereby fall under the charge of heresy on the part of his catholic opponents. They were, on the contrary, in complete agreement with his unrelenting condemnation of gnostics and Montanists. It was thus permissible for a Roman Christian from these circles, and an officeholder as well, to consider not only the Apocalypse but even the gospel of John as a forgery of the gnostic Cerinthus.[19] He reproaches it for its contradictions with the other gospels, plays Mark off against John (Epiphanius *Her.* 51.6), and betrays in

18. *Her.* 51. The attacks by Hippolytus include a work entitled *"On the Gospel and Apocalypse of John" (hyper tou kata Iōanēn euaggeliou kai apokalypseōs).* On the "alogoi," cf. E. Schwartz, *Über den Tod der Söhne Zebedaei,* Abhandlungen der Göttinger Gesellschaft der Wissenschaften (1904), pp. 29 ff.; Jülicher-Fascher, *Einleitung*[7], pp. 257, 485; M. Meinertz, *Einleitung in das NT*[4] (Paderborn, 1933), p. 256 (the *Roman* alogoi, the *Roman* presbyter Gaius).
19. Epiphanius *Her.* 51.3. If Gaius excludes 1 John from the charge, he agrees in this judgment distinguishing the gospel from the epistle with the churchman Papias and probably also with Polycarp, whose acquaintance with 1 John is certain, while it is at least not demonstrable that he knew the Fourth Gospel.

general an extraordinary sympathy for the earthly life of Jesus as presented by the synoptics. Of course, the reasons thus advanced are not the true cause for his rejection of John. Rather, he sensed in the gospel of John a spirit of heresy with which his Roman-ecclesiastical attitude could not be reconciled.

If we listen to the sources without prejudice, it seems to me that this is the result: a current of caution with regard to the gospel of John runs continuously through *ecclesiastical* Rome, that center of orthodoxy, right up to almost the end of the second century—a mood that manifests itself through silence and through explicit rejection. Even the silence becomes eloquent if one notices that people such as Ptolemy, Heracleon and Tatian, who are sharply attacked by the church, can treasure the gospel for similar reasons. Gaius in his own way gives expression to a feeling which dominated Roman orthodoxy [211] ever since the Fourth Gospel appeared on its horizon and which doubtless accounts for Justin's attitude when he consciously appeals to the synoptics for support, just as do the alogoi. Apparently the gospel of John was introduced into the world capital by personalities whose recommendation could not be accepted by the "church" there. Up until the end of the epoch with which we are dealing, it had still not overcome such reservations. To around the close of the second century, history is unable to name a single orthodox Roman for whom the Fourth Gospel had been of any significance. The line of orthodox admirers is first attested in Rome with the *Muratorian Canon* at the beginning of the third century, for the Roman origin of the ancient gospel-prologues is not certain.[20] That there were, however, at the time the prologues were composed (around 180), already orthodox theologians in the West who acknowledged the gospel of John as apostolic and valued it accordingly, is adequately attested by Irenaeus. But he reveals no Roman influence thereby. Apparently it was the close relationship between Gaul and Asia (cf. EH 5.1.3 and 17) that permitted the Asian Irenaeus, who even in his old age was proud of having been in contact, through Polycarp, with "John and the others who had seen the Lord" (EH 5.20.5-7), to accept a gospel attributed to the apostle John more unreservedly than was possible for Rome with its consciousness of responsibility as champion in the battle against heresy—and without any special preference for the apostle of Asia.

20. Cf. Harnack, *Evangelien-Prologe*, pp. 16 f.

If we go back to the period prior to Justin, I still remain convinced that it is impossible to demonstrate that any of the apostolic fathers used the Fourth Gospel.[21] That is particularly noteworthy in the case of Polycarp, of whose bond with Rome based on a common enmity toward heresy we already are aware (above, 107). A survey of the gospel-like material [22] seems to me to suggest that the situation with respect to Polycarp is quite similar to that of the Roman Clement, with whom he is so intimately familiar.

The first letter of Clement (about 95/96) as well as the letter of Polycarp (about twenty years later) make no use of the Fourth Gospel. And [212] just as, in my opinion, the hypothesis is fully justified that the former, like its contemporaries the first and third evangelists, knew the gospel of Mark and also a sort of "sayings-source," so also with regard to Polycarp we need not suppose anything different. Nor has C. Taylor been able to convince me that *Hermas* offers more concrete evidence here.[23] Furthermore, I am particularly indebted to 2 *Clement* for strengthening the conviction that even for the later part of the period of the apostolic fathers, the question concerning which of the *canonical* gospels was, or were, in use by Christians, is justified only to a very limited degree.[24]

This awareness should also guide us as we investigate whence Ignatius, who lived quite a bit earlier, came to know something of the life of Jesus. Many think he had access to the Fourth Gospel. But the oft-cited "reminiscences" are ambiguous and do not lead to a firm conviction of dependence; on the contrary, they make the absence of any actual quotations appear to be be all the more curious.[25] In any event, he does not appeal to that gospel for his great confessional statements concerning Christ in which to some extent he is in harmony with the gospel of John—for Christ's pre-existence, deity,

21. See Bauer, *Johannesevangelium*[3], p. 244.
22. Conveniently collected in *The New Testament in the Apostolic Fathers*, by a committee of the Oxford Society of Historical Theology (Oxford, 1905). [For a more recent investigation, see H. Köster, *Synoptische Überlieferung bei den apostolischen Vätern*, TU 65 (1957). On 1 Clement and the epistle of Polycarp in particular, see R. M. Grant, *1 Clement* (= Grant, AF 2, 1965), p. 103; and Schoedel, *Polycarp . . . Papias*, p. 5.]
23. C. Taylor, *The Witness of Hermas to the Four Gospels* (1892). [For a recent survey of Hermas' relation to the New Testament, see G. F. Snyder, *The Shepherd of Hermas* (= Grant, AF 6, 1968), pp. 14-16.]
24. [For a recent survey of the material, see H. H. Graham, *2 Clement* (= Grant, AF 2, 1965), pp. 133 f.]
25. [See now R. M. Grant, *Ignatius* (= Grant, AF 4, 1966), p. 24.]

and status as "Logos." And for many things that seem to us to be "gospel"-like in nature and might have come directly or even indirectly from a written gospel, John simply does not enter the picture.

The Fourth Gospel knows nothing of the claim that Mary was a descendent of David,[26] or that the Tetrarch Herod took part in the crucifixion (*Smyr.* 1.2). The birth from a virgin (*Eph.* 19.1; *Smyr.* 1.1) and the conception by the Spirit (*Eph.* 18.2; cf. 7.2) are also foreign to John, just as is the whole concept of the great mystery which occured at that time (*Eph.* 19.1). In the same context, we also read nothing in John about the colossal appearance of a star which emphasized the importance of this moment of world history (*Eph.* 19.2), nor similarly that at the end of the life of Jesus the heavenly, earthly and subterranean powers were witnesses of the crucifixion (*Trall.* 9.1). The only passage that Ignatius really *quotes* from a written gospel—containing the famous saying of the risen Lord that he is no "bodiless demon" (*Smyr.* 3.2)—likewise does not belong to the [213] gospel of John, nor for that matter to any of the canonical gospels, and none of the church fathers ever claimed to find it in them.[27]

The situation with Ignatius is basically the same as with Justin (above, 205 f.). Both believe in the heavenly pre-existence of Christ, and yet the gospel writings which both of them use begin only with the miraculous conception of Jesus. In *Trallians* 9.1, Ignatius sets before his readers the decisive main points concerning the earthly life of Jesus, as he knows it from the gospel traditions, in express opposition to his docetically oriented opponents. But despite his enthusiastic emphasis on Christ's flesh and blood (8.1), he does not follow the pattern of the Johannine prologue by beginning with the entry of the heavenly being into our sphere; and while echoing the phrase "he became flesh" (*sarx egeneto*, John 1.14) which so fully conforms to his own faith (*Eph.* 7.2), he requires the confession of "Jesus Christ, who was of the family of David, who came from Mary, who was truly born, both ate and drank, was truly persecuted under Pontius Pilate, was truly crucified and died, . . . was truly raised from the

---

26. Ignatius *Eph.* 18.2, *Smyr.* 1.1, *Trall.* 9.1; cf. W. Bauer, *Leben Jesu*, p. 15.
27. Origen traces the story back to the "*Teaching of Peter*" (*On First Principles* 1.preface.8), Jerome to the *Gospel of the Hebrews* (*Illustrious Men* 16), while Eusebius admits that he does not know whence Ignatius derived this information (EH 3.36.11). [See also Grant, *Ignatius*, pp. 115 f.]

dead . . ." (9.1 f.). Thus Ignatius apparently is as little aware of being dependent upon the Fourth Gospel for his conviction that Christ the divine being assumed flesh as is Justin. The same conviction also is expressed by 2 Clement (9.5) and Hermas (59 [= Sim. 5.6].5), but neither is in any way indebted to John.

Rather, the hypothesis that Ignatius used the gospel of Matthew might seem more appealing; [28] but no really convincing evidence can be adduced even for this. Nevertheless it is certain that this gospel, if it does play some role, by no means exhausts what Ignatius thinks he knows about the life of Jesus. What was especially valuable for Ignatius in the tradition concerning Jesus was that which revealed the divine glory of the Lord,[29] and what further [214] appeared to be appropriate for proving, in opposition to the view of the docetics, that Jesus had been a real human with flesh and blood throughout his entire life, as well as after his resurrection (cf. especially Trall. 9.1). I have no doubt that his opponents also had at their disposal gospel writings that vouched for the correctness of their teaching, and that they also knew sayings of the Lord to which they could appeal. Unfortunately, the gospels of both parties elude reliable descriptions today.

On the other hand, it appears to me to some extent demonstrated that the Gospel of John had a difficult time gaining recognition in the "church." But it succeeded. In Asia, the "apostolic" protector of the indigenous orthodox church took it under his wing.[30] And neither the Asian Irenaeus, nor the "gnostic" Clement in Alexandria, nor the Montanist Tertullian in North Africa (whose inclinations in that direction were much older than his break with the church) were in a position to doubt or even to challenge the tradition that was thus

28. In the opinion of B. H. Streeter, The Four Gospels (London: Macmillan, 1924), pp. 500 ff., with which, e.g., F. C. Grant agrees in The Growth of the Gospels (New York: Abingdon, 1933), pp. 14, 233, the gospel of Matthew originated in Antioch.
29. He proved this, however, with gospel material of a different type and origin than was used by the fourth evangelist, for whom this was also a concern of utmost importance.
30. Even if the Fourth Gospel had already been brought into relationship with the apostle John before it came into the sphere of influence of the church, that does not produce any difficulties. Peter also is claimed to be the author of the heretical gospel that bears his name, as well as being the patron of the ecclesiastical gospel of Mark. And John the son of Zebedee was also the hero of the gnostic Acts of John.

produced. When the gospel canon was defined, which was to be valid for the entire church, Rome found itself overruled, to put it rather crudely. The resistance offered previously, and perhaps more instinctively than consciously, was abandoned all the more willingly since the reasons which had caused Rome to view the Fourth Gospel in a suspicious light no longer retained their old force around the year 200. At that earlier time, the danger of heresy was a burden to Rome, but now the gospel of John could perform a valuable service in the construction and establishment of the ecclesiastical proclamation of Christ, as it had developed, without fear of undesirable side effects.

If we have correctly understood and described the position of the "church" with respect to the biblical gospels, then the peculiar order which they assume in its canon becomes self-explanatory. Irenaeus (AH 3.1.1 [= 3.1.2]) and the Muratorian list already attest the order Matthew, Mark, Luke, John. At first, [215] if we may begin after the period when one had to be content with just Mark and "Q" (see above, 209), the church made use of only the first two gospels, and probably arranged them according to size, following a principle that prevailed also with respect to the collection of Pauline epistles. After some delay, and not without encountering resistance, Luke followed, and only at the very last was John included. The idea that the chronological sequence of composition determined their order is merely an attempt to come to terms with an arrangement that originally had been established for different reasons.

Alongside the scriptures of the Old Testament and the Lord in the gospels, appear *the apostles* as the third authority of Christianity (see already the New Testament reference in Eph. 2.20). Their incomparable significance for the faithful does not need to be verified once more from the statements of the latter. Nor is it necessary to demonstrate that the apostles, by whom the tradition from the earliest Christian times is supported (as we already know), possessed enormous value for the ideological struggle. The apostles are introduced explicitly into the fight against the heretics by the epistle of Jude (17-19), which is paralleled in 2 Peter (3.2 ff.), or by Polycarp (*Phil.* 6.3); these passages neatly link the prophets, the Lord, and the apostles into a firmly knit order of battle. As the Jesus of the church

212

already has not only pointedly uprooted the opinions of the heretics, but also has precluded the possibility of their having any authority among the right-minded by providing an accurate picture of their coming for the future (Justin *Dial.* 35.3 ff., using Matt. 7.15; 24.11, 24 = Mark 13.22), so the apostles after him do the same thing to the same end (Jude 17-19; 2 Pet. 2.1 ff; 3.2, 17). By means of gospels, which are said to derive directly or indirectly from them (or from their circle), they produce the traditional basis for the view of Christ represented at any given time. And even apart from this aspect of literary activity, the apostles stand as the focus of a voluminous literature—letters by an apostolic author, acts of apostles, apocalypses —which frequently is intended to do battle against quite clearly divergent views and doctrines, sometimes in service of the "church," sometimes of its opponents.

The apostle Paul holds claim to a special place. It may be even more necessary here than elsewhere to approach the evidence without prejudice. What is the significance [216] of the Apostle to the Gentiles in the ideological struggle? Where do we encounter his influence? Where is there a sense of obligation to him? Once again we will proceed by moving back from the end toward the beginning. At the same time, we would do well to remember what we have already discovered to be the probable history of many a community founded by Paul. We need to be clear about the fact that the Apostle did not always succeed in maintaining a firm hold over what he possessed. Even outside the circle of the Jewish Christians,[31] with their bitter hatred of Paul and the resulting blunt rejection of everything influenced by him, we hear him disparaged.[32]

Hegesippus took his stand as a follower of the Old Testament and the Lord, but aroused our doubts (above, 196 f.) as to whether he really had listed completely, as he apparently intended, the fundamental basic authorities for all orthodox churches of his time. We have denied that this was the case for those at Corinth and Rome, where the apostle Paul with his collection of letters must have stood

---

31. On the attitude of the Jewish Christians toward Paul, see my treatment in Hennecke[2], pp. 127 f., [and in Hennecke-Schneemelcher, 2: 71. See also below, 236, 262 f.].
32. See above, 149 n. 5. Appeal may also be made to James 2.14-26 as evidence of how difficult it was to retain an undistorted recollection of the Apostle to the Gentiles.

alongside the Old Testament and the Lord around the year 180. But for Hegesippus himself that does not yet seem to have been the case, so that for him "the law and the prophets and the Lord" were, in fact, ill disposed toward this supplementation by means of Paul. This follows not only because in the other relevant passage he also simply refers to "the divine scriptures and the Lord" (above, 196 n. 3). It is much more significant that he was acquainted with the first epistle of Clement to Corinth (EH 4.22.1 f., 3.16), but not with 1 Corinthians. Rather, in the second passage mentioned above (196 n. 3), in a manner expressing complete ignorance, he immediately plays off against it "the divine scriptures and the Lord," particularly the saying of the Lord "Blessed are your eyes, since they see, and your ears, since they hear" (according to Matt. 13.16).[33] In 1 Corinthians 2.9, however, quite the opposite is said—"The good things prepared for the just no eye has seen nor ear heard," etc. Now in the fifth book of his *Memoirs* Hegesippus declares that this saying [217] is preposterous and only deception and opposition to Scripture could express itself in this manner (above, n. 33). But even if 1 Corinthians is unknown, then, as we shall also see, Paul is thereby completely removed from the picture. In view of everything we know about who showed preference for the content of 1 Corinthians 2.9,[34] there can be no doubt who those people were who conducted themselves with such enmity toward truth—they were the gnostics, with whom Hegesippus also crosses swords elsewhere (EH 4.22.5).

When we move back from Hegesippus to one of similar stripe, Papias, and ask what this bishop of a community that belonged to the regions reached by the Apostle to the Gentiles and was already in existence during Paul's lifetime (Col. 4.13) thought of Paul, it appears to me that again only one answer is possible—nothing. We are already to some extent prepared for this since we fittingly connected Eusebius' failure to record any expression of opinion by Papias concerning

33. Stephen Gobarus, according to Photius, *Library*, codex 232. [To clarify the argument, the context is reproduced here: " 'The good things prepared for the just (*ta hētoimasmena tois dikaiois agatha*) no eye has seen nor ear heard nor have they ascended to the human heart' (cf. 1 Cor. 2.9). Hegesippus, an ancient and apostolic man, says in the fifth book of his *Memoirs*—I do not know quite what he meant—that these words were spoken vainly, and those who said them lied against both the divine scriptures and the Lord who said 'Blessed are your eyes. . . .' "]
34. See Bauer, *Johannesevangelium*[3], pp. 4 f.

the Gospel of Luke with the fact that the Third Gospel was the gospel used by the heretic Marcion (see above, 184 f., 187). When EH 3.39.12-17 informs us that Papias valued the Apocalypse quite highly, that he used the apostolic gospels of Matthew and of Mark/Peter along with other traditional materials from the circle of the twelve and finally that he also cites from 1 John and 1 Peter, while in the same context various persons of the apostolic age to whom Papias appealed are mentioned by name (EH 3.39.2-10), its silence about Paul and his letters is completely clear, and cannot be interpreted any differently from the corresponding approach toward the gospels of Luke and John. Papias must have assumed a negative attitude here as well, even if it also may have manifested itself only through silence. That, in fact, the remains of the literary activity of Papias never show anything even vaguely resembling Pauline coloration is only mentioned in passing, since if this observation had to stand alone, it would prove precious little in view of the paucity of the remnants of Papias. Taking everything together, however, we find in Papias a churchman who, in addition to the Apocalypse and the genuine gospel tradition emanating from the bosom of Palestine, holds those two writings in highest regard which indicate their ecclesiastical orientation in a particularly clear way, the one [218] by its origin in Rome and its Petrine authorship [1 Peter], the other by its explicitly anti-gnostic thrust [1 John]. The letters of Paul (so long as we still must disregard the pastoral Epistles) could in no way compete with such writings, especially since they were compromised through the patronage of people like Marcion.

Justin, the contemporary and coreligionist of Papias, was no more successful than the latter in acquiring anything from the Apostle to the Gentiles. That is even more peculiar in his case since he carried on his activity in Rome, where "Peter and Paul" was the watchword, and at least Romans and 1 Corinthians were available. But in the case of Justin also, one must sharply minimize the claims of Pauline reminiscences in order to arrive at an acceptable result.[35] Such allusions are of no help to me, since at best they spring up occasionally from the subconscious but evidence no kind of living relationship with Paul. Or what is one to think of this matter in view of the fact that it does not occur to the apologist to mention Romans 13 when

35. On this matter, cf. Bousset, *Evangeliencitate Justins*, pp. 121-123.

he argues that the Christians have always patriotically paid their taxes (*Apol.* 17)—Theophilus of Antioch refers to this chapter (*Autolycus* 1.11,3.14); or that 1 Corinthians 15 in no way plays a role in Justin's treatise *On The Resurrection*—Athenagoras calls the apostle to mind in his treatment (*On the Resurrection* 18)? Rather, for Justin everything is based on the gospel tradition. And if a third question may be allowed, how is one to explain the fact that in the discussion of the conversion of the gentiles and the rejection of the Jews (*Apol.* 49) any congruence with Romans 9-11 is omitted, despite the fact that they both, apologist and apostle, appeal to Isaiah 65.2? In this light, the fact that the name of Paul is nowhere mentioned by Justin acquires a special significance that can hardly be diminished by the observation that the names of the other apostles also are absent. In one passage we hear of John, the apostle of Christ, as the author of Revelation (*Dial.* 81.4); and even though the names of the apostles are not mentioned on other occasions, there are repeated references to their "Memoirs." With respect to Paul, not only is his name lacking, but also any congruence with his letters. But for a learned churchman who carried on his work in Rome around the middle of the second century to act thus can only [219] be understood as quite deliberate conduct.[36] And if pressed to suggest a reason for this, it would seem to me that the most obvious possibility here would also be the reference to Marcion.

The fact that in Rome, unlike Hierapolis, the gospel of Luke did not experience a temporary rejection together with the letters of Paul is surely due to geographical considerations. Perhaps one might wish to explain in a similar manner the fact that another churchman, who stood in the forefront of the battle with heresy and whom we know especially as an opponent of Marcion, Polycarp of Smyrna, has a much more positive relationship to the letters of Paul than did Justin.

---

36. It is fitting also to be reminded of Celsus, who could hardly have gained his insight that orthodoxy represented the "great" church over against the heretics (Origen *Against Celsus* 5.59; cf. 5.61 where the ecclesiastically oriented Christians are *hoi apo tou plēthous*, "those of the multitude") anywhere but in Rome, and thus it was apparently there that he pursued his basic studies of the religion he combatted. For him also, the gospels are overwhelmingly of the synoptic type, and he also surely knows certain Pauline ideas, but not letters of the Apostle to the Gentiles. Cf. K. J. Neumann, RPTK³, 3 (1897): 774.42 ff.; H. J. Holtzmann, *Lehrbuch der historisch-kritischen Einleitung in das Neue Testament*³ (Freiburg im B., 1892), p. 111.

Still, it is more accurate to find the reason for this in chronological rather than geographical limitations, and to remind ourselves that Polycarp wrote his epistle to the Philippians a good while before Marcion appeared. Thus he needed to feel no reservations about using Paul for support as he attempted to strengthen the backbone of the ecclesiastical minority in a Christian community that the Apostle to the Gentiles had founded and to which he had sent epistolary instructions (see above, 71-74). For him the blessed and illustrious Paul, with his wisdom, was a most valuable ally—Polycarp knew full well that the Apostle to the Gentiles had instructed the Philippians not only orally, but also by means of letters.[37] And although Polycarp apparently was not even exactly clear as to the number of such letters, and does not avoid the kind of language illustrated by the matter-of-fact way in which his ecclesiastical consciousness associates "the other apostles" with Paul (9.1), this is insufficient reason to doubt that he was acquainted with the canonical epistle to the Philippians. Concerning the other Pauline epistles, it seems to me that there are clear indications only for his having read 1 Corinthians and probably also Romans. Galatians and Ephesians also might have belonged to his collection, but I cannot free myself from doubts concerning the pastoral [220] Epistles.[38] Polycarp clearly agrees with Papias, however, in the use of 1 Peter, which Eusebius had already noted (EH 4.14.9), and of 1 John (Polycarp *Phil.* 7.1).

We have already heard of the sympathy which the Antiochian churchman Ignatius, probably stimulated by Rome, showed toward the apostles Peter and Paul (above, 112, 117). In contrast to Polycarp, Ignatius does not betray any knowledge (as yet) of 1 Peter, nor of 1 John. But when we then inquire further as to the influence of Paul and his epistles, the result also is not very impressive. To be sure, alongside obvious deviations Ignatius advocates ideas, or perhaps better, attitudes that we similarly observe in the Apostle to the Gentiles who, like Ignatius, was facing martyrdom, and here and there Ignatius comes close to Paul with regard to external form. But a direct, fully conscious dependence on the letters of Paul still does

---

37. Polycarp *Phil.* 3.2. On the plural "letters," see Bauer, *Ignatius, ad loc.* (p. 287), [and also Schoedel, *Polycarp . . . Papias*, pp. 14 f.].
38. Cf. M. Dibelius, *Die Pastoralbriefe*, Handbuch zum NT 13[2] (1931) on 1 Tim. 6.7 and 10 [this commentary subsequently has been revised by H. Conzelmann, 1955[3] and 1964[4]]. See also below, 222-225 and 226 f.

not occur. In the single letter of Polycarp, who can be called a spiritual disciple of Paul only in a very limited way, the latter is mentioned by name three times (3.2, 9.1, 11.2-3), and once a Pauline saying is explicitly quoted (11.2 = 1 Cor. 6.2). But in the seven letters of Ignatius, with the exception of the Roman watchword concerning Peter and Paul (*Rom.* 4.3), Paul appears only in *Eph.* 12.2 in a passage which does not exactly attest an extensive knowledge of the content of a relatively large number of Paul's letters. There Ignatius explains that Paul mentions the Ephesians "in every letter." That this is not true for our collection is generally acknowledged, and I regard as wasted effort all attempts to prove that it is at least approximately correct. As a matter of fact, if we exclude the pastoral epistles and the inscription of Ephesians, the city of Ephesus is mentioned by Paul only in 1 Corinthians (15.32, 16.8). And it is precisely that letter of the Apostle to the Gentiles, and indeed only that letter, which Ignatius assuredly had read. As for other letters of Paul [221] only a possibility exists [39]—this may be sufficient for those who are sympathetically disposed, but it cannot be forced upon anyone.

The reason I will have nothing to do with the question of indirect influence is the futility of an argumentation based on only halfway satisfactory evidence. Although such an influence cannot be denied for Paul in those decades in general, we are in no position to define and delimit it with precision in this particular instance any more than in others. My awareness of the extremely fragmentary nature of our knowledge also prevents me from speaking on this matter even with limited confidence. I cannot possibly adopt a procedure which draws straight lines between the few more or less sure points that can still be ascertained, and thus manages to make connections between relatively remote items—connections the possibility and nature of which remain completely obscure. Paul and Ignatius are separated by a full half century that was quite rich in events of great significance for the

---

39. If Ignatius also knew Ephesians (compare the inscription to his Ephesian letter with the Pauline Eph. 1.3 ff.; this has the best claim after 1 Corinthians), and already knew it as a letter to Ephesus (which is unlikely on account of Marcion [who seems to call it "Laodiceans"]), then the plural implied in the words "every letter" would be explained. [Grant, *Ignatius,* p. 43, accepts an older interpretation that takes the phrase *en pasē epistolē* to mean "in an entire letter," referring to Ephesians alone.] Of course, it would be explained almost equally well if it were conceded that the passage refers to Romans (16.5) and 2 Corinthians (1.8) with their references to Asia (see below, 221).

Christian cause, and within which the development of Christianity in Antioch is almost completely unknown to me. The history of Paul has not encouraged me to expect that this city, where the Christian community did not belong to his circle during his lifetime and which received no letter from him, should suddenly open itself to him and to his writings (see above, 63). The period after Paul's death would seem to us to have been much more a time of diminution of the Pauline sphere of influence, rather than expansion. And what we may still have been in a position to ascertain concerning the shape of Christian life in Antioch to the time of Ignatius (above, 65-67) indicates that influences other than that of Paul were at work there and connects Ignatius to them, despite all his resistance.

Of course, all doubt would fade away if in the essentials of his teaching Ignatius were perceptibly dependent on statements from the Pauline epistles. But that is not the case. The only letter that could with certainty be ascribed to Ignatius' use was, as we saw above, 1 Corinthians—that unit among the major Pauline letters which yields the very least for our understanding of the Pauline faith. And it is not even a "dogmatic" passage such as 1 Corinthians 15 that had bewitched Ignatius. But the Pauline proclamation certainly can not overflow into the postapostolic age through the channel of 1 Corinthians. [222] If the preservation and promulgation of the Apostle's preaching really had been the intention behind the original circulation of Pauline letters in this period, then Romans and the terribly neglected second letter to the Corinthians, which completely sank into oblivion alongside the first, would have had to provide the source to a much greater extent that actually took place. But in our investigation of the impact of the Pauline writings, whenever we come from the marshy ground of "reminiscences" and "allusions" to firmer territory, again and again we confront 1 Corinthians. This was true for Polycarp (see above, 217), is true for Ignatius, and will also be true for *1 Clement.* It seems to me that the last named, *1 Clement,* holds the solution to the riddle of why 1 Corinthians, which is so meager in didactic content, should have preference— an esteem that accorded first place to it in the oldest collection of Pauline letters of which we are still aware.[40]

40. In the *Muratorian Canon.* Marcion also attests this attitude, even if he himself inserts Galatians before it. Cf. Jülicher-Fascher, *Einleitung*[7], pp. 546 f.

We already know what made 1 Corinthians so valuable to the author of *1 Clement*. He was not at all concerned with the Pauline gospel; in that case he would have put Romans, which also was available to him, to a different use than he actually does.[41] 1 Corinthians was an extremely important weapon for him in the conflict against Corinth (see above, 114), and perhaps it had been passed along to him by his allies there. Since the most obvious interpretation of *1 Clement* 47.1 indicates that at the beginning of the controversy the author knew only *one* letter of Paul to Corinth, it seems that the entire Corinthian heritage from Paul had not already made its way to Rome during peaceful times for purposes of edification.[42] Whatever Clement appropriates from 1 Corinthians makes a point against the adversaries in Corinth—1 Cor. 1.11-13 = *1 Clem.* 47.3; 1 Cor. 12.12 ff. = *1 Clem.* 37.5-38.1; and even a portion of the [223] hymn concerning love, 1 Cor. 13.4-7 = *1 Clem.* 49.5. And from that time on, the purpose of 1 Corinthians was firmly established for the church: "First of all, to the Corinthians, censuring the heresies of schism" (*primum omnium Corinthiis schismae haereses interdicens, Muratorian Canon,* lines 42 f.). But it is really rather peculiar and in need of an explanation that this extensive and multifaceted epistle is supposed to have had only this purpose.[43]

If we are not content to believe that it was by an accident of fate that, in the course of scarcely twenty years, precisely 1 Corinthians came to be firmly established and given special honor within the churches of Rome, Smyrna, and Antioch, then it must have been *that* church in which 1 Corinthians first came to be prized so highly— indeed, the only church that had a discernible reason for such an attitude—it must have been Rome that took the initiative. Rome did not want to withhold such an approved weapon from its allies in the fight against heresy. On this occasion Smyrna also may have re-

41. Strictly speaking, he uses it only for the purpose of moral admonition—*1 Clem.* 35.5-6, following Rom. 1.29-32; *1 Clem.* 33.1, following Rom. 6.1.
42. It also seems that the letter to the Philippians was not yet used in Clement's Roman church. Otherwise he surely also would have remembered Phil. 2.1-12 when he refers to the example of the humble Christ (16.17) and when he matched Paul against the Corinthians (47.1).
43. Indeed, the *Muratorian Canon* is so greatly under the influence of this attitude, which has been transmitted to it, concerning the purpose of the epistle, that even 2 Corinthians is pictured as not having any different aim (lines 42 and 54 f.).

ceived the epistle to the Romans, the use of which cannot be established for contemporary Antioch, although that possibility is not thereby excluded. Perhaps at that time both communities also obtained 2 Corinthians from the world capital, a document that Rome surely brought home as valuable booty from its Corinthian campaign. Some sort of compelling evidence of such possession, to be sure, can be offered at present neither for Smyrna nor even for Antioch. But such considerations may be left aside, even though they might throw a ray of light, albeit a woefully weak one, on the lengthy and obscure history of the collection of Pauline epistles.[44] [224] It appears to me to be to some degree probable that 1 Corinthians was put at the disposal of the orthodox communities in Smyrna and Antioch by Rome, about the year 100. That it at that time may also have received the widely discussed "ecumenical" stamp (1.2)[45] is a suggestion that may be excusable in a book that is forced to rely so heavily on conjectures.

The small collections of Pauline letters, which were cherished at the beginning of the second century in the "churches" of Rome—doubtless just as in similarly oriented Corinth, in Antioch and Smyrna[46]—were then surpassed and replaced by Marcion's more complete collection. I would regard him as the first systematic collector of the Pauline heritage. He who ruthlessly rejected the Old

44. The situation with regard to the collection of the Pauline epistles is entirely different from that of the letters of Ignatius. The latter were written one after another and then were immediately brought together. With Paul, those letters which are surely genuine cover a period of a decade, and were sent to at least six different, in part widely separated localities (Galatia, Colossae, Philippi, Thessalonica, Corinth, Rome). Further decades were required to establish the prerequisites according to which pseudo-Pauline letters could be added (Ephesians, 2 Thessalonians; prior to the year 110 according to Jülicher-Fascher, *Einleitung*[7], p. 67), and last of all the pastoral Epistles. That in a period when Pauline influence was declining, extant collections of his letters had been systematically completed everywhere at once is doubtful to me, and I can hardly regard it as really proven that Polycarp possessed a collection of ten, to say nothing of thirteen, Pauline writings [—regardless of what he had of the letters of Ignatius].
45. Cf. Harnack, *Briefsammlung*, p. 9; Jülicher-Fascher, *Einleitung*[7], p. 472; Lietzmann, "Zwei Notizen zu Paulus," pp. 3-5 [= 151-153]. In this way, Lietzmann's question in his commentary *An die Korinther, ad loc.*, also would be answered: "Why should the redactor have dealt only with 1 Corinthians in that manner, while sparing all the other epistles?"
46. Here the development flourished most extensively, since Polycarp possessed especially wide-ranging connections. He was an Asiatic, but also was in touch with Antioch and Rome, and even had contacts in Macedonia.

Testament and everything of primitive Christian tradition that stemmed from Palestine, was plainly bent on giving his teaching as broad a Pauline foundation as possible, while on the other hand, he was in a position to realize his aspirations since he was a well-traveled, educated, affluent person with numerous connections. It would not surprise me if we owed to his perception the short communication of Paul to Philemon, this purely private letter that hardly would have been read in communities prior to Marcion. And whoever wonders with Harnack why "the letter to the Galatians has been preserved for us at all" [47] perhaps may also feel himself indebted to Marcion, since prior to his activity sure traces of Galatians are lacking, while the uncertain traces are sharply limited to Polycarp.

It is well established that Marcion came from Pontus, the neighbor of Galatia, and as he travelled out into the world, he could not have avoided the communities to which Paul had addressed his communication. Possibly he had already become acquainted with this letter in his native land. In any event, it is certain that it was from Galatians [48] [225] and not, say, from Romans with its concise explanation that Christ was the end of the law (10.4), that Marcion got the idea about how he could break the back of the Old Testament, so highly treasured by so many Christians, and drive the Jewish apostles of Jerusalem from the field. Then on his journey through Asia Minor, and as he went further westward until he reached Rome, he may have collected everything that anyone here or there in the Christian communities possessed from Paul. Perhaps, together with the note to Philemon, he also brought to the West at that time the epistle to the Colossians, of which we are unable to detect even the faintest trace prior to Marcion.[49]

In line with this approach, it is difficult for me to believe that Marcion had already known the pastoral Epistles, which are not included in his canon. He who with utmost passion was in hot pursuit of every line from Paul—he had to be!—and who because of the paucity of traditional material would hardly permit any large scale wastefulness, also would have pressed these three epistles into his

47. Harnack, *Briefsammlung*, p. 72.
48. That is the only way to explain the fact that in Marcion's holy scriptures, Galatians stands first in the collection of Paul's letters.
49. With the exception of Ephesians, if it is spurious; but we do not know when and where it made use of Colossians.

service by reworking them. There would have been even less reason to reject all of them together insofar as the epistle to Titus, which from Marcion's perspective would not be wedded for better or worse to the epistles to Timothy,[50] offered very little of offense to him. But if this assumption is correct and is taken seriously, the further hypothesis seems to me valid that the pastoral Epistles still were not in existence at the time that Marcion made his decision as to the extent of the Pauline material. I see no way to accept Harnack's view:

> Around the year 140, Marcion knew a collection of only ten letters; in all probability he did not reject the pastoral Epistles, but simply did not know them. But we are in the fortunate position of being able to trace back to around the year 100 not only the collection of the ten letters, but even that of the thirteen letters, for Polycarp's letter to the Philippians at the time of Trajan shows us through its quotations and allusions that [226] our present collection, including the pastoral epistles, was already in use both in Smyrna and in Philippi. The Pastorals thus had been added to the collection of ten letters already prior to Marcion, and the older collection was supplanted immediately in almost all the churches. Not only the original collection but also that containing 13 letters take us back to the end of the first century as the *terminus ad quem!* [51]

Thus there is portrayed for us here a Marcion who comes through Asia to Rome, but the pastoral Epistles elude him despite the fact that they have been in use—and indeed not sporadically here and there, but as parts of a collection in official use—for more than a generation, and even right in Smyrna, a city with which Marcion was in contact during his journey.[52] Such a Marcion seems to me to be an impossibility, and for that reason the observations that led Harnack to his conclusions should be assessed differently. The basic reason for assigning an early date to the Pastorals is, for Harnack and many others, the notion that Polycarp reproduces "three passages from the pastoral Epistles in his letter." [53] Whoever agrees with me in con-

50. Just as little as it was for those heretics who, according to Clement of Alexandria, rejected only the two epistles to Timothy (*Strom.* 2.[11.]52), while we hear of Tatian that he recognized just the epistle to Titus (Jerome *Preface to the Commentary on Titus* 7 = Vallarsi ed. p. 686; Migne PL 26).
51. Harnack, *Briefsammlung*, p. 6.
52. Harnack, *Marcion*², p. 28° [referring to Polycarp's rebuke of Marcion; above, 70].
53. Harnack, *Briefsammlung*, p. 72.

cluding from the negative stance of Marcion toward the Pastorals that prior to him (to say nothing of the time of Trajan) they cannot already have received recognition as letters of Paul (to choose a very guarded form of expression), will explain those "quotations" either (1) by denying that they reflect any direct dependence [54] but instead derive from the common use of an established stock of ideas (as in the corresponding case of the contacts between Ignatius and the Fourth Gospel; see above, 209 f.), recalling that such connections also exist between the Pastorals and *1 Clement,* and to close the triangle, even between *1 Clement* and Polycarp—connections that reflect a standardized way of speaking common in ecclesiastical circles; or, (2) if the citations appear quite unambiguous to him, he will have to conclude that it is the Pastorals that are derivative, and their author was dependent on Polycarp.[55] That author doubtless comes from the same circle of orthodoxy as Polycarp. All the arguments against such an order of dependence do not in the least neutralize the force with which Marcion resists the assumption [227] that the pastoral Epistles had already been regarded with veneration within Christendom prior to the beginning of his activity.[56]

If we want to understand the origin of the pastoral Epistles, we must remember that just as the gospel of John began its existence as a heretical gospel, so Paul also enjoyed the favor of the heretics to a great extent. Marcion simply represents a high point, and is by no means a unique case. Zahn thoroughly demonstrated the close relationships of Valentinus and his school to the Apostle to the Gentiles;[57] according to Clement of Alexandria *Strom.* 7.(17.)106, Valentinus is supposed to have listened to Theodas, an acquaintance of Paul. The Valentinians "maintain that Paul has made use of the basic concepts of their system in his letters in a manner sufficiently clear to anyone who can read" (Zahn, 751). "The manner in which they cite the Pauline letters is just as respectful as the manner we find

54. Cf. M. Dibelius, *Pastoralbriefe,* pp. 6, 53, 55.
55. [H. F. von Campenhausen has even argued that Polycarp was the author of the Pastorals; see below, 307. On the problem in general, see also Schoedel, *Polycarp . . . Papias,* pp. 5, 16, etc.]
56. Moreover, even the *Muratorian Canon* preserves the recollection that the pastoral Epistles were added at first as a supplement to a collection that had ended with the letter to Philemon (lines 59 ff.).
57. Zahn, *Geschichte,* 1.2 (1889): 751-758.

used by the teachers of the church of the *following* [58] decades and centuries" (756). "The teaching of Valentinus is just as inconceivable without the letters of Paul as without the prologue to the Fourth Gospel, and it is no accident that Paul is preferred by all Valentinians as the preacher of the hidden wisdom who speaks out most clearly" (758). It is demonstrable that Basilides also made use of Romans and 1 Corinthians, and there may be some truth to Jerome's claim that Basilides treated the pastoral Epistles in the same way as Marcion (in the passage cited above, 223 n. 50). I need not continue naming other gnostics who appreciated Paul.[59] Second Peter 3.16 will have occurred to everyone in this connection. And for the Montanists, Paul was just as indispensible as a witness to the activity of the spirit in primitive Christianity as was the gospel of John with its Paraclete. Even the *Muratorian Canon* (lines 63-68) complains that heretics are producing false letters of Paul in order to make propaganda for their false teachings by using the stolen prestige of the Apostle to the Gentiles. [228]

In this light, the reluctance with which the representatives of the church made use of the Apostle to the Gentiles around the middle of the second century (Papias, Justin, Hegesippus; above, 213-215) seems to me to be explicable. Perhaps, as the situation developed, some would have preferred henceforth to exclude Paul completely and to rely exclusively on the twelve apostles. But it was already too late for that. Rome (together with the "church," which it led) had already accepted too much from the Apostle to the Gentiles, had appealed to him too often, suddenly to recognize him no longer. He had become a martyr-apostle of Rome—had helped it to develop the popular slogan "Peter and Paul"; and even if Rome did not really know how to begin to put to use Paul's letter to the Romans, 1 Corinthians had proved itself to be extremely productive for purposes of church politics in the hands of Rome. By that means, Paul and his letter came to have permanent claims on the "church." There were other cases as well where Christianity subsequently had to come to terms with all sorts of things that it had originally accepted without ques-

58. Italics mine. However, I reject Zahn's continuation as an unproved prejudice; "That was precisely the phraseology that Valentinius found to be dominant in the church and that his school appropriated."
59. Cf. R. Liechtenhan, *Die Offenbarung im Gnostizismus* (Göttingen, 1901), p. 79.

tion and from which it could not simply retreat as circumstances changed. Thus initially one spoke without embarrassment, in accordance with the facts (and it is easy enough to find additional examples) about how Jesus also had been baptized; he was happy to be able thus to anchor the Christian practice to the life of Jesus. But then, in the struggle with evil or contrary antagonists, he took great pains to make a convincing case for the superiority of Jesus over John, or to explain just what Jesus could have expected to gain by being baptized for the forgiveness of sins.

Thus, despite all heretical misuse, Paul had to be retained as the "church's" apostle. But it was, of course, desirable henceforth to mark him unequivocally with the ecclesiastical and anti-heretical stamp. In the light of this, I am inclined to see the pastoral Epistles as an attempt on the part of the church unambiguously to enlist Paul as part of its anti-heretical front and to eliminate the lack of confidence in him in ecclesiastical circles. As its answer to the heretical Apostle of the epistles to Laodicea and Alexandria, "forged in the name of Paul" (*Pauli nomine finctae, Muratorian Canon,* lines 64 ff.) the church raised up the Paul of orthodoxy by using the same means.[60] Such a need may have been felt even prior to Marcion. But since it [229] is difficult to find satisfactory evidence that the pastoral Epistles already were in existence prior to him (see above, 222-224), there is really no reason why it could not have been *his* appearance that gave the church the decisive impulse for their production. Indeed, if Polycarp cannot serve as the *terminus ad quem* for the pastoral Epistles, explicit attestation requiring knowledge of them occurs first with the churchman Irenaeus, who begins his great work *Against Heresies* with the words "of the apostle" from 1 Timothy 1.4 (AH 1. preface).

However unpopular this view currently may be and however little I myself shared it a short time ago, it no longer seems to me today to be improbable that 1 Timothy 6.20 refers to Marcion's *Antitheses* —perhaps even before they were put into written form.

I cannot accept the outlook which rejects such a late origin for the Pastorals because "in that case a reference to the great gnostic

60. This sort of analysis of the purpose of the Pastorals does not, of course, exclude the other view which sees them as a weapon in the conflict with the heretics. Cf. above, 76.

systems would be expected." [61] We do, in fact, know of an orthodox author who doubtless flourished subsequent to Basilides, Valentinus, and Marcion, and yet makes no clear reference to these teachings; but in spite of this he wants to draw the Apostle to the Gentiles into the ecclesiastical phalanx of heresy fighters in much the same way as we have suspected of the author of the pastoral Epistles. I am referring to that presbyter in Asia who produced the *Acts of Paul* at about the same time that the Asian Irenaeus, motivated by the same ecclesiastical spirit, opposed the gnostics with the help of the Pastorals. These *Acts* speak in language "clearly saturated with reminiscences of the pastoral Epistles." [62] Their author also has Paul advocating, by means of a letter (so-called *3 Corinthians;* see above, 42 n. 99), the ecclesiastical viewpoint in opposition to a gnostic aberration that cannot be clearly identified.

The price the Apostle to the Gentiles had to pay to be allowed to remain in the church was the complete surrender of his personality and historical particularity. If already in the pastoral Epistles he has strayed far from his origins, in the *Acts of Paul* and the *Epistle of the Apostles* he has become merely the docile disciple of the twelve from whom he receives his instructions.[63] [230] But even this sacrifice did not really help him. Wherever the "church" becomes powerful, the bottom drops out from under him and he must immediately give way to the celebrities from the circle of the twelve apostles. We have seen this same process taking place in Ephesus, in Corinth, in Rome and Antioch, with variations only on account of the differing locations and their respective histories (see above, 83 f., 112-118). And we soon reach the point where the church no longer needs the apostle to the nations for any mission, but divides up the entire world among the twelve. To some extent, Paul becomes influential only as part of the holy scriptures acknowledged in the church—not the personality of the Apostle to the Gentiles and his proclamation, but the *word* of Paul [or, the *word* "Paul"] whenever it is useful for the development and preservation of ecclesiastical teaching. But that involves

61. As in Dibelius, *Pastoralbriefe*, p. 6.
62. Rolffs in Hennecke[2], pp. 196 f. [See now also Schneemelcher in Hennecke-Schneemelcher, 2: 348.]
63. See above, 114 n. 6, and cf. C. Schmidt "Ein Berliner Fragment der alten *Praxeis Paulou*," Sb Berlin 6 for 1931, pp. 5 f. [= 39 f.].

looking beyond the limits of the period presently under discussion. In our period we observe how the introduction of the pastoral Epistles actually made the collection of Paul's letters ecclesiastically viable for the very first time. Perhaps 1 John, which has a pronounced anti-heretical tone and came to be valued quite early in the church (Polycarp, Papias), performed a similar service for the heretical gospel of John.

10

The Beginnings

Let us sketch once more the state of affairs that had developed at the beginning of the second century. Orthodoxy, so it appeared to us, represented the form of Christianity supported by the majority in Rome—a Christianity which, to be sure, still had to contend strenuously with the heretics throughout the entire second century and even longer. Indeed, in the middle of the second century the controversy rose to the intensity of a life and death struggle, the outcome of which has been of decisive significance not only for Rome but for Christianity in general. Already around the year 100 the Roman church had extended its influence to Corinth. In the course of the following decades the majority came to agree with Rome in some of the churches in Asia Minor, and a minority in some others—as also elsewhere, in Philippi and Antioch. However, east of Phrygian Hierapolis we could hardly discern any traces of orthodoxy. Christianity and heresy were essentially synonymous there (see above, 80 f., 171-173).

Rome, on the other hand, was from the very beginning the center and chief source of power for the "orthodox" movement within Christianity. At the beginning of the second century, Christianity as a whole still is called the "catholic church" by Ignatius (*Smyr.* 8.2; cf. *Martyrdom of Polycarp* inscription, 8.1, 19.2), but by the end of that century it has become divided, as far as the Roman or Roman influenced outlook is concerned, into two distinct parts, the catholic (*Muratorian Canon,* lines 66, 69, 61 f.) or "great" (see above, 216 n. 36) church on the one hand and the *massa perditionis* [condemned multitude] of the heretics on the other. As a matter of course,

229

Rome possessed the most tightly knit, perhaps the only more or less reliable anti-heretical majority, because it [232] was farthest removed from the oriental danger zone and in addition was by nature and custom least inclined or able to yield to seemingly fantastic oriental ways of thinking and oriental emotions that becloud clear thought. The sober sense of the Roman was not the proper seed-bed for Syrian or Egyptian syncretism.[1] To be sure, his church also had to undergo the experience that all ungodliness flows together at the center of the world. But the appreciation for rules and regulations, law and order, asserted itself all the more and gained the upper hand. This extremely powerful organism, although under great stress, knew how to rid itself even of the highly dangerous poison of Marcionism in the middle of the second century. In view of the actual circumstances, the Roman did not demand the impossible;[2] he was by nature fitted to be an organizer, and this gave him a sharp weapon for the battle against heresy. This weapon would prove to be all the more effective since, as we already know, from very early times Rome did not lack the necessary material means for carrying out its far-reaching plans.

Relying on the above and supported by the conviction that Rome [233] constituted the church founded in the world capital by the

1. I am well aware that there were many Orientals among the Roman Christians of the most ancient period, and will not invoke the Latin names in the list of greetings in Rom. 16 against that fact. But the easterners Paul, and even more so Peter, the man of the Old Testament and of the synoptic tradition respectively (see below, 238 f.), and Ignatius (just in case he also was heard in Rome) instituted their towering personalities in Rome not on behalf of a pronounced syncretism, but on the contrary, provided considerable obstacles to it. Notwithstanding the Greek language of *1 Clement,* directed to the Corinthians, a person like Clement is pronouncedly Roman and demonstrates what Roman leadership was striving for and what it hoped to avoid. And Justin, with his enthusiastic predilection for the millennial kingdom, is not Roman but oriental, and seems to me to leave the impression that his inclinations are by no means shared in general in his environment. He does distinguish between "godless and impious *hairesiōtai*" and the orthodox (*Dial.* 80.3-5). But the latter are further subdivided by him into those who share the "pure and pious outlook (*gnōme*) of the Christians" only in a general way (80.2), and others who are "entirely correct in outlook" (*orthognōmones kata panta;* 80.5)—i.e. who possess the correct *gnōme* in *all* particulars. The last named share his chiliastic persuasions, while the others will have nothing to do with such a notion. That these others constituted a majority in Rome can be seen from the somewhat earlier *Hermas,* who makes apocalypticism subservient to practical ecclesiastical aims; [on *Hermas* and apocalyptic, see further Grant, *Introduction to the Apostolic Fathers* (= Grant, AF 1 [1964]), pp. 113 f., and Snyder, *Hermas,* pp. 9 f.].
2. On this and on what follows, cf. chap. 6 above.

greatest apostles, Rome confidently extends itself eastward,[3] tries to break down resistance and stretches a helping hand to those who are like-minded, drawing everything within reach into the well-knit structure of ecclesiastical organization. Heresy, with its different brands and peculiar configurations that scarcely even permitted it to be united in a loose association reflecting common purpose, had nothing corresponding to this by way of a similar offensive and defensive force with which to counter. Only a few heresiarchs such as Marcion were able to draw together their followers throughout the world into an ecclesiastical structure. But Marcion himself, the most dangerous of all, to a large measure paralyzed his own cause insofar as he excised with his own hand the source of natural increase for his community by his inexorable rejection of procreation.[4] In the long run he simply had to drop out of the picture—all the more since the organization and the concept of church offices which he advocated also ultimately failed to produce the same tight and efficient structure as developed in the church.[5]

A united front composed of Marcionites and Jewish Christians, Valentinians and Montanists, is inconceivable. Thus it was the destiny of the heresies, after they had lost their connection with the orthodox Christianity that remained, to stay divided and even to fight among themselves,[6] and thus to be routed one after another by orthodoxy. The form of Christian belief and life which was successful was that supported by the strongest organization—the form which was the most uniform and best suited for mass consumption—in spite of the fact that, in my judgment, for a long time after the close of the post-apostolic age the sum total of consciously orthodox and anti-heretical Christians was numerically inferior to that of the "heretics." It was only natural that the compact ecclesiastical outlook with its concentrated energy would more and more draw to itself the great mass of those who at first, unclear and undecided, had stood in the middle resigned to a general sort of Christianity, and who under different circumstances could even have turned in the opposite direction. And

3. There is no "west" for Christian Rome in the earliest period.
4. Harnack, *Marcion*[2], pp. 148 f.
5. Cf. Harnack, *Marcion*[2], pp. 146 f.
6. As an example of this, it suffices to refer to the conflict between the followers of Marcion and of Bardesanes in Edessa; see above, 29.

it appears to be no less self-evident [234] that the Roman government finally came to recognize that the Christianity ecclesiastically organized from Rome was flesh of its flesh, came to unite with it, and thereby actually enabled it to achieve ultimate victory over unbelievers and heretics.

Something further must be taken into consideration in order to understand the victory of this kind of orthodoxy. The course of Christianity was directed toward the West from the very beginning. One could almost say that it was driven straight into the arms of Rome by its development. Many a crucial matter might have been different if the actual Orient had not simply excluded the new religion for a long time, thus making it impossible for marked and undiluted eastern influences to become operative. In Edessa, Christianity is more recent than Marcion, and in Egypt its first certain traces are found in the person of the gnostic Basilides during the reign of Hadrian. The Palestinian Jewish Christians were not able to make inroads into Babylonia, with its heavy Jewish concentration, nor was Paul able to gain a firm foothold in Nabataean Arabia. As far as we can see, Damascus, the city of Paul's conversion, no longer plays a role in his later life,[7] not to mention the fact that he also had included the other eastern areas only in his final plans. This was not because the Orient was under control and Paul would not work in what was not his own territory, but because these regions at first simply rejected Christianity. Samaria was closed, because even at the time of the Samaritan Justin everybody there worshipped the god Simon, not the god [235] Jesus (*Dial.* 120.6, *Apol.* 26.2-3); and trans-

---

7. For a long time we hear nothing about Christianity in Damascus. The suggestion in the *Chronicle of Arbela* that Christians might have been there around the year 200 (ed. with German translation by E. Sachau, Abhandlungen der preussischen Akademie der Wissenschaft, 6 for 1915: 59), is more than balanced by the silence of Eusebius, even where he speaks of the conversion of Paul (EH 2.1.9 and 14). I cannot agree at all with the favorable assessment of the historical worth of the most ancient parts of the *Chronicle of Arbela*, which belongs to the sixth century, by such people as Sachau, Harnack (in the 4th German ed. of *Mission*, pp. 683-689, especially 684 [this material is lacking in the ET, at p. 146]), and others. I find it impossible to reconcile the claim that there could have been Christianity—and that of an ecclesiastical sort—east of the Tigris already around the year 100 with the picture that I have constructed on the basis of older and better sources. If the beginnings here go back to the apostle Addai, as is claimed for Edessa by the *Doctrine of Addai*, extreme caution seems to me to be necessary (see above, 20). I have no fear that *Arbela* represents the fixed point from which my world could be turned upside down.

Jordania also was closed together with the adjacent areas, perhaps because of competing groups such as the baptist sects, which were still of grave concern to Mani,[8] but above all because of the presence of an extremely vigorous paganism.[9] Prevented by superior forces from turning aside toward the East, Christianity moved northward, clinging close to the hellenized coast of Phoenicia and Syria, and taking a sharp turn westward burst forth over Asia Minor toward Rome and Europe.

It was in Asia Minor (and more precisely primarily in its western part), in Macedonia, and in Greece that Paul engaged in successful activity. He established nothing in his homeland of Cilicia and Tarsus itself, despite extensive efforts (Gal. 1.21). What he held together by virtue of his own personality fell to pieces, was fought over, and was divided up after his death. Lycaonia and Pisidia soon disappear from the tradition. Of Galatia we learn that the capital, Ancyra, which is still a notoriously heretical city for Jerome (*Commentary on Galatians* 3.8 f.), might have been completely lost to Montanism (the anti-Montanist in EH 5.16.4). Corinth comes completely under Roman influence, and in the second century the "church" sought also to appropriate Ephesus by means of John as one of the twelve apostles. In this, of course, it meets with resistance from the heretics. And we observe the same struggle in the Pauline communities of Phrygia, which for the most part reject "right" belief (above, 81 f.)—and where they do accept it, in the person of Papias of Hierapolis, they deny any connections with Paul (see above, 214 f.). If our analysis was correct, Philippi, for the most part, soon embraced gnosticism, and perhaps one must conclude the same concerning Thessalonica (see above, 73-75).

This need not imply any deliberate defection from the Apostle to the Gentiles. After all, we noted that in Phrygia it was precisely orthodoxy that rejected Paul (above, 214 f.). Perhaps the Macedonian gnostics were just as self-conscious of being the genuine disciples of Paul as was Marcion. [236] In the long run almost any gentile Christian could attach himself to the Apostle to the Gentiles so as to re-

8. Schmidt and Polotsky, *Mani-Fund*, 62.1. [On the baptizing sects, see J. Thomas, *Le mouvement baptiste en Palestine et Syrie* (Gembloux, 1935).]
9. One thinks, e.g. of the position of Emesa or of Heliopolis-Baalbek with respect to Christianity. Cf. Harnack, *Mission²*, 2: 123, 125 (= 4th German ed., pp. 658, 660).

ceive legitimization from him—the author of 2 Peter already complains about this (3.16). One such Paulinist could, unencumbered by the weight of a Jewish heritage, develop Paul's extreme pessimism with respect to the material world into a doctrine of the demiurge, while another could omit this last step, as the Apostle himself had done. This one might put the whole Old Testament behind him, because "Christ is the end of the law" (Rom. 10.4), while that one might find the same sort of justification for continuing to revere it as "holy, just, and good" (Rom. 7.12). The "strong" as well as the "weak" (those who practice abstinence) stood equally close to him. His christology bordered on docetism with its repeated statements about the Christ who was to be considered as a man (*homoiōma*; Rom. 8.3, Phil. 2.7) abetted by his silence about the Lord's career on earth, while his talk about the "Christ in the flesh" (e.g. Rom. 1.3, 9.5) "born of woman" (Gal. 4.4) also permitted the complete humanity to be maintained firmly. Paul supported a belief in bodily resurrection—nevertheless, this involves neither flesh nor blood (1 Cor. 15.42-50). He was a pneumatic like none other (cf. 1 Cor. 14.18, 2 Cor. 12.1-4), but was also the advocate of ecclesiastical order (e.g. 1 Cor. 14.26-36). And although it is true that orthodoxy exulted in the high regard for church and apostles shown in Ephesians, and that the connections between Ephesians and certain churchmen (1 Peter, Ignatius, Polycarp, and even *Hermas*) can hardly be ignored because of their frequency (even though the decisive argument for proof of literary dependence is lacking), it is also true that the gnostics attributed their speculation about the aeons to this epistle and to Colossians.[10]

But the elasticity of the Pauline outlook did not become important only for those who came after him; it possessed significance already for Paul himself and for his epoch. Paul's as yet quite rudimentary organization of thought patterns, in combination with his apostolic openness that leads him to become everything to everyone so as to win all (1 Cor. 9.22), allows him to display a spirit of toleration that scarcely knows what a heretic might be—that is, "heretic" in the sense of a fellow Christian concerning whom one is convinced that his

10. Cf. Heinrici, *Valentinianische Gnosis*, pp. 184 f., 192; Zahn, *Geschichte*, 1.2: 751.

divergent stance with regard to the faith bars him from the path of salvation. Paul is far from being under the illusion that even in his own communities everyone believes and thinks exactly as he does. Nevertheless, it is instructive to observe the position he takes with regard to divergencies, especially by comparison to the view of later times. [237] According to Paul, the adherents of Cephas and of Apollos in Corinth are not heretics, but represent legitimate varieties of the new religion, as also do the teachings of the other independent apostles such as a Barnabas or a Titus. (It is unfortunate that we know so very little about the last named and his position, and can only suspect that he was of extraordinary significance; in any event, Titus was not, like Timothy, satisfied simply to enlist in the service of the Pauline proclamation.) The faith as it was cultivated in the house church of Aquila and Priscilla and in similar conventicles— how would it have looked? Through detailed explanations the Apostle endeavors to persuade the Corinthian Christians who reject bodily resurrection (1 Cor. 15.12)—perhaps the Alexandrianism of Apollos is at work here. For Justin, such people are only "so-called Christians" (*Dial.* 80.3), and Polycarp does not hesitate to use the expression "firstborn of satan" (*Phil.* 7.1). It is only with reference to a most serious moral deviation that the Apostle proposes exclusion from the community by handing the offender over to the devil (1 Cor. 5.1-5). In the pastoral Epistles the same sentence is levelled against Hymenaeus and Alexander because they have "made shipwreck of the faith" (1 Tim. 1.19 f.).

Furthermore, the religious outlook of the Pauline circle may have picked up additional traits through men who, like Epaphras in Colossae (Col. 1.7), and perhaps also in Laodicea and Hierapolis, proclaimed abroad the Pauline gospel to the extent that they understood it and elaborated upon it. Possibly the aforementioned Epaphras is not entirely blameless for the fact that in the community he established at Colossae, peculiar syncretistic ideas were introduced such as the worship of the cosmic elements—or perhaps it would be more accurate to suggest that such ideas already were present from the very beginning in Colossae but that Epaphras did not take the trouble to eliminate them. Paul receives news about how things stand. But instead of reacting by attacking with a club, he develops his view in the calm confidence that the Christian religion will again eliminate from itself whatever is alien to it, and thus not compatible with it.

On one occasion,[11] to be sure, we see him flare up indignantly and hear him hurl his anathema against a divergent view—[238] this is in Galatians, where it is a matter of preventing a gentile Christian community from falling back into Judaism. But even here it is not the overt Jewish Christianity as advocated, for example, by the "pillar" James that is considered heresy and the object of Paul's wrath. Brethren are transformed into false brethren only at that moment in which, in defiance of the agreement reached in Jerusalem, an attempt is made to fasten the yoke of legalism on the necks of liberated gentile Christians.

The Judaists, for their part, thought and felt differently, and demonstrated this again and again by the fact that they were unable to admit that the Pauline gospel could be adequate even for gentiles. Rather, they were fully convinced that this proclamation *as such*, because of its inadequacy, separated men from the messianic salvation. Thus, if one may be allowed to speak rather pointedly, the apostle Paul was the only heresiarch known to the apostolic age— the only one who was so considered in that period, at least from one particular perspective.[12] It could be said that the Jewish Christians in their opposition to Paul introduced the notion of "heresy" into the Christian consciousness. The arrow quickly flew back at the archer. Because of their inability to relate to a development that took place on hellenized gentile soil, the Judaists soon became a heresy, rejected with conviction by the gentile Christians. Basically, they probably had remained what they had been in the time of James the Just, but the majority of the faithful ultimately came to deviate so much from them that the connection had to break. Thus the Judaists become an instructive example of how even one who preserves the old position can become a "heretic" if the development moves sufficiently far beyond him.

11. The thrust of the polemic in Phil. 3 and in Rom. 16.17-20 is not entirely clear —or in any event, can be interpreted in different ways—and may be left aside at this point.
12. I am restricting myself here to what is attested. Whether the Judaists also came into conflict with others who preached Christ apart from the law, and how they dealt with such, is not reported to us.

That Jewish Christianity was repulsed in no way implies that the gentile Christians at first had constituted a religious entity of their own, apart from their rejection of excessive Judaistic demands and their confession of Jesus as Lord. On the contrary we must suppose that the variety of types was quite considerable; [13] and the location where, in any given case, Christianity became indigenous was of great significance. [239]

In Egypt the environmental conditions for the new religion were such that its initial development basically took a form that appeared to the later church to be heresy. In Asia Minor and further to the west Paulinism was in operation. But not only did this Paulinism bear within itself various possibilities, but alongside it there were other forms of the religion of Christ—compatible with it, alienated from it, or wholly independent of it. To the extent that the Apostle to the Gentiles took a stand with respect to them, even when he felt them to be defective, he still did not detest and condemn them as heretical.

It is not until the postapostolic era that the tensions increase and press for a solution. The explanation for this lies at first in the decline of the eschatological expectation, which made the faithful in-

---

13. In this regard, there is no change during the entire period treated in this book. [239] What was so particularly striking about the new religion for Celsus, who attentively observed and thoroughly studied the Christianity that he attacked (Neumann, RPTK³, 3: 772-775), is a rather disconcerting wealth of ideas, outlooks, and practices that mill about in confusion without achieving any arrangement or unity (Origen *Against Celsus* 5.61-63). Celsus finds as the sole point of agreement within Christianity, which in other respects is disintegrated into fragments, the statement that "the world is crucified to me and I to the world" (5.64 f., citing Gal. 4.14). Indeed, at one point he mentions in passing that part of the Christians have knit themselves together into the "great church" (5.59; see above, 216 n. 36), and finds these people to be peculiar for their close relationship to Judaism from which they had derived the story of creation, the genealogy of mankind, and some other things. But the picture is hardly brought into clearer focus thereby; in any event, the overriding impression remains one of extreme diversity. In a bewildering way, the lines cross one another. And from our perspective, the model according to which Celsus constructed his picture of Christendom is sometimes the orthodox Christian, but at other times the heretic or an undefinable mixture of the two. Surely actual heretics provide the pattern when Celsus says that the Christians boasted of their sorcery and magic, and made use of foreign names and various magical formulas (6.38-40). Indeed, he has seen barbaric books full of names of demons and other abominations in the possession of certain Christian "presbyters" (6.40). Obviously the accusation of sorcery by the pagan civil authorities against the new religion also renders feasible or even encourages the idea that Christianity actually presented such an image when considered from *one* point of view. Is there anything that did not have its place alongside everything else in primitive Christianity!

creasingly unable and unwilling to tolerate disturbances and difficulties as defects of a brief transitional period. If one has to prepare for a lengthy stay, he longs for orderliness and harmony in the house. Thereafter, the respective contending forces reinforced their positions during this period. [240] The advances that Christianity makes in the pagan world have to be purchased by means of conscious and unconscious compromise with the syncretistic spirit of the times. And on the other side, the two factors that above all represent a counter balance to the syncretistic-gnostic religiosity acquire increased significance for the faithful—the Old Testament and the primitive tradition, rooted in Palestine, of the life and teachings of the earthly Jesus.

It seems to me that down to the year 70, and especially where Christians who were free from the law attempted to win gentiles to their religion, Christianity disengaged itself as clearly as possible from Judaism and its approach because of an instinct for self-preservation that is as understandable as it is legitimate.[14] After the failure of the Jewish revolt, this was no longer a danger and the new faith could without apprehension appropriate resources and procedures from its surviving competitor—above all, it could abandon any reservations it might have had toward the Old Testament.[15] Surely this book was of incalculable importance for the proof from prophecy, and for other needs of an apologetic sort and of Christian theology in general, and also for the structure and the enriched content of the worship service. But then the dangers inherent in such a relationship were dissipated insofar as the destruction of the temple had removed the relevance of a significant portion of the law and there was no longer any prospect of forcing circumcision and Mosaic observances on the believers from the gentile world.

With regard to the other major item mentioned above, the authentic tradition of the life of Jesus, it is unfortunate that we have such a depressing paucity of information concerning its significance for the gentile preaching and the gentile Christians of the apostolic age. But we do know that Paul made little use of it in his preaching.[16] He

14. I have sought to demonstrate this from a different point of view in *Wortgottesdienst*, pp. 19 ff.
15. Nevertheless, this reticence toward the Old Testament continues to persist in certain areas where the proximity of a strong Jewish influence is considered doubtful (cf. 1 John, gospel of John, Ignatius).
16. On this, see Bauer, *Johannesevangelium*[3], pp. 245 f.

proclaimed the pre-existent Lord Christ, who descended from above, died on the cross, and after the resurrection was exalted again to heaven, whom he had encountered near Damascus. And since Paul deliberately refused to approach the gentiles as a Jew, but in his dealings with them [241] exercised remarkable self-restraint in his use of the Old Testament,[17] his converts were especially susceptible to sliding over to the gnostic side. Marcion was not the first to turn in this direction under Paul's influence. Something similar had suggested itself for Philippi and the Pauline communities in Phrygia.

We must look to the circle of the twelve apostles to find the guardians of the most primitive information about the life and preaching of the Lord, that tradition in which Jesus of Nazareth shows himself to be alive so as effectively to stand in the way of those who, preoccupied with their syncretistic conception of the heavenly redeemer and filled with a dualistic contempt for matter, deprive his earthly life of its main content. This treasure lies hidden in the synoptic gospels, and we must once again lament that we know so little about their place of origin and their influence on the outside world, even in their earliest stages. Similarly, we have scarcely any trustworthy information about any activity of the personal witnesses of the life of Jesus outside of Palestine. The only sure trail once more leads back, in the person of Peter, to Rome. Here Mark stands beside Peter already in the first century (1 Pet. 5.13). And it was here, according to the ancient gospel prologues,[18] that the gospel of Mark originated. For *1 Clement* it is quite sufficient to assume that its author was acquainted with the gospel of Mark and with a form of the *logia* collection which, judging from the gospels of Matthew and Luke, still must have been in existence in his day. In Rome, the synoptic gospels later emerge for the first time as ecclesiastical books used liturgically, with the claim that they are memoirs of the apostles, and they provide support for Justin in his battle against all the heresies.

Likewise, the Roman confession springs from a synoptic foundation and makes the presence of Jesus commence with his being begotten through the Holy Spirit and his birth from the Virgin.

---

17. Cf. Bauer, *Wortgottesdienst,* pp. 39-46.
18. Harnack, *Evangelien-Prologe,* pp. 5 f. (= 324 f.), on the prologues to Mark and Luke. [For the texts, see also Aland, *Synopsis,* pp. 532 f.; ET in Grant, *Second Century,* pp. 92 f. See also above, 186 (n. 84).]

We may further deduce from *1 Clement* that in Rome, at least the leading circles which were authoritative in ecclesiastical and theological matters were in exceptionally close contact with the Old Testament. Finally, we also notice that among all of the Pauline letters, it is Romans that is most noticeably colored by the Old Testament, and also that those New Testament authors who in other respects display clear [242] connections with Rome, the authors of 1 Peter and Hebrews, live, as it were, in the Old Testament. By means of such observations, we suggest additional reasons that must have made Rome an opponent of gnosticism from the very beginning, and the headquarters of a Christianity that was ecclesiastical in that sense.

It is indeed a curious quirk of history that western Rome was destined to begin to exert the determinative influence upon a religion which had its cradle in the Orient, so as to give it that form in which it was to achieve worldwide recognition. But as an otherworldly religion that despises this world and inflexibly orders life in accord with a superhuman standard that has descended from heaven, or as a complicated mystery cult for religious and intellectual connoisseurs, or as a tide of fanatical enthusiasm that swells today and ebbs tomorrow, Christianity never could have achieved such recognition.

Appendix 1

On the Problem of Jewish Christianity

by Georg Strecker

In the preceding investigation, Walter Bauer posed for himself the task of examining critically the widely held view that "for the period of Christian origins, ecclesiastical doctrine . . . already represents what is primary, while heresies, on the other hand, somehow are a deviation from the genuine" (above, xxiv). He concluded that this understanding of history which has dominated ecclesiastical historiography since Eusebius is not correct, but that for broad areas the heresies were "primary." It is surprising that he did not buttress this conclusion *in extenso* with reference to the problem of Jewish Christianity. This is especially remarkable because here the generalization drawn by the ecclesiastically approved view of history would be most clearly open to refutation—Jewish Christianity, according to the witness of the New Testament, stands at the beginning of the development of church history, so that it is not the gentile Christian "ecclesiastical doctrine" that represents what is primary, but rather a Jewish Christian theology.[1] This fact was forgotten quite early in the ecclesiastical heresiological tradition. The Jewish Christians usually were classified as "Ebionites" in the ecclesiastical catalogues of sects or else, in a highly one-sided presentation, they were deprecated as an insignificant minority by comparison with the "great

---

1. Cf. already above, 236; also H. Koch's review of Bauer (see below, p. 287) with reference to the "most ancient Jewish Christianity in Palestine": "Here also the dogmatically determined historiography of the heresiarchs accused the 'Ebionites' of apostasy or of relapse into Judaism while in reality they were merely the 'conservatives' who did not go along with the Pauline-hellenistic developments" (345).

church." Thus implicitly the idea of apostasy from the ecclesiastical doctrine also was applied [246] to them.[2] The more recent treatments have for the most part followed the older pattern of ecclesiastical historiography without contradiction.[3] From the fact that there is only a sparse tradition of Jewish Christian witnesses they incorrectly conclude that Jewish Christianity was actually insignificant, without taking into consideration that our knowledge is determined by the ecclesiastical tradition and that even the various titles of Jewish Christian literature [4] seem to demand some critical reservations with respect

2. Cf. among others Jerome *Epistle* 112.13: "As long as the Nazoreans want to be both Jews and Christians, they are neither Jews nor Christians." See also below, 272 ff.
3. Cf. for example A. von Harnack, *History of Dogma*, 1 (ET by N. Buchanan from German 1894[3] ed.; London: Williams and Norgate, 1894; repr. New York: Dover, 1961): 290 f.; [= 4th German ed. of 1909, p. 313; but in this appendix on Jewish Christianity, Harnack does not point specifically to the year 70 as a watershed; see also p. 330 = ET 308 f.] cf. also H. Lietzman, *History*, 1: 183: after the destruction of Jerusalem "Jewish Christianity lacked not only a racial, but also a religious basis for its former claims, and thus was forgotten in the mainstream church. It sank into oblivion in the lonely deserts of east Jordan"; also O. Cullmann, "Ebioniten," RGG[3], 2 (1958): 297 f., speaks of a "process of retardation into a heretical sect"; M. Simon, *Verus Israel: Étude sur les relations entre Chrétiens et Juifs dans l'Empire Romain (135-145)* (Paris: Boccard, 1948; supplemented reprint 1964), p. 313, claims that "Jewish Christianity outside of Palestine, in view of its initial Israelite recruitment, represents only a rather sporadic phenomenon without much extent. In Palestine itself, the Ebionites are a minority in relation to the mainstream church, in uninterrupted regression and condemned by their position itself to disappear sooner or later." It is inexplicable that L. E. Elliott-Binns quotes this with approval (*Galilean Christianity*, Studies in Biblical Theology 16 [Chatham: SCM, 1956], p. 77 n. 4), even though he correctly recognizes the disparity between actual Jewish Christianity and the uniform characterization of it in the heresiological tradition (78; cf. also 50). The year 70 is usually regarded as the time of transition into the "sectarian situation" —e.g. A. von Harnack, *Mission*[2], 1: 63; H.-J. Schoeps, *Theologie und Geschichte des Judenchristentums* (Tübingen: Mohr, 1949), p. 7; J. Munck, "Jewish Christianity in post-Apostolic Times," NTS 6 (1959–60): 103-116. The influence of the destruction of the Jerusalem temple on Judaism and on Jewish Christianity is quite often overestimated. Such influence was small wherever Jewish Christianity, like diaspora Judaism, had come to be largely independent of the temple cult. Naturally, Jewish Christianity like "official" Judaism, was capable of adapting itself to the new situation. It has been demonstrated elsewhere that the tradition of the flight of the primitive Jerusalem community to Pella during the Jewish war is a legend without historical value and therefore may not be used in this connection; see G. Strecker, *Das Judenchristentum in den Pseudoklementinen*, TU 70 (1958), pp. 229 ff. The defense by Elliott-Binns of the historicity of that event (*Galilean Christianity*, pp. 65-71; in opposition to S. G. F. Brandon) cannot remove the fundamental doubts about the quality of the tradition. His thesis about a unification of the Jerusalem and Galilean communities in Pella (pp. 68 f.) is pure speculation.
4. Cf. G. Strecker, "Ebioniten," RAC 4 (1959), pp. 492 ff.

to the judgment of the mainstream church. Therefore no further justification is required for [247] the attempt to apply Bauer's conception of history to Jewish Christianity as well.

Jewish Christianity is, to be sure, a complex thing. It is found both in a Palestinian as well as a hellenistic environment and it was subjected to various influences. Hellenistic Jewish Christianity does not represent a closed unity, but the transition from Jewish Christianity to gentile Christianity is fluid, as is shown on the one hand by the adoption of gentile Christian forms by Jewish Christians and on the other by the Judaizing of Christians from the gentile sphere. The latter process is not only to be assumed for the earliest period— as a result of the direct effects of the Jewish synagogue upon the development of gentile Christianity—but is also attested for the later period.[5] And to what extent can a boundary be drawn with precision between Palestinian and hellenistic Jewish Christianity? Further, there is the problem of genetic definition: if the Christians of Jewish descent are designated "Jewish Christians," it must be asked what criteria there are for so doing. Relationships at the level of the history of tradition should also be explored—as, for example, between the later Jewish Christians and the primitive Jerusalem community or the Jewish Christianity of the New Testament. And is it possible to regard the Jewish Christianity of the New Testament as a unity? The testimony of the Pauline letters as well as the statements (admittedly questionable in particular instances) of the other New Testament writings suggest the opposite already in the early period.[6] A multi-

5. Cf. John Chrysostom *Adversus Judaeos* (PG 48, 844 and 849 f.); Simon, *Verus Israel*, 379 f. The large-scale work of J. Daniélou, *Theology of Jewish Christianity* (ET by J. A. Baker from the 1958 French; Chicago: Regnery, 1964) has a misleading title. That sort of Jewish Christianity, the theology of which it attempts to present, never existed as an entity that can be identified in terms of the history of religions. Actually, this book is an undoubtedly worthwhile presentation of Semitic (Jewish) forms of life and thought within Christian theology. But even in this respect the book is incomplete and has not taken into consideration hellenistic analogies nor the problem of the history of tradition. For a critical evaluation, see the valuable review by A. Orbe, "Une théologie du judéo-christianisme," *Recherches de science religieuse* 47 (1959): 544-549; in addition, Munck, "Jewish Christianity," 108 ff.
6. In taking up the thesis proposed by W. Lütgert, W. Schmithals has indeed argued that besides Pauline Christianity, there existed a comprehensive counterchurch of Jewish Christian gnosticism; see the bibliography given below, p. 307 [the shorter studies on Galatians, Philippians, and Romans have now appeared in revised form in *Paulus und die Gnostiker*, Theologische Forschung 35 (Hamburg: Evangelisher Verlag, 1965), along with an article on "Die historische

tude of problems that go far beyond the [248] restricted range of an "appendix" arise. Thus some limitations must be set. We shall deal with the legalistic Jewish Christianity situated in Greek-speaking Syria, and will examine from the perspective of this investigation (1) the indirect witness of the *Didascalia* and then (2) the Jewish Christian *Kērygmata Petrou* ("Proclamations" or "Sermons of Peter"; abbreviated KP) source of the pseudo-Clementines, and compare our results with (3) the so-called ecclesiastical position, which in this instance means with the statements about Ebionitism made by the ecclesiastical heresiologists.

1. *The Didascalia.* The author who, around the first half of the third century, wrote the *Didascalia* in Syria [7] claims that he is setting forth the "catholic doctrine" (title; 24 [204.8 f. = 6.12.1], etc.) and

---

Situation der Thessalonicherbriefe"]—on 1 Thessalonians, see also p. 64 n. 123 of the article on Galatians. [248] On the problem of Philippians, cf. also the investigation by H. Koester listed below, p. 308, which modifies the conclusions of Schmithals somewhat.

7. On this matter, see the following: P. Galtier, "La date de la Didascalie des Apôtres," *Revue d'Histoire Ecclésiastique* 42 (1947): 315-351; B. Altaner, *Patrology* (ET by H. C. Graef from the German 1958[5] ed.; London: Nelson, 1960), p. 56 (see German 1960[6] ed. with A. Stuiber, p. 48); J. Quasten, *Patrology* 2: *The Ante-Nicene Literature after Irenaeus* (Utrecht: Spectrum, 1953), 147; G. Bardie, "Didascalie des Apôtres," *Dictionnaire de Spiritualité*, 3 (Paris, 1955): 863-865; Harnack, *Geschichte*, 2 (*Chronologie*).2: 488 ff. (his suggestion of post-Novatian interpolations is not convincing). [In what follows, references to *Didascalia* are given according to its normal (broad) chapter divisions, with page and line from Connolly's ET (see below) and the equivalent passage from the *Apostolic Constitutions* (by book, section, and paragraph, following Funk's ed., listed below) appended in that order—e.g. *Didasc.* 8 (80.21 = 2.27.7) means chapter 8 of *Didascalia*, material found on p. 80 line 21 of Connolly's ET, which parallels *Apostolic Constitutions* 2.27.7. The standard German translation by (H. Achelis and) J. Flemming, which is referred to by page and line in the original form of this appendix, has also been consulted at every point.] For the text of the *Didascalia*, reference has been made to the following editions and studies: P. Bötticher (P. de Lagarde), *Didascalia apostolorum syriace* (Leipzig, 1854); M. D. Gibson, *The Didascalia Apostolorum in Syriac*, Horae Semiticae 1 (London, 1903); H. Achelis and J. Flemming, *Die syrische Didaskalia*, TU 10.2 (1904), with variant Syriac readings on pp. 225-235 [Achelis is responsible for the commentary on pp. 257-387; Flemming for the text, German translation, notes, and pp. 243-247]; F. X. Funk, *Didascalia et Constitutiones Apostolorum* (in two volumes, Paderborn, 1905; reprint 1960), a reconstruction of the text in Latin according to the Latin and Syriac evidence, and a comparison with the *Apostolic Constitutions;* R. H. Connolly, *Didascalia Apostolorum: the Syriac version translated and accompanied by the Verona Latin fragments* (Oxford: Clarendon, 1929), an ET of the Syriac text and comparison with the Latin fragments. Cf. also E. Tidner, *Didascaliae Apostolorum Canonum Ecclesiasticorum Traditionis Apostolicae versiones Latinae*, TU 75 (1963). [For an ET of the Ethiopic version, see J. M. Harden, *The Ethiopic Didascalia* (London: SPCK, 1920).]

that he represents the "catholic church, holy and perfect" (9 [86.1 = 2.26.1]; cf. 8 [80.21 = 2.25.7], etc.). The consciousness of catholicity appears to permeate the church of his time—in any event it presents itself as such when the recommended practice of fasting is defended by reference to the custom "of all the faithful throughout the world" (21 [180.19 f. = 5.12.5]), and becomes concrete in the dispute with the heretics, "who have erred by thinking that there are other churches" (23 [199.1 f. = 6.5.5]) and "who with evil words blaspheme the catholic church which is the receptacle of the holy spirit" (25 [212.30 = 6.14(18).7]). In opposition to them, it is necessary to preserve the catholicity of the church by making a clear break with them (25 [210.24 ff. = 6.14(18).1-2]) and to deal with the believers who have fallen away to their side either by [249] excluding them from the church's fellowship or by converting them from their error (25 [210.20 ff. = 6.14(18).1; and 214.14 ff. = 6.14(18).10]). The author supports the "catholic doctrine" which he represents through the apostolic claim made by his work in its title and in the fiction of apostolic authorship that it maintains throughout. Thereby he gains a legitimation that could not be achieved on the basis of his own authority, and at the same time his work acquires a universality corresponding to the presupposed missionary activity of the apostles (25 [214.24 ff. = 6.14(18).11]). On the surface, it seems that the catholic ideal has been widely realized. In opposition to the dangers of heresy, a firmly established episcopal office guarantees the purity of the church.[8] The reference to the "holy scriptures" is a polemical thrust at the heresies—it is a familiar indication of a "catholic" self-understanding.[9] Even the triadic structure of the credo fits into this framework.[10]

Thus in the *Didascalia* the claim of catholicity and the claim of orthodoxy go hand in hand. But are we dealing with anything more than a claim? It is true that when the author speaks about traveling

---

8. Cf. the instructions for the office of bishop in chapter 4 (28 ff. = 2.1-6). It is significant that the admonition which is characteristic for the *Didascalia*, to use church discipline with moderation, is justified by reference to the dangers that threaten the outsiders from the side of the heresies (7 [64.28 ff. = 2.21.2]).

9. *Didasc.* 20 (172.12 = 5.7.14), 24 (204.12 = 6.12.2), 25 (212.39 = 6.14[18].7), 26 (242.13 f. and 244.7 ff. = 6.21[27].1 and 2); cf. Bauer, above, 195 ff.

10. *Didasc.* 19 (167.3 ff. = 5.6.10), 24 (204.10 ff. = 6.12.1), 26 (258.13 ff. = 6.23[30].8—cf. the codices!)—in pointed confrontation with the heretics; cf. especially the passage listed from 24, where the short form of the credo is attached to an implicit warning against the heresies.

245

Christians he makes a distinction between adherents of the church and heretics (12 [120.28 ff. = 2.58.1]), but the question remains completely open as to how extensive is the ecclesiastical background referred to here. Considering the forms in which the "catholic doctrine" of the *Didascalia* appears, it is striking that it diverges significantly from the character of "orthodoxy" with which we are familiar. To be sure a monarchial episcopate is presupposed, but the concept of succession that was for the most part simply taken for granted in the mainstream church of the third century is not mentioned. This is all the more surprising since the apostolic fiction maintained by the book plainly requires such a basis for the episcopal office.[11] **[250]** The use of the New Testament scriptures also is striking. The stereotyped reference to the "holy scriptures" is expanded as an exhortation to read "the holy scriptures and the gospel of God" (2 [20.4 f. = 1.7.17]), or "the law, the book of the kings and the

---

11. Cf. Achelis(-Flemming), *Didaskalia,* p. 270. The more or less contemporary "basic writing" that underlies the ps.-Clementines (see below, 258), on the other hand, reports the installation of Clement or of Zachaeus by the apostle Peter on the basis of a supposed order for the episcopal consecration—ps.-Clementine *Epistle of Clement to James* (ET in ANF 8: 218-222), *Hom.* 3.60 ff., *Rec.* 3.65 f. (cf. Strecker, *Judenchristentum,* pp. 97 ff.). On this problem, see also W. **[250]** Ullmann, "The Significance of the Epistula Clementis in the Pseudo-Clementines," *Journal of Theological Studies* 11 (1960): 295-317; this is an expansion of the presentation, "Some Remarks on the Significance of the Epistula Clementis in the Pseudo-Clementines," *Studia Patristica* 4, TU 79 (1961): 330-337. According to Ullmann the *Epistle of Clement to James,* which is in the form of a testament of Peter to Clement, endeavors to establish the legal basis for the transmission of Peter's authority to the papacy ("Remarks," 334 and elsewhere). Ullmann correctly recognizes that the *Epistle of Clement to James* presupposes the concept of apostolic succession, but he is wrong in his contention that the reference to the Roman community determines the character of the letter. From the viewpoint of literary analysis, the *Epistle* derives from the author of the "basic writing" behind the ps.-Clementines. Correspondingly, its content relates directly to the ps.-Clementine story. As an introduction to the work, this epistle was fashioned in connection with the other introductory writing, the *Epistle of Peter to James* (below, 260 n. 57), and attempts to prepare for the significance of the speeches of Peter that are referred to in what follows, and at the same time to indicate that the journeys of Peter and Clement ended in Rome. Herein lies the purpose of the *Epistle of Clement to James,* not in the establishing of a foundation for the Roman claim, of which no indications are found elsewhere in the Clementine romance. How little the Roman claim lies in the background is disclosed through a comparison with the episcopal installation of Zachaeus in Caesarea; Zachaeus is also the successor of Peter (*Hom.* 3.60.1, *ant' emou!*), and is even legitimated through being an eyewitness (*Hom.* 3.63.1).

prophets, and the gospel" (2 [14.12 ff. = 1.5.2]), or even "law, prophets, and gospel" (4 [34.21 ff. = 2.5.3]). The designation "gospel" apparently means the gospel literature, which is the most important part of the New Testament canon for the author.[12] The gospel of Matthew is preferred.[13] But acquaintance with the gospel of Mark is not to be ruled out, and knowledge of Luke [251] and of John is highly probable.[14] Thus caution is in order with respect to the con-

12. Achelis(-Flemming), *Didaskalia*, p. 333. In *Didascalia* 8 (81.29 f. = 2.25.1) the introductory formula ["in David and in all the prophets and in the gospel also, our savior prays for our sins . . ."] alludes to an episode from the story of Jesus (cf. Luke 23.34 [and the similar "gospel" material about how "our savior made intercession for sinners before his father," found in *Didasc.* 6 (52.14 ff. = 2.16.1); cf. also 24 (212.10 f. = 6.14[18].4)]), just as elsewhere the "gospel" introduces only synoptic material, and not quotations from the canonical epistles (the "apostolos"). [But see n. 14 below on possible "gospel" material from John.]
13. Cf. Achelis(-Flemming), *Didaskalia*, pp. 318 ff. [and Connolly, *Didascalia*, lxx ff.]. Matthew is the only gospel cited by name (21 [182.11 = 5.14.11]—"but in the gospel of Matthew it is written thus. . ."). This introductory formula can hardly be the result of an interpolation as was suggested by Connolly (*ad loc.* and p. lxxi); rather, it is confirmed by the content of the quotation. Reference is made to Matt. 28.1 f., which is part of the material peculiar to Matthew, and the quotation from Matt. 12.40 that follows has been shown to belong to the Matthean redactional material (see G. Strecker, *Der Weg der Gerechtigkeit: Untersuchungen zur Theologie des Matthäus*, FRLANT 82 [1962]: 103 f.).
14. Achelis(-Flemming), *Didaskalia*, p. 319 ff. [and Connolly, lxx f.]. According to Harnack, *Geschichte*, 2 (*Chronologie*).2: 492 f., the gospel of John was "not used as an evangelical platform," but the testimonies adduced by Achelis (pp. 241 and 320) should not be belittled. With a high degree of probability John 6.38 f. (in 11 [118.3 ff. = 2.55.2]), 7.24 (in 11 [114.23 f. = 2.51.1]), and 12.25 (in combination with Matt 10.39, in 19 [166.16 f. = 5.6.7]) are cited. Therefore one also will have to favorably evaluate allusions to John 13.4 f. and 14 f. in *Didasc.* 16 (150.10 ff. and 16 = 3.13.4 f. ["in the gospel"!]). To be sure, the Syriac manuscript Harrisianus does not contain a translation of this passage. However, this omission includes the larger context and is insignificant in view of the numerous omissions in this manuscript. Finally, the possibility also must be left open that the pericope concerning the adulteress in *Didasc.* 8 (76.16 ff. = 2.24.3) was accessible to the author because it was included in his copy of the Fourth Gospel (cf. certain manuscripts of John 7.53 ff.)—contrary to Achelis(-Flemming), 319, and Connolly, lxxi f. Even though Papias and the *Gospel of the Hebrews* transmitted a similar narrative, according to the report of Eusebius (EH 3.39.17), there is still no proof that the *Didascalia* is dependent on them. The fact that the notice of Eusebius and the *Didascalia* agree in avoiding the word "adulteress" is not a sufficient argument. Against this hypothesis it can be argued (1) that no other connections can be established between the *Didascalia* on the one hand and Papias and/or the *Gospel of the Hebrews* on the other—for the latter, such connections are not to be expected since the *Gospel of the Hebrews* is native to Egypt and not to Syria; and (2) that the content of the pericope as it was known to Papias and to the *Gospel of the Hebrews* cannot be determined any longer, but verbal agreements exist in part between *Didascalia* and John 7.53 ff.

jecture that the author made use of a harmony of the gospels [15]—in view of the freedom of the manner of quotation and the citation of mixed texts from Old and New Testament writings, the use of such a harmony can hardly be established. This holds true with one exception. It is almost universally recognized that the author either directly or indirectly used the so-called *Gospel of Peter*, [16] a compilation based on the canonical gospels. The surprising agreements in the account of Jesus' passion can hardly be explained otherwise, particularly the statement that it was Herod, not the procurator Pilate, who had Jesus crucified (21 [190.4 = 5.19.5]), but also in a more general way the exoneration of Pilate that immediately precedes this passage, the dating of the resurrection of Jesus in the night [252] preceding Sunday (21 [190.10 f. = 5.19.6]), and the emphasis upon fasting during holy week.[17] The casual manner in which this gospel is used (formulas of citation do not occur [18]) is all the more significant since we are dealing with the gospel of "Syrian-Antiochian heretics" (see above, 66) and Serapion of Antioch already devoted an official refutation to the book.[19] As the *Didascalia* shows, Serapion's judgment was not able to prevail very quickly throughout the area of the Syrian church. The outlook of its author with respect to what may be considered "catholic doctrine" is rather different from that of the occupant of the bishop's throne in Antioch.[20]

---

15. Harnack, *Geschichte*, 2 (*Chronologie*).2: 494.

16. Cf. [Connolly, *Didascalia*, lxxv ff.;] C. Maurer in Hennecke-Schneemelcher, 1: 179 ff.; L. Vaganay, *L'évangile de Pierre*[2] (Paris: Gabalda, 1930), pp. 167-169; Harnack, *Bruchstücke des Evangeliums und der Apokalypse des Petrus*, TU 9.2 (1893[2]). Harnack also attempts, without much success, to trace John 7.53 ff. back to the *Gospel of Peter*; cf. on the contrary Vaganay, pp. 186 f.

17. Compare *Didasc.* 21 (190.6 ff. = 5.19.6), "thus it is fitting for you to fast on Friday and Saturday and also to take your vigil and watch on Saturday," and *Gospel of Peter* 5.27, "on account of all these things we fasted and sat there and cried night and day until Sabbath." See also below, 250 n. 26.

18. With the possible exception of 21 (183.4 ff. = 5.14.14-15), where the relationship to the *Gospel of Peter* is not entirely clear ["and he said to us, teaching us, 'Are you fasting. . . ?' " These words are spoken in the presence of Levi after the resurrection—cf. *Gospel of Peter* 14.60 and n. 25 below].

19. EH 6.12 (see above, 115); Zahn, *Geschichte*, 1.1:177-179, and 2: 743 ff.; Harnack, *Geschichte*, 1.1: 11.

20. Eusebius, on the other hand, later included the *Gospel of Peter* among the heretical writings; EH 3.3.2 and 3.25.6 ff.

We will bypass the question of *Didascalia*'s relation to the rest of the canon [21] and also the problem of its use of so-called agrapha, in which it does not go beyond the bounds of what is common in patristic literature of the third [253] century.[22] But in connection with what has been said, we must refer to the relation of the author of the *Didascalia* to Judaism.[23] Of course, one should not overestimate

21. The number of canonical New Testament writings presupposed by *Didascalia* is not as extensive as Achelis had affirmed (*Didaskalia*, pp. 321 ff.). In addition to the four gospels, the *Gospel of Peter*, and the book of Acts, there is clear acquaintance with some Pauline epistles, especially the Pastorals (Achelis, pp. 322 f.; [cf. Connolly, lxxii]). But in regard to the remaining canonical works, judgment must be reserved. The idea that the author knew Hebrews is not supported by any real evidence. Nor is it demonstrable that his Pauline corpus comprised fourteen letters, as Achelis supposed (323; [cf. Connolly, lxxii]). Knowledge of the catholic Epistles is also questionable. The parallel between *Didascalia* 12 (122.29 ff. = 2.58.4) and James 2.2 f. does not prove that James is being cited because, as Achelis himself acknowledged (322), it is precisely the colorful statements of the version in James that are absent from *Didascalia*. It is self-evident that use of 1 John cannot be inferred from the fact that the Johannine gospel is quoted. Only for a knowledge of 1 Peter is there some basis: *Didascalia* 1 (2.6 = 1. introduction) seems to refer to 1 Pet. 1.2, *Didasc*. 4 (32.26 = 2.3.3) to 1 Pet. 4.8, and *Didasc*. 9 (86.1 f. = 2.26.1) to 1 Pet. 2.9 (Achelis, 322; [Connolly, lxxii]). There is no denying the existence of these parallels. Moreover, the material in *Didasc*. 4 is presented as a direct quotation. But surprisingly, the quotation is said to be spoken by the "Lord," so that one must ask whether this logion was actually transmitted to the author of the *Didascalia* as part of 1 Peter, or whether it may not have been independent of that document. This supposed evidence also is compromised by the discovery that the passage ultimately derives from an Old Testament text (Prov. 10.12) even though the wording in *Didasc*. 4 is closer to the text of 1 Peter [253] than to that of the Old Testament. The same applies to the material in *Didasc*. 9, where the text that supposedly is cited (1 Pet. 2.9) actually is an indirect quotation of Exod. 19.6 and 23.22 (LXX). As was true in the case of *Didasc*. 4, the wording of *Didasc*. 9 is closer to the New Testament text than to the Old Testament. But this is hardly decisive. The text in question appears in a series of ecclesiological predications which were well known and probably orally transmitted. The same is true of *Didasc*. 1, where the wording of 1 Pet. 1.2 is not reproduced exactly either. The conclusion that the author of *Didascalia* knew 1 Peter is not compelling, to say the least. Finally, with reference to the Apocalypse [cf. Connolly, lxxiii], even Achelis recognized that the few allusions do not go beyond the stock of commonly used liturgical formulae in the ancient church (323 f.). There is thus no reason for assuming that the author of the *Didascalia* knew and used the Apocalypse.
22. Cf. Achelis(-Flemming), *Didaskalia*, pp. 336 ff.; [Connolly, lxxiii; and above, n. 12].
23. Details in Achelis(-Flemming), *Didaskalia*, p. 361; C. Schmidt, *Studien zu den Pseudo-Klementinen*, TU 46.1 (1929): 252; L. Goppelt, *Christentum und Judentum im ersten und zweiten Jahrhundert* (Gutersloh: Bertelsmann, 1954), pp. 205-207. [Cf. also Connolly, lxxxviii f.]

the evidence that will be cited here. The fact that the author speaks of the Jews as "brothers" in chapter 21 (184.31 = 5.14.23, and 187.8 = 5.17.1) is based on the Old Testament [24] and perhaps goes back to a literary source that could also have contained the idea of intercessory fasting for the brethren from the Jewish people.[25] Behind it lies an understanding of the history of salvation that concentrates primarily upon the past and less upon the current situation (cf. 21 [184.17 ff. = 5.14.22], 23 [198.10 ff. = 6.5.4 ff.]). Nevertheless, this assessment of Judaism also has a root in the author's present experience, as is indicated by the fact that the *Didascalia* betrays a detailed acquaintance with Jewish customs and teachings. The following examples will suffice: the unusual etymological derivation of the Jewish name from the Hebrew root *YDH* in chapter 13 (126.22 = 2.60.3—" 'Jew' means 'confession' ' "); the precise presentation of Jewish [254] sabbath customs; [26] the distinction between the passover and the feast of the unleavened bread,[27] the dating of the

---

24. The former passage continues: "For even if they hate you, we must call them brothers, for thus it is written for us in Isaiah, 'Call those who hate and despise you "brothers," because the name of the Lord is praised' " (Isa. 66.5).

25. In terms of its content, *Didasc.* 21 (180.29 f. = 5.13.1, "when you fast, pray and intercede for those who are perishing, as we also did when our savior suffered") has parallels in the *Gospel of Peter* 5.27 (see above, 248 n. 17). The later citation in *Didasc.* 21 (183.5 ff. = 5.14.15) seems to be a resumption of the same tradition, which Achelis already claimed was part of the *Gospel of Peter* (327)— "but he [the Lord] said to us, teaching us, 'would that you not fast these days for my sake; or do I have need that you should afflict your soul? [cf. Isa. 58.4-5]. But for the sake of your brothers you did it, and you will do it on these days on which you fast, on the fourth [day] of the week [= Wednesday] and on Friday, for all time" [see also above, n. 18]. The possibility that a source lies behind this material becomes more probable in view of the way it differs from its present context; it refers to fasting on Wednesday and Friday, [254] but immediately thereafter *Didasc.* 21 (183.18 ff. = 5.14.17) speaks of fasting during the holy week, from Monday "till the night after the sabbath." With respect to the designation of the Jews as "brothers" it follows that it was originally contained in the source which was either closely related to or identical with the *Gospel of Peter* (above, and n. 18), and was placed into the larger context by the author of the *Didascalia*. Accordingly, it is on the basis of this source used in chap. 21 (180.29 f. = 5.13.1, and 183.5 ff. = 5.14.15) that the intercession was made to relate to the Jewish people even in the subsequent treatment (184.22 = 5.14.22, 185.3 ff. = 5.14.24, 185.10 f. = 5.15.1), without being limited to them, as is clear from the earlier reference to gentile unbelievers (180.10-181.1 = 5.12.4-5.13.1).

26. *Didasc.* 21 (191.4 ff. = 5.20.1 ff.). However, the injunction for Sabbath observance "you shall not lift your foot to do any work, nor shall you speak a word with your mouth" (191.16 ff. = 5.20.5) is not derived from a Jewish tractate (Achelis) but from Isa. 58.13; see Connolly, lxxxviii [following Funk, *ad loc.*].

27. *Didasc.* 21 (192.18 = 5.20.10); cf. Achelis(-Flemming), *Didaskalia*, p. 361; Josephus *Antiq.* 3.(10.5.)248 f.

lament over the destruction of Jerusalem on the ninth of Ab.[28] These are statements which one may not explain simply by assuming that the author had been of Jewish origin. Such a hypothesis cannot be based upon observations that in reality do nothing more than to identify various items of information.[29] Hence it is more probably the case that there was an active relationship between Christians and Jews in the author's world. Even though with regard to particulars the question of the extent to which such a contact contributed significantly to the development of the outlook of the author and the practice of his community must remain open,[30] it is quite clear that the Syrian environment of the *Didascalia* supports an intensive influence of Jewish thought and conceptual material.

The "catholic doctrine" of the *Didascalia* unfolds itself in the controversy [255] with the "heresies." This problem is treated in chapter 23, "On Heresies and Schisms" (194 ff. = 6.1.1 ff.). Already at the beginning of the *Didascalia* the problem of heresy is mentioned,[31] and it is called to mind repeatedly in what follows.[32] The heresies form a constant danger to the church (23 [199.21 ff. = 6.5.8]). Hence the warning at the start of chapter 23, "guard yourselves against all hateful, reprehensible, and abominable heresies and flee them as you

---

28. *Didasc.* 21 (191.23 = 5.20.6). It is true that a clear distinction between Jewish and Jewish Christian influence cannot always be made. Thus some of the texts that have been cited may have derived from Jewish Christian influence (see below). Nevertheless, the distinction itself should not be abandoned—it is suggested by the author of *Didascalia* when on the one hand he can speak of the "Jews" (13 [126.22 = 2.60.3] or of "the people" (21 [189.19, 190.26 f., 191.7 ff. = 5.19.2 and 9, 5.20.2 ff.], etc.), and on the other of the "dear brothers" who came "from the people [and] became believers" (26 [233.7 f. = 6.18 (23).11]).

29. Contrary to Achelis(-Flemming), *Didaskalia*, pp. 384 f., and Quasten, *Patrology*, 2: 147. Even though the author knows of a replacement of Israel by the church in the development of salvation history (21 and 23; see above, 249 f.), he does not reveal any special sympathy for the fate of the Jewish people—in contrast to Rom. 9-11, for example.

30. Goppelt, *Christentum und Judentum*, p. 206, states that the instructions to the bishop, the "juridical functions," and the community's "simple ideal for living" are examples of the "high estimation" for the "Jewish tradition." But with respect to the orders of office and community the author is primarily dependent on Christian traditions as is indicated, for example, by his extensive use of the pastoral Epistles.

31. *Didasc.* 5 (38.1 = 2.6.17). The sinners have "fallen into the pernicious corruption of the heresies concerning which the decisive word is (still) to be spoken."

32. *Didasc.* 7 (64.28 ff. = 2.21.3), 12 (120.32 = 2.58.1), 13 (128.16 = 2.62.3), 23 (194 ff. = 6.1.1 ff.), 25 (210.20 ff. = 6.14[18].1).

would a blazing fire" (197.22 ff. = 6.5.1), and the instruction in chapter 25 to have no fellowship with the heretics (210.24 ff. = 6.14[18].1). Nor are references to the frightful ultimate fate of the heretics lacking in these contexts (194.13 ff. = 6.1.2, 197.25 ff. = 6.5.2, 212.29 ff. = 6.14[18].7 ff.).

Apparently the author presupposes the existence of a number of heresies. This is not merely part of the fictitious character of this work, with its apostolic claim addressed to the church's past, present, and future, but is also based on actual experiences (cf. chaps. 7 and 12, above n. 32). What actual picture emerges? Following a general warning about heresies in chapter 23 (199.21-31 = 6.5.8 f.), the author presents the "beginning of heresies," namely, the appearance of Simon Magus from his confrontation with the apostles in Jerusalem (!) to the macabre contest of the miracle workers (Simon Magus and Peter) in Rome (200.1-202.6 = 6.7-9). Of course, this does not permit us to draw an inference as to the present situation of the author. The presentation is rather reminiscent of the accounts of the apocryphal acts of the apostles.[33] But even the summary presentation of the heresies that follows in *Didasc.* 23 is not immune to criticism. In a very schematic manner "all heresies" are accused of rejecting "the law and the prophets," blaspheming "God almighty," and denying the resurrection (202.8-11 = 6.10.1). In addition there are the false teachings of particular groups—"many of them taught that a man should not marry, and said that if one did not marry, that would constitute sanctification" (202.12-14 = 6.10.2; cf. 204.14 ff. = 6.12.1); "others of them taught that a man should eat no meat . . ." (202.15 f. = 6.10.3). These assertions, like the preceding portrayal of the heresy of Simon [256] Magus, do not seem to presuppose the existence of an actual situation of controversy, but remain remarkably schematic and lack concreteness. Similarly, they are taken up again only in brief summary statements, without the addition of more specific information.[34] Apparently the author follows an established

33. Cf. Lipsius, *Apokryphen Apostelgeschichten,* 2: 59 ff., 321, 328 (but here the text of the Didascalia is regarded as an abbreviation of the report found in *Apostolic Constitutions* 6.9). Hegesippus already associated Cleobios with Simon Magus (Eusebius EH 4.22.5; cf. Hilgenfeld, *Ketzergeschichte,* p. 32; F. X. Funk, *Die Apostolischen Konstitutionen* (Rottenburg, 1891), p. 74, [and also his *Didascalia* 1: 317 f.].

34. Cf. *Didasc.* 24 (202.23-204.4 = 6.11.1-2, 204.9 ff. = 6.12.1), 26 (240.22 ff. = 6.20[24].1).

pattern of presentation that does not reveal any connection with his own situation. This leads to a further observation—the false teachings to which *Didascalia* refers can be identified with the gnostic theological ideas opposed by the "great church." [35] But in the actual body of the *Didascalia* gnostic influences can be confirmed neither in a positive nor in a negative (antithetical) manner. The heresiological statements summarize material formulated and transmitted in the church tradition. It is a different matter with the last part of the heresiological characterization that is given in *Didasc.* 23—"others said that one should abstain only from the flesh of swine, and should eat what the law declares to be clean, and ought to be circumcised according to the law" (202.17-20 = 6.10.4). In contrast to the gnostic rejection of the Old Testament, the ceremonial law of the Old Testament is here expressly acknowledged as binding. In a subsequent section the author will apply to the above-mentioned "heresy" a notion peculiar to him concerning the "second legislation" (24 [204.1-4 = 6.11.2]; see below, 256). This makes it likely that the former passage contains a reflection of a concrete situation. While the question may remain open whether this notice originally was attached to the older traditional formulation—the above-mentioned repetition of the basic wording in chapter 24 would support this—or whether it was composed by the author, it is certain that the author connects the relevant doctrinal position to the present. Thus we are here provided with the clue by means of which we can reconstruct the "heresy" opposed by the author of the *Didascalia.*

It has already become clear that the heretical group under discussion is not to be characterized as a vegetarian Jewish Christianity [257] that rejected marriage, the eating of meat, and the Old Testament, such as is attested by Epiphanius.[36] Instead, the fundamental

35. It suffices to refer to the summary treatments of Hilgenfeld, especially with regard to the teaching of the Syrian gnostic Cerdo (*Ketzergeschichte*, pp. 316 ff. and especially 332 f.). According to Harnack, the characterization found in *Didascalia* conforms to "the Marcionites" (*Marcion*[2], p. 341°). However, it is difficult to make a distinction between gnostic and Marcionite outlooks here, as is often true with such isolated assertions. Against Harnack it can be argued that Marcion does not seem to have rejected explicitly the idea of an eschatological resurrection; and further, that in our passage the *Didascalia* ascribes the prohibition of marriage and of eating meat not to one single group but to different heretical groups.
36. Cf. Achelis(-Flemming), *Didaskalia*, pp. 355 f.; Schoeps, *Theologie*, pp. 179 n. 3, and 191.

acknowledgment of the Old Testament law is assured. Of course, the author can also clothe his polemic in the kind of Old Testament terminology that does not allow us to recognize its actual setting. The assertion that in the true law "no distinctions with regard to food, no burning of incense, no sacrifices and burnt offerings" were mentioned (26 [218.21 ff. = 6.16.2]) can be regarded only as literary decoration at a time subsequent to the destruction of Jerusalem.[37] But in other respects the dependence on the Old Testament still can refer to current situations. The ritual baths after sexual contamination (26 [242.6 ff. = 6.21(27).1 ff.]; cf. 24 [204.25 ff. = 6.12.2]) reflect Lev. 15.16 ff. without being derived in a literary sense from that passage. The explicit nature of the controversy and also the direct or indirect address to the heretics indicate a current situation. The observance of the sabbath is also counted among the characteristic features of the heretics, as the context attests (26 [233.7 ff. = 6.18(23).11]); probably this is true also of circumcision, to which not only the last part of the statement quoted above (on 253) refers but also the emphatically positive description of ecclesiastical life (24 [204.21 = 6.12.2], "spiritual circumcision of the heart"; 26 [218.25 = 6.16(20).2], "uncircumcision"). Finally, it is possible that the observance of the Old Testament food laws is to be included here, although it is mentioned only in the summary passages in chapters 23-24 (202.17 ff. = 6.10.4, 204.1 ff. = 6.11.2; see above, 253).

According to Connolly and W. C. van Unnik,[38] the heretics of the *Didascalia* were "Judaizing Christians" who had adopted some aspects of Jewish observance but not the totality of Jewish regulations. Therefore they did not actually live in association with Judaism and are not to be designated as Jewish Christians.[39] But while it cannot be denied that Syriac Christianity exhibits strong Judaizing tendencies, one should not connect the people addressed in the *Didascalia* with such trends. Since they are interested in Jewish observances,

---

37. Cf. also *Didasc.* 9 (98.15 ff. = 2.35.1), and perhaps 26 (216.3 f. = 6.15.1, and 252.3 f. = 6.22[28].1)?
38. Van Unnik, "De beteeknis van de mozaische vet voor de kerk van Christus volgens de syrische Didascalie," *Nederlandsch Archief voor Kerkgeschiedenes* 31 (1939): 65-100. [Connolly, lxxxiii, does not explicitly argue for such an interpretation, despite Strecker's claim, but seems to leave the question open.]
39. Van Unnik, "Beteeknis," pp. 95 ff. Cf. similarly J. Thomas, *Mouvement baptiste*, pp. 406 f.; Simon, *Verus Israel*, pp. 362 ff.

they are explicitly [258] designated "heretics," [40] a verdict which would be extraordinary with respect to Judaizing Christians, whose basic mistake did not so much involve questions of faith as questions of ecclesiastical discipline. The same can be said with reference to their practice of circumcision, which provides tight bonds to Judaism and goes far beyond mere "Judaizing." [41] Therefore, the deduction is more likely that we are dealing here with Jewish Christians. It is not accidental that the author, at the beginning of his instruction about the "second legislation" (or "repetition of the law") in chapter 26, spoke to those who "from among the people have turned to faith in God our savior Jesus Christ" (216.1 ff. = 6.15[19].1), just as in chapter 21 he also interpreted the quotation from Isaiah 9.1 f. by referring it to the church made up of Jews and gentiles (186.4 ff. = 5.16.2 ff.).

In spite of the apparent close connection between the Jewish Christian "heretics" and the community of the author, it is not to be assumed that they actually belong to the community of the *Didascalia*. [42] It is striking that where the order of the congregation and its spiritual life is especially treated, a Jewish Christian peril is not mentioned. Controversies concerning the authority of the bishop and the other office holders would hardly be absent in the event of a struggle within the community. The question of how "catholic doctrine" is to defend itself against heresy is not concerned with the problem of the inner life of the community, but the community is presupposed as a self-contained entity that seeks to defend itself against sin and apostasy (cf. *Didasc.* 5 ff. [37 ff. = 2.7 ff.]). The Jewish Christian "heretics" stand outside the community of the *Disascalia*.

With this result we have reached a point of departure for the question concerning the relationship between heresy and catholicism in the world of the *Didascalia*. Apparently a complete separation was not involved; rather the previously mentioned contacts permit

---

40. *Didasc.* 23 (202.17 ff. = 6.10.4), 24 (203.23 ff. = 6.11.1 f.); in 26, compare also 242.6 = 6.21(27).1 with 240.22 ff. = 6.20(24).1.

41. The objection that no christological heresy is mentioned (van Unnik, "Beteekenis," p. 96) does not carry much weight, because first of all it is doubtful whether the author of the *Didascalia*, in view of his very practical purpose, would even be aware of such a deviation; second, it is not impossible that the Jewish Christians who are addressed were in agreement with the community of the *Didascalia* in christological matters.

42. Contrary to Schmidt, *Studien*, pp. 253, 260.

the assumption of a lively relationship in which the leading role of "catholic doctrine" was not considered to be incontestable. The powerful language with which the faithful are warned against "heresy" [259] in chapter 23 (194.7 ff. 6.1.1, 197.22 ff. = 6.5.1, 1.99.1 ff. = 6.5.5, etc.) is eloquent proof of this. The statements made by the author about the form and content of the Jewish Christian "heresy" make it seem questionable that it formed an actual sect.[43] It is instructive to note that it is in his confrontation with his Jewish Christian opponents that the author develops the theory, so central for the *Didascalia,* of the "second legeslation" (or "repetition of the law") —i.e. the contrasting of the Old Testament decalogue [= the "real" law] with the ceremonial rules [the *deuterōsis* or "second legislation"] which had been added after the generation in the wilderness worshipped the golden calf (26 [216.1 ff. = 6.15(19).1 ff.]). Although it cannot be established as probable that the author himself constructed this theory in dependence upon a Jewish Christian theological concept,[44] since a corresponding interpretation of the Old Testament had long been used even in ecclesiastical circles in the controversy with Judaism,[45] its pointed application to the Jewish Christian situation (cf. 26 [216.1-5 = 6.15(19).1]) shows that the Jewish Christian "heretics" had a special importance in the world of the *Didascalia.* We can even go a step further; the fact that the author addresses the Jewish Christian "heretics" with the term "dear brothers"

43. Cf. *Didasc.* 26 (240.1 = 6.19[24].3)—they live "in the dispersion among the gentiles." Of course, this also applies to Judaism after the year 135. But the context refers to Jewish Christianity.

44. Contrary to Schmidt, *Studien,* pp. 262 ff., and Schoeps, *Theologie,* p. 180. The theory of false pericopes, which is found in the "KP" document of the ps.-Clementines (see above, 244, and below, 257 f.), cannot be considered as a predecessor since it shows no dependence on Exod. 32; nor does it contrast two stages of written law, but rather, contrasts the falsification of the law with the oral revelation of "the true prophet" (see Strecker, *Judenchristentum,* pp. 162 ff.). The criticism of the Old Testament in the *Didascalia* comes somewhat closer to the Jewish Christian "AJ II" source of the ps.—Clementines [= *Rec.* 1.33-44.2 and 53.4b-71, according to Strecker, *Judenchristentum,* pp. 221-254, and in Hennecke-Schneemelcher, 2: 106], which like the *Didascalia* sees the starting point of the outdated legislation in the veneration of the golden calf by the generation in the desert (*Rec.* 1.36), and holds that sacrifice is replaced by baptism (1.39). However, the author of the *Didascalia* thinks, among other things, of the elimination of the ritual baths through Christian baptism (cf. 26 [224.17 f. = 6.17(22).1, and 248.10 ff. = 6.21(27).7]), while for the "AJ II" source the Jewish ritual laws of purification do not belong to the "second legislation." [For an extended discussion of the concept of *deuterōsis* or "second legislation" in the *Didascalia,* see Connolly, lvii-lxix.]

45. As is pointed out correctly by van Unnik, "Beteeknis," pp. 86-95.

(216.3 = 6.15[19].1, 233.7 = 6.18[23].11) can now no longer be understood as a self-evident *captatio benevolentiae* [attempt to gain good will] resulting from pastoral concern, but can also include the acknowledgement that the Jewish Christian "heresy" actually predominates. The reckoning of the dates for fasting as observed in the author's community is expressly [260] traced back to the reckoning by "believing Hebrews" (21 [187.12 f. = 5.17.2]). Since the designation "believers" in a similar context means only Christians and not Jews, this statement can only be referred to Jewish Christians.[46] The influence of the Jewish Christian "heresy" on the "catholic" ecclesiastical orientation of the *Didascalia* is evident there. The author presupposes Jewish Christian influences. Furthermore, he considers the possibility that the "heretics" might accept those who have been excluded from the church (7 [64.28 ff. = 2.21.2]) or that they themselves might even take part in the worship in his community.[47] As a result, the notion that the "heretical" Jewish Christians were the ones who separated themselves from the church seems much less probable than that the church of the *Didascalia* itself was faced with the task of separating itself from the "heretics."[48] The opposite view is no longer as self-evident as the heresiological outlook would like to imagine, and it is not difficult to conclude that in this part of Syria Jewish Christianity occupied a dominant "orthodox" position superior to "catholicism."

2. *The "Kērygmata Petrou" Source.* We would not be able to draw this conclusion with confidence if we were not in the position of being able to appeal to a direct witness for Jewish Christianity in Greek-

---

46. It could be argued that the preceding sentence, "begin [your fasting] when your brothers who are of the people keep the passover" (187.7 f. = 5.17.1), already should be considered as a reference to the Jewish Christian opponents. This accords with the reading in Epiphanius (*Her.* 70.10.2— *hoi adelphoi humōn hoi ek peritomēs*), which, however, is regarded as doubtful by Connolly (note, *ad loc.*), following Funk (*Didascalia* 2: 7). That the author of the *Didascalia* recognized the connection between the Jewish Christian practice of fasting and the Jewish practice is revealed also by the instructions, "thus you must fast when that people is celebrating the passover" (21 [192.16 f. = 5.20.10]). Therefore a serious objection against the available textual tradition cannot be raised. [The point being argued by Funk and Connolly is that Epiphanius has paraphrased the original Syriac, which they accept as a satisfactory text.]

47. *Didasc.* 12 (120.31 f. = 2.58.1). The fact that these statements are formulated in the plural ("heresies") does not, in view of the tremendous influence of the Jewish Christians, exclude the possibility that they are primarily under consideration.

48. Cf. also Achelis(-Flemming), *Didaskalia*, p. 357.

speaking Syria. The *Kērygmata Petrou* source (= KP, "Proclamations of Peter") contained in the "basic writing" that underlies the pseudo-Clementines contains a Jewish Christian theology that is approximately contemporaneous with the author of the *Didascalia* or perhaps a few decades earlier. This document, which was literary in character but can be reconstructed only in part, is especially valuable for our inquiry since we cannot assume that it was literarily dependent on the *Didascalia* or vice versa, in spite of their geographical proximity.[49] KP is a [261] pseudo-Petrine treatise. It contains material about (1) the "true prophet," how he passed through the world, and his relationship to the hostile female prophecy; also about (2) the exposition of the law by the "true prophet" with material about the "false pericopes"; connected with this are (3) anti-Pauline statements, which attempt to show Paul as an opponent of Peter and as one who was not approved by James, the representative of the true doctrine and bishop of Jerusalem; finally (4) material about baptism is given in which the strongly legalistic character of the work becomes evident.[50]

An important piece of evidence for establishing geographical locus and orientation in terms of the history of theology is the testimony a writing gives with respect to the New Testament canon. The *KP* source is acquainted with the four canonical gospels, the Acts of the Apostles, Galatians and 1 Corinthians.[51] It is significant that neither the catholic epistles nor the Apocalypse are known. Thus there is a basic distinction between the attitude of the *Kerygmata* and the situation that obtained in the West and in wide areas of the East at that time, in which the catholic epistles were in use and the validity of the Apocalypse was only partially contested.[52] However, even at a later period these writings were slow to find acceptance in northern

49. Cf. above, 256 n. 44; Strecker, *Judenchristentum*, p. 215 n. 2.
50. For a treatment of various details as well as a reconstruction of the "basic writing" and the KP source, cf. Strecker, *Judenchristentum, passim*. A summary presentation with selected texts in translation is found in Strecker, "The Kerygmata Petrou," in Hennecke-Schneemelcher 2, 102-127 [in the same volume, see also J. Irmscher's introduction to the ps-Clementines on 532-535].
51. Strecker, *Judenchristentum*, p. 218.
52. Cf., among others, J. Leipoldt, *Die Entstehung des neutestamentlichen Kanons*, 1 (Leipzig, 1907): 58 f.

and eastern Syria.[53] Even the *Didascalia* does not yet show acquaintance with the catholic epistles and the Apocalypse, as was noted above (249 n. 21). This establishes a relation between the KP document and the *Didascalia*, and confirms the view that both are to be placed in a Syrian locale.

It is noteworthy that, in contrast to the assumption of the ecclesiastical heresiologists,[54] the Jewish Christian *Kerygmata* show no knowledge of a Jewish Christian gospel.[55] Therein the *Kerygmata* [262] stand even closer to the "catholic" tradition than does the *Didascalia* which, as we have seen (248 f.), shows a positive relationship to the apocryphal *Gospel of Peter* in spite of Serapion's negative verdict. This and the fact that the *Kerygmata* quote as a matter of course the four gospels that later became canonized is a fundamental argument for the view that the Jewish Christianity represented by the *Kerygmata* had not cut itself off from the "great church," but lived in a situation in which it could candidly accept the development toward the New Testament canon.

This can be corroborated through another line of approach. When we take into consideration the fact that the Pauline letters and the book of Acts are not quoted with approval in the KP document,[56]

53. Zahn, *Geschichte*, 1: 373 ff.; Leipoldt, *Entstehung*, pp. 74, 222; Bauer, *Der Apostolos der Syrer*, pp. 76 f.
54. Cf. Irenaeus AH 1.26.2 (= 1.22), on the Ebionite use of "Matthew"; below, 277 f.
55. G. Quispel ("L'évangile selon Thomas et les Clémentines," *Vigiliae Christianae*, 12 [1958]: 181-196) attempted to prove that a Jewish Christian gospel is cited respectively in the so-called *Gospel of Thomas* and in the ps.-Clementines. [262] However, this attempt is not convincing. It presupposes that the ps.-Clementine quotations from scripture disclose the use of an apocryphal Jewish Christian gospel (cf. the contrary view in Strecker, *Judenchristentum*, pp. 117 ff.), and takes into consideration neither the literary stratification of the ps.-Clementine romance nor the demonstrably free manner of handling scriptural evidence on the part of the ps.-Clementine editor. Contrary to Quispel, cf. also A. F. J. Klijn, "A Survey of the Researches into the Western Text of the Gospel and Acts (1949-1959), Part 2," *Novum Testamentum*, 3 (1959): 176 f.: E. Haenchen, "Literatur zum Thomasevangelium," *Theologische Rundschau*, 27 (1961): 165, 168.
56. It is true that in *Hom.* 3.53.3 we find the influence of a reading which is also attested in Acts 3.22 f. But the parallel passage in *Rec.* 1.36.2 differs. Thus it is not impossible that the (alleged) influence of Acts is to be attributed to a later stratum of tradition in the development of the ps.-Clementine romance. On the problem of anti-Paulinism, see below, 263 f.

it would appear that only the Old Testament and the four gospels are quoted as holy scripture. This is without precedent in Greek-speaking Syria around the year 200, but has a striking parallel in the canon of the Edessene Christians, who besides the Old Testament, used only the four gospels, and these in the harmonized form found in Tatian's *Diatessaron* (see above, 30 ff.). Of course the *Kerygmata* are not to be assigned to Edessene Christianity; they were not originally written in Syriac and betray no acquaintance with the *Diatessaron*. But this parallel probably can enable us to fix more precisely their geographical position and their place in the spectrum of the history of theology—it makes it clear that the Jewish Christianity of the KP was located on the dividing line between Greek and Edessene Syria. This type of Jewish Christianity is a witness for the history of the development of the New Testament canon in this region. It is [263] subject to the fluctuation which is characteristic of the formation of the New Testament canon in the developing mainstream church.

This fundamental openness toward a line of development taken by the "great church" is especially significant since the milieu in which the Jewish Christianity of the *Kerygmata* emerged also presupposes influences that are non-ecclesiastical—namely, Jewish and pagan. That Judaism is an important factor in the environment of the author can already be learned from the prefixed "Epistle of Peter to James" (= EP) which serves as an introduction to KP [57] and explicitly presents the followers of Moses (EP 1.2) as an example to the disciples of Jesus (EP 2.1). It becomes obvious that behind EP there is not only an appeal to history (Moses handing over his teaching office to the seventy, Num. 11.25), and not only a literary fiction (the reference to a Jewish Christian body of seventy brethren should probably be considered such, based on Luke 10.1!), but there are actual references to contemporary Judaism. Thus it is expressly stated that Judaism could serve as an example "to this very day" (EP 1.3), and the document goes beyond biblical allusions in mentioning particular details of a Jewish mode of instruction such as the Jewish confessional formula (EP 1.3 and 5) and especially the idea of the

57. [This *Epistula Petri* (= EP) and another short document called the *Contestatio* or "Testimony Regarding the Recipients of the Epistle" were prefixed to KP already in the "basic writing" behind the ps.-Clementines, according to Strecker. See his treatment in Hennecke-Schneemelcher, 2: 102-115, which includes an ET (by G. Ogg) of these two introductory writings; see also above, 184 n. 78.]

"contradictions of the scriptures," which are brought into harmony by means of a Jewish "guiding principle" or rule (EP 1.4 f.). This derives from a Judaism which is not really "official" but rather "heretical," from which other statements of the KP documents also come, such as the explanation of the theory of false pericopes in particular.[58] It is also characteristic of KP that its Jewish Christian self-understanding affirms the continuity between ancient Israel and Judaism—not only because the followers of Moses serve as an example in EP, but also because the figure of the true prophet Jesus is important in this connection. He is to guarantee the continuity between the old and the new Israel (*Hom.* 8.5-7), and thus on the basis of this coordination of contents which finds no essential conflict between the law of Moses and the proclamation of the "true prophet," the teaching of Moses and the message of Jesus are identified.[59] It is only logical that [264] with such a common foundation, contact with Judaism would also be maintained. The absence of an anti-Jewish polemic, which was so freely practiced in the "great church" of the same period,[60] also suggests that the Jewish Christianity of the *Kerygmata* existed in close relationship to Judaism. This corresponds to the situation regularly encountered with Jewish Christianity, which normally grew from the soil of Palestinian or hellenistic Judaism.

The Jewish Christianity of the *Kerygmata* was also in close contact with paganism. Even though the fictitious nature of the introductory

58. Cf. Strecker, *Judenchristentum*, pp. 166 ff.
59. Cf. EP 2.5, *Hom.* 9.19.3, etc.; Strecker, *Judenchristentum*, pp. 151 f., 163 ff. The nature of the Judaism confronted by the *Kerygmata* cannot be dealt with in detail here. That it does not refer to the Essenic Judaism of the Qumran sect has been shown elsewhere: see Strecker, *Judenchristentum*, pp. 215 ff. [cf. J. A. Fitzmyer, "The Qumran Scrolls, the Ebionites, and their Literature," *Theological Studies*, 16 (1955): 335-372 (reprinted in K. Standahl, *The Scrolls and the New Testament* [New York: Harper, 1957], pp. 208-231)]; contrary to Schoeps, *Theologie*, pp. 252 ff., 316, and also *Urgemeinde-Judenchristentum-Gnosis* (1956), pp. 68 ff.; K. Schubert, "Die [264] jüdischen und jüdenchristlichen Sekten im Lichte des Handschriftenfundes von 'En Fešcha," *Zeitschrift für katholische Theologie*, 74 (1952): 1 ff.; O. Cullmann, "Die neuentdeckten Qumrantexte und das Judenchristentum der Pseudoklementinen," *Neutestamentliche Studien für R. Bultmann*, ZNW Beiheft 21 (1954): 35 ff.; K. Rudolph, *Die Mandäer 1, Prolegomena: Das Mandäerproblem*, FRLANT 74 (1960): 226 f. and *passim*. The Qumran texts are, however, an important witness for the diversity of Judaism in the period of the New Testament and earlier.
60. Cf. e.g. Justin, *Dialogue;* Tertullian *Adversus Judaeos.* In contrast to Matt. 23.25 f., the critique of Pharisaic attitudes is not applied to the totality of the Pharisees in the *Kerygmata* (*Hom.* 11.29.1).

epistle should not be underestimated, on the basis of Peter's plea "not to pass on to any one of the gentiles the books of the *Kerygmata*, not even to a member of our own tribe before he has passed probation" (EP 1.2, 3.1), we may conjecture that the author's situation brought him into confrontation with gentiles. Perhaps this is true also of the statement that "some of the gentiles" have rejected Peter's "lawful" proclamation (EP 2.3). It becomes especially clear from the baptismal instruction of the *Kerygmata* (*Hom.* 11.21-33 and parallel material) included in the discourses of Peter at Tripolis (*Hom.* 8-11 = *Rec.* 4-6). Just as the external framework, which was part of the "basic document," presupposes a gentile audience (*Hom.* 11.1.1 f.), the content of the baptismal instruction does likewise. It alludes to the polytheistic cult of idols (*Hom.* 11.21.4, 11.31.1, etc.), which is also characterized by "lust" (*epithymia—Hom.* 11.26.1; cf. 11.11.5, 11.15.1 and 4 ff., etc.). It contains the demand for the adoption of ritual cleansings, which it presupposes are not being observed by the hearers.[61] Accordingly, it is the gentile populace (not the Jewish) that is the main objective of the Jewish Christian missionary activity. [265]

The fact that the Jewish Christianity of the *Kerygmata* carried on its discussion with both Jewish and gentile parties, coupled with the realization that the KP document reflects tendencies at work in the development of the canon of the ecclesiastical mainstream, should not encourage us to draw far-reaching inferences concerning an actual or even simply a geographical classification of KP within the sphere of the ecclesiastical mainstream. And even though a basic openness toward the tendencies at work in the development of the New Testament canon of the ecclesiastical mainstream is evident, the form and the content of the Jewish Christian theology of the *Kerygmata* are not determined by a confrontation with the "great church." Although the teaching on baptism in the KP document provides an insight into the practices of the Jewish Christian mission to gentiles, it is characteristic that this missionary activity does not reveal opposition on the part of a mainstream mission. The Jewish Christian theological tenets of the *Kerygmata* do not imply a polemical atti-

61. *Hom.* 11.28. But *Hom.* 11.30.2 states, on the contrary, that the hearers observed "things that pertain to purity" (*ta tēs hagneias merē*) during the time of idolatry. *Hagneia* apparently must be understood in a wider sense. It does not designate ritual practices but signifies an ethical attitude (cf. *Hom.* 11.31 ff.).

tude toward the "great church." Apparently a serious controversy with the representatives of the "great church" has not (yet) taken place. It was not necessary because the real partner in the discussion was not the "great church" and because, as has been said, the formation of this type of Jewish Christianity took place primarily in a Jewish and pagan setting.

It should, of course, be asked whether the anti-Paulinism of the KP document contains a polemic against the "great church." [62] One could get that impression from the *Epistula Petri*. Here Peter says that already in his lifetime some of the gentiles have rejected his "lawful preaching" since they "have preferred the lawless and senseless teaching of the hostile man" (EP 2.3 f.). This material seems to reflect a later development, subsequent to Peter's death. This becomes even clearer in Peter's prediction: "But if they falsely assert such a thing while I am still alive, how much more will those who come later venture to do so after my death" (EP 2.7). One must conclude that the author is aware of Pauline teachings in his immediate environment or its wider setting. But this conclusion is as far as one can go in this respect, for the anti-Paulinism of the *Kerygmata* does not reveal an actual controversy taking place between the ecclesiastical mainstream and Jewish Christianity. The author remains [266] bound to his sources, the Pauline letters and the picture of Paul in Acts. His knowledge derives essentially from literary sources. This is also indicated by particular references that have the appearance of citations.[63] The anti-Pauline statements of the *Kerygmata* thus can confirm that the Jewish Christianity of KP did have access to the writings of the mainstream church, but they do not lead us back to an actual controversy. From a formal point of view, their purpose is to give

62. In my opinion it is an assured result of scholarship that the *Kerygmata* originally polemicized against Paul alone, and not in some sort of combined fashion against Simon-Paul or Marcion-Paul (cf. Strecker, *Judenchristentum*, pp. 187 ff., 154 n. 1). The suggestion has recently been made by W. Schmithals [266] that from the very beginning the polemic was directed against Simon-Paul (*Das kirchliche Apostelamt*, FRLANT 79 [1961], p. 153 n. 305; p. 198 n. 481). But this does not take into consideration the problems involved in reconstructing the Jewish Christian element in the ps.-Clementines. One must begin with an analysis of the introductory writings, the *Epistula Petri* and the *Contestatio* (see above, 260 n. 57). They show no demonstrable confusion of the "hostile man" (*ekthros anthrōpos*, EP 2.3) with Simon Magus, but the identification with Paul is evident in the allusions to Gal. 2.11 ff. (EP 2.4).
63. Cf. the examples listed in Strecker, *Judenchristentum*, p. 218.

color to the apostolic fiction of Peter's doctrinal discourses as expressed especially in the reference to the controversy between Peter and Paul in Antioch.[64] With reference to content, their purpose is the explication of the Jewish Christian self-understanding. The pseudo-Petrine doctrinal discourses as a whole are not directed primarily against Pauline thought, but their anti-Paulinism should be interpreted as a specific expression of the Jewish Christian legalistic system.[65]

From this perspective the picture of the Jewish Christianity of the *Kerygmata* comes into focus. If the references to the Pauline letters and to Acts are set aside as a literary matter, then the relationship to the "great church" can be defined with more precision. There appears to exist no direct interconnection nor any genetic dependence, but the structural elements of the theology of the *Kerygmata* must be attributed to an earlier independent Jewish Christian tradition. This follows from the fact that the citation of gospel texts is made in a rather unpretentious manner with such introductory formulas as: "For thus the prophet has sworn to us saying" (*Hom.* 11.26.2), "for he said thus" (EP 2.5), "and when he said" (*Hom.* 3.50.2), etc. Apparently the readers made regular use of the gospel writings being cited. [267] Insofar as the author is explaining the theology of the *Kerygmata* by means of the citations,[66] he is not resorting directly to the tradition of the "great church"; rather, the Jewish Christianity of the *Kerygmata* presupposes a tradition which may have developed in the region bordering Osröenian Syria, and which paralleled in part that stream of tradition represented on the other side by the "great church."

How much the theology of this Jewish Christianity must be considered to be fundamentally autonomous is further indicated by its

---

64. EP 2.4; *Hom.* 17.19; Gal. 2.11 ff.
65. The warning against false "prophets, apostles, and teachers" as well as the admonition to accept only messengers who have been approved by the "bishop" James (*Hom.* 11.35.3-6 and par.) could be construed as indicating the presence of a current polemic. But this warning also is related to the basically literary anti-Paulinism (the sequence of offices is paralleled in 1 Cor. 12.28). Furthermore, the motif of James is related to the apostolic fiction and cannot be transferred to the period [267] of the author. Even here, the contemporization indicates nothing more than the presence of a legalistic self-understanding.
66. The quotations from the gospels underline the validity of the law (EP 2.5), the doctrine of the falsified pericopes in the scriptures (*Hom.* 3.50.1), the anti-Paulinism (*Hom.* 11.18.1), and the teaching on baptism with its related injunctions to purity (*Hom.* 11.26.2, 11.29.2).

teaching on baptism. On the one hand this appears against the background of gnostic dualism. The original materialism of this dualism is taken over by the *Kerygmata,* with some modifications, but it is still assumed that the "first birth" (*prōtē genēsis*), the natural origin of man, is identical with enslavement to lust (*epithymia, Hom.* 11.26 and par.). This recalls the deprecation of the cosmos in gnostic systems.[67] But at the same time a judaistic interpretation is also apparent—the task of the Spirit at baptism is not related to a sacramental event but rather to the evaluation of the good deeds of the baptized. The Spirit "offers the good works of the baptized as gifts to God" (*Hom.* 11.26.3 and par.). Not the act of baptism but man's ethically related "fear" (*phobos*) brings about the rebirth—i.e. the exchange of man's natural destiny for "being born to God" (*Hom.* 11.26.1, 11.27.2 and par.). Therefore in the last analysis the rationale for the act of baptism consists solely in the divine command (*Hom.* 11.26.1 and par.). This peculiar doctrine of baptism also leads to the baptismal exhortation (*Hom.* 11.27.3 ff. and par.), which is clearly distinguished from the unique baptismal instruction that precedes by its directions concerning ritual baths of purification (*Hom.* 11.28.2, 11.30.1). This distinction is also indicated by the specific terminology used: while the *baptisma* or the passive voice *baptisthēnai* are regularly used for the act of baptism, the lustrations are designated by *kathareuein* or *loutrō plunein;*[68] [268] and while baptism as an act of initiation is connected with "rebirth" (*Hom.* 11.24.2, 11.26.1 ff; *Contestatio* 1.2) with the phrase "living water" appearing in this context (*hydōr zōn; Hom.* 11.26.2 and 4; *Contestatio* 1.2), this designation is not applied to the lustrations which can be repeated. It is apparent that directions of this sort have no parallels in mainstream gentile Christian practices, but express the genuine

---

67. Cf. Strecker, *Judenchristentum,* pp. 158, 199 f.
68. *Hom.* 11.28.1 ff.; also *Hom.* 11.30.1 f., 11.33.4 (*baptizesthai* or *baptistheisē*). K. Rudolph also called attention to this terminological distinction, but at the same time he emphasized the unity of baptism and lustrations because the significance [268] of the water as "a vehicle of divine power" is present in both (*Die Mandäer* 1, 241; cf. 235). Since KP does not really seem to attest a magical-sacramental character for the baptismal act, it would be more accurate to speak of a moralistic understanding as the common basis for baptism and lustrations. This also distinguishes the Jewish Christianity of the *Kerygmata* from the views of baptism and lustrations held by the Elchasaites and Mandaeans. Moreover, the *Book of Elchasai* also distinguishes between baptism and lustrations (cf. Strecker, "Elkesai," RAC 4 [1959]: 1181), and thus reveals its originally Christian nature; cf. also below, 269. [For ET of the fragments of the "Book of Elchasai," see Hennecke-Schneemelcher, 2: 745-750, by J. Irmscher and R. McL. Wilson.]

Jewish Christian character of the material.[69] The KP source also bases its injunctions for the ritual baths on the Old Testament Jewish law (cf. Lev. 15.24, 18.19) or on the instructions of the "true prophet" who summons men to surpass the pharisaic way of life (*Hom.* 11.28.1, 11.29.1 ff.; cf. Matt. 23.25 f.).

The consequences of the peculiar Jewish Christian legalistic outlook are not fully developed in the *Kerygmata*. Baptism serves as the sole rite of initiation, not circumcision.[70] But *Contestatio* 1.1 advises that the books of Peter's proclamations be transmitted only to a "circumcised and believing" candidate for the teaching office. This, however, does not imply that circumcision had the function of a rite of initiation, since the immediate context does not deal with the introduction into the community, nor with baptism, but only with the transmission of the books. Furthermore, the earlier statement in EP 3.1, which has the same purpose, [269] does not mention any requirement of circumcision. Although the supposed evidence in *Contestatio* 1.1 also may permit the conclusion that the author knew of circumcised persons who were members of the Christian community, it seems that this passage should be understood primarily as a literary intensification of the rule found in EP 3.1, and that inferences of a more far-reaching sort cannot be drawn. Since statements corresponding to this cannot be demonstrated elsewhere in KP, it is probably correct to suppose that in the Jewish Christianity represented by the *Kerygmata* baptism has taken the place of circumcision. However, this does not imply that the Jewish Christian practice of baptism has been borrowed from the ecclesiastical mainstream, although the parallelism with ecclesiastical baptism extends beyond the mere act—if baptism

69. For Jewish ritual baths, cf. Babylonian Talmud *Berakot* 21b (3.4); Josephus *Against Apion* 2. 203; W. Brandt, *Die jüdischen Baptismen*, ZAW Beiheft 18 (1910): 44 f., 52, 55; A. Oepke, "louō," TDNT 4: 300 f. = TWbNT 4: 303 f.
70. This was correctly emphasized by E. Molland, "La circoncision, le baptême et l'autorité du décret apostolique (Actes XV 28 sq.) dan les milieux judéo-chrétiens des pseudo-Clémentines," *Studia Theologica*, 9 (1955): 1-39 [repr. in Molland, *Opuscala Patristica* (Oslo, 1970)], against Schoeps (*Theologie*, pp. 115, 138). Molland's position with respect to source analysis, however, is untenable; it follows O. Cullman (*Le problème littéraire et historique du roman pseudo-clémentin* [Paris, 1930]) in positing a "Journeys of Peter" source (*Periodoi Petrou*) between the "basic writing" and KP, but fails to recognize that the demonstrable multiplicity of special sources behind the "basic writing" makes it necessary to stratify the tradition further at this point.

is performed, according to the mysterious circumlocution, "in the thrice-blessed name," it is hardly possible that any formula other than the ecclesiastical triadic formula is meant.[71] But according to what has been said it is evident that the witnesses for the baptismal practice do not stand in contradiction to the independent character of the *Kerygmata,* but they enable us to recognize the stream of tradition that is common to the *Kerygmata* and to the "great church," just as was true of the use of the "canonical" gospel writings (above, 258-260).

Can we conclude from all this that the Jewish Christianity of the KP document was not a sectarian conventicle—that it cannot be considered as a sectarian minority that stood over against an orthodox majority?[72] K. Rudolph has disputed these results and affirmed a close relationship to the so-called baptizing sects on the grounds that in his view the "living water" in the *Kerygmata* stands in opposition to the fire, baptism by water is in contrast to sacrifices, and ritual baths play an important role.[73] However, his argumentation does not really take into account the problem of the literary criticism of the ps.-Clementines, but he endeavors to take his point of departure from the "contents of the entire complex insofar as they are instructive for our purposes."[74] On the contrary, it is necessary to stress that this

71. *Epi tē trismakaria eponomasia, Hom.* 11.26.3. In *Hom.* 11.26.2, according to the extant text, Matt. 28.19 is expressly quoted along with John 3.5. This citation of Matthew belongs to a later stage of the tradition. The parallel passage in *Rec.* 6.9 shows that the triadic formula of Matt. 28.19 is not yet found in the "basic writing." But even in the earlier form of the quotation (in *Hom.* 11.26.2) the influence of Matthew's gospel seems to be present in the phrase "you will never enter the kingdom of the heavens" (*ou mē eiselthēte . . . tōn ouranōn*), which reflects Matt. 5.20 [cf. John 3.3 and 5, and the variants].
72. Cf. Strecker, *Judenchristentum,* p. 215.
73. Rudolph, *Die Mandäer,* 1: 240.
74. Rudolph, *Die Mandäer,* 1: 240 n. 1. E. S. Drower also is content to state: "My own interest in the *Homilies* is, of course, confined to similarities found in them [270] to the secret teaching of the Nazoraeans" (*The Secret Adam: A Study of Nasorean Gnosis* [Oxford: Clarendon, 1960], pp. 45 n. 1, 88 ff.). Similarly P. Beskow (*Rex Gloriae: The Kingship of Christ in the Early Church* [Stockholm: Almqvist and Wiksell, 1962]) does not wish to contribute to the "confusion" concerning the question of the sources of the ps.-Clementines by introducing a "new basis for source division" (256). One would hardly have expected such a major undertaking in an investigation dealing with the kingship of Christ. But it is not unreasonable to require that even this type of investigation should at least take a position worthy of the name on the problem of the ps.-Clementine sources. In its present form Breskow's work itself contributes to the "goodly measure of confusion" on this subject insofar as this author, in spite of his failure to take

[270] sort of approach does not do justice to the complicated stratification of traditions reflected in the ps.-Clementines, and overlooks the fact that the specific meaning of the supposed Jewish Christian "contents" varies with each changing situation in the history of tradition—thus the "contents" can be identified only by means of literary-critical classification. But even apart from the methodological problem, Rudolph's thesis is open to serious objections. Although the antithesis between baptism and sacrifice appears not only in the"AJ II" source of the ps.-Clementines (in *Rec.* 1.39 and 55; see above, 256 n. 44), but is also found in *Rec.* 1.48.5, the latter is part of a context (*Rec.* 1.44.3-53.4a) in which the author of the "basic writing" gathered together heterogeneous materials. Thus one would obviously suppose that the passage in *Recognitions* 1.48.5 had been influenced not by the KP source but by the context (*Rec.* 1.39 belongs to "AJ II"). This assumption is confirmed by the fact that the KP document does not contain such an antithesis between baptism and sacrifice elsewhere. The rejection of temple sacrifices found in the *Kerygmata* is not relevant to the present problem.[75] And finally it is doubtful on principle that the antithesis between sacrifice and baptism constitutes a sufficient criterion for connecting the KP document with the "baptizing sects," since this sort of direct relationship cannot be affirmed for the "AJ II" source, in spite of the admitted antithesis, and since the antithesis between baptism and sacrifice is not clearly evidenced in the literature of the actual baptizing sects.[76] [271]

---

a position on the source critical problem, thinks he is in a position to make the straightforward claim, as startling as it is unfounded, that "It is sufficient for our purposes to point out that in one section of PsC there is a deposit of Greek speculation, which has nothing whatever to do with more or less hypothetical 'Ebionite' concepts" (256).

75. In reply to Rudolph, *Die Mandäer*, 1: 240 n. 4.

76. It should be noted that the "AJ II" source speaks of a contrast between a single act of baptism over against sacrifice and not of an antithesis between various ritual baths and the sacrificial cult (cf. also *Rec.* 1.55 and 69 f.). This indicates a Christian [271] background. Wherever ritual baths were practiced alongside baptism within the Christian sphere, a careful distinction is made (cf. above, 265 f.). The antithesis of ritual baths and sacrificial cult presupposes another environment, namely, a Jewish world of ideas; it is not even generally found among the baptizing sects, and what evidence exists is ambiguous (for the Essenes cf. Josephus *Antiq.* 18.[1.5.]19; for the *Book of Elchasai* [above, 265 n. 68], Epiphanius *Her.* 19.3.6 f.—but is this from the Elchasaites?). This sort of contrast is not present in the Jewish Christian literature of the ps.-Clementines.

An allusion to the practice of the baptizing sects could perhaps be seen in the notion of the "daily baths of Peter," if it were possible to trace this idea back to the KP document.[77] But this cannot be demonstrated. First of all, the pseudo-Clementines do not speak of "daily" baths of Peter. The "basic writing" only mentions occasional baths (*Hom.* 8.2.5, 10.26.2 and par.). The editor of the *Homilies*-recension has elaborated on this motif in secondary fashion, but still has not understood it in the sense of "daily" baths (cf. *Hom.* 10.1.2, 11.1.1, 14.3.1; etc.). It is only in Epiphanius that such a reference occurs (*Her.* 30.2.4, 30.15.3, 30.16.1, 30.21.1), which is a typical example of the liberties he takes with his sources. Secondly, it is clear that the notion of "Peter's baths" cannot be traced back to the KP source, but is a legitimate part of the narrative framework of the Clement romance. Thus it would seem plausible that the idea was inserted by the author of the "basic writing" since he is responsible for the narrative of the romance. This is consistent with the archaizing manner of presentation used by the author of the "basic writing," who also employs Judaizing features elsewhere.[78]

Of course, it cannot be denied that the KP document refers to injunctions for ritual baths. But it has already been shown that in the *Kerygmata* the ritual baths are distinguished from baptism proper and that they reflect not a gnostic but a genuinely Jewish background.[79] These baths [272] do not go beyond the Jewish sphere of thought and therefore cannot be used as an argument to show that the *Kerygmata* belongs in the same category as the so-called baptizing sects. The *Book of Elchasai* (above, 265 n. 68) serves as a counter-example. Its injunctions for ritual baths depend not so much on Jewish as on Christian presuppositions, and its demand for a

---

77. So. K. Rudolph, *Die Mandäer*, 1: 240, n. 5.
78. Strecker, *Judenchristentum*, pp. 213, 257 f.
79. Above, 267 f. Rudolph has demonstrated that Jewish commandments for ritual baths are also known in Mandaeanism (*Die Mandäer*, 2, *Der Kult* [1961]: 109 ff.). Beyond that, he sought to establish that the Mandaean baptism could, in the final analysis, be traced back to Jewish ritual baths (402). This hypothesis is rather daring, since unambiguous examples of the repetition of the Mandaean baptismal bath are not given (if we ignore the modern reports, which can hardly be utilized as evidence for the more ancient period). This criticism should not detract from the significance of Rudolph's work. Without doubt, his detailed presentation of recent literature and the results of his discussions on particular problems of basic importance make this investigation one of the most valuable contributions to the present state of Mandaean studies.

baptismal bath for "grievous sinners" (Hippolytus *Ref.* 9.15.1 f.) and for baths at time of sickness (*Ref.* 9.15.4 ff. and par.) can with more justification be considered elements of a baptizing sect.[80]

Finally, the notion of "living water" does not provide grounds for a real argument. The expression does occur in gnostic literature,[81] but nothing can be made of this fact because one should in principle make a differentiation between baptizing the gnostic circles, and only in particular instances can an identity be established.[82] Moreover, the notion is not limited to gnosticism, but is met also in the ecclesiastical milieu,[83] quite apart from the fact that in the KP source this expression appears exclusively [273] in connection with the water of baptism and is not used in relation to ritual baths (see above, 265 f.).

In conclusion it can be said that Rudolph's attempt to postulate a sectarian situation for the Jewish Christianity of the KP by connecting it with the so-called baptizing sects is not convincing. We can now affirm with greater assurance that the Jewish Christianity of the *Kerygmata* should be understood in the context of Bauer's hypothesis.[84] The relations to the "great church" are primarily on a liter-

80. Strecker, "Elchesai," cols. 1171 ff. E. Peterson ("Die Behandlung der Tollwut bei den Elchasaiten nach Hippolyt," *Frühkirche, Judentum und Gnosis* [New York: Herder, 1959], pp. 221-235; a revised form of "Le traitement de la rage par les Elkésaïtes d'après Hippolyte," *Recherche de science religieuse,* 34 [1947]: 232-238] has attempted to prove that the lustrations of the Elchasaites were not intended to avert sicknesses, but that sicknesses named in the *Book of Elchasai* symbolize sin. "Madness" (*Ref.* 9.15.4) is to be understood as "concupiscence" (227 ff.). But Peterson's proposal leaves unanswered the question of why the *Book of Elchasai* can in other places refer to sexual sins without circumlocution (Hippolytus *Ref.* 9.15.1 and 3) if in fact it spoke symbolically in this passage. Furthermore, Peterson did not take into consideration the fact that in the Elchasaite traditions cited by Epiphanius, lustrations against sicknesses also are mentioned (Epiphanius *Her.* 30.17.4). Finally, Hippolytus quotes another fragment in which Elchasai's injunctions to ritual baths are explicitly directed to sick people (*Ref.* 9.16.1). In the original form of his essay, Peterson attributed this last passage to an interpolator (237), which must be taken as an admission of the weakness of his approach. The fact that this interpretation is not repeated in his revised version is no improvement, since he does not provide an alternative solution.
81. Strecker, *Judenchristentum,* p. 202.
82. Contrary to Rudolph, *Die Mandäer,* 1: 245; 2: 379.
83. *Didache* 7; perhaps also *Barnabas* 11.11, etc.; T. Klauser, "Taufet in lebendigem Wasser! Zum religions-und kulturgeschichtlichen Verständnis von Didache 7, 1-3." *Pisciculi* (Festschrift for F. J. Dölger, Münster, 1939), pp. 157-164.
84. Only the historical problem is posed here. A dogmatically conditioned definition of the concept of "heresy" would not advance the historical analysis. This must also be said of H. Köster's article "Häretiker im Urchristentum" (RGG³, 3 [1959]: 17-21; see below, 307 n. 21), which takes its point of departure from the "faith of the community in the revelation of God that took place once and for

ary level and there is no indication of an active confrontation. Rather this Jewish Christianity has its own theology, independent of mainstream Christianity, which precludes the possibility that it is "sectarian" in nature. The widespread notion that Jewish Christianity separated itself from the "great church" and subsequently led a cloistered existence as a sect (cf. above, 242 n. 3) must be revised. It is much more probable that in the world from which the *Kerygmata* derives, Jewish Christianity was the sole representative of Christianity and the problem of its relationship to the "great church" had not yet arisen. This conclusion is indirectly supported by Bauer's recognition that other parts of Syria also served as the original homeland for non-ecclesiastical gnostic [274] groups, and the situation did not indicate the prior presence of ecclesiastical orthodoxy (above, pp. 1 ff.). It is also supported by the witness of the *Didascalia* which, as has been demonstrated above, reflects confrontations between a "catholic" community and a Jewish Christianity that apparently enjoyed unrestricted prominence in Syria up to that time. This verdict stands even if the Jewish Christians addressed in the *Didascalia* are not to be identified with the community of the author of KP. The evidence of the *Didascalia* confirms from the ecclesiastical viewpoint the situation of Syrian Jewish Christianity as it is presented in the *Kerygmata*. In this part of Syria around the end of the second and beginning of the third century Jewish Christianity is independent of the "great church," and has an appearance that does not conform to the usual heresiological characterization.

-----

all," and considers as "heretical" (1) an overemphasis on the time-bound historical character of the revelation or, (2) the absolutizing of the transcendent content of the revelation (18). However, Köster's presentation of the "heretics" is not based on this theological point of departure but proceeds phenomenologically on the basis of statements by New Testament writers concerning the Christian groups which are opposed to them (18 ff.). This discrepancy can be interpreted as constituting an indirect admission that sufficient criteria for the historical application of the theological concept cannot be developed, but rather that the historical phenomenon of "heresy" resists theological classification. This also is evidence for the correctness of Bauer's thesis. If the theological definition of heresy were consistently applied to the whole New Testament and were not used simply to describe anti-ecclesiastical groups, this would not only lead to difficulties, but the problem would also be raised as to what extent the theology of the New Testament writers or of the traditions used by them should be exempt from the concept of "heresy" in that sense. Against such a schematic application of a theological understanding we could also point to the usage of *hairesis* in the New Testament, which does not yet suggest the later heresiological-dogmatical meaning.

3. *The Ecclesiastical Attitude and "Ebionism."* In the heresiological classifications Jewish Christianity has a well established position under the rubric "Ebionites." In the older secondary literature the Hebrew equivalent of this name [*'ebionim* = "poor"] was traced back to a messianic self-designation of the primitive community.[85] However, while this explanation seems quite plausible at first sight, it cannot be verified. In the Pauline letters those references to the "poor" (*ptōchoi*) which relate to the situation of the Jerusalem community and have been interpreted in the above sense do not demonstrably require anything but a literal interpretation. They are not messianological in nature.[86] Even if it is admitted that [275] at an early period a broad stream of piety based on a Jewish ideal of poverty found acceptance in Christianity,[87] there is no reason to assume that the earliest community as a whole followed that ideal. The reports in Acts about a general community of goods in the Jerusalem community are largely legendary or else Lukan generalizations of non-typical isolated epi-

85. E.g. Holl, *Gesammelte Aufsätze,* 2: 60; Lietzmann, *An die Römer*4, 122 ff.
86. Rom. 15.26, Gal. 2.10. E. Bammel's attempt to the contrary is not convincing. His argument that the expression *ptōchoi* in Rom. 15.26 could not have the literal meaning "poor" because "then it is inconceivable that the collection would be continued after the need for it had disappeared" (TDNT 6, 909 = TWbNT 6, 909.5 f.) is not decisive because it has not been proven that the reason for the collection was a specific emergency in Jerusalem—Acts 11.27-30 cannot be used in support of this thesis (Strecker, "Die sogenannte Zweite Jerusalemreise des Paulus," ZNW 53 [1962]: 67-77). It is not impossible, on the contrary, that the collection resulted from a general concern for the socially deprived, and that the Jerusalem authorities would have added legal overtones to its accomplishment. When in Rom. 15.26 *tōn hagiōn* appears as partitive genitive describing *tous ptōchous* ("the poor from among the saints"), this certainly does not convey a "general meaning" which "would not definitely exclude non-Christian Jerusalem" (Bammel, TDNT 6, 909 = TWbNT 6, 908.33 f.; G. Klein also disagrees, "Die Verleugnung des Petrus," ZTK 58 [1961]: 320, n. 5; this essay has been reprinted in *Reconstruktion und Interpretation: Gesammelte Aufsätze zum Neuen Testament* [München: Kaiser, 1969]), but employs the eschatological designation of the community that is frequent in Paul ("saints"—Rom. 1.7, 1 Cor. 1.2, 2 Cor. 1.1, etc.). Thus *ptōchoi* refers to only one group within the community and not to the community as a whole, and a literal interpretation of "poor" is the most logical. This can also be demonstrated for Gal. 2.10 (A. Oepke, *Der Brief des Paulus an die Galater*2, Theologische Handkommentar zum Neuen Testament 9 [Berlin: Evangelische Verlagsanstalt, 1960], p. 54), and is confirmed by 2 Cor. 9.12 (*ta hysterēmata* [!] *tōn hagiōn*).
87. Cf. e.g. Luke 6.20 f., 12.13 ff., 16.19 ff.; James 1.9 ff., 2.5 ff., 5.1 ff., etc.; M. Dibelius, *Der Brief des Jakobus,* Meyer Kommentar 15 (Göttingen: Vandenhoeck & Ruprecht, 1956; expanded by H. Greeven, 19579, 196411, etc.), p. 37 ff.

sodes.[88] The title *Ebiōnaioi* appears first in Irenaeus (AH 1.26.2 [= 1.22]), and even if it was already used as a fixed designation for the sect prior to Irenaeus, as is probable (see below, 278), it does not date back to earliest Christian times with that meaning since it does not occur at all in Justin's statements about Jewish Christianity (*Dial.* 47). Therefore it is not probable that it was originally used as a general Jewish Christian self-designation; instead, we assume that the name was originally applied to a specific Jewish Christian group which felt especially obligated to uphold the Jewish ideal of poverty. Later the title was transformed by the heresiologists into a general designation for "sectarian" Jewish Christianity. Such a schematic procedure corresponds to the usual heresiological pattern, as will become clear. Thus critical discretion with regard to the data of the church fathers is mandatory as we proceed to investigate their accounts in detail.

After the first part of his *Dialogue with Trypho the Jew*, which deals with the transitory value of Jewish ceremonial law (9-42), Justin speaks of the divine majesty of Jesus in a second section (43-118). At the intersection of these two major sections there is an excursus criticizing those Christians who combine the observance of the Jewish law with faith in Christ (47). Trypho's question, whether a member of the Jewish people can be saved if he believes in Jesus as the Christ but also observes the Mosaic commandments [276] is answered as follows: (1) Jewish Christians can be saved if they hold fast to the Jewish law without demanding such observance from others nor regarding it to be necessary for salvation (47.1)—this is Justin's view, even though there are gentile Christians who reject any social contact with Jewish Christians (47.2). (2) Jewish Christians who force their gentile brothers to keep Jewish observances or who withhold fellowship from them are not acknowledged as true Christians by Justin (47.3). (3) For those who have been misled by Jewish Christians to accept Jewish observances, salvation is possible if they hold fast to the confession of Christ (47.4a). (4) Christians who have turned

88. Acts 2.44 f., 4.36 f., 5.1 ff.; E. Haenchen, *Die Apostelgeschichte*[4], Meyer Kommentar 3 (1961), *ad loc.* Epiphanius later traced the name of the Ebionites back to the community of goods in the earliest community of Acts 4-5 (*Her.* 30.17.2) [See also J. A. Fitzmyer, "Jewish Christianity in Acts in the Light of the Qumran Scrolls," in *Studies in Luke-Acts*, ed. L. E. Keck and J. L. Martyn (1961) p. 244.]

to Judaism and forsaken faith in Christ and who are not converted prior to their death will not be saved (47.4b). (5) The descendants of Abraham who live in accordance with the Jewish law and who are not converted to Christ, but in their synagogues curse the be-, lievers in Christ will not be saved (47.5). In spite of its logical arrangement this list cannot be attributed to mere abstraction. It presupposes actual knowledge about the "Jewish" attitude. This is demonstrated not only by the concluding reference to the Jewish "eighteen benedictions" (*Shemoneh Esreh*) [89] but also by the fact that in other passages, Justin also is well-informed about Judaism,[90] not the least of which are the statements that according to Jewish Christian theology Christ had been a "man from among men" (48.4) and "had been elected" to be Messiah-Christ (48.3, 49.1).

From Justin's data the following can be discovered about the form and the self-understanding of the Jewish Christianity known to him. The general mark of identification relates to Jewish observances, namely the observance of circumcision and sabbath (47.2), of months and purification (cf. 46.2). Of course, sacrifice is no longer part of Jewish cultic practice, as is stated elsewhere (46.2). Justin's witness about the large variety of beliefs and practices within Jewish Christian theology is significant. The indefinite formulation "for there are also some" (*kai gar eisi tines*, 48.4) already indicates that an adoptionistic christology was not a general feature of all Jewish Christian circles. In fact, the presence of a preexistence [277] Christology in Jewish Christian literature can be demonstrated.[91] On the other hand, an adoptionistic christological confession is considered possible also among gentile Christians (48.4). Above, all there were different approaches to the gentile mission—legalistic Jewish Christianity wavers between a basically tolerant attitude that grants gentile Christians freedom from the law (47.1 f.), and another attitude that expects gentile Christians to maintain Jewish observances also (47.3).

89. On this subject, see H. Strack-P. Billerbeck, *Kommentar zum Neuen Testament aus Talmud und Midrasch*, 1 (München: Beck, 1926): 406 ff.; 4 (1928): 208 f.; K. G. Kuhn, *Achtzehngebet und Vaterunser und der Reim* (1950).

90. E.g. on Jewish teachings concerning the Messiah in *Dial.* 8; A. von Harnack, *Judentum und Judenchristentum in Justins Dialog mit Trypho. . .* , TU 39.1 (1913), *passim*.

91. Jerome *Commentary on Genesis* 1.1; ps.-Clementine *Rec.* 1.43 f.; Strecker, "Ebioniten," col. 497.

The heresiological situation reflected in this account is somewhat clearer. In the gentile Christian church the appraisal of legalistic Jewish Christianity apparently has not yet advanced beyond the stage of expressing a personal point of view. This is indicated by the introductory words "as it seems to me" (*hōs men emoi dokei,* 47.1-2) and also by the extremely personal tone of Justin's statements in general,[92] and his references to other possible points of view (47.2, 48.4). There is nothing to indicate the existence of a developed heresiological stance, or even an official ecclesiastical differentiation. Nor is there evidence that Jewish Christians were classified with other "heretical" groups. A basic tolerance is possible in which the norm of behavior can depend on the attitude of the Jewish Christians, with the principle that the person excluded from the church's fellowship is the one who excludes himself (47.2 f.). It is therefore quite consistent that the concept *hairesis* is not applied to Jewish Christians. Here Justin's assessment of Jewish Christianity differs greatly from his presentation of other religious groups. The parties of Judaism are designated "heresies" (62.3, 80.4). Above all, gnostics and Marcionites are numbered among the *haireseis* (*Dial.* 35.3, 51.2, 80.3 f.; *Apol.* 26.8). If Justin's *Syntagma* described "all heresies"[93] it would not have included heretics of Jewish Christian provenance, but probably dealt primarily with gnostic-Marcionite teachings.[94]

The author Hegesippus is quoted by Eusebius as an outstanding representative of the correct doctrine (EH 4.21 f.) whose travels, by his own admission, were aimed at confirming that "the law, [278] the prophets, and the Lord" possess authority "in every transmission of doctrine[95] and in every city" (EH 4.22.3). To the extent that the preserved fragments permit us to recognize the outline of his own conception, Hegesippus shows parallels to Justin's heresiological thought in a surprising way. The danger that threatens the church originates primarily from gnostics (EH 4.22.5; see above, 189). The

---

92. "I am of the opinion" (*apophainomai,* 47.2,4,5), "I am not in agreement" (*egō ou sunainos eimi,* 47.2), "I do not accept" (*ouk apodechomai,* 47.3), "I suspect" (*hypolambanō,* 47.4).
93. *Apology* 26.8, syntagma kata pasōn tōn gegenēmenōn haireseōn syntetagmenon.
94. *Apol.* 26 names the heretics Simon (Magus), Menander, and Marcion.
95. This is the meaning of *diadochē;* for a discussion and bibliography cf. Altaner, *Patrology,* 149 f. (see the German 6th ed. with A. Stuiber, p. 118), and above 196 n. 2.

concept *hairesis* is applied to Jewish groups,[96] but a corresponding characterization of Jewish Christianity is lacking. The name "Ebionite" apparently is unknown to him, and the problem of the relationship between Jewish Christianity and orthodoxy is never raised. The ab-sence of that sort of question is not necessarily due to the Jewish Christian tradition in which Hegesippus undoubtedly stands, which even permits him to view the Jerusalem community as the authentic prototype of orthodoxy (EH 3.32, 4.22.4). For our purposes, his witness is all the more valuable since it cannot be demonstrated that he was dependent on Justin.[97] Thus, with Justin, Hegesippus is an important informant concerning the openness of the heresiological situation in the second half of the second century.

Justin's literary influence is noticeable in the writings of Ireneaeus, in which Justin's work against Marcion is cited (AH 4.6.2 [= 4.11.2]) and Justin's literary heritage has also been utilized in general.[98] It is therefore all the more surprising that Irenaeus' reports concerning the Ebionites do not refer back to the position taken by Justin to which we have already referred. Irenaeus describes the *"Ebionaei"* in AH 1.26.2 (= 1.22), subsequent to the heresiological characteriza-tion of Cerinthus (26.1 [= 21]) and prior to the treatment of the Nicolaitans (26.3 [= 23]), Cerdo (27.1 [= 24]), and Marcion (27.2 ff. [= 25.1-2]). They are said to acknowledge the creator God, possess a christology similar to Cerinthus and Carpocrates,[99] and [279] use only "the gospel according to Matthew." The apostle Paul is rejected

96. EH 2.23.8 f., *tines oun tōn hepta haireseōn tōn en tō laō. . . ;* cf. 4.22.5. The names of the seven Jewish heresies are found in EH 4.22.7; cf. also 3.23.3 and 6 (also 3.19 and 3.32.2).

97. Cf. Hilgenfeld, *Ketzergeschichte,* pp. 30 ff., contrary to A. von Harnack, *Zur Quellenkritik der Geschichte des Gnostizismus* (1873), pp. 36 ff.

98. Cf. AH 5.26.2 (= 5.26.3)—is this material taken from Justin's *Syntagma?* See Bardenhewer, *Geschichte*², 1: 407. [On the general problem of Justin's lost *Syntagma,* see P. Prigent, *Justin et l'Ancien Testament* (Paris: Gabalda, 1964).]

99. The *"non"* must be deleted; it disturbs the meaning of the text which ap-parently intended first to emphasize the contrast between Ebionites and Cerinthus-Carpocrates, and then the agreement with them. The deletion is confirmed by Hippolytus *Ref.* 7.34 (*ta de peri ton christon homoios tō Kērinthō kai Karpokratei mytheuousin*) and also through Irenaeus' description of Ebionite christology in AH 3.21.1 (= 3.23) and 5.1.3. [279] The reading could have originated through assimilation to the preceding *"dominum"* (cf. Harvey's note, *ad loc.*).

by them as an apostate from the law. They have their own peculiar interpretation of the "prophecies" (*prophetica*), practice circumcision, and also observe the Jewish law in general.

No doubt, this description is influenced by the immediate context— e.g. in the emphasis on God's creatorhood. But it is also clear that the statements which in part are rather general in tone presuppose a concrete tradition not only in the reference to the similar christological ideas of Cerinthus and Carpocrates but also in the other reports, even though at first glance they may seem to be rather unintelligible. The statements receive partial explanation through the other passages: In AH 3.21.1 (= 3.23) Irenaeus mentions that the Jewish translators Theodotion and Aquila do not read *parthenos* ("virgin") [100] in Isa. 7.14 but *neanis* ("young woman") and that the "Ebionites," who regard Jesus as a natural son of Joseph, follow them (cf. also 3.21.9 [= 3.29]). Here a "natural christology" is clearly reported as the christological position of the Ebionites (cf. 5.1.3). This confirms the reference back to Cerinthus and Carpocrates (1.26.2 [= 1.22]) for whom the notion of a natural birth of Jesus is also asserted (1.25.1 [= 1.20] and 1.26.1 [= 1.21.1]). Perhaps this christology can shed new light upon the obscure remark about the "peculiar interpretation of the prophets" among the Ebionites (1.26.2 [=1.22]). Is Irenaeus thinking of the interpretation of Isaiah 7.14 along the lines of an Ebionite christology? For support one could refer to Symmachus' translation, which like that of Theodotion and Aquila reads *neanis*— if indeed Symmachus had been a Jewish Christian.[101]

AH 3.11.7 (= 3.11.10) contains a brief notice about the gospel of Matthew which was the sole gospel used by the Ebionites and, as

100. This is the reading of the "Septuagint"; cf. the detailed discussion of this passage in Justin *Dial.* 43 f., 66 ff. (esp. 84).

101. Cf. Origen's *Hexapla;* Hilgenfeld, *Ketzergeschichte,* p. 440. According to Eusebius EH 6.17, Symmachus was a Jewish Christian; this is supported by Harnack, *Geschichte,* 1.1: 209-212; 2.1: 165 f.; *History of Dogma,* 1: 305, n. 1 (= 5th German ed., 1: 327 n. 1); Schoeps, *Theologie, passim.* But according to Epiphanius, Symmachus had been a Samaritan who defected to Judaism (*On Weights and Measures* 16). [For a survey of the subject, see H. B. Swete, *An Introduction to the Old Testament in Greek* (Cambridge: University Press, 1902², supplemented ed. by R. Ottley, 1914, repr. KTAV 1968), pp. 49-53; also S. Jellicoe, *The Septuagint and Modern Study* (Oxford: Clarendon, 1968), pp. 94-99.]

Irenaeus remarks, contradicts their specific christology. Obviously, Irenaeus is thinking of the canonical gospel with its doctrine of the virgin birth in the infancy narrative (Matt. 1.18 ff.) which cannot be brought into harmony with an adoptionist christology. But it must be asked whether such a contradiction ought to be postulated for Jewish Christianity? [280] It can only be claimed if the Ebionites mentioned by Irenaeus actually used the canonical Matthew. But it is more probable that behind the phrase "gospel according to Matthew" is hidden another gospel writing similar to the canonical gospel or perhaps even dependent on it, but not identical with it. This is true of the so-called *Gospel of the Ebionites* which, according to Epiphanius, was a mutilated Matthaean gospel.[102] The infancy narratives are lacking in the latter, so that the assumption of a contradiction is resolved if we suppose that Irenaeus' notice reflects some confusion.

That Irenaeus could have confused the *Gospel of the Ebionites* with the canonical Matthew is conceivable since he does not have independent knowledge of the Ebionites. The fact that his report contains only a few concrete details that are frequently repeated[103] points in the same direction. Basically, his reports can be reduced to the information which is explicitly or implicitly contained in 1.26.2 (= 1.22). This would suggest that Irenaeus had used a fixed source corresponding most nearly to that passage, from which the remaining references are also taken. In favor of this assumption is the fact that the name "Ebionites" is first attested in Irenaeus, where it seems to be taken for granted as the designation for legalistic Jewish Christianity. Irenaeus probably found this name in the suggested source.

---

102. Epiphanius *Her.* 29.9.4, 30.13.2, 30.14.2; cf. P. Vielhauer on "Jewish-Christian Gospels" in Hennecke-Schneemelcher, 1: 117 ff.

103. AH 5.1.3 deserves notice as a further reference to the Ebionite christological confession. Here the comment is offered that instead of a "mixture of the heavenly wine" (*commixtio vini caelestis*) the Ebionites accept "only worldly water" (*solam aquam saecularem* [?]—on the textual problem cf. the editions of Stieren or Harvey, *ad loc.*). Epiphanius later speaks of a Jewish Christian meal with unleavened bread and water (*Her.* 30.16.1). However, one must question whether our passage ought to be interpreted in the light of Epiphanius' information or whether commonly held Christian notions about a meal with water have, in secondary fashion, here been transferred to Jewish Christianity (cf. G. Gentz, "Aquarii," RAC 1 (1950): 574 f.). There is danger of over-interpreting this section since its thrust is to be understood christologically and not sacramentally. AH 4.33.4 (= 4.52.1) also deserves notice with its general pronouncement of judgment against the Ebionites. The anti-Pauline passage in AH 3.15.1 to which Hilgenfeld refers (*Ketzergeschichte*, p. 421, n. 711) is not relevant to this discussion, as is indicated by its immediate and its wider context.

This is not the place to inquire into the more comprehensive question as to the source materials from which Irenaeus' report about the Ebionites is derived. No detailed argumentation is necessary to show that this source cannot be identified with the *Syntagma* of Justin. [281] The name Ebionites as well as the content of Irenaeus' report and its heresiological presuppositions are completely alien to Justin. This difference in outlook marks a development in the patristic evaluation of Jewish Christianity. The complex nature of Jewish Christianity, which was self-evident to Justin, is now no longer seen. Jewish Christianity now is classified as a self-contained unit alongside of other groups. The designation *Ebiōnaioi*, which probably originated in a concrete situation and was not a general label, has become the name of a sect. The term loses its original theological significance and is degraded to a heresiological technical term. A tendency toward schematization, which becomes characteristic of subsequent heresiology, comes into operation.

In *Ref.* 7.34, Hippolytus is largely dependent on Irenaeus' report.[104] His claim that the Ebionites acknowledge God as creator together with the explicit comparison of the Ebionites with the heretics Cerinthus and Carpocrates and the summary statement about "Jewish customs" are reminiscent of Irenaeus, AH 1.26.2 (= 1.22). Even his subsequent observations only appear to go beyond what is found in Irenaeus. Hippolytus' reflections on the elevation of Jesus to the position of Messiah-Christ add nothing really new but merely transfer to the Ebionites what Irenaeus said about Cerinthus or Carpocrates.[105] For the remainder, Hippolytus has introduced into his

104. It is assumed that Hippolytus wrote this work; see also Harnack, *Geschichte,* 2 (*Chronologie*). 2: 211, n. 2. The frequently noted attempts of P. Nautin (*Hippolyte et Josipe* [Paris, 1947] and *Hippolyte, Contre les hérésies. Étude et édition critique* [Paris, 1949]) to attribute Hippolytus' literary activity to an almost unknown Josippus or to an equally little known Hippolytus lead to even greater difficulties than those involved in the objections Batiffol once raised against the commonly accepted literary-historical judgment concerning Hippolytus (*Anciennes littératures chrétiennes: La littérature grecque* [Paris, 1897], pp. 156 f.). Contrary to Nautin cf., among others, M. Richard in *Mélanges de science religieuse,* 5-10 (1948–1953) and *Recherches de science religieuse,* 43 (1953): 379 ff.; H. Elfers, "Neue Untersuchungen über die Kirchenordnung Hippolytus von Rom," *Abhandlungen über Theologie und Kirche,* Festschrift für K. Adam, ed. M. Reding (Düsseldorf, 1952), pp. 181-198. [For further bibliography on the discussion, see Altaner, *Patrology,* p. 185, and Quasten, *Patrology,* 2: 169.]
105. The distinction between "Jesus" and "Christ" as well as the idea of his adoption are found in Irenaeus' treatment of Cerinthus (AH 1.26.1 [= 1.21]; cf. the reference in 1.26.2 [= 1.22]; a relationship to Jewish Christianity is already attested in Justin *Dial.* 48.3-49.1). On the other hand, the anthropological sig-

discussion terminology and concepts from the Pauline doctrine of justification. Of course, this does not represent an independent tradition, but it expresses the intention to theologize and conceptualize [282] which characterizes the whole of Hippolytus' "Philosophumena" (cf. *Ref.* preface.11). The *Epitome* of the work repeats the same material in abbreviated form—the sketch of Ebionite tenets derived from Irenaeus and Hippolytus' own Paulinizing judgment (*Ref.* 10.22). Finally, it is also significant that for Hippolytus the sequence of heresies immediately preceding his section on Ebionites corresponds to Irenaeus' schema. Thus the genesis of this material in terms of its literary history is not problematic.

On the other hand it is remarkable that in the next chapter, *Refutation* 7.35, "Ebion" is mentioned as the supposed hero from whom the Ebionites derived their name. This is the first appearance of that name in the heresiological literature and it cannot be traced back to Irenaeus. Where did this name originate, for which there is obviously no historical basis? [106] Reference could be made to Lipsius' witnesses for the *Syntagma* of Hippolytus,[107] which likewise mention "Ebion": Pseudo-Tertullian *Against Heresies* 48 (11); Epiphanius *Heresy* 30.1 f; and Filaster *Heresy* 37 (9). But since E. Schwartz's brilliant explanations [108] this attestation has become questionable: Filaster probably used Epiphanius; Pseudo-Tertullian is still "an unknown quantity which first must be solved" (p. 38); and the treatment in Epiphanius is demonstrably confused while the sources he employed still have not been identified.[109] In order to answer our

---

nificance of the adoption [i.e. anyone who lives as Jesus did can become "Christ"] derives from the report about Carpocrates (AH 1.25.1 [= 1.20.1]; Hippolytus *Ref.* 7.32.3).

106. Hilgenfeld, *Ketzergeschichte*, pp. 436 ff., shows unusual confidence in the reports of the church fathers when he accepts as genuine a monothelitic tract which, according to the witness of Anastasius (seventh century), was attributed to Ebion.

107. [R. A. Lipsius, *Zur Quellenkritik des Epiphanios* (Vienna, 1865).]

108. Schwartz, "Zwei Predigten Hippolyts," *Sitzungsberichte der Bayrischen Akademie der Wissenschaften*, 3 (München, 1936): 36 ff.

109. On the indiscriminate use of the ps.-Clementines by Epiphanius, cf. Strecker, *Judenchristentum*, pp. 265 f., and "Elkesai," 1175 f. Indeed, on the basis of the reports on the Nazoraeans M. Black asserts that Epiphanius' treatment is trustworthy (*The Scrolls and Christian Origins: Studies in the Jewish Background of the New Testament* [New York: Scribner's, 1961], pp. 67 ff.). But his argument only shows in exemplary fashion that Epiphanius' literary efforts are capable of producing such an impression.

question, therefore, it would be better not to make use of Lipsius' threefold attestation. Nevertheless, it should be discussed whether this designation could derive from the *Syntagma*. Tertullian, who also refers to "Ebion," [110] encourages this possibility. It is therefore impossible to regard Hippolytus' *Refutation* as the place of origin for this name since Tertullian belongs to an earlier period. Since Tertullian also made use of local Roman tradition [283] elsewhere [111] the possibility cannot be excluded that he was here under the direct or indirect influence of the *Syntagma* which was composed much earlier than the writing of the *Refutation* and perhaps immediately after the appearance of Noëtus in Rome.[112] This possibility is supported by the fact that in the immediate context, also without any parallel in Irenaeus, Hippolytus deals with the Byzantian Theodotus who appeared in Rome and was excommunicated by Bishop Victor.[113] Theodotus is mentioned also in chapter 3 of Hippolytus' homily against Noëtus.[114] Both the excommunication of Theodotus and the composition of the writing against Noëtus suit the time of origin of the *Syntagma*. Thus it is reasonable to conclude that *Refutation* 7.35 as a whole is based on the *Syntagma*. Perhaps we may go one step further and assume that it was Hippolytus himself who, on the basis of false etymology, conjectured that the founder of the sect had been a person named "Ebion." The context even seems to indicate how this misunderstanding could have arisen. While Hippolytus deals with "Ebionites" in *Refutation* 7.34, depending on Irenaeus, the name "Ebion" occurs in 7.35, in the chapter that goes back to the *Syntagma*,

110. *On the Flesh of Christ* 14, 18, 24; *On the Veiling of Virgins* 6.1; *Prescription Against Heretics* 33.5 and 10 f.
111. Cf. e.g. Harnack, *Marcion*², p. 17°.
112. According to Photius (*Library*, codex 121) Hippolytus' *Syntagma* covered thirty-two heresies beginning with the Dositheans and ending with the adherents of Noëtus. Its time of composition should be fixed considerably before the *Refutation* since according to the preface to book one of the *Refutation*, the earlier draft was written "some time ago" (*palai*). The grounds for Harnack's dating of the *Syntagma* (*Geschichte* 2 [*Chronologie*]. 2: 223: during the first decade of the third century) are convincing only insofar as the work could not have appeared after 210. Since Photius applied the word *biblidarion* to the *Syntagma*, it follows that it was small in size and (contrary to the widely held assumption) could not have contained Hippolytus' *Homily against the Heresy of Noëtus*, as has been demonstrated conclusively by Schwartz ("Zwei Predigten," 37).
113. *Ref.* 7.9 and 35, 10.23; Eusebius EH 5.28.6; Hilgenfeld, *Ketzergeschichte*, p. 611.
114. [Ed. by Schwartz, "Zwei Predigten"; cf. also Migne PG 10.817. ET by S. Salmond in ANF 5: 223-231.]

and is juxtaposed with the names of "Cerinthus" and "Theodotus." Therefore, it would seem that the name originated in the *Syntagma* by means of a somewhat automatic assimilation to other founders of sects—apart from the other argument based on the fact that Hippolytus provides the earliest attestation of this name.

The foundation for the later heresiological treatment of Ebionitism has been provided by Irenaeus and Hippolytus. Henceforth, the doctrine and the practice of Jewish Christians will be reported in a stereotyped manner. Observance of Jewish customs, rejection of Paul, a "natural christology," and derivation from a certain "Ebion" as founder of the sect—all of this is subsumed under the concept *hairesis tōn Ebiōnaiōn*, "Ebionite heresy." By being identified as "Ebionism," Jewish Christianity [284] becomes an established heresiological entity which is treated in the one place provided in the catalogue of sects. The heresiologists who are supposed to have used Hippolytus' *Syntagma* (above, 280) can confirm this. The individual details that they have to offer are nothing but assimilations to the extant heresiological material, and cannot claim to be derived from firsthand knowledge (cf. Pseudo-Tertullian and Filaster). This also applies to Epiphanius. The comparison with other heresies mentioned by name (*Her.* 30.1) is just as much a secondary literary embellishment as the seemingly significant reference to "the earliest" Ebionite position (*ta prōta*), which introduced a line of development in Ebionite christological outlook stretching from a "natural" (30.2) to an Elchasaitic Christology (30.3 and 17), but is really a literary device whereby the diverse sources and disorganized bits of information are held together. This indicates, to be sure, that in distinction from other heresiologists, Epiphanius had access to sources hitherto unknown in the West, but it also shows that he did not really understand the significance of these bits of information, but rather grouped them according to a general heresiological point of view in which matters of detail are not differentiated.[115]

Origen's evidence also agrees at first with the heresiological reporting. Jewish observances (*Homily* 3.5 on Genesis), rejection of Paul (e.g. *Against Celsus* 5.65 and *Homily* 17.2 on Jeremiah), and

---

115. On the heresiological outlook of Epiphanius, cf. P. Fraenkel, "Histoire sainte et hérésie chez Épiphane de Salamine," *Revue de théologie et de philosophie,* 12 (1962): 175-191. Unfortunately Fraenkel does not follow Bauer's approach.

natural christology (*Homily* 17 on Luke) also are typical characteristics of the Ebionites according to Origen. He can also designate
them as "heretics" (*Against Celsus* 5.65). However, it is remarkable
that Origen does not reflect the heresiological pattern in other respects
—e.g. the common stereotyped comparison with Cerinthus and Carpocrates is not made. It is also characteristic of Origen to interpret
the name of the Ebionites ironically as indicating "the poverty of
their spirit." [116] What is especially important is the new information
he provides. Origen knows of Jewish Christians who teach that Jesus
was born in a natural way [285] but he is also aware of others who
acknowledge the virgin birth (*Against Celsus* 5.61; *Commentary on
Matthew,* 17.12). He is informed about their literal interpretation of
the Bible (*Commentary on Matthew,* 11.12), and also about their
celebration of the passover (*Commentary on Matthew,* series 79). His
reports apparently are based at least in part on his own substantiated
observation. He is aware that the Jewish Christian rejection of Paul
continues "to this day" (*Homily* 19 on Jeremiah). And there is other
evidence to confirm that the christology of Jewish Christians cannot
be limited to the notion of Jesus' natural birth, but also has room for
declarations concerning his preexistence.[117]

The idea that Origen's knowledge of Jewish Christianity was based
on personal observation explains his exceptional attitude of openness.
Origen admits that Jewish Christian theology was more complex than
would be possible according to the heresiological pattern. Even Eusebius, who elsewhere follows Origen's presentation for the most part,
by no means remains within the limits of the heresiological pattern,
but is also aware (perhaps on the basis of personal observation) of
Jewish Christians who live in Kokaba,[118] and he knows "Ebionites"
who celebrate the Lord's day as well as the sabbath.[119] The reporting
of Origen and Eusebius differs from the usual heresiological approach
not only by virtue of its factual knowledge; chronological and geo-
graphic differences are also reflected. Whereas Origen and Eusebius

116. *On First Principles* 4.3.8; *Against Celsus* 2.1, and *passim*. This interpretation
probably originated with Origen himself. It agrees with his knowledge of Hebrew
and is not found prior to him but appears rather frequently afterward. Cf. Strecker,
Judenchristentum, p. 123.
117. Strecker, "Ebioniten," col. 496 f.
118. *Onomasticon* (ed. Klostermann, GCS, 11.1 [1904], 172); [cf. Hilgenfeld,
Ketzergeschichte, pp. 426 n. 715, 428 n. 734 (cf. n. 731)].
119. EH 3.27.5; cf. *Apostolic Constitutions* 7.23.

attest that in the eastern church the complexity of Jewish Christianity is still acknowledged (even if only with regard to particular details) in the third and fourth century, the western church had already forced Jewish Christianity into a fixed heresiological pattern by the end of the second and beginning of the third century. This pattern was the result of a gradual development since the relatively open position of Justin, (and of Hegesippus), was replaced around the end of the second century by the typically heresiological approach. It is clear from the witness of Origen and Eusebius that even after standardization took place in the West, the East remained open with respect to the actual situation. It was not until much later that the final transfer of the heresiological pattern in the East seems to have become possible. Epiphanius can be named as the first witness to this development. [286] Theodoret and the later fathers, who wrote in complete dependence on their predecessors, mark the ultimate victory of the heresiological outlook.[120]

Walter Bauer had established that the early opponents of heresy, from Clement to Dionysius of Corinth, stood in close relation to Rome (see above, 106 ff.). It can now be added that this is also true with respect to the heresiological approach itself. The Roman character of Justin's literary endeavors is well known, in spite of his Samaritan origin and his sojourn in Asia Minor. Even though it may be supposed that his source material comes partly from the East, it was given its ultimate shape in Rome. Bauer showed in detail the connections between Hegesippus and Rome (above, 103, 107). This Roman orientation is especially true of Irenaeus, the first ecclesiastical author of whose systematic heresiological activity we have knowledge. His account of the heresies grew out of the ecclesiastical situation at Lyons— out of his struggle with Valentinian gnosticism. His journey to see Eleutherus of Rome (Eusebius EH 5.4) and his entry into the passover controversy through his letter to Bishop Victor (EH 5.24.10 ff.) are sufficient evidence for recognizing the strong ties by which he and his community felt themselves bound to the Roman ecclesiastical position. And that Hippolytus represents Roman tradition does not need to be argued, in spite of his actual alienation from the official

---

120. In several respects, Jerome occupies a unique position. He has connections with both East and West. As is well known, his information is no more reliable than that of Epiphanius. We cannot deal with it in more detail here.

incumbent of the Roman episcopal chair and his corresponding enumeration among the schismatics. Without any doubt, systematically practiced heresiology begins in Rome. The later penetration into the East of the heresiological attitude toward Jewish Christianity indicates that a Roman principle gained "ecumenical" validity. In this respect, Bauer's claims receive substantial confirmation.

The variations in configuration and success of the heresiological point of view corroborate the results gained from the direct and indirect evidence for Jewish Christianity in Syria—namely, that the situation with regard to Jewish Christianity is complex, both in terms of its own theological frame of thought and also in its relationship to the "great church." This complexity contradicts the heresiological pattern. And to the extent that later Jewish Christianity can be uncovered, even greater variety is encountered there.[121] The simplistic, [287] dogmatically determined classification of Jewish Christianity as a heresy which confronts the "great church" as a homogeneous unit does not do justice to the complex situation existing within legalistic Jewish Christianity. Walter Bauer's opinion that "the Judaists soon became a heresy, rejected with conviction by the gentile Christians," and that the Jewish Christians were "repulsed" by gentile Christianity (above, 236 f.) needs to be corrected. Not only is there "significant diversity" within the gentile Christian situation, but the same holds true for Jewish Christianity. The fact that Jewish Christianity was a polymorphic entity and that a heresiological principle emanating from Rome could succeed against it only gradually provides not only a correcting supplement, but above all an additional substantiation of Bauer's historical perspective.

121. There are few witnesses, the Jewish Christian gospels cannot [287] be dated with sufficient certainty, and the reports of Jerome and Epiphanius are unreliable even when they deal with the contemporary situation rather than with past events. On the activity of Jewish Christian groups on into Islamic times, cf. A. Schlatter, "Die Entwicklung des jüdischen Christentums zum Islam," *Evangelisches Missionsmagazin*, 62 (1918): 251-264; Harnack, *Lehrbuch der Dogmengeschichte*[4], 2 (Tübingen: Mohr, 1909; repr. Darmstadt, 1964): 534 ff. [this appendix on Islam is not included in the ET, *History of Dogma*, 4 (1898)]; Schoeps, *Theologie*, pp. 334-342; Strecker, "Elkesai," col. 1177.

Appendix 2

The Reception of the Book

by Georg Strecker

revised and augmented by Robert A. Kraft *

Reviews and Notices of the Original Edition

During the years immediately following the appearance of Bauer's original edition, more than two dozen reviews or notices appeared in six different languages. For convenience, those known to the editors are listed below: [1]

"A." [= N. von Arseniew (?)], *Irénikon* 12 (1935): 682-83 [French language, Belgian Roman Catholic publication; brief summary, favorable];

"p.b.," *Religio* 11 (1935): 83-84 [Italian Roman Catholic; relatively favorable summary];

"Brs." [= H. Bruders, S. J.]. *Scholastik* 10 (1935): 589 [German language, Dutch Roman Catholic; brief and favorable summary];

* The original essay by Georg Strecker, "Die Aufnahme des Buches" (Bauer[2], 288-306), has been completely revised and expanded by R. A. Kraft in consultation with Professor Strecker for inclusion in this English edition.

1. Brief annotations are provided for some of the reviews not treated at any length in the subsequent discussion as well as basic information about the reviewer when available. Bauer himself supplied a precis of the book in *Forschungen und Fortschritte*, 10 (1934): 99-101; this has now been reprinted in the collection of Bauer's *Aufsätze und Kleine Schriften*, edited by Georg Strecker (Tübingen: Mohr, 1967), pp. 229-233. See also the detailed appreciation by W. Schneemelcher, "Walter Bauer als Kirchenhistoriker," NTS 9 (1962/63): 11-22, and the "Report on the New Edition of Walter Bauer's Rechtglaubigkeit. . . ," by Georg Strecker, *Journal of Bible and Religion* 33 (1965): 53-56.

J. Bergdolt, *Luthertum* 47 (1936): 316-17;

G. A. van den Bergh van Eysinga, *Nieuw Theologisch Tijdschrift* 24 (1935): 374-76 [Dutch Protestant];

M. Dibelius (Heidelberg), *Deutsche Literaturzeitung* 6 (1935): 443-48;

M. Goguel (Protestant Faculty, Paris), *Revue d'histoire et de philosophie religieuse* 15 (1935): 163-67;

K. Heussi (Jena), *Historische Vierteljahresschrift* 30 (1935): 410-11 [complimentary brief summary];

H. Koch (Munich), *Theologische Literaturzeitung* 59 (1934): 343-46;

J. Lebreton (Catholic Faculty, Paris), *Recherches de science religieuse* 25 (1935): 605-10;

J. Leipoldt (Leipzig), *Theologisches Literaturblatt* 57 (1936): 228-30;

"H. L." [= Hans Lietzmann, Berlin], ZNW 33 (1934): 94;

W. von Loewenich (Erlangen), *Theologie der Gegenwart* 29 (1935): 8;

E. Lohmeyer (Breslau), *Historische Zeitschrift* 151 (1935): 97-100;

C. Martin, S. J. (Louvain), *Nouvelle revue théologique* 62 (1935): 750-51;

C. H. Moehlman (Colgate-Rochester Divinity School), *Church History* 4 (1935): 236-37 [favorable summary];

J. Moffatt (Union Seminary, N.Y.), *The Expository Times* 45 (1933/34): 475-76;

M. Schmidt, *Neues Sächsisches Kirchenblatt* (20 Jan., 1935);

H. Schuster, *Deutsche Evangelische Erziehung* 48 (1937): 260;

H.-D. Simonin, O. P. (Rome), *Revue des sciences philosophiques et théologiques* 25 (1936): 342-45;

H. Strathmann (Erlangen), *Theologie der Gegenwart* 28 (1934): 192-93 [generally favorable, some reservations];

W. Völker (Halle), *Zeitschrift für Kirchengeschichte* 54 (1935): 628-631;

H. Windisch (Kiel/Halle), *Christliche Welt* 49 (1935): 138-139;

"Z." [= J. de Zwann, Leyden], *Nieuw Theologische Studien* 20 (1937): 255 [Dutch, generally favorable with some reservations];

(anonymous), *La vie spirituelle* (1936), p. 177 f.;

(anonymous), *Revue des sciences religeuses* 17 (1937): 23-24.

Continental Protestant Reviews. On the whole, continental protestant reviewers showed a positive appreciation for the book, although criticisms of this or that aspect were not infrequent.

Hans *Lietzmann,* in his very brief published notice, praises it highly as:

A splendid book. . . , a frontal attack on the usual approach to church history, vigorously carried out with solid erudition, penetrating criticism, and balanced organization. . . . It is the old thesis of Usener, once so violently rejected by Harnack, that reappears here in a new form and with new foundations. Hopefully it will be appreciated better this time for its positive significance. Bauer's book belongs to those works the value of which rests not in the sum of particular matters treated, but which by their provocative total impression force the investigation to healthy self-examination.[2]

Ernst *Lohmeyer*, near the end of a lengthy summary of the book, concedes that "it is inevitable that this book, 'more than it likes,' must make use of hypotheses that cannot be fully substantiated. But what is to be said has been said with so much caution and such careful support that the whole picture seems assured even though particular interpretations of sources and events must remain uncertain." [3]

In his extremely appreciative review, Maurice *Goguel's* only specific complaint is that "the title . . . perhaps is a bit unfortunate" since it is "too vague and would profit from having a sub-title to define the subject more closely." Otherwise, he emphasizes the value of the book as "an entirely new approach" that "throws light on a number of hitherto obscure points" and as a "point of departure" from which further studies may arise to sharpen, verify, or perhaps correct various aspects. By way of example, Goguel offers some observations of his own on Revelation 2-3 (above, 78 ff.). In short, Goguel feels that the book "has an importance out of proportion to the number of pages it contains" in that "it offers more new conclusions and fruitful suggestions than many large books three or four times

2. Bauer's files contain a private communication from Lietzmann, dated 17 April 1934, as follows:

Seldom has a book reached me at such an opportune time as your investigation has for the second volume of my *History of the Church.* How much I incline to your view, on the whole, you will realize from my [academic] genealogy. It was, after all, the thesis of my old teacher Hermann Usener that 'between the rock of the teaching of Christ and the clearly heathen lands lies a wide plain of common property' (*Das Weinachsfest Kap. I-III*[2], ed. H. Lietzmann [Bonn: Bouvier, 1911], p. XI), and I have always thought this thesis to be correct. It is now very gratifying to me to see it carried through by you with such energy, and to have the church history of all regions examined from this perspective. That is truly a fruitful adjustment which I will carefully investigate and will make fruitful in my own presentation.

The extent to which Lietzmann actually put Bauer's work to use seems limited —see his *History,* 2: 58 n. 6; 259, nn. 1 and 5; 260 nn. 2-3; and 275 n. 1. As Strecker has pointed out privately in this connection, the identification of the thesis of Usener with Bauer's approach rests on a misunderstanding.
3. Lohmeyer's personal note to Bauer, dated 29 June 1934, reads: "I have worked through your book . . . with much pleasure and agreement."

its size." Because of the positive results it provides, the method it inaugurates, and the perspective it offers for subsequent research, "this book is one of those, few in number, that marks a stage. No one who henceforth concerns himself with the history of primitive Christianity can neglect to read and study it."

Hugo *Koch* is somewhat more critical, although also complimentary, on the whole. He regrets that Bauer did not examine more systematically the early Jewish-Christianity of Palestine (and Egypt), and that he is "completely silent" about earliest Christianity in Africa; on these matters, Koch appends some suggestions of his own (e.g. above, 241 n. 1), as well as on early Roman christology and on the problem of marriage in early Christianity. Also he feels that a distinction might usefully be made between the earlier, more "gnostic," and the later, more ecclesiastical, positions of Origen. Nevertheless, although:

> one may think what he likes about [the book's] conclusions in particular matters, as a whole it is an extremely valuable scholarly investigation that for once reads the sources through other eyes than is usually the case, and hears many things from them that have not been heard for a long time. Bauer himself is well aware that the area in which he moves is often uncharted and requires careful procedure, and it cannot be said that he has neglected the necessary caution and has substituted mere conjectures for facts.

Similarly, Johannes *Leipoldt* praises Bauer for an exciting book that opens "new paths" and deals critically with some legends of modern scholarship as well as those of antiquity. "Taken as a whole, the book of Bauer will determine the course of the investigation for a long time." Nevertheless, Leipoldt finds that the book moves along almost too rapidly—there is little coherence—and hopes that Bauer will "someday paint a complete picture of how the history of the church in the second century now looks." While agreeing "essentially" with Bauer's thesis, Leipoldt has reservations at some points and mentions specifically his conviction that "the boundaries between orthodoxy and heresy "often were even more fluid" than Bauer allows, and that Bauer's interpretation of the situation behind 3 John is unlikely (above, 92 f.)—it has to do with a conflict in "church polity" between an old missions-type of Christian and a young representative of the "local episcopate" (see also below, p. 308).

In what must have been one of the last pieces he wrote before his death in 1935, Hans *Windisch* comments that "much is immediately convincing, but many things still require substantiation" in this "learned and ingenious" book. "Perhaps what is worked out in the main points is correct, but it is not exhaustive for the entire situation of the church in the second century." Nevertheless, it is welcome for its many new observations, and will help to advance scholarship along many lines.

In the same vein, H. *Strathmann* complains that Bauer's "ingenious criticism" often must employ the argument from silence and that Bauer seems excessively distrustful of ecclesiastical sources in constructing his picture. But on the whole, "the book is an extremely suggestive and forward-moving plea to rethink the history of earliest Christianity with new considerations."

From the protestant Netherlands we find J. *de Zwaan* mentioning exegetical and methodological problems accentuated by Bauer's use of the argument from silence and multiplication of hypotheses, in an otherwise favorable, brief notice. G. A. *van den Bergh van Eysinga* writes at much greater length, praising Bauer for countering the traditional Roman Catholic view that has also enjoyed wide influence among protestants, but objecting to such details as Bauer's dating for the Pauline and Ignatian letters and for *1 Clement*.

Martin *Dibelius* provides a balanced and incisive review in which he praises the book as "a bold advance," concerned with "a constructive search," and maintains that from it "a historical view of earliest Christianity can only gain, on the whole, in a constructive way, and I am the last who would or should call the author to task because of the boldness of the treatment. . . . It is a pleasure to find that there still can be an investigation that reflects the two talents that have made German scholarship the pillar of German respectability: meticulousness in investigation of the most minute aspects, and boldness of construction in larger matters." Nevertheless, Dibelius feels it his duty to ask basic questions especially about "the methodology by which the author supports his overall picture," and collects his observations under two main headings: (1) Bauer makes extensive use of the argument from silence—e.g. concerning pre-Ignatian Christianity at Antioch, Asia Minor apart from Ignatius' addressees, the orthodoxy of the Christians mentioned by Pliny, Papias' failure to mention Luke's gospel, and Polycarp's silence about a bishop at Philippi; (2) "Bauer tends to give to writings and events the purpose of which has not been clearly preserved for us an interpretation that relates to his problem"— e.g. *1 Clement*, Ignatius' concern about the monepiscopate, references to the "great number" of heretics. Nevertheless, such questions by no means negate "the importance of the whole endeavor and the seriousness of the plea for a revision of opinion" in dealing with early church history.

By far the most negative review to appear was the caustic piece by Walter *Völker* (see also below, n. 5). Although Bauer claims to be fully aware of the fragmentary nature of the sources and the hypothetical nature of much of his study, this does not prevent him from making a claim such as is found in the second sentence of chapter 6 (p. 111), complains Völker. At a number of particular points, Völker attacks Bauer's interpretations: "no less than everything is unsure" about the early situation at Edessa, "the chapter on Egypt . . . is riddled with the argument from silence," at various points the interpretation of Ignatius' letters is unacceptable as is Bauer's use of *1 Clement*.

> All in all, Bauer's book is an attempt to view the history of the earliest church in an entirely new light, and to interpret all the particulars as consistent with this new approach. Thus the heretics are valued most highly, especially Marcion. . . . In contrast, the 'church' faded strongly into the background, and only Rome championed orthodoxy. . . . The author arrives at this astonishing conclusion by frequent use of the argument from silence, by bold combinations, by unsupportable conjectures which themselves are reused as a precarious foundation for further conjectures, by inferences drawn from later periods, and finally, by the arrangement of all the particulars into the schema orthodoxy/ heresy, whereby the variegated historical events are robbed of the complexity of their causes and motivations. I cannot believe that such a reconstruction of history has prospects of becoming accepted in the protestant approach to church history (to say nothing of the Catholic); it is only the most extreme swing of the pendulum of a view that ultimately goes back to G. Arnold's estimation of the heretics, and thus it must occasion just as extreme a reaction.[4]

4. In the following year (24 May 1936), Völker wrote Bauer this note: "After a searching examination I cannot agree with the thesis ventured in part 1, but you yourself scarcely will have expected that the firm battle lines of the tradition would shatter at the first assault of the opposition."
Bauer also received personal communications from several other distinguished German scholars:
Adolf *Jülicher* (Marburg, emeritus), dated 1 Feb. 1934: "I have begun to read

English Language Reviews. Apart from a fairly lengthy favorable summary by C. H. *Moehlman,* the only real review in English came from the pen of James *Moffatt,* who found the book to be an "able, challenging monograph." Nevertheless, Moffatt thinks that Bauer's "proofs" for certain interpretations "are sometimes forced"—"he tends to take the position of the barrister rather than of the judge." The fact that at times the earliest extant written materials from an area happen to voice the faith of "queer, uncatholic movements . . . instead of the catholic . . . does not imply that the latter was non-existent." Perhaps the gnostics such as Valentinus were

> more Christian than their later critics allowed, or than even Dr. Bauer believes. . . . A historian must be sensitive to what we may call the sense of the Centre in early Christianity. I should prefer that term to "orthodoxy." And although it took the Church long to express that sense of the Centre, yet it was not absent from the early controversies. We need not read back a definite expression or consciousness of it. One merit of Dr. Bauer's treatise is that it enters a valid warning against such an unhistorical prejudice.

Moffatt also questions Bauer's estimate of the role of Rome.

> There is still a case for the other side here. Was not the Apostolic Canon of Scripture first formed, in its informal stages, in Asia Minor? Was not Asia Minor ahead of Rome in the formation of the Apostolic, Episcopal ministry? And does the Symbol not seem as likely to have emerged in Asia Minor as at Rome? Dr. Bauer's views to the contrary are sharply stated, but I do not detect any cogent, decisive arguments in support of his thesis at this point, beyond what other scholars have brought forward. The real thinking upon vital Christianity for centuries was done outside the Roman Church.

---

the first part of your new book, on the earliest church and/or Christianity in Edessa, and have already obtained from it so many unexpected and persuasive insights that it is with deep regret that I must lay the book aside for a few weeks, after which I intended to read it to the end with heightened interest. Where you yourself hesitate, neither can I arrive at any definite decision, but the main point, the priority of heretics in Edessa, seems to be demonstrated."

Rudolf *Otto* (Marburg), dated 20 Feb. 1934: "I have now partaken with thanks and admiration of your *Ketzer.* Jülicher spoke very appreciatively of it." (The same card contains handwritten notes with complimentary remarks by Frederick C. *Grant* [Seabury-Western Seminary, Illinois], W. *Macholz,* and K. *Müller.*)

Rudolf *Bultmann* (Marburg), dated 7 Feb. 1935: "The basic thesis and presentation are, it seems to me, a real advancement of research. I have learned much from it" (see also below, p. 306).

In short, Bauer has provided a "serviceable . . . reminder that catholicism or orthodoxy took much longer to shape itself than is commonly supposed, and that centrifugal tendencies in the first three centuries were probably stronger than the later Church liked to admit. [What] . . . sounds less convincing here and there . . . [is] the estimate of the data from which [this position] is deduced."

Roman Catholic Reviews. There is much variety of attitude among the Roman Catholic reviews that appeared. By far the most receptive are those from the Netherlands and Belgium. Heinrich *Bruders'* brief notice concludes that "the entire work is a constructive attempt to understand the development of Christianity without the papacy as an enclosure surrounding a unified doctrine." Indeed, N. von *Arseniew*(?) writes that "the interest of the book does not necessarily rest only with those ideas which it is well to place before the eyes of protestant readers but which represent nothing particularly new for the catholic scholar, but also in the way in which the author treats the birth of the concept 'orthodoxy' and the idea of 'heresy.' His thesis is clearly explicated . . . and gives useful material for meditating upon the seriousness of our faith."

The treatment by H. D. *Simonin*, O.P., of Rome, on the other hand, is relatively hostile. He characterizes the volume as "a hard book, difficult to read, with a vehemence and a dialectic power that is rarely met to such a degree in a work dealing with history"—a "typically Germanic" book. Simonin considers it ironical that Bauer appears as an "apologist" whose phenomenology of religion cannot seem to visualize orthodoxy "without having at every moment a church charged to guard and to teach doctrine." This has "a real apologetic value for the Roman Church" in contrast to the Anglican conception of "orthodoxy." Where Bauer errs most seriously is in the frequent use of the argument from silence and in failing to deal with the theological aspects of church history, particularly with the development of the *regula fidei*—the credal rule of faith emphasizing belief in the creator God (see below, n. 8).

The French Jesuit, C. *Martin*, has mixed reactions. He agrees that the relationship between orthodoxy and heresy is more complex than usually has been recognized, but "neither the method nor, often, the argumentation of Bauer is satisfactory." Martin's fundamental objection is that Bauer neglects most of the evidence from the New

Testament, where he thinks the issues are already rather clearly de-fined. Bauer also overplays language referring to "the whole world" being full of heretics. Even if Egypt and Syria did abound with heretics, "such a fact is not so astonishing, and theologically speaking, is only of secondary significance. Already from the outset, as the New Testament writings show, the church was more concerned with orthodoxy than with numbers. The distinction between the sects and the 'apostolic party' stands out clearly there. . . . We regret that Bauer has not given enough attention to the analysis of these writings" which are fundamental for the problem (see below, n. 6).

Finally, the distinguished French church historian Jules *Lebreton,* S. J., incorporates numerous critical comments into his fairly lengthy summary of the book. He thinks that Bauer's evidence in support of this "new schema" has been offered "not without violence," and notes the use of the argument from silence. "One reads [the book] with lively interest, but without being able to subscribe to the thesis he defends"—e.g. Bousset's hypothesis that Pantaenus was gnostic "is generally abandoned today" in favor of Munck's judgment that Pan-taenus was what Clement was after him. And however one evaluates the truth of such claims as Clement and Tertullian make for orthodoxy (*Strom* 7.[17.]106; *Prescription against Heretics* 29), they "prove to us that the catholics were conscious of being in possession of the church from apostolic times." In contrast, claims of apostolic suc-cession by the heretics are rare (see below, n. 7). Clearly, at the end of the second century orthodoxy saw itself as traditional, and viewed gnosticism as something new. When heresy occasionally did gain the upper hand (as in the rise of Montanism), it was "a passing fever and local" in extent. If Bauer had interpreted the evidence from Rome as he does the letters of Ignatius for the Antioch situation, he could argue that heresy controlled Rome also. Although he assigns to Rome a role that is "very glorious . . . very charitable for the catholic church, . . . it is not necessary, in order to make this point, to suppose that ancient and quasi-universal defections had abandoned the churches to heresy until Rome took charge. . . . What (Rome) taught corresponded in the other churches to a traditional faith, inherited from the apostles" (with references to Irenaeus AH 1.10.2 [= 1.3]).

Synthetic Summary. On the whole, the reviewers tend to agree that Bauer's general thesis is a desirable, if provocative, counter-balance to the oversimplified traditional view,[5] and some of them do not hesitate to express basic agreement with Bauer's overall view (e.g. Lietzmann, Lohmeyer, Leipoldt; cf. Koch, Windisch). The positive, constructive character of the investigation is emphasized by some (Lietzmann, Dibelius, Goguel, Bruders) as well as its negative thrust (esp. Eysinga). Its value not only as a new step, but as a stimulus to further research especially impresses Goguel (cf. also Windisch, Leipoldt, Heussi). Some of the reviewers even comment that they found it an exciting book to read—"like a novel," says Leipoldt, complimentarily—although Simonin complains that it is hard to read and "typically Germanic."

One expects to find negative comments in critical reviews, and is far from disappointed in this case. At the general level, Bauer's method and argumentation is assailed to various degrees again and again: hypotheses and conjecture play a large role (Lohmeyer, de Zwann, Völker), the argument from silence is frequent (Dibelius, de Zwann, Völker, Strathmann, Simonin, Lebreton), interpretations often are forced to fit Bauer's thesis (Dibelius, Moffatt), Bauer writes as an apologete rather than an impartial judge (Moffatt, Völker, Simonin) and shows excessive distrust for ecclesiastical authors (Strathmann), some materials are used anachronistically and the whole picture is grossly oversimplified (Völker, see n. 5 above). For Windisch, the treatment of the second century is hardly exhaustive, and Leipoldt would like to see a more synthetic overview of the situation as Bauer now pictures it.

The problem of exactly how Bauer's investigation relates, or should relate, to theological questions appears in some reviews. Goguel thinks a subtitle would help clarify the fact that Bauer is not dealing primarily with the history of doctrinal conflicts. In different ways and for different reasons some of the reviewers are concerned that Bauer tends to neglect the question of *theological* standards in the

5. With respect to Völker's extremely negative review, Strecker complains that it shows no appreciation for the fact that the traditional attitude toward the development of church history and the history of dogma can no longer be accepted as self-evident in the light of Bauer's investigation. Instead, Völker is critical of what the book intends to do and of how the material is presented, and his review places a one-sided stress on the hypothetical character of many of Bauer's particular conclusions, generalizes from the difficulties relating to individual details, and emphasizes out of all proportion the use of the argument from silence (p. 291 n. 1).

early church, whether it be the Christianity of Paul and John (Loewenich), "the sense of the Centre" (Moffatt), the presence of the "apostolic party" already in the New Testament (Martin),[6] the consciousness of possessing the catholic faith (Lebreton),[7] or the development of the *regula fidei* (Simonin).[8]

Finally, numerous more or less detailed questions are raised about various aspects of Bauer's treatment: Can anything be said with confidence about early Edessene Christianity (Völker, cf. Martin)? Is not Tatian's role more important than Bauer allows (Windisch)? In Egyptian Christianity, was Pantaenus really "gnostic" (Lebreton)? Certainly Clement has his orthodox side (Windisch, Lebreton), and the later Origen must be distinguished from his earlier, more gnostic outlook (Koch). Especially open to question are Bauer's interpretations of the evidence from Ignatius (Dibelius, Völker, Simonin, Lebreton) and from *1 Clement* (Dibelius, Völker, Lebreton; cf. Eysinga), and his overly literal reading of passages referring to the large numbers of heretics (Dibelius, Martin). And did Rome really play such a uniquely formative role (Moffatt, Lebreton)? A few other particular queries are raised by individual reviewers (cf. Dibelius, Leipoldt, Eysinga), along with Koch's observation that Bauer has completely neglected the origins of Christianity in North Africa, and has not paid

6. On Martin's claim that already in the New Testament the church was more concerned with orthodoxy than with numbers, Strecker comments: "This can hardly be supported under close scrutiny since it overlooks the differences between the New Testament writings themselves, and since the New Testament solves the problem of 'orthodoxy and heresy' (when it hints at such a problem at all) in a different way and presupposes neither the concept nor the consciousness of later 'orthodoxy'" (p. 292).

7. Strecker comments as follows on Lebreton's argument that from apostolic times, the "catholics" were conscious of being in possession of the "church": "No one has denied this. But it is questionable whether this consciousness corresponds to the facts in every instance. Lebreton's reference to the lack of a concept of an apostolic succession in heretical circles can neither be accepted in general nor does it refute Bauer's thesis *in toto*" (291). See also above, pp. 119 f., on "heretical" appeals to apostles.

8. On this matter, Strecker offers the following comments: According to Simonin, orthodoxy considers belief in the creator God to be the boundary line separating from heresy, which maintains a dualistic cosmology (see Irenaeus AH book 3). The recognition of the *regula fidei*, with which Bauer does not deal, is of fundamental significance for this question. In this way it is possible for Simonin to simplify the difficulty; but the fact remains that not all "heretics" can be considered as gnostics, or as advocating a dualistic cosmology. The example of Jewish Christianity already shows that the problem of differentiating between orthodoxy and heresy is much more complicated (p. 292).

sufficient attention to earliest Jewish-Christianity in Palestine and Egypt (see above, 241 n. 1).

Turner's Reply to Bauer

For two decades, Bauer's work had little recognizable impact in the English-speaking world. Then, in the Bampton Lectures of 1954, it was examined—and attacked—in great detail by the Anglican Professor of Divinity at Durham, Canon H. E. W. Turner.[9]

Turner's intentions are outlined clearly in the opening lecture, where he contrasts the so-called classical theory (cf. above, xxiii f.) with three modern alternative views (of Harnack, Werner, and Bultmann) that emphasize diversity in early Christian thought and "the marked difference between the developed Christianity of the fourth century and the primitive life and thought of the Church" (25 f.). Turner sets out to "bridge the gap" between these extremes by suggesting that there was "an interaction of fixed and flexible elements" in early Christianity (26-35).

On the one hand, argues Turner, three kinds of "fixed elements" appear: (1) "religious facts" such as a "realistic experience of the Eucharist," belief in God as father-creator, in Christ as historical redeemer, and in the divinity of Christ; (2) recognition of the centrality of "Biblical Revelation" (28 f.); and (3) "the Creed and the Rule of Faith" (29-31). In his discussion of the "religious facts," Turner

9. *The Pattern of Christian Truth: A Study in the Relations Between Orthodoxy and Heresy in the Early Church* (London: Mowbray, 1954). H. Koester calls this book the "only systematic treatment of the question of heresy in the early Church since W. Bauer; . . . a very learned and instructive study" (281 n. 4 of the article discussed below, n. 24), and A. A. T. Ehrhardt finds Turner's study to be "the only detailed appreciation of [Bauer's] book in English which I have found" (93 n. 1/171 n. 1 of the article discussed below, n. 13). In this connection, mention should also be made of a paper read by S. E. Johnson at the annual meeting of the Society of Biblical Literature and Exegesis on 29 December 1942, entitled "Nascent Catholicism and Rome." The abstract of this paper appeared in JBL 62 (1943), ii-iii, and reads as follows: "Bauer's *Rechtgläubigkeit und Ketzerei* is a ground-breaking study which may prove a starting point for many investigations; the fact that it asks theological, not merely literary-historical questions, accounts partly for its success. On the basis of Bauer's results it is possible to push back into the end of the first century and better understand the situation of Hebrews, James and other late New Testament books." Also, the introduction to Robert M. Grant's 1946 collection of fragments from second century Christianity (London: SPCK; see below, n. 11) reflects a positive appreciation of Bauer's thesis: "well into the second century . . . there was within Christianity no sharp dividing line between what was orthodox and what was heretical" (p. 13, with a footnote reference to Bauer's book).

gives the title *lex orandi* to that "relatively full and fixed experimental grasp of what was involved religiously in being a Christian" which he finds to have existed in the early church. "The Church's grasp on the religious facts was prior to any attempt made to work them into a coherent whole. . . . Christians lived Trinitarily long before the evolution of Nicene orthodoxy" (27 f.). This *lex orandi* "formed the instinctive basis for that exercise of Christian common sense which enabled the Church to reject interpretations of her Faith and dilutions of her life even before she possessed formal standards of belief" (28).

On the other hand, he admits, some "flexible elements" also were present in early Christian thought (31-35). There were "differences in Christian idiom," including various literary forms and "differing thought-worlds (e.g. Semitic-eschatological gave way to Greek-metaphysical). "The selection of a distinctive theological idiom, whether it be eschatology, ontology, or even . . . existentialism, illustrates one possible element of flexibility in Christian thinking. The primacy of Christ . . . will inevitably assume a different appearance in each case" (31). Many problems arose as the church sought for adequate philosophical terminology to express her theology. Finally, "the individual characteristics of theologians themselves" constituted another element of flexibility (34 f.).

Turner's second lecture, "The Relation between Orthodoxy and Heresy—An Historical Inquiry" (39-80), is devoted expressly to Bauer's monograph and to the issues it raises from the perspective of church history rather than the history of doctrine. Turner scrutinized Bauer's treatment piece by piece, often presenting objections and observations already known to us from the reviews. "We know nothing and can conjecture little more" (41) about the early history of Christianity at Edessa (40-46). Burkitt's source analysis is preferred to Bauer's for the Abgar legend; Marcion's supposed role in founding the church there is questioned as is Bauer's interpretation of the "Palûtian" passage (above, 21 f.); the claim that Ḳûne (Quna) was the first real Edessene bishop (above, 33 ff.) rests on an argument from silence. Bauer is excessively sceptical on many details, and "the evidence is too scanty . . . to support any theory so trenchant and clear-cut as Bauer proposes." Nevertheless, Turner admits that "heretical or at least sub-orthodox influences counted far more at Edessa" than in the Mediterranean area churches (45).

With regard to Alexandria (46-59), the evidence as a whole "favours the full rigour of Bauer's hypothesis even less than that of Edessa," although in both places "the full pattern of orthodoxy" develops rather late and there is "a certain shading off into heresy on the outer fringes of Church-life" (59). The gospels of the Egyptians and of the Hebrews (above, 51 ff.) may simply "represent the views . . . of splinter movements" (51); the "orthodox" Fourth Gospel circulated in Egypt earlier than Bauer allows (e.g. above, 206 ff.), as new papyri discoveries show,[10] and soon came to be used by Egyptian gnostics—who thus must have been in close proximity to orthodoxy. Bauer's inference concerning the minority position of orthodoxy prior to Demetrius (above, 53) is a possible interpretation, but hardly the only alternative. "Personal pique" may have been an important factor in Origen's trouble with Demetrius.

"The early history of the Church in Asia Minor is even less promising for Bauer's views" (59). Both Ignatius and Polycarp are "determinidly orthodox," with a "genuine grasp of doctrinal essentials and a firm practical attitude towards heresy" (59 f.). In the letters of Ignatius, "the existence of heretics on the fringe or within the Church is clearly recognized," and the implication is that "orthodoxy has already reached self-consciousness" and has a "doctrinal policy." "Nothing here supports the more daring features of Bauer's reconstruction" (63).

On the situation at Philippi (above, 73 f.), Bauer's interpretation is "much exaggerated" and does not exhaust the possibilities (64 f.). His appeal to Polycarp *Phil* 2.1 and 7.2 (above, 73 f.) is overly literal (66). He relies on a "twofold misuse of the argument from silence" in dealing with Thessalonica (67; see above, 74 f.). His "reconstruction of the events which led up to the letter of St. Clement [above, 95 ff.] is at best non-proven"—the traditional interpretation of *1 Clement* seems more likely (69-71).

With regard to Rome, "it is regrettable that Bauer did not attempt any minute analysis of the early traditions . . . comparable to his treatment of the history of the other great sees" (72). Since there were many reasons why a Christian might wish to visit Rome in the

10. Turner refers particularly to P. Rylands 457 (a fragment of John 18 from a codex, = p^{52}) and to P. Egerton 2 (fragments from a non-canonical "gospel"-like codex with some materials resembling John), both of which have been dated on paleographical grounds to sometime around the middle of the second century or slightly earlier.

second century, there is "nothing surprising" about "the convergence of orthodox church leaders upon Rome" (the names of many non-orthodox figures also are connected with that city), and it "certainly fails to establish the special significance which Bauer appears to assign it" (73). Polycarp and Polycrates seem to represent a native orthodox growth in Asia Minor, "collateral" with Rome "rather than derivative." Finally, the presence of the name of Peter (or Mark, in Alexandria) in the bishop lists of various communities (above, 111 ff. = chap. 6) probably simply reflects "the desire of the great sees to claim apostolic foundation" rather than signifying a token of gratitude to Rome (74-79).

In sum, Turner suggests that Bauer's

> fatal weakness [is] . . . a persistent tendency to over-simplify problems, combined with the ruthless treatment of such evidence as fails to support his case. It is very doubtful whether all sources of trouble in the early Church can be reduced to a set of variations on a single theme. Nor is it likely that orthodoxy itself evolved in a uniform pattern, though at different speeds in the main centres of the Universal Church. The formula 'splinter movement, external inspiration or assistance, domination of the whole Church by its orthodox elements, tributes of gratitude to those who assisted its development' represents an historical generalization too neat to fit the facts. History seldom unfolds itself in so orderly a fashion (79).

Clearly, Bauer has made "many valuable suggestions: . . . it is probable that orthodoxy may have been more hard-pressed in certain churches . . . than it has been customary to admit. Orthodoxy and heresy certainly lay side by side . . . The establishment of the monepiscopate and the achievement of fixed standards of orthodoxy evolved with varying degrees of rapidity in different parts of the Christian Church" (79 f.). Nevertheless, Bauer's presentation is open to question time and again. Turner finds the "root difficulty" to be that due to "the primarily historical character of his inquiry," Bauer

> fails to attain an adequate view of the nature of orthodoxy. . . . He is . . . concerned not so much with the nature either of heresy or orthodoxy as such as with the historical relations between those who considered themselves to be orthodox and those whom they condemned as heretical. But the virtual absence of a satisfactory treatment of the previous question inevitably vitiates his treatment to some extent.

For the nature of orthodoxy is richer and more varied than Bauer himself allows. Its underlying basis lies in the religious facts of Christianity itself. . . . It may appear in different forms at different periods without loss of continuity of life and unity of theme. For orthodoxy resembles not much a stream as a sea, not a single melodic theme but a rich and varied harmony, not a single closed system but a rich manifold of thought and life (80).[11]

In the remaining lectures, Turner devotes his attention to the theological issues that he considers basic. In "The Relationships between Orthodoxy and Heresy—A Theological Analysis" (lecture 3) he sets out to "test the claim of heresy to the name Christian" by examining some typical examples (101 ff.)—e.g. "Gnosticism as the dilution of Christianity by alien elements, . . . Marcionism as the truncation of the Christian faith to a mere fragment, . . . heresies which conserve the past without reference to the demands of the present" as "archaism," and Arianism as "the virtual evacuation of the religious content of Christianity in the interests of a barren, if coherent, metaphysic." The errors of the heresies vary and the response of the church varies. "Yet at every stage the response is made in the light of the religious realities received by the Church and revealed by the One God . . ." (148).

"The Doctrinal Basis of Heresy" (lecture 4) is the same as that of orthodoxy—"Scripture, Tradition, and Reason"—but the application of these sources differs. For the heretics, canonical scripture is used selectively or interpreted by forced exegesis, church tradition is falsified or discarded in favor of non-orthodox materials, and in the use of reason, there is a tendency to convert "logic into logistics" (230). In short, the heretics have no feeling for the organic wholeness of

11. Turner's objection to Bauer's position, and his thesis that a "penumbra" existed between orthodoxy and heresy, which he works out in detail in this book (79, 81-94, and *passim*), were already expressed in his review of R. M. Grant's *Second-Century Christianity* in *Theology*, 50 (1947): 37: "While in his Introduction Prof. Grant rightly emphasizes the infinite variety of second-century Christianity, his conclusion (following W. Bauer) that there is no sharp dividing line between orthodox and heretics needs considerable qualification. There was a large Christian penumbra of the Gnostic type, but it remains a highly debatable point to what extent this can be regarded now, or even was regarded then, as within the ambit of second century Christianity. Further, many of the passages which he quotes indicate the growth of a Christian paradosis and the reaching back into the traditions of the past. The solution of the difficulty, which might have been more clearly emphasized, is that orthodoxy was an organic thing, rejecting heresy rather as the healthy body rejects a virus, than a closed system with a hard-and-fast dividing line separating it from its competitors."

the church's faith. Lectures 5-7 deal with the use of scripture, tradition, and reason by "orthodoxy"—e.g. the formation of the New Testament canon, the development of the theory of apostolic succession (or better, the "fact of the transmission of the apostolic authority," 348) and of the creed, and the gradual cultivation of philosophically oriented theology, although this still remained secondary to the *lex orandi* (462 f.).

Turner's "Conclusions" (lecture 8) emphasize again his belief in "the essential autonomy of orthodoxy" (479; cf. 338 etc.) which "rests ultimately upon the authoritativeness of the Christian facts" as they are "mediated through the *lex orandi* of the Church" (473 f.). The independence of orthodoxy also is maintained in contrast to heresy: "The utmost that can safely be admitted is that certain stages of development may have been accelerated by the battle against heresy" (479). "The most important element in the evolution of Christian orthodoxy" is not external influences, but "a kind of Christian common sense . . . which is merely another name for the guidance of the Holy Spirit" (498).

General Influence of the Book

As the reviews indicate, Bauer's monograph was read widely on the continent, and especially in Germany. Lietzmann claims (above, n. 2) to be ready to take it into account in preparing the second and subsequent volumes of his *History,* but it does not seem to have appeared soon enough to leave any significant mark on the French Roman Catholic *History* produced around the same time by Jules Lebreton (who reviewed it; see above) and Jacques Zeiller.[12] It would be futile to attempt to catalogue here all the references to Bauer's book in continental literature. One finds it as a fairly standard item in the bibliographies and footnotes of works dealing with related issues, as for example:

Marcel Simon, *Verus Israel,* bibliography;

Hans-Joachim Schoeps, *Theologie und Geschichte des Judenchristentums,* bibliography and *passim* (cf. index);

12. J. Lebreton and J. Zeiller, *The History of the Primitive Church* (4 vols.; ET by E. C. Messenger from the 1934–35 French; New York: Macmillan, 1942–47; reprinted under the title A *History of the Early Church,* New York: Collier paperback, 1962).

Jean Daniélou, *The Theology of Jewish Christianity*, bibliography and 55, n. 1;

Hennecke-Schneemelcher, *New Testament Apocrypha*, 1: 23, 33.

Ehrhardt's Positive Appraisal. Special notice may be given here to the recent appreciation for Bauer's thesis offered by the late A. A. T. Ehrhardt, who fled Germany in 1935, leaving his position as lecturer in Roman and Civil Law at Freiburg University (Frankfurt) and subsequently became an Anglican clergyman and lecturer in church history (Manchester). Ehrhardt's lengthy article on "Christianity before the Apostles' Creed"[13] attempts to show that in the early period, "the unity of Christianity was not preserved by outward means. Baptism was not originally considered as an admission rite; . . . the Creed . . . was not considered as a constituent part of Baptism. . . , but only as declaratory, and almost accidental. . . . There is no evidence for it to have been used as a touch-stone of orthodoxy anywhere before the end of the second century" (119/198 f.).

Parts 1 and 2 are concerned respectively with "The Meaning of 'Creed' and the 'Gospels' of St. Paul and his Opponents," and "The Various Forms of the Gospel of Christ in the Later New Testament Writings." Ehrhardt finds that credal formulae existed in the early period, but they are not identical with the later apostles' creed. Nevertheless, by the time 3 John appeared, there seems to be a search for "such an authoritative statement of the right Christian doctrine" (92/170).

In parts 3 and 4, entitled respectively "Orthodoxy and Heresy in the Early Church" and "The Formation of the Creed and the Church of Rome," Ehrhardt makes frequent reference to Bauer's investigation. On the whole, he is highly appreciative:

> For the possibility of making such a survey [of the boundaries between orthodoxy and heresy around the year 100] with comparative ease, and indeed for the first attempt at analyzing Christianity before the Apostles' Creed without any doctrinal or denominational bias, we are indebted to that great New Testament scholar, the late Dr. Walter Bauer. . . . In 1934 he published a comparatively small book on orthodoxy and heresy in earliest Christianity, the result of many years of

13. HarvTR 55 (1962): 73-119; reprinted with minor corrections in *The Framework of the New Testament Stories* (Manchester: University Press; Cambridge: Harvard University Press, 1964), pp. 151-199. Page numbers will be given below from both editions.

study. However, those were the days when the small still voice of the self-denying theological scholar could hardly hope to penetrate the groans of suffering and the shouts of triumph in the German Protestant Church, where the battle for the preservation of contemporary Christianity was fought, and at best only partly won. No wonder that Dr. Bauer's book found far too little of the attention which it so richly deserved—and still deserves (93/171).

Ehrhardt is not uncritical of Bauer. He complains that the way Bauer speaks of "ecclesiastical" doctrine (above, xxiii f.), "as if the earthly existence of the Church had already had a theological significance for the earliest Christians" is "unmethodical because it presupposes that somewhere in early Christianity a *regula fidei* was invented as a touch-stone of orthodoxy at the very outset of the history of the Church, an assumption which seems to leave out of consideration the question whether or not the problem of heresy was at all visualized in the early days of Christianity." [14] Ehrhardt thinks, rather, that "the formation of organized groups was suspect in earliest Christianity" and that "the true Church" was understood in the context of divine election, parallel to the contrast between Israel and the nations (93 and n. 2/172 and n. 1).[15]

On matters of detail, Ehrhardt voices some additional protests. Although he finds Bauer's discussion of eastern Syria and Egypt to be especially persuasive,[16] the view that Marcion founded east-Syrian Christianity is "open to doubt" and Tatian's role there was probably more important than Bauer allows (94 f./173). Concerning western

14. Strecker (p. 303) comments: "Ehrhardt is quite correct in calling attention to the fact that Bauer's definition of 'orthodoxy' begins with the assumption of an 'ecclesiastical doctrine' recognizable from the beginning; but he is erroneous in concluding that this represents Bauer's own position (93/172); actually, this only shows that the book is conditioned by the way in which the problem is posed. The results leave no doubt that the existence of an orthodox ecclesiastical doctrine for the period of origins is not undisputed" (see above, p. xxiv; also below, n. 28).
15. Strecker (p. 303) doubts that Bauer would agree with Ehrhardt's statement about the formation of organized groups, and adds: "Here Ehrhardt seems to subscribe to a view in which the Christian self-awareness which derived from a consciousness of being the elect originally stood in fundamental opposition to ecclesiastical organization—a view that has scarcely any support in the early Christian literature."
16. For example, p. 93 n. 1/p. 171 n. 1: Turner has not done "Bauer's book justice, as in the case of East-Syria, so particularly in the case of Egypt." Also, concerning Egypt, "Bauer has made one of the most signal discoveries in early Church History" (95/174); his thesis for this region is "wholly convincing" and Ehrhardt accepts it "to the full" (96/174).

Syria, Ehrhardt finds that "the evidence for a strongly Gnostic movement in Antioch at the time of Ignatius is hardly overwhelming"—Ignatius probably is not representative of Antiochian Christianity, nor does he fight for "purges and excommunications," but for reconciliation. His creed is that of the martyr, like some of the creedal formulae ("gospel") of earlier times. Furthermore, Bauer has "neglected the evidence of the Didache," a writing that exercised considerable "constitutive force" in the church of west-Syria (100 ff. = 179 ff.). Nor is Bauer's "challenging" treatment of Asia-Minor prior to Ignatius "wholly convincing," especially because some of the sources to which he appeals may not be Asian (e.g. Jude, 2 Peter, Pastorals; 102 f. n. 43 = 181 f. n. 4). Although Bauer poses the question of what became of Christianity in Asia Minor in the latter part of the second century, he has not treated this matter in its entirety (103/182). Montanism as a regional movement that assimilated Phrygian ecstaticism and set in motion group conversion, had a great effect on "organized Christianity." The Catholic defence included appeals to the "Apostolic" ministry and to a closed canon of "Apostolic" scriptures, but "no recourse to any 'Apostolic' credal formula was made" (104-108 = 183-187).[17] Bauer also has "greatly exaggerated" Polycarp's relative failure to expand the influence of the Smyrnean church over other communities in Asia Minor, although he rightly draws attention to the struggles of Polycarp (105/184).

Finally, Ehrhardt disagrees strongly with Bauer's assessment of the influence of Rome on Christian leaders elsewhere (109 ff. = 189 ff.), and traces the problem largely to Bauer's failure to give "an account of the character and the organization of the Church at Rome in the

17. Strecker poses the following "critical questions" concerning Ehrhardt's assessment of Montanism (p. 303): "Was the confrontation with Montanism really of decisive significance in the establishment of the New Testament canon? Is it demonstrable that the danger of accepting Montanist scriptures into the canon ever existed for the nascent 'great church'?" In fairness to Ehrhardt, however, it should be noted that he only claims that "the closing of the 'Apostolic' canon of sacred books" helped to prevent Montanism "from making its mark in the Catholic Church," not necessarily that Montanism was the primary catalyst for closing the "orthodox" canon. Indeed, Ehrhardt refers to the fact that the anti-Montanist Roman presbyter Gaius (see EH 2.25.6, 6.20.3) rejected the book of Revelation as a composition of the gnostic Cerinthus (see EH 3.28.3, and the note of Lawlor and Oulton to 6.20.3; also above, 207), possibly because it was so similar to the "new prophecy" of Montanism. That the canon was an issue in at least some of the Montanist disputes is clear from such passages as EH 5.18.5 and 6.20.3.

second century"—"the homogeneity of the Church at Rome" in the middle of that century is particularly open to question, "at least in matters of doctrine." Ehrhardt objects to Bauer's interpretation of the situation behind *1 Clement,* and to his assessment of the role of Victor I in the "third Easter conflict" (111-117/190-197).[18] Ehrhardt concludes that "the influence of the Church at Rome . . . did not aim at doctrinal unification," although it sometimes worked out in that direction (e.g. with the rejection of Marcion and Montanism), and thus "it seems doubtful . . . that this Church should have been responsible for the spreading of the Apostles' Creed"—"Bauer has understandably refrained from enquiring into the propagation of the Roman 'regula fidei,' [but] this is nevertheless to be regretted" (117 f./ 197 f.).[19]

Contemporary German Scholarship. The most widespread and obvious influence of Bauer's position, however, is to be found among contemporary German scholars, especially those associated with Rudolf Bultmann, at first in Germany, but now overflowing to the United States. Bultmann himself appealed to Bauer's thesis in support of the contention that "faith" rather than "orthodoxy" was the distinguishing mark of earliest Christianity.[20] More recently, Helmut

18. Strecker (p. 303) questions the claim of Ehrhardt that in Asia Minor, the observance of Easter went "right back to Apostolic times" (116 f./196). Ehrhardt suggests that Victor hesitated to appeal to apostolic succession in support of the Roman position on the date of Easter precisely because observance of Easter had begun only recently in Rome, in contrast to Asia Minor.

19. On Ehrhardt's assessment of the significance of Rome, Strecker comments as follows (p. 303 f.): "Is not the role of the Roman community too greatly underrated, in opposition to Bauer? For granted that Valentinus and other 'heretics' were found in Rome, does this suffice to demonstrate the heterogeneity of the Roman community? The expulsion of Marcion shows how they were accustomed to deal with the 'arch-heretics.' [Ehrhardt, 110 n. 8/190 n. 2, suggests that Marcion's banishment "was caused by his resignation, if we may trust Epiphanius," *Her.* 42.2.] The character of the Roman community may thus have been more unified than Ehrhardt would allow. And even though an antiheretical thrust may not always stand behind the intervention into extra-Roman affairs, the importance of the Roman point of view can hardly be denied—this follows simply from the position of Rome as capital city, as Bauer rightly would have argued. The special significance of Rome is acknowledged by Ehrhardt himself when he mentions that the bishop Victor came from Africa, where Roman primacy was recognized (117/197); in any event, that calls attention to the claim of Rome, and is confirmed with reference to Asia Minor by the 'resentment against Roman presumptuousness' attested by Firmilian of Cappadocian Caesarea, if Firmilian can be considered a reliable witness here. (This is, however, not so certain as Ehrhardt assumes—Harnack, *Maricon*[2], p. 340*, rightly shows that Firmilian often wrote 'what Cyprian dictated to him.') Above all, critical questions may be raised concerning the attempt to claim that gnosticism and Montanism, along with catholicism, were the three formative factors in the history of doctrine (108 f./187 f.)."

Koester of Harvard Divinity School has listed an impressive array of recent books and articles dealing with various aspects of the problem of "heresy" in the early church, most of which were written by students of Bultmann (including himself) and "influenced by Walter Bauer's pioneering monograph," [21] a sampling of which follows (since 1950, arranged chronologically):

Hans Freiherr von Campenhausen, "Polykarp von Smyrna und die Pastoralbriefe," Sb Heidelberg for 1951, pp. 5-51; reprinted in *Aus der Frühzeit des Christentums* (Tübingen: Mohr, 1963), pp. 197-252;

Ernst Käsemann, "Ketzer und Zeuge: zum johanneischen Verfasserproblem," ZTK 48 (1951); 212-311; reprinted in *Exegetische Versuche und Besinnungen,* 1 (Göttingen: Vandenhoeck & Ruprecht, 1960); 168-187 [see further below, p. 308];

Günther Bornkamm, "Herrenmahl und Kirche bei Paulus," ZTK 53 (1956), 312 ff.; reprinted in *Studien zu Antike und Urchristentum* (München: Kaiser, 1959, 1963 [2]), 138-176; ET in *Early Christian Experience* (New York: Harper, 1970);

Walther Schmithals, *Die Gnosis in Korinth. Eine Untersuchung zu den Korintherbriefen,* FRLANT 66 (Göttingen: Vandenhoeck & Ruprecht, 1956, 1965 [2]);

———. "Die Häretiker in Galatien," ZNW 47 (1956): 25-67 (see above, 243 n. 6);

———. "Die Irrlehrer des Philipperbriefes," ZTK 54 (1957): 297-341 (see above, 243 n. 6);

———. "Die Irrlehrer von Röm. 16.17-20," *Studia Theologica,* 13 (1959): 51-69 (see above, 243 n. 6);

Ulrich Wilckens, *Weisheit und Torheit: eine exegetisch religionsgeschichtliche Untersuchung zu 1 Kor. 1 und 2,* Beiträge zur historischen Theologie 26 (Tübingen: Mohr, 1959);

20. *Theology of the New Testament,* 2 (ET by K. Grobel from the 1951 German; New York: Scribner's, 1955): 137 (55.4).
21. "Haretiker im Urchristentum als Theologisches Problem," in *Zeit und Geschichte; Dankesgabe an Rudolf Bultmann zum 80 Geburtstag,* ed. E. Dinkler (Tübingen: Mohr, 1964), p. 61 n. 1. and also his HarvTR article discussed below (see n. 24), p. 283 n. 8. For a more extensive selection, see Koester's article on "Häretiker im Urchristentum" in RGG[3] 3: 17-21. Numerous other titles might have been included in such a list—e.g. Strecker's work on the ps.-Clementines (see 242 n. 3); a relevant discussion of some aspects of the Bauer-Bultmann approach also may be found in the article by J. M. Robinson, "Basic Shifts in German Theology," *Interpretation* 16 (1962): 76-97.

Schmithals, "Zur Abfassung und ältesten Sammlung der paulinischen Hauptbriefe," ZNW 51 (1960): 225-245;

Helmut Koester, "The Purpose of the Polemic of a Pauline Fragment," NTS 8 (1961/62): 317-332 [on Phil. 3].

Dieter Georgi, *Die Gegner des Paulus im 2 Korintherbrief: Studien zur religiösen Propaganda in der Spätantike*, Wissenschaftliche Monographien zum Alten und Neuen Testament II (Neukirchen-Vluyn: Neukirchener, 1964).

A brief summary of but one of these investigations should suffice to illustrate how provocative the Bauer-oriented approach to the history of earliest Christianity has proved to be. In his inaugural lecture at Göttingen, where he was appointed to Bauer's former chair, Ernst Käsemann boldly reversed Bauer's interpretation of Diotrephes and the "presbyter" of 3 John (above, 93), and pictured Diotrephes as the authoritative leader of the community who refuses to receive the messengers of the "presbyter" and excommunicates those who support them. The "presbyter" is on the defensive; Diotrephes is accused of being power-hungry, but his "orthodoxy" is not questioned. Apparently Diotrephes is functioning "as a monarchial bishop who considers himself to be confronting a false teacher and acts accordingly" (173 f.). Since a local leader could hardly threaten with excommunication the apostle John, or even the famous presbyter named John known to Papias, the author of 2-3 John must actually be one of Diotrephes' presbyters—"a Christian gnostic who has the inconceivable audacity to write a gospel of the Christ whom he has experienced and read back into the world of gnosticism" (177 f.). The Johannine approach posed a serious threat for the "nascent catholicism" represented by Diotrephes; thus it was both logical and necessary that Diotrephes intervene. The question that remains for us is whether the "presbyter" was really a heretic, or an authentic witness (186 f.).[22]

Soon after the appearance of the 1964[2] edition of Bauer, the Bauer-Bultmann approach received general treatment in a paper read by Hans Dieter Betz (Claremont School of Theology) at a New Testament colloquium dealing with the legacy of Rudolf Bultmann.[23]

22. Subsequently, Käsemann has modified his thesis somewhat in view of criticisms such as those offered by Ernst Haenchen in *Theologische Rundschau* 26 (1960): 267 ff. See Käsemann, *Exegetische Versuche und Besinnungen*, 2 (Göttingen: Vandenhoeck & Ruprecht, 1964): 133 n. 1.

23. "Orthodoxy and Heresy in Primitive Christianity: Some Critical Remarks on

Clearly Betz thinks that Bultmann's use of Bauer's thesis is a step in the right direction: "Bultmann not only reformulates Bauer's thesis, he also sees its full impact lying within the New Testament itself: Bauer's problem is identical with the problem of the origin of early Christian theology" (300). Betz emphasizes that one must be aware of Bauer's own theological development and earlier writings to appreciate fully the synthesis presented in this volume. Bauer has put historical investigation on the right track, but "did not apply his thesis extensively enough to the New Testament" and "leaves certain facts out of consideration" such as "the fact that Paul claims to be 'orthodox' (Gal. 1-2)" (306-308).

Betz argues that we must "rethink and reformulate Bauer's thesis" for each area with which it deals, as Strecker has done for Jewish Christianity (see above, appendix 1). The historical and theological approaches cannot be sharply distinguished—indeed, it may be, as Koester argues (see below), that "the historical problem itself was regarded by the New Testament writers themselves as essentially a theological problem," that is, the question of what constitutes a legitimate interpretation of the historical Jesus. Clearly there was no "pure" form of Christianity that existed in the beginning and can be called "orthodox." Betz concludes:

> In the beginning there existed merely the 'heretical' Jew, Jesus of Nazareth. Which of the different interpretations of Jesus are to be called authentically Christian? And what are the criteria for making that decision? This seems to me the cardinal problem of New Testament studies today. The problem was raised clearly by Bauer in his book *Rechtgläubigkeit und Ketzerei*. Bultmann understood the problem rightly as the problem of the origin of Christian theology. If we are concerned today with the question of the legacy of Bultmann, we must accept as part of this legacy the concept of the historical-critical and the theological tasks as being basically one. (311)

In the same month that Betz' article was published, there appeared a wide-ranging, "hypothetical and fragmentary" sketch of just such a Bauer-Bultmann approach from the pen of Helmut Koester.[24] Koester begins by discussing the problem of "historical and theological cri-

---

Georg Strecker's Republication of Walter Bauer's *Rechtgläubigkeit und Ketzerei im ältesten Christentum*," *Interpretation* 19 (1965): 299-311.

24. "GNOMAI DIAFOROI: The Origin and Nature of Diversification in the History of Early Christianity," HarvTR 58 (1965): 279-318. Reprinted as Chapter 4 in *Trajectories Through Early Christianity* (Phila.: Fortress, 1971).

teria" applicable to the early Christian situation and decides that "the criterion for true Christian faith" is "that which has happened historically . . . in the earthly Jesus of Nazareth." The only way to evaluate the "orthodox and heretical tendencies of each new historical situation" is to determine "in which way the criterion for true Christian faith, consciously or unconsciously, structured the re-interpretation of the religious traditions and presuppositions upon which Christianity was dependent," whether Jewish, pagan, or Christian (282).[25]

In the remainder of the essay (284 ff.), Koester keeps this criterion in view in his attempt "to draw the lines from the developments of the 'Apostolic Age' and the first century A.D.—seldom considered in Walter Bauer's study—into the subsequent history of the Ancient Church" by surveying the earliest evidence from "Palestine and Western Syria" (284-290), "Edessa and the Osrhoëne" (290-306), and "The Countries around the Aegean Sea" (306-318). This is intended as "a blueprint for further work in the history of early Christian theology" rather than an attempt "to present final solutions with complete documentation," and is "heavily indebted to W. Bauer's work throughout" (284 nn. 9a and 9).

Occasionally, Koester's reconstruction comes into direct conflict with that of Bauer: for example, "Bauer was . . . probably mistaken in his assumption that the Marcionites were the first Christians to come to Edessa, presumably soon after the middle of the second century" (291). Rather, argues Koester, the tradition embedded in the newly recovered *Gospel of Thomas* probably "was the oldest form of Christianity in Edessa, antedating the beginning of both Marcionite and orthodox Christianity in that area" (293; see also below, n. 40). Even on such rare occasions, however, Koester's "sketch" fulfills its function as an extension of Bauer's investigation back into the earliest period of Christian beginnings. For the many stimulating details of Koester's provocative historico-theological treatment, the reader must be referred to the essay itself.

Summary and Prospectus

In the body of the preceding survey, an attempt has been made to allow the various authors to speak for themselves as much as

25. Koester focuses further on such an approach in his "One Jesus and Four Primitive Gospels," HarvTR 61 (1968): 203-247.

possible, and the temptation to join in the debate has been resisted (except in a few notes). At times this has not been easy; the claims and counter-claims concerning Bauer's presentation often invite the observations of a moderator or the rebuttals of a defense counsel, and it is sometimes hard to avoid commendation of or impatience with the suggested improvements, applications, or alternatives to the thesis—or to add one's own observations on points neglected by the reviewers.

General Methodology and Approach. For example, no one is more conscious of the hypothetical aspects of the inquiry than Bauer himself. Sometimes he must argue from silence if he is to say anything at all. The monograph attempts to suggest a fresh approach; as new evidence becomes available and the results of fresh investigations are made known, it is expected that various aspects of the picture will require modification of one sort or another. Historical study is a matter of weighing degrees of probability. By its very nature it is to a large degree hypothetical. There is little to be gained for historical research by simply dismissing certain of Bauer's suggestions as "conjectural." Rather, what is needed is a methodologically sound presentation of a more probable interpretation, a more adequate reconstruction of the evidence. This is not to deny that Bauer has sometimes used language suggesting more confidence in his reconstruction than the evidence would seem to warrant, and that sometimes there is no direct evidence to support his interpretation, or he has overgeneralized on the basis of ambiguous data. But this admission in itself cannot be used to brush aside Bauer's thesis without further examination. The place to join battle is, ultimately, with the examination of the various pieces of evidence and their implications, not with *ad hominem* blasts [26] and apologetic counter-charges.[27]

26. Völker, for example, notes various passages in which Bauer admits his use of conjecture, contrasts them with some less-careful statements, and on that basis hints that the whole endeavor can be dismissed. Simonin's clever classification of Bauer as an "apologete" for catholic orthodoxy also is mostly beside the point, for all its cleverness.
27. Turner's lectures present a strange juxtaposition of descriptive historical judgments on details and a general framework of confessional apologetics. This is most obvious in the final sentence of each lecture, where Turner refers doxologically to the trinitarian orientation of the church's interpretation of revelation (35, 148), expression of truth (80), faith (231, 306), experience (378), and service (463). The closing words of his book are an excellent illustration: "Despite the picture of flesh and blood contestants with mixed motives and dubious techniques

That there were people who considered themselves to be "true" followers of Jesus Christ, in contrast to other positions which they considered "false," cannot be doubted, either in the second century or in the first. If "orthodoxy" means such a self-evaluation, then Lebreton is undoubtedly correct in pointing to the "orthodox" position of Clement of Alexandria, and Betz is justified in suggesting that Paul understands himself to be "orthodox." Clearly Tertullian also exhibits such a self-consciousness, and it does not vanish in his "Montanist" period! And Marcion also saw himself in this light, as a "true" believer as over against the "false." Nor do we lack evidence that there were those for whom Paul's approach was to be condemned as contrary to their "orthodox" position.

At this level, the problem is to a large extent *semantic* in nature. The word "orthodoxy" almost inevitably conjures up a picture of established, institutionalized Christianity as it was forged in the great doctrinal debates of the fourth and fifth centuries. Is it possible to trace lines of direct and significant continuity back from this traditional "orthodoxy" (which came to wield political as well as social and theological weapons) toward the earliest period of Christianity, and to apply the title "orthodoxy" to them without confusing the issue? Is such a procedure desirable, and if so, why? Is such a procedure helpful? What happens when we find a person who is clearly a predecessor of "orthodoxy" in one sense but not in another? How do we handle a Tertullian, with his Montanist sympathies, or an Origen, condemned by some representatives of later "orthodoxy"?

It is not clear that, in 1934, Bauer saw this aspect of the problem in sharp focus.[28] Indeed, he helped clear the way for us to see it more sharply. Despite all the talk, especially by Bauer's Bultmannian heirs, of the unity of the historical and theological tasks, there *is* a strictly historical legacy left by Bauer—the obligation to ask each

---

which the Church historian will often bring to light, it is impossible for the historian of Christian thought in its classical formative period to mistake the guidance of that Spirit of Truth to Whom with the Father and the Son be now ascribed all honour, glory, dominion, and power now and forever more" (498).

28. Bauer discusses specifically only the problem of majority/minority in this context (xxii), an issue that is rather peripheral to the question of "orthodoxy/heresy," as some of the reviewers noted (cf. especially Martin). Nevertheless, it is clear from Bauer's introduction (xxiv) that he does not intend to use "orthodoxy/heresy" as value judgments—despite the fact that in their "traditional and usual use" they normally do involve value judgments. See also above, n. 14, and below.

participant in the drama how he sees his role and how it relates to other participants. This is a descriptive task. Where it deals with evaluations, they are the evaluations of the participants in their own time and place, not of the investigator. The theological aspect is unavoidably present, but it concerns the "theology" of the participants, not of the investigator. If one *then* wishes to make theological judgments about the participants from his own modern perspective, or to derive from some of them theological principles to be applied today, or to trace back into an earlier period theological outlooks that are appealing today, or in some other way to join the theological to the historical approach, that is his business; but it is not an inevitable or necessary adjunct to the descriptive-historical task. And if it be objected that pure descriptive history, totally divorced from the presuppositions and prejudices of the interpreter is impossible, that is freely admitted; but does it follow necessarily that this ought to be used as justification for neglecting the ideal goal of objective inquiry? [29]

Even more seriously than Goguel may have realized, Bauer's title has an unfortunate and misleading aspect to it. Whether one translates *Rechtgläubigkeit* hyper-literally as "right-believing," or with its traditional and idiomatic connotation of "orthodoxy," he scarcely escapes the feeling of passing theological judgment on the figures of history when the word is used. Yet in the introduction, Bauer claims that this is not his intention at all—he uses the terms "orthodoxy" and "heresy" to designate movements in history to which these terms usually are applied, but he does it for the sake of convenience, so as not to confuse the issue (xxii f.). But it has not proved to be a convenient procedure at all. Even as appreciative a commentator as Ehrhardt misinterprets Bauer's perspective at this point when he accuses Bauer of presupposing that "a touch-stone of orthodoxy" must have been available at the very outset. Indeed, Bauer does set the stage for his inquiry by using such traditional terminology—that is

29. Although Bauer's analogy between historian and judge in a court of law (xxii ff.) is not a completely happy one (the judge does pronounce judgment!), he is clear about the ideal objectivity of the historian: value judgments are not the business of the historian (xxiv), he should cast his preconceptions aside and place himself into the period and thought-world of those he examines (xxii). Whether Bauer himself has been successful in exercising such ideal impartiality is quite another matter (see esp. Moffatt's critique).

how he poses that question—but a careful reading of the introduction leaves the clear impression that for Bauer, *"the* ecclesiastical doctrine" of later orthodoxy was neither present with Jesus nor does it necessarily represent something "primary" and "genuine" in the period of Christian origins (xxiv; cf. also xxii and n. 14 above). How much less confusing the whole discussion would be in the future if, for the historical task, such traditional, theologically loaded slogans as "orthodoxy" and "heresy" could be eliminated from treatments of the early period except where they are used by the participants under discussion—and thus are actual elements within the historical reconstruction.[30]

Specific Details. With reference to content, there is much in Bauer's treatment that invites supplementation or reassessment, especially in the light of more recent discoveries and continuing research. In the 1964[2] edition, a section on Jewish-Christianity has been added;[31] Koester has made some preliminary attempts at drawing lines to the earlier phases of Christian origins by means of the New Testament (and related) writings and newly discovered materials such as the "Nag Hammadi" finds.[32] Turner has referred to papyrological discov-

30. The sort of confusion that results from this aspect of the semantic problem is well illustrated by the attempts of some of Bauer's critics and heirs to define what they would like to understand by the word "orthodoxy": for Moffatt, it is "a sense of the Centre": for Turner, a mostly unconscious feeling for unity, etc., centered in "the religious facts"; Ehrhardt speaks of "orthodoxy" in the context of a recognized *regula fidei;* others appeal to the "apostolic" criterion (e.g. Martin); for Koester, it has to do with a conscious or unconscious identification with the historical Jesus. Indeed, is there today *any* commonly accepted meaning of "orthodoxy" such as Bauer wished to presuppose?
31. The ever-growing interest in this aspect of early Christianity is evidenced by the literature cited above in Strecker's essay (esp. 242 f.), to which may now be added these more recent examples: *Aspects du judéo-christianisme,* essays from a Strasbourg colloquium (Paris: Presses Universitaires de France, 1965); B. Bagatti, *L'Eglise de la Circoncision* (Jerusalem: Impremerie Franciscaine, 1965); S. Pines, "The Jewish Christians of the Early Centuries of Christianity according to a New Source," *Proceedings of the Israel Academy of Sciences and Humanities* 2.13 (1966); and the relevant material in M. Simon and A. Benoit, *Le Judaïsme et le Christianisme Antique d'Antiochus Epiphane à Constantin,* Nouvelle Clio 10 (Paris: Presses Universitaires de France, 1968), which also includes a chapter by Benoit on "Orthodoxie et Hérésie dans le Christianisme des premiers siècles" (289-307), with a summary of Bauer's thesis (297-301).
32. Koester's probe does not extend to Alexandria-Egypt or to the western Mediterranean (North Africa, Rome, etc.). On the Nag Hammadi materials, see J. Doresse, *The Secret Books of the Egyptian Gnostics* (ET by P. Mairet from the 1958 French; New York: Viking, 1960), W. C. van Unnik, *Newly Discovered Gnostic Writings* Studies in Biblical Theology 30 (ET by H. H. Hoskins from the 1958 Dutch; London: SCM, 1960), J. M. Robinson, "The Coptic Gnostic

eries that indicate the need for some revision of detail in Bauer's presentation on Egypt.[33] Ehrhardt makes passing reference to a recently discovered letter attributed to Clement of Alexandria, which is of interest for the situation at Alexandria.[34] Other significant materials to appear in the past quarter century include Manichaean [35] and Mandaean [36] texts, the long lost homily of Melito on the passover,[37] and a previously unknown record of a discussion between Origen and Heraclides (ed. J. Scherer, 1949; compare above 166).

Still lacking are a fresh approach to the origins of Christianity in North Africa, Rome, and other western regions.[38] The situation in Asia Minor and the Aegean area also is admittedly more complex than Bauer indicated,[39] and the whole question of east Syrian Chris-

---

Library," (above, 170 n. 39), and the growing literature conveniently listed in each issue of *New Testament Abstracts* under "NT World."

33. Turner's argument, however, that the presence of the Fourth Gospel in Egypt at the beginning of the second century (p^{52}, etc.) indicates the existence of "orthodoxy" there before the gnostics came to "borrow" that gospel is open to question since it simply assumes the "orthodoxy" of the Fourth Gospel. But the affinities of that document are quite problematic, and it would not be difficult to adjust Bauer's picture to include an originally "gnostical" Fourth Gospel in circulation in Egypt at that early date. On the recent discovery of a papyrus text of "3 *Corinthians*" and its implications for Bauer's argument, see above, 42 n. 99.

34. See above, 60 n. 60. In the letter, Clement refers to a longer, "secret" form of the gospel of Mark, allegedly used by Christian "gnostics" at Alexandria.

35. For a recent survey of the subject, see G. Widengren, *Mani and Manichaeism* (ET by C. Kessler; New York: Holt, Rinehart and Winston, 1965). See also above, 49 f. n. 25.

36. See now K. Rudolph, *Die Mandäer* (above, 261 n. 59); also E. M. Yamauchi, "The Present Status of Mandaean Studies," *Journal of Near Eastern Studies,* 25 (1966): 88-96. The Mandaean discoveries had already made a large impact by the 1930's, but much additional material has been published subsequently.

37. Two relatively complete Greek manuscripts have come to light since 1935: the Chester Beatty papyrus, edited by C. Bonner (Philadelphia: University of Pennsylvania, 1940), and the Bodmer papyrus, edited by M. Testuz (Cologny-Geneve: Bibliotheca Bodmericana, 1960). Abundant versional and other textual evidence also has now been identified. A new edition of the text is being prepared by Molly Whittaker of Nottingham University, and an ET by S. Hall, also of Nottingham.

38. In his review, Koch made some preliminary observations on this subject. Of continued interest for the situation at Rome is the classic article by G. La-Piana, "The Roman Church at the end of the Second Century," HarvTR 18 (1925): 201-277; see also his "Foreign Groups in Rome during the First Centuries of the Empire," HarvTR 20 (1927): 183-394.

39. Cf. the comments of Windisch, in general, and the specific suggestions by Moffatt, Turner, and Ehrhardt. Koester discusses the earlier situation here on the basis of such evidence as Paul, Revelation, Colossians-Ephesians, Luke-Acts, the Pastorals, and (briefly) some of the early fathers.

tianity currently is receiving much attention along with the question of "gnosticism" in general.[40] Again, several reviewers regretted Bauer's failure to discuss the origin and development of the early Christian *regula fidei*, which certainly deserves treatment among themes such as those discussed in Bauer's chapter 9.[41] But this should all be viewed as part of the legacy left by Bauer for those who were to follow. He did not claim to be attempting an exhaustive treatment (xxv), but to be opening a new route for historical investigation. In this he has certainly been successful, and it is in hopes of encouraging even more careful historical scrutiny of the period of Christian origins, unencumbered by later ecclesiastical value judgments, that Bauer's pioneering volume is here made available to the English reader.

40. Whereas some of Bauer's critics ascribed a much greater role to Tatian in founding Christianity in eastern Syria (e.g. Windisch, Ehrhardt), Koester argues that "the Thomas tradition was the oldest form of Christianity in Edessa" (293) and was developed along various lines including the approaches of Bardesanes, Tatian, and later, Mani (304 f.). On the Nag Hammadi material in general, see n. 32 above; on the Thomas tradition in particular, see also the literature cited by Koester. Of the many recent works on gnosis and gnosticism, the English reader is referred especially to Hans Jonas, *The Gnostic Religion* (Boston: Beacon, 1958, 1963[2]) and to R. M. Grant, *Gnosticism and Early Christianity* (New York: Harper and Row, 1959, 1966[2]), as well as his *Gnosticism Anthology*. See also the comments of M. Smith in JBL 89 (1970): 82-84, for some timely warnings about this subject matter.
41. In addition to Ehrhardt's probe, see J. N. D. Kelly, *Early Christian Creeds* (New York: Longmans, 1950, 1960[2]).

Comprehensive Index

by Robert A. Kraft

This comprehensive index includes abbreviations, supplementary bibliographical information beyond what is contained in the notes, and other aids to the reader. Names of modern authors appear in capital letters; no attempt has been made to include the names of modern editors of ancient texts or modern translators if they are mentioned solely for that reason in the notes. Some selectivity has also been exercised with regard to proper names (persons, places) from the ancient world—those of primary significance for the subject of the book are emphasized. With regard to ancient authors such as Clement of Alexandria, Epiphanius, Eusebius, Hippolytus, Origen, and Tertullian, to whom frequent reference is made in various connections in the book, the index does not attempt to be complete. When an item appears primarily or solely in a footnote on a given page, this will normally be noted by listing page and note number as follows: 42.99 (i.e., page 42, note 99).

317

Date Due

S. B.			